American Academic Culture
in Transformation

American Academic Culture in Transformation

FIFTY YEARS, FOUR DISCIPLINES

Edited with an Introduction by
THOMAS BENDER and CARL E. SCHORSKE

Foreword by
STEPHEN R. GRAUBARD

PRINCETON UNIVERSITY PRESS • PRINCETON, NEW JERSEY

Originally published as the Winter 1997 Issue of *Daedalus: Journal of the American Academy of Arts and Sciences* (vol. 126, no. 1)

ISBN 0-691-05824-5

Princeton University Press books are printed on acid-free paper and meet the guidelines for permanence and durability of the Committee on Production Guidelines for Book Longevity of the Council on Library Resources

First Princeton Paperback printing, 1998

http://pup.princeton.edu

Printed in the United States of America

10 9 8 7 6 5 4 3 2 1

Contents

Foreword

The history of the American university in the twentieth century waits to be written. To say this is not to denigrate existing histories or to suggest that a great book, yet unwritten, waits to find its author. Rather, it is to argue that American higher education in this century has been fundamentally changed, and that the nature of these transformations is still insufficiently studied. *American Academic Culture in Transformation* is intended to contribute to a greater understanding of what has happened to four major disciplines—two in the humanities, two in the social sciences—in the last fifty years. A great debt is owed to the two historians, Carl Schorske and Thomas Bender, who recommended this study to the American Academy of Arts and Sciences and who were so instrumental in causing the draft essays commissioned for this enterprise to be discussed, criticized, and published in a special issue of the journal *Daedalus*. It is a great boon to see this material appear in this Princeton Paperback edition, reaching an audience that may not have seen its original publication.

These essays, collectively, provide a unique set of reflections on how major academic disciplines have changed in the decades since the Second World War, and what the internal and external stimuli to these changes have been. Professors Schorske and Bender, in their introduction to the volume, explain how the specific disciplines—economics, political science, philosophy, and English—came to be chosen, what themes have figured most conspicuously, what subjects have been neglected or ignored, and what the rationale for the choices and omissions has been. I do not need to repeat what they have so eloquently expressed. If my duty is to thank them, which I do most heartily, I cannot forbear to add just a few words of my own.

Recalling the remarkable insight of Robert Merton in his seminal "Science, Technology and Society in Seventeenth Century England," that "the *cultural soil* of seventeenth century England was peculiarly fertile for the growth and spread of science," one is entitled to ask what the cultural soil of twentieth-century America has been, and what intellectual flora and fauna it has nourished. Where has the soil been too barren to allow for growth? To ask such questions is to confront an even more difficult dilemma: Is there in fact an "American academic culture," or ought we, more properly, speak of academic *cultures*, specific to particular disciplines and professions? No one reading this book will fail to note the immense changes that have so significantly altered American scholarship in the last half century; but the explanation for these transformations may not be entirely satisfying. Who can doubt, for example, the influence of the Vietnam War and the civil rights struggle on American scholarship? Yet it is obvious from this study of even a handful of disciplines that while such events fundamentally altered the intellectual agendas in certain areas, it scarcely affected others. More importantly, perhaps, when one considers how few of the world's leading universities were touched at all by these events, and how much more fundamental were the changes produced in these societies by the carnage of World War II and also by the mass prosperity of recent decades, one has to ask whether the foreign institutions are pursuing intellectual agendas substantially different from those presently obtaining in the United States. If so, what are the likely consequences of such disparity in what is studied, in what is deemed important?

Alfred North Whitehead, among many others, recognized early that science was an international enterprise, and that this determined what research was pursued. Many humanists and social scientists like to believe that their disciplines are no less international, and there are compelling reasons for saying that such a claim is not simply an expression of hubris. Yet it is perfectly reasonable to ask whether the scholarly agendas common to France, Germany, and the United Kingdom, for example, not to speak of Japan, India, and China, outside the broad domain of the natural sciences, fundamentally resemble those that prevail today in the United States. If they are different—this may just possibly be one of their most conspicuous strengths—this raises a fundamental question of what the nature of the international dialogue in these areas is, and which disciplines in the United States, if any, are today enjoying some sort of "imperial" influence, comparable in many ways to the influence Germany enjoyed in many scholarly areas in the last century, and that the United States enjoyed in the decades immediately after the Second World War.

To ask that question is to ask a really embarrassing one: Is America threatened with becoming parochial in these last years, in its scholarship but also in many other ways as well? Indeed, at a time when so many insist on claiming that we live in a "global village," that technology makes us all near neighbors, is there evidence of new kinds of provincialism in many disciplines in the humanities and the social sciences, and what does this portend for the future? If we have all become "provinces," where, then, is the center? And will it hold into the next millennium?

To ask these questions is to ask another scarcely less fundamental to our inquiry. Is it possible that relations with specific countries in western Europe, particularly in the long years of the Cold War, allowed for certain kinds of international scholarship, and indeed introduced certain biases in that scholarship, but that no comparable interchange was possible with any part of the communist world, or indeed with great parts of the so-called "developing world"? Indeed, have the exchanges between American academics and those in Asia, in societies as diverse as those of Japan and India, ever achieved the level of intimacy that became common, for example, with the United Kingdom and France? And, even in Europe, in those countries that were never in the communist sphere, have American academic relations with certain ones been significantly closer than with others? What have the intellectual consequences of this been? If new technologies allowed for greater and closer exchanges between the United States and western Europe, is it at all evident that the burgeoning societies of Latin America have figured comparably in American scholarship, or that major efforts have been made to understand and involve scholars from the vast and differentiated Muslim world? In short, even as air travel and fax machines, E-mail and the like have allowed for exchanges that would have been wholly inconceivable in 1945 or even in 1968, entire areas of the world have been virtually excluded from the purview of American academics.

There is every reason to believe that the kinds of intellectual relations built up with certain European scholars in the last half century will only deepen in the decades ahead, and that a truly international scholarship in the humanities and the social sciences will evolve, different in many respects from what heretofore has been common. Indeed, a question that must be asked is what needs to be done to foster such international ties on a worldwide basis, and what ought American academics be doing to help construct institutions at home and abroad sympathetic to forms of scholarship that will be decidedly less parochial, less nation-bound, less susceptible to the vagaries of specific local ideologies? We are only at the beginning of an intellectual process that has made scholarship in the natural sciences truly international, but that has not to date been replicated either in the humanities or the social sciences. Perhaps that ought to be our next major scholarly assignment: to aim for research that is more responsive to thought abroad, that is, more critically aware of what is happening in intellectual circles distant from the United States.

Stephen R. Graubard

Acknowledgments

This project was created and developed under the auspices of the American Academy of Arts and Sciences. The Academy provided not only generous financial support, but also the unstinting organizational assistance of its able staff. To Dr. Joel Orlen, who led its work with patience, responsiveness, and efficiency, we owe particular thanks. The Academy further provided at its house in Cambridge hospitality for the first of two conferences central to the project. The Huntington Library in San Marino, California, hosted the second. We are indebted to Dr. Robert Ritchie, its director of research, for his early interest in the project and for making it possible to hold the conference in the Huntington's delightful surroundings. Tracy Tullis of New York University, the *rapporteur* for the Huntington conference, produced a critical record of the proceedings, which was of the greatest value in the construction of this book.

The Andrew W. Mellon Foundation provided the principal funding for the project. We thank in particular Dr. Harriet Zuckerman, the Foundation's vice president, for her immediate and encouraging response to our plans and her unobtrusive but very useful suggestions for their development. Alberta Arthurs, recently retired director of the Arts and Humanities Program of the Rockefeller Foundation, was instrumental in providing further financial support to assist in the work's publication.

This study originally appeared in *Daedalus,* the journal of the American Academy of Arts and Sciences. To no one do we owe a greater debt than to its editor, Stephen R. Graubard. He was closely associated with the project from its beginnings in the

Academy's Committee on Studies, and his advice was especially helpful in finding the best ways to bring the results of the conference into published form. We also wish to thank his staff for their editorial work on the *Daedalus* issue.

In the introduction we have named scholars who helped us on our way. To these we should like to add acknowledgment of the wise counsel of Kenneth Prewitt, who contributed to our understanding of the social sciences, especially political science. Finally, thanks must go to the uncounted and unnamed colleagues in various disciplines with whom we discussed the project over its several years of development.

American Academic Culture
in Transformation

Thomas Bender and Carl E. Schorske

Introduction

The humanities and social sciences in the United States have lately been shaken by debates about both method and mission. Questions have been raised about the nature and definition of American academic disciplines, the role of ideology and political commitment in scholarship, the possibility of objectivity, the status of theory, and the place of knowledge in the larger culture and polity.

Such questioning is not unique to the United States, nor is it unprecedented in our history. Struggling as they have in the past with the cultural politics of their complex and multicultural society, Americans are again presenting urgent societal claims to the educational and scholarly community. Social demand does not, however, adequately explain the current discussion. There is a deeper historical background to these debates that bears examination and deserves attention in its own right. The controversies so much discussed in the past decade grow out of this history, but they do not constitute the whole of its significance. The achievement of new levels of disciplinary professionalism over the course of a half century has generated its own needs and produced its own internal tensions as well as changed relations to the larger public realm. To achieve greater self-awareness of the present circumstance of American academic culture, we need a fuller and clearer sense of the dynamics, phasing, and patterns of its change.

There has been little inquiry into this history, for reasons that are easy to grasp. The world of scholarship is generally oriented toward the production of fresh perspectives and the articulation of new disciplinary knowledge. Hence neither the individual

3

scholar nor the academy as a whole is inclined to pause from its normal pursuits to take itself as its subject and examine its own transformations and condition. This study, launched by the American Academy of Arts and Sciences, presents the yield of a collective attempt at such an examination.

It is a vast topic. Our strategy for addressing it has relied upon a combination of case study method, comparative analysis, and contextualization. We begin by examining selected disciplines separately. We asked scholars of different generations whose own work contributed to the transformation of their fields to write as participants in and witnesses of those changes. In order to identify larger, transdisciplinary patterns, and contextual explanations of changes, we supplemented the internal and self-conscious analysis by discipline with an external, more distanced, comparative one.

This strategy is reflected in the structure of the volume: After a broad historical sketch of the general social, political, and intellectual context of the postwar university in Part I, Part II presents separate essays on individual disciplines, at least two on each. As one moves from one discipline to the next, from one generation to another, one begins to recognize the phasing of change, patterns of persistence and innovation, and evidence of both commonality and difference.

Part III is organized synchronically to make these larger features visible. Utilizing the internal disciplinary narratives, its authors seek patterns across the disciplines in temporal phases, situating disciplinary change in broader cultural and political developments. These synoptic essays also explore the wider causes and implications of academic change. We hope that this combination of firsthand testimony and critical commentary will encourage readers to reach beyond their natural interest in their own or closely associated disciplines to reflect on the relation of disciplinary change to the development of the larger academic enterprise and its societal context.

The inquiry has involved a number of scholars in two formal conferences, one held at the house of the American Academy of Arts and Sciences in Cambridge, Massachusetts, the other at the Huntington Library in San Marino, California. The conferences included participants from a broad array of humanistic and social scientific disciplines, representing several generations, diverse methods, and a range of professional styles.[1]

After the first meeting, we determined that the best way to proceed was to narrow the focus to four disciplines as the foundation of the inquiry; English, philosophy, economics, and political science were selected. Our choices identified what we called pluralized disciplines, which we contrasted with more tightly unified ones. In both the humanities and the social sciences, we selected one discipline with a "strong ego" and inner consensus, and another, more eclectic, even fractured discipline, even one rethinking its foundations. We were also concerned to include disciplines with different relations to a public beyond the academy, from those aspiring to address a general public to those with sharply defined and particular audiences. For the humanities, philosophy represented an example of a firmly bounded and well-policed discipline, marked after 1950 by high self-confidence and a rather limited public face. We understood English to be more pluralistic, inclusive, contested, increasingly seeking to assume a general public role. In a rough sense, economics and political science represent a similar contrast within the domain of the social sciences.

Any such choice is, of course, necessarily limiting, always establishing a particular perspective that at once masks and reveals. Our choices—as well as the half century span of our inquiry—give less prominence than one might expect to many issues that have been widely contested during the past decade. Two of the disciplines we have studied, economics and philosophy, have been among the least affected by the challenges posed by new and often politically driven fields such as feminism, the study of race, or

---

[1]These participants, some of whom were at both conferences, were: M. H. Abrams, Svetlana Alpers, Annette Baier, Michael Baxandall, Thomas Bender, Marhsall Cohen, Mark Edmundson, Catherine Gallagher, Stephen Graubard, Russell Hardin, David A. Hollinger, Gerald Holton, Barbara Johnson, Mark Johnston, Stanley Katz, Ira Katznelson, Robin D. G. Kelley, David M. Kreps, Charles E. Lindblom, Alexander Nehamas, Joel Orlen, Hilary Putnam, Richard Rorty, José David Saldívar, Carl E. Schorske, Daniel Selden, Philip Selznick, Elaine C. Showalter, Neil Smelser, Rogers M. Smith, Robert M. Solow, Margaret Somers, Catharine Stimpson, George W. Stocking, Jr., Emily D. T. Vermeule, and Michael Woodford.

multiculturalism. On the one hand, this disciplinary silence suggests that common perceptions of the ubiquity of discussions of race, gender, and ethnicity in academe are exaggerated. On the other hand, their silence prompts one to ask why these disciplines have been so oblivious to such pressing cultural concerns.

Despite our awareness of the importance of the natural sciences both in shaping the internal culture of the academy and in establishing the terms of the academy's relation to the larger society and polity, we have not included them here. We decided that extending our inquiry into the natural sciences would so expand the scale of the project as to make it unmanageable. Indeed, we understand this project as an initial foray that will, we hope, encourage further inquiry that may include the natural sciences and other fields not pursued here.

Once the disciplines were selected, a small planning committee was created that included, besides the two editors, specialists in each of the four fields: Catharine Gallagher (English), Alexander Nehamas (philosophy), Michael Woodford (economics), and Ira Katznelson (political science). These disciplinary specialists wrote brief working papers outlining the phasing and patterns of change in their fields. By revealing differences among the disciplines as well as their commonalities of intellectual orientation and the chronologies of change across them, the papers enabled us to develop our plan of work.

The most important cross-disciplinary illumination was the identification of a virtual refounding of all four disciplines in the 1940s and 1950s. The refounding was a complex process, striking for the simultaneity with which a commonality of intellectual style appeared across the disciplines. This redefinition of the human sciences responded in part to the wish to escape the ideological legacy of the 1930s, in part to the new pressures of the Cold War. Yet the changes were also spurred by the appeal of newly available theories and techniques that could satisfy professional aspirations to rigor. This postwar reconstruction and its salience in the fifties in all four disciplines became the baseline for the study.

Following the disciplines from this moment of refounding impressed upon us the further periodization for the project. Between roughly 1960 and 1975, all disciplines were confronted by developments in the larger culture and society, but they responded in different ways. Each had to struggle with the ideals, accomplishments, and limitations of the postwar academic agenda, with its devotion to the model of science, its commitment to objectivity, its confidence in the power of formal analysis, and its dislike and distrust of ideology or any other contamination of disciplinary autonomy and purity. The current condition of academic culture represents the different resolutions of the challenges of that period.

The hold of the discipline over the academic intellect is powerful, as many of the essays in Part II show. Largely self-enclosed, the essays reveal the internal sequential development in a series of scholarly foci. Given their disciplinary commitments, many of the practitioners did not find it congenial to approach the development of their disciplines in a contextual fashion. They largely ignored the possibility of external sources of disciplinary change, whether by way of ideas from other fields or through the influence of broader political, cultural, or social phenomena. This unanticipated pattern in the narratives provides important evidence of the capacity of the disciplines and their protocols to channel the imagination of even the most vigorous academic mind. The notion of academic culture as a whole is surely not entirely imaginary, but it is clear from our study that it has only a limited hold on the academic consciousness of our time.

The project, as developed on the basis of the working papers by Gallagher, Katznelson, Nehamas, and Woodford as well as with guidance from the conventional chronology of postwar American intellectual history, assumed a three-period phasing of academic change: the period of the postwar foundation, the challenges of the sixties, and the present. The structure of the project based upon this understanding of the phases of historical development led us to seek contributors who had come of age professionally during these periods. We expected distinctively generational perspectives, which were to be the basis for historical commentary emphasizing synchronic analysis across the disciplines within the larger context. In fact, the participants, regardless of generation, tend to play down or even omit entirely the middle phase, the 1960s, as an autonomous period of intellectual production. The personal testimonies in Part II show a strikingly high level of agreement on a two-phase rather than a three-phase model of historical change. By contrast, the historians writing in Part III, more disposed to external forms of explanation of intellectual life, insist upon the separate importance of the 1960s, not so much as a moment of academic revolution but rather as a trigger of changes that would work through the disciplines in different ways into our own historical moment.

*   *   *

This book largely defines itself in the movement between two modes of inquiry, one emphasizing the practitioner's perspective, which is discipline-focused, the other seeking to map the larger configurations of academic culture across several disciplines and to analyze these in a historical context. What have been the yields of this dual approach to the transformation of academic culture? How much has the strategy illuminated, how much distorted or concealed from view? The reader will form his own answer to these connected questions, but they deserve brief consideration here.

The disciplinary witnesses were chosen on the basis of their representation of the most influential and innovative tendencies of their fields in a given phase of development. This principle of selection obviously privileged the professional mainstream. It resulted inevitably in a simplified picture of the pluralistic reality prevailing in the more divided disciplines, such as political science and English, and in a neglect of the scholarship of the marginalized within the most united disciplines, economics and philosophy. Yet the focus on dominant scholarly tendencies also produced a positive result. It revealed with unexpected clarity first the commonalities, then the divergencies among the disciplines as they responded to historical change. It showed how the first period under review, 1945–1960, witnessed the establishment of the primacy of analytic method and a quest for epistemological certainty not only within each discipline but across the whole spectrum. The strongly positivistic, neo-Lockean intellectual foundations given to all four disciplines in the 1950s—even the New Criticism in English had some of its roots in Lockean language theory—set the terms for subsequent developments in the disciplines. Against this common background in the early Cold

War era, the difference in the responses of the disciplines to the crises of the sixties and seventies stands out in sharp relief. At one end of the spectrum was English, where involvement of the scholars with the moral claims of ethnic and gender minorities occasioned a virtual revolution in the definition of the discipline's aims, scope, and methods. Not only did the formal analytic of the New Criticism come tumbling down, but the very legitimacy of literary art as the center of their profession was assailed by younger literary scholars seeking to establish cultural studies as a metadiscipline. At the other end of the spectrum, economics maintained its method-centered distance from the social problems and issues that, in the 1930s and 1940s, had been important to its mission. Cannot English thus be seen to have assumed in altered form the role of social criticism that economics had abandoned? This shift in roles, if such it was, points beyond the academy to America's two major domestic crises in our century, and the deep differences between them. In the 1930s, the national crisis was economic. Depression vaulted economics and the social sciences to center stage, to lead the academy's response to society's ills and needs. In the 1960s, with capitalism returned to strength and ethnic and gender questions challenging the status quo in fundamental ways, culture replaced the economy as the crisis area. Therewith the humanistic disciplines—especially English and history—became the principal carriers of the academy's social-critical function.

The upheavals of the 1960s that projected cultural and minority issues into the center of American public life fostered a virtual intellectual revolution in the discipline of English. In philosophy and political behavioralism, it evoked a response less drastic, that of reform. Practitioners in both the latter fields, without abandoning the scientific canons of the 1950s, expanded their applications to accommodate issues previously excluded or ignored. The intra-disciplinary narratives in this volume as well as Katznelson's comparative synchronic analysis of the 1960s record these adaptations of the astringent scientific orthodoxies of the fifties to address new societal demands for community and the recognition of minority cultures. Here the developing intellectual substance of the disciplines is shown in a direct relationship with historical change.

In the process of adaptation to new social claims, more flexible inter-disciplinary ties were formed. In political science, economic thinking informed rational choice theory, while analytic philosophy fortified political value theory. Analytic philosophers after 1970 also reached out to address ethical and socio-political questions previously regarded by the strictest of their founding fathers as not properly philosophical. The economists, as their research and teaching expanded into management science, law, and other practical professions, drew once again upon descriptive disciplines such as sociology and anthropology, which mainstream theorists had abandoned as incompatible with their scientific standards. But these excursions did not affect the theoretical and methodological identity established for economics in the early postwar years, when the aspirations of its most creative scholars to scientific rigor narrowed its social scope. The academic intellectuals who espoused the American civil rights and cultural identity politics of the sixties offered no serious critique of economics as a discipline any more than they challenged capitalism as a system, however much they sought to open its opportunities more widely. More than any other field here studied, economics, impervious to the winds of social change, maintained the intellectual foundations established in the early postwar years.

However justified it has proven to be in mapping changes where scholarly identity is largely defined and empowered, the use of the dominant tone-setters in the individual disciplines as the primary vehicle of our account has also resulted in obscuring or neglecting some significant elements in academic transformation. Three of these deserve particular mention: the marginalization of subdisciplines; the changing nature and roles of inter-disciplinarity; and the influence of European ideas.

Wherever the postwar redefinition of an academic field produced the virtual hegemony of a single school of thought, as in philosophy and economics, certain questions and/or approaches to the discipline were soon delegitimized or sidelined. Some subfields were absorbed into other disciplines: the history of economic thought and discarded parts of philosophy found room in history departments; problems of poverty and class, in sociology departments. The host disciplines, however, adapted the immigrant intellectual substances to their own perspectives. In the process, their vital relation to their mother-disciplines was lost.

In the case of pluralized disciplines such as political science and English, our stress on the most salient tendency in the field in each period has resulted in serious underrepresentation of scholarly subgroups of persistent vitality. Thus in politics departments, political theory grounded in classical philosophy not only had a continuous life during the ascendancy of behavioralism, but acquired a new influence in the aftermath of the upheavals of the sixties, when the issues of community and political culture gained an urgency that behavioral science was ill-suited to deal with. In English, where scholarly variety has long been characteristic, the concentration on the problems of the culture wars in this study has, despite our best intentions, produced a reductionist picture of a field whose multiplicity of outlooks has been if anything increased by its crisis of identity.

A second consequence of the project's organization by individual discipline has been an insufficient attention to the role of interdisciplinary formations in our academic culture. Their study would have had great value in tracing the changing relations between different parts of the academy and the sectors of the society their work serves, and in illuminating the emergence of new transdisciplinary scholarly communities that may redefine the academy's intellectual and institutional structures.

While some subject-centered fields were inter-disciplinary by long tradition—classics or oriental studies, for example—two new kinds of programs rose to prominence in the mid-century. In the 1950s, after Sputnik, area studies of foreign societies were established all over the country. Designed to produce a knowledgeable group of scholars and specialists who would increase America's capabilities as a world power, they were generously funded by the government and the Ford Foundation. Social scientists and historians played a leading role in these programs. Such programs have offered a continuing function for scholarly methods marginalized in their disciplines of origin.

American studies, autochthonously generated by the universities, was developed largely by humanists. Literary scholars committed to strengthening the relationship of their discipline to history when the New Criticism was decontextualizing it played a major role. In contrast to the foreign area programs, American studies, whose origins lay in the New Deal years, drew faculty and students of a socially critical persuasion, in contrast to the more policy-oriented foreign area programs where "experts" were educated. In this respect, both types of programs contributed to the increasing polarization of the social sciences and the humanities that has marked the last half century.

The foreign area and American studies programs have been not so much inter-disciplinary as multidisciplinary. Subject-matter centered, they brought together several disciplines to shed their particular lights on a common object. While they did not fuse methods or create a new metadiscipline, they provided an institutional frame that served as both model and spawning ground for post-sixties cultural identity programs such as women's studies and black studies. This was particularly true of American studies. The special nature of cultural identity problems also stimulated and spurred theoretical approaches that challenged disciplinary identity definitions.

As new common analytic, theoretical, and ideological outlooks penetrated a wide variety of disciplines in the 1980s, metadisciplinarity began to succeed multidisciplinarity. In this study, the essays on English are attentive to this development. The choice of disciplines represented, however, does not do justice to the pervasiveness of metadisciplinary intellectual tendencies in many fields that may yet produce some institutional reorganization of academic culture. David Hollinger's final essay surveys the evidences of the recent search for a transdisciplinary community of discourse. In strongest contrast to the autonomistic thrust that characterized the disciplines in the 1950s, their current porosity suggests that any future study of academic culture would profit from a greater concentration on substantive intellectual trends that work their changes across and despite disciplinary boundaries, and that may yet breed new taxonomies of learning.

Our disciplinary narratives yielded a new awareness of the changing affiliations of American scholarship with European intellectual life. In refounding its academic culture in the early postwar years, as we have noted above, America in its quest to secure both liberalism and intellectual certainty returned to its Anglo-

Saxon philosophical roots. Of continental thought, Austrian philosophical and economic ideas, themselves deriving from English empirical rationalism, were fruitfully absorbed into their respective American fields. French and German influences, however, stifled by Nazism, cut off by the War, and little relevant to the quest for a stable liberal capitalist order at home in the postwar decade, lost their important traditional place in American social science and philosophy. (Max Weber and Tocqueville were notable exceptions.)

When it resumed in the 1950s, the postwar flow of ideas across the Atlantic reversed its direction, switching from west to east as American scholarship in many fields acquired a primacy in Europe that was the intellectual accompaniment of the nation's world power. When issues of culture and community moved to the center of the American stage, however, new continental influences entered American academic culture. The liberal Anglo-Saxon thought of the fifties, oriented toward science, was ill-suited to deal with the problems of community, identity, and affective values that erupted in the sixties and that have been with us ever since. In the ever-widening area of cultural studies, continental philosophic and critical thinking has become a major factor in recasting the function and substance of scholarship. The development of transdisciplinary intellectual discourse and the shifting impact of European ideas of different kinds and provenance have thus become closely intertwined. Both are among the many problems touched upon but not resolved in this study. For, whatever its accomplishments in clarifying the dimensions of the broad but under-cultivated field of academic culture, our inquiry is offered as a beginning only, seeking to draw readers into the issues raised and to prompt further investigation and reflection.

PART I

HISTORICAL CONTEXT

Thomas Bender

Politics, Intellect, and the American University, 1945–1995

B Y MOST MEASURES, the half century following World War II
has been the "golden age" of the American university.[1] The
period was haunted by the bomb, McCarthyism undermined academic freedom, and the Cold War distorted intellectual
agendas. Other qualifiers could be named. Yet one cannot but be
impressed. The American research university simultaneously adapted
and actively furthered a dramatic expansion and significant diversification of its student body and faculty while its research and
graduate training capacity was greatly strengthened. It was a remarkable transformation, with both quantity and quality rising.
Recognizing new constituencies and opportunities for expansion,
universities sought and gained both private and public support.
On the government side alone, there was a massive reallocation of
resources; between 1950 and 1970 governmental expenditures for
higher education rose from $2.2 billion to $23.4 billion, and to
$31 billion in 1991.[2]

There was a pattern of leveling up: by 1970 or so, research and
training was no longer dominated by a select few institutions—
Chicago and the Ivies. Distinction was as likely to be found in
major public institutions (Berkeley, Ann Arbor, Madison) as private ones, though recent developments, since about 1985, threaten
to reestablish this divide as major private institutions have gained
resources relative to public ones.[3] All areas of the country became
home to major research institutions, and the number of institu-

*Thomas Bender is University Professor of the Humanities and Professor of History at
New York University.*

tions with stature as major research and graduate training campuses increased from about twenty to more than 125 in the half century.[4] But if there has been some leveling at the top among the institutions examined in this inquiry, considerable differentiation still marks the 3,600 institutions of higher education in the United States, where a half million faculty teach. Over the past half century this decentralized system has become nationalized even while remaining differentiated, making difference feel more hierarchical now than in 1940 when institutions, including Harvard, Berkeley, and Princeton, were more local, even parochial in outlook.[5]

Before World War I, many of the most ambitious and talented American scientists and scholars had sought advanced training abroad. During the interwar years, however, the American university became self-sufficient, and the academic leaders of the postwar era were mostly American trained, though in some fields they were significantly influenced by the émigré scientists and scholars who fled European fascism.[6]

The American research establishment had taken form during the interwar years, and postwar developments would build upon these foundations. Two characteristics in particular would have struck visitors from major research centers in Europe. First, there was (and is) the American combination of advanced research and undergraduate teaching in a single institution. Second, visitors would be surprised by the number and diversity of decentralized institutions, each organized more by local opportunity than by national policy. Partly from these two circumstances, there was more space and more opportunity in the American system for innovation and for the incorporation of new disciplines and fields. The fact that change could occur faster and with less bureaucratic conflict in the loosely organized American system would become an advantage in the years of growth after the war.

Before the war, national academic systems were rather insular, but the postwar years witnessed the development of an international scholarly community, sustained in part by exchange programs supported by the United States government (e.g., Fulbright scholarships) and major foundations. In the natural sciences, where resources were so important, the United States came to dominate this internationalized research environment, but there was an important international role for the United States in the social sciences, especially in sociology (briefly) and economics (continuing). More recently, the end of the Cold War has promoted a new level of international visibility for American academic experts, and in a broader context the advent of global academic communication has been both advanced and dominated by American research and scholarship.

The quantity and quality of American research cannot be measured with any precision, but some crude indicators are available. For example, 80 percent of all citations in electronic retrieval systems are in English.[7] And the awarding of Nobel Prizes indicates an increasing recognition of American research: before 1946, one in seven Nobel Prizes went to Americans, while between 1946 and 1975 Americans received one in two.[8] Notwithstanding the attention given to a few French ideas recently imported into the United States, American research universities are massive exporters of research and importers of graduate students, mostly in science but also more generally. With no intention of trivializing the matter, one can say that only American scholarship, research, and advanced training have the international stature and appeal of American movies, popular music, software, and basketball.

Yet the public has taken little notice of this success; indeed, in a spirit of disappointment Americans may even be initiating its dismantling. Within academe, moreover, there is a pervasive sense of unease, and the origins of this self-doubt precede the current financial crisis of higher education. In fact, there is a certain paradox in the success of academe. Its recognized achievements (disciplinary excellence in the context of dramatic expansion) have not strengthened academic culture as a whole. It has even produced conflicts about its mission, particularly its civic role, and there has been a weakening of the informal compact between the university and society.

Academe is also a victim of larger transformations in American society. The incorporation of higher learning into the center of American established institutions, including the government, has enhanced the university, but it has also made it vulnerable to a larger disaffection with those institutions. Universities have also been focal points (and sometimes at the leading edge) for increasingly controversial efforts to overcome racial and sexual injustices.

The most compelling aspirations of the universities—whether one speaks of advanced scholarship or progressive social interventions—have prompted more criticism than congratulation.

What follows is a brief and necessarily selective elaboration of the phases and contexts of change in American academic culture. It highlights some of the more important social, intellectual, and political trends that have intersected and affected the trajectory of academe's ascent and apparent loss of standing.

MAKING THE GOLDEN AGE

The period following World War II was one of two great moments of academic reform in the United States—the other coming after the Civil War, when the sixty-seven land grant colleges were created and the modern American research university was established. In the half century following the founding of The Johns Hopkins University in 1876, educational leaders augmented a substantial university system in the United States. But it still fell short of the highest ambitions of the research community, a point underscored in Abraham Flexner's scathing report of 1930 on the universities of the United States, Great Britain, and Germany.[9] Twenty years later a major appraisal of the state of American scholarship praised progress but saw most of it as very recent. Prewar social science and humanities research, it seemed in 1953, was too often marked and marred by "fact-finding," "over-specialization," and "trivial investigations."[10] Moreover, the style of academic life had begun to change since the war. A genteel profession became more diverse and worldly. Postwar academics were less gentlemanly and more professionally ambitious, fired by aspirations to upward mobility.

There was a strong sense that the postwar era would demand more from universities, both as teaching and as research institutions. Harvard commissioned a study of its curriculum, producing, in 1945, *General Education in a Free Society,* otherwise known as the famous "Red Book." Two years later the President's Commission on Higher Education presented its multivolume report, *Higher Education for a Democracy* (1947). Both envisioned an expansion of education: more students and wider responsibilities for the future direction of society. The Red Book made a case for studying science and the texts of the European humanist tradition, associating them with freedom and democracy. This argument, framed against the backdrop of fascism and communism, preserved a role for history and the historical disciplines in a blueprint for a higher education oriented to contemporary concerns. The President's Commission pointedly criticized economic and racial barriers to equal education, and the language was strong enough on the issue of racial injustice to prompt several commissioners, including the scientist Arthur H. Compton and historian Douglas S. Freeman, to note their dissent. The report was attentive to the diversity of the American people, and it urged reforms that would make higher education responsive to their various needs and interests but at the same time committed to a curriculum sufficiently unified to nourish a common culture and citizenship. The report explained that "liberal education," the lineage of which was distinctly aristocratic, must be converted into its democratic counterpart, "general education," which is "directly relevant to the demands of contemporary society."[11]

The next half century would witness the predicted expansion of access to higher education, but it is not clear that university faculty expected to make much accommodation to these changes, nor does it appear that any special needs or aspirations of these new students were considered by the faculty and administration. The faculty of elite institutions provided the vision for the Golden Age of the postwar university, and its priorities reflected their interests.[12] Between 1940 and 1990, federal funds for higher education increased by a factor of twenty-five, enrollment by ten, and average teaching loads were reduced by half.[13]

The nationalization of higher education tended to establish a single standard for excellence—the model of the major research university. Ernest Boyer complained that just when American higher education opened itself to a larger and more diverse student body, "the culture of the professoriate was becoming more hierarchical and restrictive."[14] This process seems also to have advanced a growing commitment to (and internalization of) meritocratic standards. Family backgrounds, regional loyalties, and ethnic backgrounds generally counted for less, and the universities became the principal carriers of the universalistic values then described as "modern."[15] One must recognize the historical incorporation of these values into the core meaning of the university to understand the threat presented by supposed challenges to them today. Much that seems upsetting today might have been less provocative to the interwar American university.[16]

Faculty values—research opportunities, better colleagues, better students, greater autonomy—drove university development and established the standards by which universities were judged and ranked, at least those universities that aspired to distinction (and in a nationally competitive market, more and more were urged toward such aspirations). The goal of raising academic standards in appointments tended to empower elite scholars and departments over administrators, and it reduced the claim of institutional or local particularities. Indeed, the historian Richard Freeland argues that "the central constituencies of the academic culture were the scholarly disciplines and the learned societies they sponsored, for it was these groups that could confer a reputation for excellence."[17] So radical was this transformation that Christopher Jencks and David Riesman called it, in the title of their book of 1968, *The Academic Revolution.*

This pattern of change freed faculty for a stronger research orientation, and it enabled a firmer sense of academic autonomy and disciplinary professionalism. Whereas the Red Book had asked philosophers to investigate and teach "the place of human aspirations and ideals in the total scheme of things," the postwar discipline, embracing the inward-looking and donnish analytical movement, eschewed such a civic role. In retrospect it appears that the disciplines were redefined over the course of the half century following the war: from the means to an end they increasingly became an end in themselves, the possession of the scholars who constituted them. To a greater or lesser degree, academics sought some distance from civics. The increasingly professionalized disciplines were embarrassed by moralism and sentiment; they were openly or implicitly drawn to the model of science as a vision of professional maturity.[18]

The proper work of academics became disciplinary development and the training of students for the discipline. The authors of the Red Book recognized this possibility and pointed out that "one of the subtlest and most prevalent effects of specialism has been that. . .subjects have tended to be conceived and taught with an eye...to their own internal logic rather than their larger usefulness to students."[19] Talcott Parsons, who taught at Harvard, reflected the dominant mood in an address to the American Sociological Association in 1959. He argued that as a scientific discipline sociology "is clearly primarily dedicated to the advancement and transmission of empirical knowledge" and only "secondarily to the communication of such knowledge to non-members."[20]

The transformation of academic culture was possible, in part, because the onset of the Cold War mobilized the state to invest heavily in research and scholarship, especially in science and in area studies.[21] One of the great developments of the postwar university, in fact, was the academic enclosure of international studies, which had earlier been widely distributed among missionaries, journalists, and travel writers, and international business.[22]

But the needs of the Cold War state were not the only reasons for investment in higher education. The postwar years were marked by an awareness of expanding resources and a level of abundance that would permit massive investment in the universities, especially the biggest and best ones. After a decade of scarcity, the GNP grew over 100 percent between 1939 and 1945. There was a sharp but brief dip in economic growth between 1945 and 1947, but the rebuilding of Europe and the building of a permanent war economy sustained growth almost without interruption for two decades. The titles of two widely read books capture the mood: David Potter's *People of Plenty* (1954), followed by John Kenneth Galbraith's *The Affluent Society* (1958).[23]

It is difficult today to grasp the magnitude of the infusion of new funds into the university, especially the most select research universities, in the quarter-century following World War II. By far, the greater portion of these investments went to the natural sciences and engineering, but substantial funding went to the social sciences, and this support may well have artificially sustained a very high level of professional development and a sense of autonomy. For the period from 1946 to 1958, foundation support for academic social science amounted to more than $85 million, 48 percent of which went to three institutions (Harvard, Columbia, and Berkeley).[24] Between 1959 and 1964, the big three foundations (Rockefeller, Ford, and Carnegie) bestowed nearly $100 million on political science departments, half of which went to the same three institutions.[25]

But it was not only applied knowledge nor international studies nor politically useful knowledge that was supported. Theoretical work in both the natural and social sciences was nourished, as was humanistic scholarship. Indeed, postwar Americans were newly sympathetic to the claims of scholarship and art, a point noted at the time by the critic Lionel Trilling.[26] The depression had discredited the business elite, who had historically been a major source of anti-intellectualism in the United States.[27] Intellectuals inside and outside of the government gained status, partly because of the policy success of Keynesian economics, an academic theory of acknowledged utility.

In the twenty years following World War II, American intellectuals, according to Edward Shils, were welcomed into the centers of American power and influence.[28] Americans had become vastly more receptive to what Clark Kerr in 1963 called the university's "invisible product, knowledge."[29] Policy studies were developed in major university institutes, but the less practical disciplines were supported as well, as evidence of the cultural achievements of a new world power. John F. Kennedy symbolized this new sensibility, both for the technocrats he brought into his administration and for his apparent cultural sophistication. His interest in art and intellect implied a qualitative liberalism that led to the creation of the National Endowments for the Arts and Humanities in 1965.

The new and broadened respect for humanistic learning was important, but the idea of research was especially associated with science. Much of science's appeal derived from its promise of new technologies and economic development, a mantra regularly invoked by university presidents before state legislators. It was a successful strategy in the short run, but over time it left science and the research university vulnerable. Quite unexpectedly, it invited radical critics of the 1960s to blame the university for society's ills and for complicity in the war. Conservatives, who had always had reservations about state support for research except for that in the defense-related category, grew increasingly skeptical. By the 1980s public support had seriously eroded, with serious consequences not only for science but for the standing of academic research in general.

Reference to the G.I. Bill is commonplace in discussions of the expansion of higher education, and I must reiterate its importance here. In 1947–1948, the Veterans Administration paid the tuition for almost half the male college students in the United States, and by 1962 higher education had received $5 billion from that source on behalf of veterans of World War II and the Korean War.[30] Mostly due to the impact of the G.I. Bill, the number of college students doubled between 1938 and 1948. Those who recall the Quonset huts on college campuses will have a sense of the true magnitude of this population increase. But it was an opportunity as well, making new resources available, especially to public universities. The G.I. Bill paid out-of-state tuition rates for soldiers no matter what their residence. This produced windfalls for many universities, especially the University of California, which in 1947–1948 took in more than $12 million from out-of-state fees. That surplus revenue, combined with the general growth of the California economy, supplied Robert Sproul and Clark Kerr with the unrestricted financial resources that enabled them to leverage Berkeley to the premier position it had achieved by 1960.[31]

But enrollment was driven by other forces as well: a new awareness of the value of college degrees and the prosperity to sustain the ambitions of an expanding middle class. The rate of the rise in college enrollment kept accelerating. Between 1960 and 1980 the number of college students tripled, the largest percentage increase since the period from 1875 to 1895, the first era of massive educational reform.[32] The magnitude of this increase no doubt accounts in part for the strains within the university and between the university and society.

Not only did the numbers of students increase, but so did the range of their social backgrounds. Enrollments had been increasing since the late nineteenth century, but as recently as 1940, the student body of American higher education remained largely upper middle class in origin. Only after the war did American higher education become a mass phenomenon, increasing its representative character every decade thereafter. If our campuses as a whole still fail to be genuinely representative, urban campuses, even of elite research institutions, come close. By the 1970s, the changes in class origins, gender ratios, race, and ethnicity were beginning to transform the culture of the university, even as the university expanded the cultural resources available to increasingly diverse cohorts of students.

As universities grew and moved to the center of American society, so did the professoriate and intellectuals generally.[33] Indeed, the 1950s witnessed considerable self-consciousness among intellectuals. Aware of themselves as a rising class, they wrote endlessly about the role and status of intellectuals in the United States. This enhanced position coexisted with a worry that mass society would provide no home for serious intellect.[34] Intellectuals often portrayed themselves as beleaguered, seeking a haven in a hostile world, and they defended the university as a free space for intellect. With the rise of McCarthyism, such defensiveness and the need for this sort of safe place in universities became all the more important; Richard Hofstadter responded by writing a history of academic freedom that emphasized its legitimacy and importance in the McCarthy era.[35]

POSTWAR CULTURE

The immediate postwar mood in the United States was one of relief, but it was not a period of relaxation. There was an undercurrent of uncertainty, even terror. The bomb, the specter of an expanding communism, and the ever-present preparation for war transformed the conditions of life. Was the United States, even if more worldly and more powerful, up to the challenges of the era? Public policy and private aspirations both pointed to the promotion of a consumer society, marked by a landscape of corporations, suburbs, and shopping centers that redefined middle-class life. While science offered progress, many worried; while modernity beckoned, there was a pervasive sense of alienation in this new world, something evident in the most notable literature and painting of the period.

Even as Americans embraced a bright and shiny world of consumer products, American intellectuals became more sensitive to the problem of evil than at any time since the seventeenth century. It was almost predictable that Perry Miller, the distinguished Harvard professor of American literature, would in 1949 publish an intellectual biography of Jonathan Edwards that self-consciously made him a contemporary, or that the neo-orthodox theologian Reinhold

Niebuhr would become a beacon for a new "realism" in American liberal thought, even for many nonbelievers.[36] More generally, literary studies rediscovered and celebrated those American writers, particularly Nathaniel Hawthorne and Herman Melville, who challenged American optimism, who were sensitive to the power of blackness, and who expressed a tragic sense of life. Freud, who had been misinterpreted in the 1920s as a proponent of sexual liberation, became for intellectuals in the 1950s a darker Freud, the Freud who wrote *Civilization and Its Discontents* (1930).[37]

From one perspective, the postwar years are notable for a revival of religion. Among intellectuals Reinhold Niebuhr exerted enormous influence, and at a more popular level church membership was growing rather dramatically. Yet it was also a moment of triumphant secularism in the academy, and by the end of the 1970s the secularism and liberalism of the educated classes and the religiosity of other, less cosmopolitan Americans marked a major fault line in American culture and politics that would be manifest in the political and cultural conflicts of the 1980s and 1990s.[38]

It is too easy to overlook how deeply encompassing Christian academic culture was before 1945. We remember T. S. Eliot's literary prescriptions, but we should also recall his important political intervention in 1940, with a small book on *The Idea of a Christian Society*.[39] The academic humanities were the possession of Christians in the 1940s. Lionel Trilling's appointment in English at Columbia in the late 1930s was highly unusual, and before World War II there were no Jews in any Yale College department. In the context of what David Hollinger has denoted a *Kulturkämpfe* in the United States, scientists and others mobilized in the 1940s against an aggressive and worrisome religious resistance to science, modernity, and cosmopolitanism. It was with such dangers from religious as well as political ideologies in mind that Robert Merton, Sidney Hook, and other secularists sought to establish a cluster of modern, Enlightenment values: science, democracy, cosmopolitanism.[40]

All of this would change after 1945. American intellectual culture, academic and literary, would be de-Christianized.[41] There were rapidly growing religious movements that had significant potential, later realized, for anti-intellectual hostility to the arts and to academic culture, but in 1950, a secular and scientific culture was established in the American university, enough so that William F. Buckley could make a mark attacking it.[42] Protestant dominance within the faculties of American research universities and elite colleges, especially in the humanities, was dissolved by a dramatic influx of Jewish scholars and scientists and, much later, a smaller influx of Catholics.

In 1936, on its three hundredth anniversary, Harvard altered its university seal, dropping *Christo et Ecclesiae,* leaving only *Veritas,* with three open books. The change signaled the progress of a secular, scientific understanding of knowledge. Heretofore, whether formally articulated or not, religion had provided the moral authority and basis of cultural unity for higher education, even for the new research universities. But by the middle third of the twentieth century, it was assumed that the university would be held together by the ideal of inquiry, which would unify scholars investigating the whole domain of knowledge. This vision was not new; it had been articulated in the United States by Harvard's Charles W. Eliot in the late nineteenth century. But the context was new; now academic culture was thoroughly secular. Under such circumstances, as Julie Reuben has recently argued, the idea of research lacked the capacity to provide the unifying authority to sustain an academic culture that amounted to more than the aggregate of autonomous disciplines.[43] Indeed, it may even be, as she suggests, that this combination of secularization and specialization paved the way at Harvard and elsewhere for the introduction of a formalism in philosophy and other disciplines that fostered a separation of method from a substantive ethics.

The increasing emphasis on scientific method and objectivity, along with a shrinking menu of social questions to be examined, derived in part from the advent of substantial foundation support for the social sciences in the interwar years. To an extent, the emphasis upon objectivity represented an obvious caution about offending powerful donors. But it served scholars in a deeper way: it legitimated political interventions by denying any political character to the act. "If their findings were morally neutral, objective descriptions of institutional and human functions," as Edward Purcell has written, then social scientists did not have to face the question of value or take responsibility for the "actual consequences" of their interventions.[44]

The growth of federal support, beginning with the establishment of the National Science Foundation (NSF) in 1950, led to the elevation of peer review to a sacred level.[45] The policy of peer review protected the academic freedom of scholars and shielded foundations, the NSF, and, later, the National Endowments from criticism. But, by privileging audiences of peers, this development encouraged a focus on the model of science, an emphasis on method, and a narrowness of reference in social studies and humanistic scholarship. The unintended but distinct long-term effect of this reorientation of research authorized disciplinary (even subdisciplinary) autonomy and a certain distancing of academic work from society at large. By the 1990s this structure of self-governance by peers would be characterized in important sectors of the larger public as elitist and irresponsible, and it became the focus of attacks on the National Endowment for the Arts and, to a lesser extent, the National Endowment for the Humanities.

A sense that ideology had made the first half of the twentieth century an age of disaster encouraged a quest for certainty at mid-century. Much as Descartes had been driven to secure a ground for absolute knowledge in the aftermath of the revocation of the Edict of Nantes and in the midst of the religious wars of the seventeenth century, intellectuals in the mid-twentieth century, witnesses of war and totalitarian ideologies, may have been drawn to epistemologies of certainty as an antidote. One can imagine, as Stephen Toulmin has, that in such circumstances the dream of certain knowledge as an alternative to ideology, perhaps even to politics, would have an appeal.[46] This impulse is clear in philosophy, political science, and economics; the case of literary studies is more complex, for the New Criticism combined a quest for analytical precision with a hostility to the science from which this program derived its cultural value.

By 1950 the intolerance generated by McCarthyism and the Cold War moved academics and intellectuals generally to make themselves and their work less vulnerable to attack. For example, Marx was replaced by Freud, the word "capitalism" dropped out of social theory after the war,[47] and class became stratification. Economics, in its Keynesian and consumerist emphases, was oriented to growth and consumption, turning away from reform and distribution questions.[48] The creation of the Department of Social

Relations at Harvard in 1946, under the leadership of Talcott Parsons, was an important interdisciplinary initiative, but it also marked a revealing shift in academic outlook, one exemplified by Parsons himself: his interests shifted from history and political economy to sociology, cultural anthropology, and psychology, especially psychoanalysis. Interest in transformative theories of society, in short, waned.

More broadly, Arthur Schlesinger, Jr., staked out a progressive position that was clearly distinguishable from Marxism and communism. In *The Vital Center* (1949), he articulated an ideology of freedom that promoted liberal internationalism and domestic reform.[49] But his tract was not quite a clarion call of Enlightenment optimism. Acknowledging the influence of Reinhold Niebuhr's neo-orthodox thought, he stressed human limits. History, as he saw it in 1949, "is not a redeemer, promising to solve all human problems in time; nor is man capable of transcending the limitations of his being. Man is generally entangled in unsolvable problems; history is consequently a tragedy in which we are all involved."[50] Nonetheless, this skeptical or ironic attitude fostered an activist posture in intellectuals committed to the Cold War.

For those who wanted to get on with disciplinary scholarship, such times recommended particular methodologies, more scientific and less engaged. The political scientist David Easton has found in McCarthyism a stimulus for the development of a more scientific and objective political science, for it provided a "protective posture for scholars." It was, he suggests, a gain for political science, even if "for the wrong reasons."[51] But one must be careful in generalizing. A precise sense of chronology and generational succession is needed. For some academics, particularly in the immediate postwar group, talk of method carried a progressive agenda, much as had been the case with the development of the new method of historical economics in the last third of the nineteenth century. But in many cases, increasingly over the postwar decades, the method had its own fascinations.

If such was the path of philosophy and the social sciences toward sharper and more precise models of knowledge, the humanities, or at least parts of history, literary studies, and anthropology, turned in the opposite direction, interestingly, for some of the same reasons. In the face of absolute ideologies, such figures as

Lionel Trilling in literature and Richard Hofstadter in history stressed the extraordinary complexity of social life, urging restraint and a sense of the tragic in history.[52]

Both groups—those seeking simplicity and those stressing complexity—were nervous about the politics of mass democracy. For one group, expertise might obviate excessive participation by the thoughtless masses. The other group, cognizant of totalitarian mass societies in Germany and the Soviet Union and of the worries of émigré scholars about such societies, expressed their distaste for populism, which they demonized, associating it with anti-modern, unrealistic, and intolerant politics.[53] More comfortable with elites than with the masses, these quasi-democrats envisioned a moderate pluralism in which negotiation among elites forestalled enthusiastic democracy and promoted sound policy.[54]

The social sciences seemed to hold special promise for addressing the challenges of the postwar era. Gunnar Myrdal's *An American Dilemma* (1944), commissioned by the Carnegie Corporation, represented both the ambition of social sciences and the hope invested in them.[55] After Hiroshima, both John Dewey and Robert Maynard Hutchins, combatants on so many educational issues, agreed that social knowledge must now catch up to technological knowledge, with universities taking the lead. Within forty-eight hours of Hiroshima, in an act as comic as it was important, Talcott Parsons and four fellow social scientists submitted a letter to the *Washington Post* asserting that in light of "the startling news of the atomic bomb," the social sciences had a vital role in the now urgent challenge of peace. Human intelligence could solve "human problems as well as. . .those of atomic physics." The letter urged a high-level study to "explore the needs which the social sciences must fill in a world equipped for suicide." Continuing this argument, Parsons later argued successfully for the inclusion of the social sciences in the National Science Foundation.[56] Parsons did not turn his hand to the study of the atomic age; rather he devoted himself to the development of a discipline of sociology. By outlining a general theory of social action and explanations of social development at the societal scale (modernization theory), he sought to endow the social sciences with the status of the physical sciences.

Other social scientists did, however, turn to the task of describing and understanding contemporary culture. Indeed, the postwar era saw the emergence of the "social-science intellectual," and David Riesman, senior author of the best-selling *The Lonely Crowd* (1950), became the most widely known. It was specifically as a social scientist that he appeared on the cover of *Time* magazine in 1954.[57] Byron E. Shafer has recently observed that "the immediate postwar years were to be the glory days for the social sciences. . . . They had achieved practical wartime applications; they had acquired new research techniques; they possessed nearly unlimited aspirations. They could finally hope to join the 'true' sciences, simultaneously advancing knowledge of social life and addressing real social problems."[58] At this golden moment, method and social purpose worked together.

Only later would method and disciplinary development extrude the civic work so central to the historical aspirations of the social sciences, leading to the circumstance recently reported in the *New York Times*: a survey by the American Economic Association found that nearly two-thirds of graduate economics professors consider their calling "too unrelated to the real world."[59] It is revealing that no present-day social scientists invite the general interest of intellectuals in the way David Riesman, Ruth Benedict, B. F. Skinner, or even Robert Merton, Talcott Parsons, Daniel Bell, or Edward Shils did in the 1950s.[60]

The end of ideology, a common phrase used to describe the political and intellectual orientation of the 1950s, not only assumed the exhaustion of Marxism in the West, but it implied a shift from historical to analytic, process to structural, economistic to culturalist approaches to the study of society and thought. Like the phrase "consensus history," the end of ideology presumed that the big questions were settled. Political conflict, therefore, would be within a consensus, thus inviting a style of social research in what Robert Merton called the "middle range," an approach that elaborated on theoretical questions susceptible to rather direct empirical verification.[61] Parsonian social theory, less empirical, similarly assumed a consensus on core values.[62]

There were similar developments in other disciplines: intense study and theory construction within tight bounds. The New Criticism in English represented, among other things, an increase in professional ambition and a sharpening of the object of study—the literariness of a work. The analytical turn in philosophy abandoned the discipline's expansive Deweyan vision, but it promised verifiable and universal truth. In political science, also, behavioralism eschewed ideology and limited context in order to produce remarkably fruitful middle range problems and theory. Economics moved from institutional analysis and description of the economy to rigorous models and the manipulation of massive data sets newly available after the war.

Academic intellect in the 1950s and thereafter increasingly located itself in a larger international arena and began actively to study contemporary societies beyond the Northern Atlantic, but at the same time it turned inward to the study of the United States. While the influx of European émigré scholars Europeanized certain fields to a degree, ranging from political theory to political sociology, musicology, and the history of art, there was a simultaneous proliferation of interdisciplinary American studies programs that later became the staging ground and model for initiatives on behalf of African-American studies, women's studies, and ethnic studies.[63]

Gradually, but especially in the past quarter-century, the core intellectual tradition of general education that had earlier been presumed to represent the best of European culture was increasingly supplemented by engagement with the art, ideas, and experience of Americans. This shift partly explains the identification of the university with the society in 1968 and afterward, an association implausible during the interwar years. This blending of the university into society (or vice versa) today provides the context for many of the battles over historical representation and literary canons. The "culture wars" as we know them would not be fought on campus had this Americanization of academic culture not occurred.[64]

A commitment to American nationalism grew stronger and more celebratory as well soon after the war, something noted by historian Merle Curti.[65] American nationality was distinctive, exceptionalist; it was at once pluralistic and consensual. Myrdal's famous study of race relations, for example, was built upon a confidence that there was an American consensus, a universally shared American creed. Will Herberg made a similar argument in his widely read *Protestant-Catholic-Jew* (1955).[66] Religious difference need not divide the society, for there was agreement on the idea of religion itself. This complacent and consensual nationalism would be sharply challenged after 1968.

If many leading intellectuals (Reinhold Niebuhr, Arthur Schlesinger, Lionel Trilling, Sidney Hook, George Kennan, and Perry Miller, among others) embraced a humanism marked by a tragic sense, it was also an era of sentimental humanism committed to representing the unity of man. Such was the appeal of Carl Jung's notion of archetype, of Joseph Campbell's *The Hero With A Thousand Faces* (1949),[67] and of the anthropology of Ruth Benedict. Perhaps the most widely known gesture of this sort was the *Family of Man* exhibition. Organized by Edward Steichen at the Museum of Modern Art in New York in 1954, it broke attendance records at the museum and was seen by more than nine million people over the course of a seven-year government-sponsored international tour. Haunted by the fear of nuclear annihilation (the last segment was a six-by-eight-foot image of the hydrogen bomb), the exhibit acknowledged differences among humans. Yet it was determined, in the words of Edward Steichen, that it would "arrange these pictures so they stress alikeness." Otherwise, "we have lost out."[68]

Even with their deep belief in American exceptionalism, or perhaps because of it, educated Americans after the war were quite receptive to European high culture. More than ever before it seemed to belong to Americans, who had, after all, saved Europe. With the expansion of higher education, a larger part of the American elite became familiar with and sympathetic to the European humanist tradition. The Aspen Institute, founded in 1945 by Walter Paepcke, a Chicago businessman who headed the Container Corporation of America, Henry Luce, the founder of the *Time-Life* empire, and Robert Maynard Hutchins, president of the University of Chicago, provides an example of this superficial Europeanization of American culture. The Institute sought to sustain the value of culture in a commercial society, and it aimed to use art and culture as a salve for a war-torn world. In 1949, it sponsored a festival commemorating the two hundredth anniversary of the birth of Goethe, a figure who represented the ideal of a cosmopolitan humanist. Such an event, and others like it, were expected to heighten the stature of American culture, making it commensurate with its postwar international leadership in politics and economics. Aspen also presaged the movement of artists and progressive business leaders who supported the public art movement, the creation of Lincoln Center and similar institutions in other cities, and the establishment of the National Endowment for the Arts in the early 1960s.[69]

The utterly unexpected challenge to assumptions of political consensus and to the authority of European high culture in the 1960s severely weakened the self-confidence and public standing of the social sciences and humanistic scholarship. Many social scientists, recognizing that they had a strong base in the academy, turned inward, focusing more on the development of their disciplines than upon describing, explaining, and participating in the society around them.[70]

Humanists moved in two directions. Some greatly expanded the domain of the humanities, examining a broader range of cultural expression, while others assumed an increasingly defensive posture. The unstable balance between responsibility for the custody of the tradition of European humanism and the task of cultivating the critical intellect did not survive the 1960s. As early as 1961, in a famous essay entitled "On the Teaching of Modern Literature," Lionel Trilling expressed his concern that the critical side might be pressed too far.[71] By the 1980s the two orientations within the humanities that at their best complemented each other became competing academic ideologies.

TOWARD THE 1960s

The intellectuals of the 1950s had come late to modernism, as Irving Howe once remarked.[72] But modernism had work to do for Howe's generation. It helped to free art from the contamination of politics, a legacy of the ideological wars of the 1930s, and in the midst of a mass culture that fed upon but threatened to devalue art, modernist claims for the autonomy of art established a categorical difference that intellectuals valued.[73] The classic statement of the cultural commitments of these modernists was an essay by Clement Greenberg, "Avant Garde and Kitsch," published in the *Partisan Review* in 1939. Greenberg had no problem distinguishing art from pretenders to art or a poem from a non-poem, and he articulated the formal challenges of modernism in his brilliant art criticism in the 1940s and 1950s.

For Greenberg's generation, the work of criticism was to establish "hard and fast cultural distinctions, exclusions, hierarchies." By the 1960s, this austere, formal, and highly intellectualist understanding of art seemed too limited, too constraining. A new generation, less fearful of contamination by the plenitude of cultural expression surrounding them, more sympathetic to a native tradition represented in literature by Walt Whitman rather than Melville, and more liberationist in feeling, looked to a "redemption of the senses."[74] It was very much in this context that Paul Goodman, Herbert Marcuse, and Norman O. Brown came to be favored intellectuals in the 1960s. Susan Sontag provided the clarifying text in her famous essay, "Notes on Camp," published in 1964,[75] but there were at the same time a number of other important indicators of change: Allan Ginsberg, Andy Warhol, and the Judson Church minimalists all challenged the categories that had seemed so fundamental in the 1950s.

When Allen Ginsberg, who had graduated from Columbia in 1948, returned a decade later for a reading in McMillin Theatre, the stage was set for delineating the difference between the 1950s and the 1960s. Ginsberg had studied the major texts of European humanism with Lionel Trilling, but he had also discovered a native tradition that began with Walt Whitman. His arrival in the sacred precincts of the humanist tradition was a jolt to the prevailing assumptions at Morningside Heights. Diana Trilling, in a famous account that might have been remembered as an anticipation of Norman Mailer's "New Journalism" had it been on the progressive rather than the reactionary side of the cultural divide, recoiled at the proposition that *Howl* was literature and thus properly sponsored (and certified) by the university.[76]

Once Andy Warhol represented a Brillo box and a Campbell's soup can as art, how could Greenberg's categories stand? On seeing the Brillo box and other works of art by Warhol in 1964, the philosopher and art critic Arthur Danto recognized that art could not be treated simply as a matter of vision, of image. In time, he realized that Warhol, more than Marcel Duchamps, more than anyone else, had forced a fundamental question: what is the nature of art?[77] Warhol also knowingly challenged the conventional modernist distinction between art and business. "After I did the thing called 'art,'" he reflected, "I went into business art...for business is the best art."[78]

The group of poets, musicians, artists, and dancers who came together at Judson Memorial Church in 1963 mixed all the arts, creating what later came to be known as performance art. For them the fact of the performing body was more important than any objectified genre. Feeling that all things were possible, there was a playfulness, a mixing of high and low, academic and vernacular, physical and spiritual. They sought, as critic Sally Barnes has written, "to *embody* democracy."[79]

Such developments in the larger intellectual and artistic culture posed serious challenges to academic culture in general and the humanities in particular. Most of the humanities disciplines are object-focused, and these larger cultural changes, well before Derridean theories of deconstruction entered the academy, put in question the status of the object of humanist inquiry. Moreover, given the rigidity of the categories that defined not only proper objects of inquiry but also disciplinary terrains, the university found it difficult to engage the contemporary culture. By the end of the 1960s the gap between the university and advanced culture had widened to the point of open conflict.

If these changes in the cultural domain threatened to subvert the ways of humanistic scholarship, political developments overwhelmed the social sciences, which had been preoccupied with notions of pluralist consensus and equilibrium models. Such approaches to social analysis had provided no warning that transformative social movements were taking shape. Economics, which had been celebrated for finding the secret of growth, lost some of its luster when the pervasiveness of poverty was discovered in the 1960s. And as the 1960s became the 1970s and the American economy suffered a condition popularly called "stagflation," economists and the public wondered why their models seemed to lack the capacity to explain what was happening.

Social criticism before 1963 had mostly described the follies of white, middle-class consumers, complaining about suburban life, tailfins on cars, organization men, or "other-directed" moderns. By 1963, when Martin Luther King led the March on Washington, one can detect a shift marked by Michael Harrington's *The Other America* (1962) and Nathan Glazer's and Daniel Patrick Moynihan's *Beyond the Melting Pot* (1963).[80] Henceforth the focus of social criticism became class, race, and ethnicity, with issues of gender to follow a decade later. The "rights revolution" of the 1960s and 1970s empowered groups, largely because inequalities were often associated with group designations. It was reasonable for groups suffering discrimination to so organize and identify themselves, but Americans began to worry by the 1980s that the much celebrated value of individualism was being threatened along with a broader sense of the civic.

The political origins of the 1960s are in the mid-1950s, when Rosa Parks refused to go to the back of a bus in Montgomery, Alabama, and when the United States allowed itself to be drawn into Indochina following France's failure there. By the late 1960s, however, the issues of life-style, war, poverty, and race converged, making for a volatile compound that produced riots in cities and divided university campuses. Some academics were radicalized in the process; others retreated to more conservative positions. The middle ground narrowed to the vanishing point. The university is still struggling to accommodate the tensions produced by the continuing coexistence of the rigid categories embraced in the 1950s and the expansive commitments and sensibilities associated with the 1960s.

Perhaps the most important legacy of the 1960s has been a loss of faith in elite institutions, among which universities were included. The failure of the policies advocated by "the best and the brightest" in Vietnam and the "dirty tricks" and casual disregard of law and the Constitution by the Nixon White House produced a legitimation crisis, weakening both political and cultural authority in the United States. Academic experts, once identified with grand hopes, had become a part of the problem, not a part of the solution. It is a chastening story, the course from high optimism about the collaboration of academic expertise and state action reflected in the Full Employment Act of 1946 to the reaction by the Left and the Right against the state and expertise in the 1970s. The demolition of the Pruitt-Igoe housing project in St. Louis in the mid-1970s came to symbolize the failure of a dream.

Liberal and radical academics, who in varying degrees had embraced a politics of participatory democracy in the 1960s, lost confidence in the conventional political process by the end of the 1970s. Many of these academic intellectuals redefined politics in cultural terms; the campus became the world. This move made academic culture and the syllabus, more than the class system and the conditions of community life, the locus of political energy.[81] There was also a celebration, often quite romantic, of the everyday life of ordinary folk and marginal peoples. Elitism became a pervasive worry, and this sensitivity weakened a commitment to the intellectual culture and disciplinary traditions that were (and are) the principal resources of academic intellect.

The Right, by contrast, mobilized against the government, particularly attacking assistance to the poor, to education and scholarship, and to the arts. The political intellectual, historically associated with the Left, came to be identified with the Right and with a program hostile to government support of art and intellect. In the 1980s, conservative intellectual journalists, ensconced in privately-funded positions, initiated extravagant attacks on academics—damning them either as boring and narrow pedants or as unrealistic leftist revolutionaries.[82]

The ride through and beyond the sixties was sometimes rough. But one can say that along the way intellectual life was opened up and many social and cultural practices were liberalized. It made a difference, as so many commentators have remarked, that students and faculty in universities began to dress alike after the sixties.[83] This weakening of traditional hierarchies and authority had wide ramifications, from classroom practices to the definition of research topics. It mattered, too, that students and faculty had been politically mobilized; no one can doubt that the moral and political commitments of the sixties brought issues of race, class, and gender (and new models of society, conflict, and stability) into academic work. The concern with power and exclusion that was so pervasive in the academy of the 1960s stimulated interest in the relation of the Euro-American center to other peoples and to issues of hegemony, colonialism, and domination. The European intellectual tradition that had provided a foundation for higher education (and freedom and democracy) in the Red Book of 1946 came to be associated by the academic avant-garde with forms of domination.

But if new critical perspectives and a pluralization of disciplinary practices were authorized, there is also a legacy from the sixties of disillusionment. And there has been a continuing conservative backlash.

The ambitious, white, male, Europe-oriented, and quite privileged professional culture of major research universities that had taken its style and intellectual agenda from the 1950s could not sustain itself through the last quarter of the twentieth century. After about 1971, with some variation by discipline, there was a serious and continuing job crisis in academe, especially in the humanities, and this weakened the claims of established hierarchies. The shortage of jobs, along with federal affirmative action regulations and pressure from women and African-American scholars, transformed the process of academic recruitment. Jobs were openly advertised; the "old boy" network lost legitimacy and its former power to place students. Not only did this change promote greater equality of opportunity among job candidates, but it also reduced the advantage of a small cluster of traditionally powerful departments in each discipline.

There was an influx of women into the professoriate, especially in history and literature; they were followed by a substantial increase in African-American scholars and more generally by men and women of distinctly modest and often ethnic backgrounds. The presence of these new social groups in academe changed its culture and promoted attention to issues of race, class, and gender. But more generally, it produced a more varied and thus more complicated academic culture that found it difficult to speak with one voice. As leadership was fragmented (or diversified), so was scholarship.[84] But this infusion of new talent and the breaking of forms propelled the disciplines, making the era one of remarkable intellectual invention, with new concepts and approaches marking research, especially in history, political theory, anthropology, literature, and art history.

THE CULTURAL TURN

What I have termed a cultural turn encompasses a number of trends—historicism, the linguistic turn, hermeneutics—that are, of course, distinct and even in conflict. Yet the term captures a leading tendency of the intellectual culture of our time, distinguishing it from the broadly analytic emphasis of the immediate postwar years.[85] The concept of culture, developed by Franz Boas with relativistic and pragmatic implications, spans the century, and by mid-century the idea had been absorbed by many disciplines. Just after the war, a commentator on academic trends in the United States remarked (rightly, as it turned out) that the idea of culture was "one of the most important and emancipating of all twentieth-century contributions to knowledge in the social field."[86]

It was in the 1960s, however, that our present understanding of the cultural approach began to take shape. A profoundly influential challenge to the positivistic and analytical intellectual strategies of the 1950s came in a brief, elegant book by Thomas S. Kuhn, addressing a fairly esoteric issue in the philosophy of science. That book, *The Structure of Scientific Revolutions* (1962), was quickly and eagerly read (and often misinterpreted) by scholars in the humanities and social sciences.[87] Kuhn offered a historicist interpretation of scientific knowledge that incorporated rich sociological insight identifying communities of inquirers as the authority for knowledge claims. Although Kuhn (unlike some of his readers) believed in a referential theory of knowledge and the progressiveness of science, the implication of his work was a loosening of the connection between object and the interpretation of it. There was little sympathy for Kuhn's book among analytical philosophers, but it did take some of the glitter off the more extravagant claims of *the* scientific method in the humanities and social sciences. It complicated an earlier generation's assertion of a natural nesting of science, democracy, and toleration. Kuhn's work, moreover, provided a platform for Richard Rorty's more radical critique of the epistemological project of philosophy.[88]

Moving in a complementary direction, Clifford Geertz defined the human experience as interpretive; a human, he wrote in an oft-quoted phrase, is "an animal suspended in webs of significance he himself has spun." Having earlier studied economic development in Indonesia, Geertz now outlined an approach to social inquiry little concerned with issues of transformation or with the explanation of change over time. Rather, he proposed what he called a "thick description" of cultural moments, most famously a Balinese cockfight.[89] Both Kuhn and Geertz, as well as Quentin Skinner, J. G. A. Pocock, Bernard Bailyn, and others who were deeply involved in this shift toward hermeneutics, emphasized subjective meaning (rather than social causation) as the focus of social inquiry. They understood culture (or language) as constraining, as having deterministic implications, yet, unlike later commentators, they all assumed the possibility of innovation—"revolutions," in Kuhn's phrase. And Kuhn even ventured a theory of scientific change.

With Michel Foucault, whose works were first taken up in American academic discourse in the late 1960s and the 1970s, the deterministic implications of this move were vastly expanded; the human subject tended to disappear, trapped in existing "epistemes" and external linguistic structures. Foucault directly challenged the humanist tradition and the progressivist claims of the Enlightenment.[90]

Foucault built his scholarship on structuralism and went beyond it; much the same happened in the human sciences generally.[91] The key American moment came in October 1966, when The Johns Hopkins University hosted a conference funded by the Ford Foundation on "The Languages of Criticism and the Sciences of Man." This intergenerational, international, and interdisciplinary conference, which eventually included one thousand humanists and social scientists in a two-year series of follow-up colloquia and seminars, established a broad interdisciplinary base for the introduction of French theory into the American academy. The pattern of this infiltration of American academic culture was peculiar. Although much of this thought had its origin in French philosophy, it had almost no impact in American philosophy departments.[92] Nor did it affect economics or political science, save for political theory, a marginal subfield much invigorated by its capacity to absorb theory and contemporary issues. The main impact was in less firmly bounded disciplines—literary study, anthropology, and, to a lesser extent, history.

Surprisingly, perhaps, the impact of French theory coincided with an accelerating increase in the humanistic study of American culture that fostered new fields and new theories. The study of American literature and culture, for example, has moved very near the center of humanistic inquiry in the United States today— something quite unprecedented.[93] The domain of American litera- ture has been vastly expanded in the past twenty years, with new interest in non-canonical texts, in writings by African Americans, women, Native Americans, writers of the southwest borderlands, and other previously marginalized or unnoticed literatures.

It was not simply that American academics began to study race or gender or ethnic identity with a new seriousness, but this work, impelled as often as not by a commitment to identity politics and drawing upon both Foucault and Jacques Derrida, deconstructed presumptively natural categories. Race, gender, and "oriental," for example, were not "natural" or transparent categories but rather historical or cultural constructions that constituted forms of power. Edward Said, Natalie Davis, Evelyn Fox Keller, Joan W. Scott, Henry Louis Gates, Jr., Werner Sollors, Carole Pateman, Mary Poovey, Judith Butler, and Anthony Appiah, among others, working in different disciplines and with different methods and perspectives, developed these highly influential critiques.[94] This work, which is often associated with multiculturalism and cultural studies, is strongly supported by American foundations, particu- larly the Rockefeller Foundation. It has a considerable interna- tional presence, more than American humanistic scholarship has had in the past. When foreign scholars turn to American research, especially in the American field, they are quite likely to follow the literature of race, gender, ethnic identity, and the like.

The work of the American pragmatists became the subject of new interest at home and abroad in the 1980s.[95] Only a few American philosophers moved in this direction, but they were notable ones such as Richard Rorty and Stanley Cavell. Literary critics, historians, and political theorists reinvigorated the prag- matic tradition, which offered a moderate response to the Nietzschean challenge promoted by Foucauldians and others.[96]

In some ways, the linguistic turn was a rediscovery of the semiotic theories of an American, Charles S. Peirce, the brilliant and eccen- tric philosopher who a century earlier was among the founders of

American pragmatism. But his was not the pragmatism of John Dewey, for whom truths were tested by experience and by consequential action in public. Although regard for Dewey's program is increasing today, Peirce's approach to the study of signs, texts, or discourses has been dominant. In this mode of scholarship there is very little indication of an inclination or a capacity to bring textual analysis into relation with the examination of institutions, and that is worrisome. As Edward Said has written of contemporary scholarship in the humanities, there is a danger of collapsing the social into the text; in much current practice there is little or no effort to bridge the gap between academic theory and the local politics of everyday life.[97]

Contrary to the author's intention, *The Structure of Scientific Revolutions* fed an unease about science and about the Enlightenment legacy more generally. Commitments to universalist categories became problematic in the 1980s, largely because the North Atlantic local had too often been presumed to be a global universal. Species-centered discourse was severely weakened; the emphasis was on *ethnos,* on the situated speaker or interpreter. This shift fairly marks the emergence of academic postmodernism, which emphasizes the local, the particular, the fragmentary.[98] More recently there has been a move—as surprising as it is disturbing—by religious traditionalists to build upon the postmodern critique of the academy's commitment to science and objectivity. For them postmodernism authorizes a challenge to the secularism of the research university. If there is no objectivity in science, they say, then why not give religious perspectives equal credibility with science in the academy?[99]

PROSPECTS

The biggest changes since 1945 fall under the rubric of demographics: there is now a much larger and, more importantly, a far more diverse professoriate. Greater roles have been taken by women and African-American scholars in setting intellectual agendas, both in the domain of race and gender studies and more generally. Academic culture has in a sense been de-Europeanized. Although European ideas, models, and traditions remain predominant, even for those who challenge them, they are no longer transparent.

They are interrogated and contextualized. The most energetic, even aggressive, work in literature, history, anthropology, and cinema studies is now exploring other cultures and the notions of "difference" and "otherness."

Although the culture wars continue, the theory wars have concluded. There are signs that a reengagement with history is underway, which promises a more dialogic (and fruitful) relation between theory and history in the humanities and social sciences. One sees this development in literature within the broad array of critical practices comprehended, some more historical than others, under the rubric "The New Historicism." In the social sciences, despite and to some degree in reaction to the imperial quest of rational-choice theorists for a simplified and unified social science, there is a renewed interest in institutional approaches and more complex models in economics and political science. Philosophy is the most resistant to the general drift toward some form of historicism, to the point that Richard Rorty, who has made a strong move in this direction and is perhaps the most widely read American philosopher, is no longer considered a philosopher at all by most graduate professors in the discipline. Philosophy also makes the strongest disciplinary claims for self-referential autonomy, rendering its relation to the larger intellectual public the most problematic. In its practice, if not its content, philosophy seems to have moved the least from the model developed in the 1950s.

At present, the humanities more generally seem to be moving in two directions, both under the sign of a cultural or historical turn. One eschews essentialism and emphasizes the contingent; even the most basic conventional categories of identity are treated as unstable, as cultural or historical constructs—race, gender, sexuality. Opening up such questions—provided it does not ignore the various domains of experience and institutional forms of power—has the promise of both scholarly fruitfulness and civic value.[100]

But much current scholarship in the humanities, seemingly guided by the same compass, points in a different direction. A particular deconstructive style rather crudely, and I think unintentionally, restores essentialism: one's situation, especially circumstances of race or gender, all too readily, even tautologically, determines ideology. All unmaskings have tiresomely similar denouements. Many advocates of this version of cultural studies embrace what they call a postdisciplinary academy, and they are hostile to the notion of disciplines as they have developed since the Enlightenment.[101]

Thus one tendency in the broad domain of culture studies fruitfully combines the methods of the humanities with the topical concerns once identified with the social sciences to open new terrain. Another, however, rather discouragingly closes the circle prematurely. As the space of academic inquiry opens up, as more diverse methods and approaches are adopted, one might anticipate a new cosmopolitanism among humanists. Unfortunately, such is not the case; if anything, there has been, as David Damrosch has observed, "an increase of factionality and coterie behavior."[102]

Looking past such factionalism, one finds a broad divide in academic culture today. One cluster of scholars resides in a variety of humanities disciplines (including history and anthropology). They share weak borders, openly-declared value commitments, and a historical/cultural sensibility, which produces, inevitably, a tendency toward particularism. Another group, identifying mostly with the social sciences—in mainstream economics, political science, law, sociology, and some versions of ethics—is more oriented to tight subfields (often interdisciplinary) and to methods affirmed as objective that attend little to considerations of time and place. The gap between these two interpretive frames, which roughly tracks the borders between the social sciences and the humanities, is more difficult to bridge now than at any time in the past half century.

Taking a longer view, however, one is naturally struck by important continuities, both substantive and structural, especially in the social sciences. Issues of scientism, objectivity, formalism, and the claims of rational-choice theory in the social sciences emerged in the 1920s.[103] The humanities have changed in much more fundamental ways than the social sciences since that decade, when they were archaeological and philological, dealing not at all with the aesthetic issues that are so much the issue today. Whatever the changes in content, however, it is striking how little the structure of the university has altered since the 1920s, when the present pattern of departments and divisions emerged. The department remains the basic organizational unit. Very few new departments have been created anywhere since World War II, and even fewer have been abolished. The units of university organization no longer clearly denote the actual intellectual work sustained, yet they manage to provide an effective structure for it.

The relations between the university and the public have surely been better at other times. While some disciplines and subdisciplines have established sub-publics (economics, for example, is oriented to government and business elites, and feminist scholarship is oriented to a wider, interdisciplinary, even interactive, but still particularistic audience), the notion of a general public seems to be attenuated. The dissolution of a public sphere and the limited role of academic intellect in whatever survives of that sphere is worrisome. A democratic culture and polity invites and needs an open dialogue on all questions pertaining to the human condition. Restoring a place for academic knowledge in the public culture and a role for public discussion in academic culture ought to be a high priority of both academic and public leaders. Yet we must not dream of a perfect rapprochement, of a seamless web of discourse uniting the language of daily life with that of the academy.

The university ought never be too comfortable in and with society—and vice versa. To say that the university ought to be connected to society is not to say that it might properly be a synecdoche for the world. But neither should it claim a position of transcendence.[104] There ought to be a degree of friction deriving from the critical spirit that is central to academic intellect. Our thinking about the modern university, as Wendy Steiner has recently observed, is contradictory. We imagine it at once "hermetically sealed from reality and centrally constitutive of it." But, she insists, "the value of the university, like art, lies in its simultaneous relevance and irrelevance to reality, in a balance that we continually renegotiate."[105]

ENDNOTES

[1]See Clark Kerr, *The Uses of the University,* 4th ed. (Cambridge, Mass.: Harvard University Press, 1995), chap. 6; Richard Freeland, *Academia's Golden Age: Universities in Massachusetts, 1945–1970* (New York: Oxford University Press, 1992); Roger L. Geiger, *Research and Relevant Knowledge: American Research Universities Since World War II* (New York: Oxford University Press, 1993); and Hugh Davis Graham and Nancy Diamond, *The Rise of the American Research University* (Baltimore, Md.: Johns Hopkins University Press, 1996).

[2]Robert Wuthnow, *The Restructuring of American Religion: Society and Faith Since World War II* (Princeton, N.J.: Princeton University Press, 1988), 155; David Damrosch, *We Academics: Changing the Culture of the University* (Cambridge, Mass.: Harvard University Press, 1995), 51.

[3]Clark Kerr, *The Great Transformation in Higher Education, 1960–1980* (Albany, N.Y.: State University of New York Press, 1991), 35–37.

[4]Kerr, *The Uses of the University*, 149; Jonathan R. Cole, Elinor G. Barber, and Stephen R. Graubard, eds., *The Research University in a Time of Discontent* (Baltimore, Md.: Johns Hopkins University Press, 1994), 380–381.

[5]On differentiation and the importance of *where* faculty are employed, see Burton R. Clark, "Faculty: Differentiation and Dispersion," in Arthur Levine, ed., *Higher Learning in America, 1980–2000* (Baltimore, Md.: Johns Hopkins University Press, 1993), 162–178; on localism, see Freeland, *Academia's Golden Age*.

[6]It should be noted that in the 1940s a large number of distinguished European academics joined American university faculties. Between 1933 and 1943, the Emergency Committee in Aid of Displaced Foreign Scholars helped 269 academics find positions in the United States.

[7]David L. Featherman, "What Does Society Need from Higher Education," *Items* 47 (1993): 41. Of course, Great Britain, a considerable center for scholarship, and the substantial English-speaking research establishments in the countries of the former British empire both contribute to this figure.

[8]Data on Nobels from Wuthnow, *The Restructuring of American Religion*, 155.

[9]Abraham Flexner, *Universities* (New York: Oxford University Press, 1930).

[10]Merle Curti, "The Setting and the Problem," in Merle Curti, ed., *American Scholarship in the Twentieth Century* (Cambridge, Mass.: Harvard University Press, 1953), 15.

[11]Portions of the Report are conveniently available in Richard Hofstadter and Wilson Smith, eds., *American Higher Education: A Documentary History*, 2 vols. (Chicago, Ill.: University of Chicago Press, 1961), II, 970–990; quotation from p. 990.

[12]See Richard M. Freeland, "Pragmatism Won't Save Us But It Can Help," in Robert Orrill, ed., *The Condition of American Liberal Education* (New York: College Entrance Examination Board, 1995), 158–162.

[13]Kerr, *The Uses of the University*, 142.

[14]Ernest L. Boyer, *Scholarship Reconsidered* (Princeton, N.J.: Carnegie Foundation for the Advancement of Teaching, 1990), 12–13.

[15]This is a major theme of Christopher Jencks and David Riesman, *The Academic Revolution* (Garden City, N.Y.: Doubleday, 1968).

[16]The ease with which quotas for Jewish students were deployed in the interwar years, particularly at the most elite private universities, is evidence of the weakness of universalist principles in that era.

[17]Freeland, *Academia's Golden Age*, 168.

[18]See René Wellek, "Literary Scholarship," in Curti, ed., *American Scholarship in the Twentieth Century*, 111–145; Louis Wirth, "The Social Sciences," in Ibid., 33–82.

[19]Harvard University, Committee on the Objectives of a General Education in a Free Society, *General Education in A Free Society* (Cambridge, Mass.: The University, 1946), 71, 74.

[20]Quoted in Terence Halliday, "Sociology's Fragile Professionalism," in Terence Halliday and Morris Janowitz, eds., *Sociology and Its Publics: The Forms and Fates of Disciplinary Organization* (Chicago, Ill.: University of Chicago Press, 1992), 6. Pages 3–12 contain an interesting comparison of the professionalism of Parsons and the more civic professionalism of Morris Janowitz.

[21]On the mobilized state and its contributions to research, see Walter McDougall, *The Heavens and the Earth: A Political History of the Space Age* (New York: Basic Books, 1985).

[22]See Robert A. McCaughey, *International Studies and Academic Enterprise: A Chapter in the Enclosure of American Learning* (New York: Columbia University Press, 1984).

[23]David Potter, *People of Plenty* (Chicago, Ill.: University of Chicago Press, 1954); John Kenneth Galbraith, *The Affluent Society* (Boston, Mass.: Houghton Mifflin, 1958).

[24]Geiger, *Research and Relevant Knowledge*, 105–106.

[25]Albert Somit and Joseph Tanenhaus, *The Development of American Political Science* (Boston, Mass.: Allyn and Bacon, 1967), 168–169.

[26]See Thomas Bender, *Intellect and Public Life* (Baltimore, Md.: Johns Hopkins University Press, 1993), 107; Edward Shils, *The Constitution of Society* (Chicago, Ill.: University of Chicago Press, 1982), chap. 10, esp. p. 259.

[27]See Richard Hofstadter, *Anti-Intellectualism in American Life* (New York: Knopf, 1963). Religion, according to Hofstadter, was the other major source.

[28]Shils, *The Constitution of Society*, chap. 10.

[29]Kerr, *The Uses of the University*, xiv.

[30]James B. Gilbert, *Another Chance: Postwar America, 1945–1968* (Philadelphia, Pa.: Temple University Press, 1981), 22.

[31]Geiger, *Research and Relevant Knowledge*, 41.

[32]Freeland, *Academia's Golden Age*, 88; Damrosch, *We Academics*, 24.

[33]See Daniel Bell, *The Coming of Post-Industrial Society* (New York: Basic Books, 1973); Daniel Bell, *The Reforming of General Education* (New York: Columbia University Press, 1966).

[34]See, for example, Allan Tate, "The Man of Letters in the Modern World," *Hudson Review* 5 (1952): 335–345. Bernard Rosenberg and David Manning White, eds., *Mass Culture: The Popular Arts in America* (Glencoe, Ill.: Free Press, 1957) is both an artifact of the growing awareness and concern about mass culture in the 1950s and a convenient anthology of both commentary and analysis.

50   Thomas Bender

[35]Richard Hofstadter and Walter Metzger, *The Development of Academic Freedom in the United States* (New York: Columbia University Press, 1955).

[36]Perry Miller, *Jonathan Edwards* (New York: W. Sloane Associates, 1949); on Niebuhr, see Richard W. Fox, *Reinhold Niebuhr: A Biography* (New York: Pantheon Books, 1985); for a secularist embrace of Niebuhr's realism, see Arthur Schlesinger, Jr., *The Politics of Hope* (Boston, Mass.: Houghton Mifflin, 1962), chap. 9.

[37]Sigmund Freud, *Civilization and Its Discontents* (New York: J. Cape and H. Smith, 1930).

[38]See Wuthnow, *The Restructuring of American Religion,* 158–163.

[39]T. S. Eliot, *The Idea of a Christian Society* (New York: Harcourt, Brace and Company, 1940). His more important book, *Notes Towards the Definition of Culture* (New York: Harcourt, Brace, 1949), sustains this notion, particularly in an appendix on "The Unity of European Culture."

[40]See David Hollinger, *Science, Jews, and Secular Culture: Studies in Mid-Century American Intellectual History* (Princeton, N.J.: Princeton University Press, 1996), chap. 8. For two key essays of the time, see Robert Merton, "A Note on Science and Democracy," *Journal of Legal and Political Sociology* 1 (1942): 115–126; and Sidney Hook, "The New Failure of Nerve," *Partisan Review* 10 (1943): 2–23.

[41]Hollinger, *Science, Jews, and Secular Culture,* chap. 2.

[42]William F. Buckley, *God and Man at Yale* (Chicago, Ill.: Regnery, 1951).

[43]Julie A. Reuben, *The Making of the Modern American University* (Chicago, Ill.: University of Chicago Press, 1996). On the vocation of inquiry in the nineteenth century, see David Hollinger, "Inquiry and Uplift: Late Nineteenth Century American Academics and the Moral Efficacy of Scientific Practice," in Thomas L. Haskell, ed., *The Authority of Experts* (Bloomington, Ind.: Indiana University Press, 1984), 142–156.

[44]See Edward Purcell, *The Crisis of Democratic Theory* (Lexington, Ky.: University Press of Kentucky, 1973), 26; Bender, *Intellect and Public Life,* 103. See also Mark C. Smith, *Social Science in the Crucible: The American Debate Over Objectivity and Purpose, 1918–1941* (Durham, N.C.: Duke University Press, 1994).

[45]See Henrika Kuklick, "Boundary Maintenance in American Sociology: Limitations to Academic Professionalization," *Journal of the History of the Behavioral Sciences* 16 (1980): 209.

[46]See Stephen Toulmin, *Cosmopolis: The Hidden Agenda of Modernity* (New York: Free Press, 1990).

[47]John Kenneth Galbraith's *American Capitalism* (Boston, Mass.: Houghton Mifflin, 1956), which develops the concept in a way that dissolves conflict, confirms my point.

[48]See Gilbert, *Another Chance,* 204; Alan Brinkley, *The End of Reform* (New York: Alfred A. Knopf, 1995).

[49]Arthur Schlesinger, Jr., *The Vital Center* (Boston, Mass.: Houghton Mifflin Co., 1949).

[50]Arthur Schlesinger, Jr., "The Causes of the Civil War," in Schlesinger, Jr., *The Politics of Hope*, 47; originally published in *Partisan Review* (1949).

[51]David Easton, "Political Science in the United States: Past and Present," in David Easton and Corrine S. Schelling, eds., *Divided Knowledge: Across Disciplines, Across Cultures* (Newbury Park, Calif.: Sage Publications, 1991), 44.

[52]See Lionel Trilling, *The Liberal Imagination* (New York: Viking Press, 1950); Richard Hofstadter, *The Progressive Historians* (New York: Knopf, 1969), 442. Daniel Bell makes this point in his book, *The Social Sciences Since the Second World War* (New Brunswick, N.J.: Transaction Books, 1982), 51.

[53]See Daniel Bell, ed., *The New American Right* (New York: Criterion Books, 1955); Richard Hofstadter, *The Age of Reform* (New York: Knopf, 1955), esp. chaps. 1–3.

[54]For a classic statement of this pluralism, see Robert Dahl, *Who Governs?* (New Haven, Conn.: Yale University Press, 1961). For critiques, see Michael Rogin, *The Intellectuals and McCarthy: The Radical Specter* (Cambridge, Mass.: MIT Press, 1967); and Peter Bachrach, *The Theory of Democratic Elitism: A Critique* (Boston, Mass.: Little, Brown, 1967).

[55]Ellen Lagemann, *The Politics of Knowledge: The Carnegie Corporation, Philanthropy, and Public Policy* (Middletown, Conn.: Wesleyan University Press, 1989), 124.

[56]Paul S. Boyer, *By the Bomb's Early Light: American Thought and Culture at the Dawn of the Atomic Age* (New York: Pantheon Books, 1985), 160–173, quotations from p. 168.

[57]David Riesman, *The Lonely Crowd* (New Haven, Conn.: Yale University Press, 1950); *Time* (27 September 1954).

[58]Byron E. Shafer, "On Being the Same but Different," *TLS* (29 March 1996): 7.

[59]Richard Parker in *New York Times Book Review* (28 January 1996): 29.

[60]Clifford Geertz may come close, but he makes the point, for it is mainly as a humanist who has assimilated anthropology to literature that his current reputation rests.

[61]For Robert Merton's classic formulations, see Robert Merton, *Social Theory and Social Structure* (Glencoe, Ill.: Free Press, 1949; rev. and enl. ed., 1957). On the appeal of this approach to foundations, see Lagemann, *The Politics of Knowledge*, 148.

[62]See Talcott Parsons, Robert Bales, and Edward Shils, *Working Papers in the Theory of Action* (Glencoe, Ill.: Free Press, 1953). At the level of high theory, this analysis provided the intellectual foundations for what Shils called "consensual pluralism."

[63]On the role of American studies, see Linda K. Kerber, "Diversity and the Transformation of American Studies," *American Quarterly* 41 (1989): 415–431.

[64]See Michael Geyer, "Multiculturalism and the Politics of General Education," *Critical Inquiry* 19 (1993): 507–508; David Bromwich, *Politics by Other Means* (New Haven, Conn.: Yale University Press, 1992), 119.

[65]Curti, "The Setting and the Problem," 32.

[66]Will Herberg, *Protestant-Catholic-Jew* (Garden City, N.Y.: Doubleday, 1955).

[67]Joseph Campbell, *The Hero With A Thousand Faces* (New York: Pantheon Books, 1949).

[68]Quoted in Eric Sandeen, *Picturing an Exhibition: The Family of Man and 1950s America* (Albuquerque, N.Mex.: University of New Mexico Press, 1995), 4.

[69]On Aspen and the cultural movement it represented, see James Sloan Allen, *The Romance of Commerce and Culture: Capitalism, Modernism, and the Chicago-Aspen Crusade for Cultural Reform* (Chicago, Ill.: University of Chicago Press, 1983).

[70]See Frederick F. Siegel, *Troubled Journey: From Pearl Harbor to Ronald Reagan* (New York: Hill and Wang, 1984), chap. 8.

[71]Lionel Trilling, *Beyond Culture: Essays on Literature and Learning* (New York: Viking Press, 1965), 3–30; originally published in *Partisan Review* (1961).

[72]Irving Howe, *Selected Writings, 1950–1990* (San Diego, Calif.: Harcourt Brace Jovanovich, 1990), 240.

[73]See Andreas Huyssen, *After the Great Divide* (Bloomington, Ind.: Indiana University Press, 1986), vii-xii.

[74]Morris Dickstein, *Gates of Eden: American Culture in the Sixties* (New York: Basic Books, 1977), 4, 9.

[75]Susan Sontag, "Notes on Camp," in Susan Sontag, *Against Interpretation* (New York: Farrar, Straus, & Giroux, 1966), 275–292; originally published in *Partisan Review* (1964).

[76]Diana Trilling, "The Other Night at Columbia," in Diana Trilling, *Claremont Essays* (New York: Harcourt, Brace, and World, 1964), 153–173; originally published in *Partisan Review* (1958). See also Lisa Phillips, ed., *Beat Culture and the New America, 1950–1965* (New York and Paris: Whitney Museum of American Art and Flammarion, 1995).

[77]Arthur Danto, *Beyond the Brillo Box: The Visual Arts in Post-Historical Perspective* (New York: Farrar, Straus & Giroux, 1992).

[78]Quoted in Allen, *The Romance of Commerce and Culture*, 4.

[79]Sally Barnes, *Greenwich Village, 1963* (Durham, N.C.: Duke University Press, 1993), 10.

[80]Michael Harrington, *The Other America* (New York: Macmillan, 1962); Nathan Glazer and Daniel Patrick Moynihan, *Beyond the Melting Pot* (Cambridge, Mass.: MIT Press and Harvard University Press, 1963).

[81]See Jonathan Arac, *Critical Genealogies: Historical Situations for Postmodern Literary Studies* (New York: Columbia University Press, 1987), 314–315; Bruce Robbins, *Secular Vocations: Intellectuals, Professionalism, and Culture* (London: Verso, 1993); Bruce Robbins, "'Othering' the Academy: Professionalism and Multiculturalism," *Social Research* 58 (1991): 355–372; the exchange between Andrew Ross and Richard Rorty in *Dissent* (Fall 1991): 483–490 and (Spring 1992): 263–267; and the statement by Ross quoted by Stanley Fish in Stanley Fish, *Professional Correctness: Literary Studies and Political Change* (New York: Clarendon Press, 1995), 117: the academy "is a massive public

sphere in itself, involving millions of people in this country alone, and so the idea that you break out of the academy into the public is rather a nonsense."

[82]Of many examples, see Roger Kimball, *Tenured Radicals: How Politics Has Corrupted Higher Education* (New York: Harper & Row, 1990).

[83]Geiger, *Research and Relevant Knowledge,* 253.

[84]For an account of this development in the discipline of history, see Thomas Bender, "Wholes and Parts: The Need for Synthesis in American History," *Journal of American History* 73 (1986): 120–136.

[85]Identifying the same cluster of developments, Dorothy Ross uses historicism as an equally useful general identification in "Panel on the Johns Hopkins Seminar of History and Politics," *Studies in American Political Development* 8 (1994): 394.

[86]Curti, "The Setting and the Problems," 5. A key work here was Caroline Ware, ed., *The Cultural Approach to History* (New York: Columbia University Press, 1940).

[87]Thomas S. Kuhn, *The Structure of Scientific Revolutions* (Chicago, Ill.: University of Chicago Press, 1962).

[88]See Richard Rorty, *Philosophy and the Mirror of Nature* (Princeton, N.J.: Princeton University Press, 1979), esp. chap. 7.

[89]Clifford Geertz, *The Interpretation of Cultures* (New York: Basic Books, 1973), 5, 6. Almost all the essays in this volume were originally published in the 1960s. For the earlier work, see Clifford Geertz, *Agricultural Involution: The Process of Ecological Change in Indonesia* (Berkeley, Calif.: University of California Press, 1963); *Peddlers and Princes: Social Change and Economic Development in Two Indonesian Towns* (Chicago, Ill.: University of Chicago Press, 1963); and *The Social History of an Indonesian Town* (Cambridge, Mass.: MIT Press, 1965).

[90]His key early works include *Madness and Civilization* (New York: Pantheon Books, 1961); *Birth of the Clinic* (New York: Pantheon Books, 1963); *The Order of Things* (New York: Pantheon Books, 1966); and *The Archaeology of Knowledge* (New York: Pantheon Books, 1969). Even more influential were *Discipline and Punish* (New York: Pantheon Books, 1975); and *History of Sexuality*, vol. I (New York: Pantheon Books, 1976).

[91]See Richard Macksey and Eugenio Donato, eds., *The Structuralist Controversy* (Baltimore, Md.: Johns Hopkins University Press, 1972).

[92]For an interesting study of the pattern of absorption of French theory in the United States, see Michele Lamont, "How to Become a Dominant French Philosopher: The Case of Jacques Derrida," *American Journal of Sociology* 93 (1987): 584–622.

[93]Julie Thompson Klein, "Knowledge, America, and Liberal Education," in Orvill, ed., *The Condition of American Liberal Education,* 146.

[94]See, for example, Edward Said, *Orientalism* (New York: Pantheon Books, 1978); Natalie Z. Davis, *Society and Culture in Early Modern France* (Stanford, Calif.: Stanford University Press, 1975); Evelyn Fox Keller, *Reflections on Gender and Science* (New Haven, Conn.: Yale University Press, 1985); Joan W. Scott, *Gender and the Politics of History* (New York: Columbia University Press, 1988); Hannah F. Pitkin, *Fortune is a Woman: Gender and Politics in the Thought of*

Niccolo Machiavelli (Berkeley, Calif.: University of California Press, 1984); Werner Sollors, *Beyond Ethnicity: Consent and Descent in American Culture* (New York: Oxford University Press, 1986); Carole Pateman, *The Disorder of Women* (Stanford, Calif.: Stanford University Press, 1989); Henry Louis Gates, Jr., *Figures in Black: Words, Signs, and the "Racial" Self* (New York: Oxford University Press, 1987); Mary Poovey, *Uneven Developments: The Ideological Work of Gender in Mid-Victorian England* (Chicago, Ill.: University of Chicago Press, 1988); Judith Butler, *Gender Trouble* (New York: Routledge, 1990); and K. Anthony Appiah, *In My Father's House: Africa in the Philosophy of Culture* (London: Methuen, 1992).

[95]Jürgen Habermas is the most well-known European student of the American pragmatists, but see also the extremely insightful exploration of American pragmatism as theory by the German Hans Joas, *Pragmatism and Social Theory* (Chicago, Ill.: University of Chicago Press, 1993).

[96]For a fine historical argument locating pragmatism in this context, see James L. Kloppenberg, *Uncertain Victory: Social Democracy and Progressivism in European and American Thought, 1870–1920* (New York: Oxford University Press, 1986). See also his recent and important survey of the current place of pragmatism in American academic culture: "Pragmatism: An Old Name for Some New Ways of Thinking," *Journal of American History* 83 (1996): 100–138.

[97]Edward Said, "Opponents, Audiences, Constituencies, and Community," in Hal Foster, ed., *The Anti-Aesthetic: Essays on Postmodern Culture* (Port Townsend, Wash.: Bay Press, 1983), 147.

[98]On this shift, see David A. Hollinger, "How Wide the Circle of 'We': American Intellectuals and the Problem of Ethnos Since World War II," *American Historical Review* 98 (1993): 317–337.

[99]See George Marsden, *The Soul of the American University* (New York: Oxford University Press, 1994). For a critique, see Thomas Bender, "Putting Religion in its Place," *Culturefront* 3 (Fall 1994): 77–79.

[100]See the somewhat crudely argued but well-targeted warning of Masao Miyoshi, "A Borderless World? From Colonialism to Transnationalism and the Decline of the Nation-State," *Critical Inquiry* 19 (1993): 726–751, especially his concluding remarks on pp. 750–751.

[101]The issues here are illustrated in the recent and rather messy contretemps surrounding *Social Text* (Spring/Summer 1996): 46–47; Alan Sokal, "A Physicist Experiments With Cultural Studies," *Lingua Franca* (May/June 1996): 62–64; and the responses by Andrew Ross, Sokal, and others in *Lingua Franca* (July/August 1996): 54–64.

[102]Damrosch, *We Academics*, 9.

[103]Dorothy Ross, *The Origins of American Social Science* (New York: Cambridge University Press, 1991), Part IV.

[104]Here I extrapolate from Michael Walzer's notion of the intellectual as a "connected critic" in Michael Walzer, *The Company of Critics* (New York: Basic Books, 1988).

[105]Wendy Steiner, *The Scandal of Pleasure* (Chicago, Ill.: University of Chicago Press, 1995), 138.

PART II

TRAJECTORIES OF
INTRA-DISCIPLINARY CHANGE:
PARTICIPANT PERSPECTIVES

Robert M. Solow

How Did Economics Get That Way and What Way Did It Get?

M Y EXPOSURE TO ECONOMICS as a discipline began in September 1940 when I enrolled as a freshman in the elementary economics course at Harvard College. I will try in this essay to make sense of the evolution of economics over a span of more than fifty years.

An analogy that comes to mind is from *The Boston Globe*. The Sunday edition occasionally publishes pairs of photographs of urban landscapes. They are taken from the same spot, looking in the same direction, but are at least thirty, forty, or fifty years apart. One shows a corner of the city as it looked then and the other as it looks now. Some buildings have disappeared, some new ones have been built, and some of the old ones are still there but with altered facades. This description is also true of the landscape and structure of economics, and I would like to provide a few then-and-now snapshots. The difference, however, is that with economics something more is called for; the pictures have to be connected. I would like to tell a story about how and why the architecture of economics changed. It will be a sort of Whig history but without the smugness.

* * *

There were three textbooks that were used in the 1940 economics course at Harvard. One was a standard principles text by Frederic

Robert M. Solow is Institute Professor Emeritus at the Massachusetts Institute of Technology.

Garver and Alvin Hansen. Hansen had been at Minnesota with Garver but by 1940 was a professor at Harvard and—although we freshmen had no inkling—the leading figure in bringing the ideas of John Maynard Keynes's *General Theory of Employment, Interest and Money*[1] into American economics. The second text was a large introductory book called *Modern Economic Society* by Sumner Slichter,[2] also a member of the Harvard faculty and usually referred to as the dean of American labor economists. The book was more about economic institutions and their functioning than about theory. The third text was a little green volume by Luthringer, Chandler, and Cline about money and banking, one of a series of little green books. (Lester Chandler of Princeton was the only one of the authors whose name we ever heard again.) It was a pretty boring text, as I remember, but fortunately we only had to read bits of it. This is actually an important point, and I will come back to it later.

Even a quick physical comparison of a good contemporary elementary text with Garver and Hansen and Slichter tells us something. Leaving aside the typographical changes—color, wider margins, larger type—the modern text is sprinkled with diagrams, tables, even simple equations, whereas the older ones present page after page of unbroken prose. In some seven hundred pages, Garver and Hansen have fewer than forty tables or figures. Some of them represent the working-out of numerical examples of simple propositions, and the rest, maybe half, contain data about the US economy. Similarly, there are fifty-five graphs, again divided between a small number of analytical diagrams and a larger number of graphical presentations of actual data. Slichter is not radically different in his nine hundred pages.

The modern counterpart, while no more intellectually demanding for the student (perhaps even less so), is full of diagrams, tables, and equations. The use of analytical diagrams is probably ten times as intense, and the volume of real-world data presented is correspondingly greater. Propositions are often stated in the form of equations, but these are almost always simple statements (i.e., two intuitively understandable quantities must be equal); there is not a lot of heavy mathematics in these texts. (The older books mention one equation, the Quantity Equation.) The numerical example, hallowed in economics since the days of David Ricardo, is still in use, but it is no longer the analytical workhorse.

The older books are long on classifications—kinds of goods, kinds of industries, kinds of labor—and on descriptions of public and private institutions. The first 260 pages in Slichter's text are exclusively descriptive of the US economy as it then was. I would guess that fewer than one hundred of the next six hundred pages are devoted to the development of analysis or to the application of analysis. Most provide more institutional descriptions, very sensible discussions of economic policy, and serious looks at recent history as it would be seen by an economist. No one should underestimate the value of these historical reflections. They are, in a way, the application of analytical ideas. But there is a not-so-subtle difference. The modern textbook presents and uses economic analysis as a tool to be directly applied to contemporary or historical situations. The student is shown how to map real events into the categories that appear on the axes of the diagrams or the terms in the equations. The older texts are simply more discursive. The underlying ideas are treated more like categories that resonate to this or that bit of history or policy; the authors ruminate more than they analyze.

One sees this clearly in the way these two books present the idea of supply and demand. This is the one piece of analysis that gets careful treatment. Characteristically, however, Garver and Hansen are very good on how one should think about different kinds of commodities—perishable or not, bought frequently or seldom, standardized or not—but the student is not encouraged to make literal use of the apparatus of supply and demand curves. Both books spend time discussing monopolistic elements in real-world markets, but most of the discussion is institutional. There is, of course, no serious treatment of monopoly price because there was very little known at the time.

I do not want to be misunderstood. Garver and Hansen and Slichter were serious people. Their reflections on the workings of the economy are worth reading. They inspire bursts of nostalgia; words like "civilized" came to mind. The point is that the modern text takes a different approach. Of course it explains more; the intervening sixty years of economic research have not been wasted. But it is the tone that I want to emphasize. The modern text treats economics as a collection of analytical tools to be applied quite directly to observable situations.

It is plain from this comparison that there was a significant change between 1940 and 1990 in economics as a discipline and also in the way it sees itself. Perhaps this sea change deserves to be called a transformation. One way to describe it is to say that economics became a self-consciously technical subject, no longer a fit occupation for the gentleman-scholar. And I mean that literally: nowadays economists arrive at their conclusions by using an evolving collection of analytical techniques, most of them non-intuitive, the sort that have to be learned laboriously. The shift of the center of gravity from Great Britain to the United States (and to the G.I. Bill veterans at that) may have helped the process along. Judicious discussion is no longer the way serious economics is carried out. Of course, that is not all that happened in fifty years. A lot of new knowledge was acquired, most of it by virtue of those analytical techniques. New branches of economics appeared, some of them because new facts and institutions emerged, some of them for internal intellectual reasons. Not many subfields seem to have disappeared, though there was some rearrangement as a more unified macroeconomics absorbed segments like "business cycles." At the most general level, however, the change in tone was as I have described it.

Many outside observers and some critics from within the profession have interpreted this development as a sweeping victory for "formalism" in economics. The intended implication is that economics has lost touch with everyday life, that it has become more self-involved and less relevant to social concerns as it became more formal (and more mathematical). I think that this view of the discipline rests on a misconception about the change in the way mainstream economists go about their work. Barking may well be justified, but not up the wrong tree.

If "formalist economics" means anything, it must mean economic theory constructed more or less after the model of Euclid's geometry. One starts with a few axioms, as close to "self-evident" as they can be—although this is harder to do when the subject matter is more complicated than points and lines in a plane—and then tries to work out all the logical implications of those axioms. Formalist economics starts with a small number of assumptions about the behavior of individual economic agents, and a few more about their interactions with each other, and goes on to study what can then be said about the resulting economic system.

The past fifty years have indeed seen formalist economics grow and prosper. But it has not grown very much. Only a small minority within the profession practices economic theory in this style. To tell the truth, not many more pay any attention at all to formalist theory. Generally speaking, formalists write for one another. The formalist school contains some extraordinarily able people, and of course it attracts economists who not only are talented at mathematics of a certain kind but enjoy it. It is not surprising, therefore, that outsiders think that there is a lot of formalism in economics, just as half a cup of blood spread around a bathroom can make it look like a scene from *Psycho*. Nevertheless, it is an illusion. Modern mainstream economics is not all that formal.

* * *

What the outsider really sees is *model-building,* which is an altogether different sort of activity. In college classrooms in the 1940s, whole semesters could go by without anyone talking about building or testing a model. Today, if you ask a mainstream economist a question about almost any aspect of economic life, the response will be: suppose we model that situation and see what happens. It is important, then, to understand what a model is and what it is not.

A model is a deliberately simplified representation of a much more complicated situation. (I have no reference for this, but I think I remember that the philosopher J. L. Austin wrote somewhere that "one would be tempted to describe oversimplification as the occupational disease of philosophers if it were not their occupation." Exactly.)

The idea is to focus on one or two causal or conditioning factors, exclude everything else, and hope to understand how just these aspects of reality work and interact. There are thousands of examples; the point is that modern mainstream economics consists of little else but examples of this process.

What follows are three of them, described in the sketchiest terms. Suppose we are interested in the effects of taxation on the willingness to work. (God knows that is a reasonable thing to be interested in.) The usual approach goes something like this: Imagine a typical person of working age who enjoys both consumer goods and leisure, and whose tastes for them can be described in a simple and well-behaved way. This person has a certain amount of nonwage income, from property or from transfer payments of various kinds. He has the option of working any number of hours at a wage rate determined by the market. Part of his income is taxed away according to some known schedule. We have to assume that this person does the best he can to satisfy his tastes for leisure and for the goods that his after-tax income can buy.

We now ask the question that led to this model in the first place. How will he respond to higher tax rates—by working more or fewer hours? If he makes no adjustment, he will have the same amount of leisure time but have fewer goods. That may suggest that he work longer hours, giving up some leisure time for more goods. With the higher tax rates, however, each hour worked brings less in the way of goods, suggesting that work has become less attractive. He may choose, therefore, to work fewer hours. It may make a difference whether the tax system imposes different rates on wage and nonwage income. Perhaps it depends on the details of his preferences; not every person need react in the same way. This model asks for some deeper analysis, which it gets.

Notice all the casual oversimplifications. Not everyone can choose how many hours to work. People do not buy "consumer goods" in general; they buy hundreds of different things, some of which go particularly well with leisure. Some people, but not others, have some control over the intensity with which they work. There are customs and norms that affect the behavior of different groups. All of this sort of talk is cheap. The point of the exercise is to simplify and see where it leads. Alternative simplifications are possible, and making those choices is the art of the model-builder. How do we judge success? It is a good question, and I will return to it soon.

Here is a different type of example. Anyone who has looked at the history of business cycles knows that net investment in inventories by businesses is highly volatile and can easily account for most of the top-to-bottom change in production during a recession. It is therefore a matter of some importance that we understand the nature of inventory fluctuations. There are plenty of reasons for firms to hold inventories and to change the amount of inventories they hold. Production schedules are efficient when they are smooth, but sales can fluctuate unpredictably (or predictably, as from season to season). Inventories of finished goods provide a buffer, enabling firms to meet a fluctuating demand with smooth production. Inventories of goods-in-process and, to a lesser extent, raw materials and components may be tied fairly closely to current production. Some firms build up inventories in anticipation of future sales, or they may try to run their inventories down if they expect sales to be slack. Inventories of raw materials may provide a way to speculate on the prices of raw materials, buying more than needed when the price is low and using up the surplus when the current price is high. Finally, firms may find themselves with inventories that are lower or higher than they actually want: higher because sales have been disappointing, lower if sales have been unexpectedly strong. Even this list is not a complete inventory of reasons for holding and changing inventories. And there are potentially important conditioning factors that have been completely left out: relations with suppliers and customers and financial constraints, for instance.

Modeling inventory fluctuations is a matter of finding a way to represent some or all of these motives so that they can be weighed against one another in much the same way that a profit-seeking firm will have to weigh them as it decides what to do. Notice that last month's unintended inventory fluctuations will have an effect on this month's plans, so that the behavior to be described has a dynamics of its own. How do we judge success? Good question, and I will come to it soon.

Lastly, I give yet a third example because it illustrates a quite different point. Ten years ago, Elhanan Helpman modeled a group of countries trading with one another under very special circumstances. Each country specialized completely in producing a single variety of good. In the eyes of consumers, each country's "own" variety served as a symmetrically imperfect substitute for each other country's variety. Consumers, however, all had the same set of tastes, no matter where they lived. Under these restrictive assumptions and a few others, he showed that there would be a simple formula relating the volume of a country's trade to its size. In reality, countries do not specialize in producing a single good, and consumers do not have the same tastes wherever they are. Nevertheless, Helpman's formula seemed to work quite well for a group of OECD (i.e., advanced) countries. The moral might be that, in reality, production patterns are a lot more specialized than tastes.

Recently, however, other economists tried out the Helpman formula on a group of non-OECD countries, including some in Latin America and Africa. It seemed to work pretty well for them too. Paradoxically, perhaps that success casts some doubt on the Helpman model: one would not expect the less advanced countries to exhibit the same specialization in production and commonality of tastes that is plausible for OECD countries. After all, there may be quite different models that imply a similar relation between the size of a country and the volume of its trade. It appears that measuring success may not be a simple notion.

A good model makes the right strategic simplifications. In fact, a really good model is one that generates a lot of understanding from focusing on a very small number of causal arrows. Model-building is not a mechanical process. Some people are better at this sort of thing than others. Economic models are usually stated mathematically, but they do not have to be. They can be described in words, as I have been doing, or in diagrammatic form, or in computer flow charts for that matter. But mathematics turns out to be a very efficient way to express the structure of a simplified model and it is, of course, a marvelous tool for discovering the implications of a particular model. That is probably why outsiders tend to think of model-building as just more formalism. That is a mistake. The mere use of mathematics does not constitute formalism. Maybe the sharpest way to make this point is to say that the mathematics in these models is almost never deep. There are exceptions, of course. Nevertheless I venture the estimate (safe because it is unverifiable) that there is little or no correlation in fact between the difficulty or mathematical depth of an economic model and its value as science. God is in the details, or perhaps in the absence of details. There is something to be said for both.

The interesting question is *why* economics stopped being club-bable and became technical sometime in the 1940s and 1950s, and *why* model-building took over as the standard intellectual exercise. I think one has to allow for the possibility that it is, after all, the best way to do economics, and we are just seeing the survival of the fittest in another context. That would be Whig history with a vengeance. I confess to some sympathy with that view, but only within limits. I would add that the model-building approach is peculiarly vulnerable to unproductive controversy of a particular kind. I will discuss this later when I talk about measuring success (one model at a time).

I have a different hypothesis to suggest—that technique and model-building came along with the expanding availability of data, and each reinforces the other. Each new piece of information about the economy, especially if it is quantitative information, practically sits there and begs for explanation. Someone will eventually be clever enough to see that it is now feasible to construct a model. Reciprocally, alternative models have to compete on some basis. They are not usually fancy enough to compete on the basis of elegance or depth or the intellectual equivalent of pectoral development. They compete on the basis of their ability to give a satisfying account of some facts. Facts ask for explanations, and explanations ask for new facts.

There is another partner in this evolutionary spiral: the development of new methods of data analysis and statistical inference. The other highly visible change in the style of academic economics since 1940 has been the explosion of econometrics from an esoteric minority taste to an essential part of a Ph.D. education—at least one chapter in most of the dissertations produced in a major department. I will say a little about this vertex of the triangle later.

The spread of model-building coincided in time with the development and diffusion of Keynesian economics. This was an accident, but an accident with consequences: the heyday of Keynesian economics provides a wonderful example of the interplay among theory, the availability of data, and the econometric method. *The General Theory* dates from 1936; Simon Kuznets's book on national income accounting appeared in 1938.[3] Both were no doubt related to the depression of the 1930s, but that is just history. The point is that Keynesian theory needed the national income and product accounts to make contact with reality, and the availability of national income and product accounts made Keynesian macroeconomics fruitful (and helped to shape it).

When I mentioned at the very beginning that my freshman textbook of money and banking was a bore, this is what I had in mind. It was the only vestige of macroeconomics that we were taught—although the unemployment rate in 1940 was still about 14 percent!—and it consisted of a few details about the fractional-reserve banking system and the way it provides credit and generates cash. There was such a thing as business-cycle theory, but it was regarded as a sort of special topic. The textbook writers before 1940 had neither the theory nor the data required to give a coherent account of macroeconomics as part of the core of the subject.

Keynes more or less invented macroeconomics. He was not much of a model-builder himself, but he opened up a gold mine for those who came after. Suddenly there were models of aggregate consumption and aggregate investment, small but complete models of aggregate output and employment, and data against which they could be tested and perhaps improved. Econometricians had new problems of statistical inference to solve. And it all seemed so *important*.

The General Theory was and is a very difficult book to read. It contains several distinct lines of thought that are never quite made mutually consistent. It was an extraordinarily influential book for my generation of students (along with John Hicks's *Value and Capital*[4] and Paul Samuelson's *Foundations of Economic Analysis*[5]), but we learned not as much from it—it was, as I said, almost unreadable—as from a number of explanatory articles that appeared on all our graduate-school reading lists. These articles reduced one or two of those trains of thought to an intelligible *model*, which for us became "Keynesian economics." The most important of those articles were by John Hicks and Oskar Lange, but there was a whole series of them, by Brian Reddaway, David Champernowne, and others. This story provides a different sort of illustration of the clarifying power of the model-building method.

It is very likely that the war, as much as the depression, worked in the same direction. The panoply of wartime policy—Treasury finance, price and production controls, logistics of various kinds—involved economists in social engineering. Any routinization of policy, even nonintrusive policy, leads inevitably to technical questions. What will be the consequences if we do A? Vague generalities will not do for an answer; demands for quantification are just around the corner. Policy A can usually be undertaken with more or less intensity. The powers that be will not only want to quantify the consequences but they will have the power to measure where no one had measured before. Models happen.

If they happen in connection with the availability of data, as I have suggested, then success will be measured by the ability to "explain" the data. Fitness is goodness of fit. (I put "explain" in quotes to emphasize that there need be no claim to fundamental explanation. A model of inventory accumulation will likely eventuate in an equation that relates inventory spending to a small number of observable variables. If that equation actually holds to a fair degree of approximation, the model explains the data.)

There is, however, a twist, and I think it is important. If the logic of model-building, in economics anyway, is a drastic simplification, then one cannot expect any model to fit the facts in every detail. There are examples of models—and not only in economics—that have been judged to be very successful because they manage to account for fairly gross, large-scale patterns that are actually observed and measured. In practice, two consequences seem to follow.

The first is a persistent temptation to add explanatory variables in order to improve the fit. The variables do not follow from the model, or else they would already be there. But it is usually easy to think of reasonable auxiliaries, things that "should" plausibly affect inventory investment even if they were not included in the original, narrowly-focused model. Trouble arises because data are scarce in economics; more cannot be generated by experimentation. So there is a danger of "overfitting": adding variables that work in the data at hand but will turn out to be irrelevant in the next batch, making them therefore deeply irrelevant.

This plays into the second and more fundamental problem. In the nature of the case it will often happen that two quite different models can fit the facts just about equally as well. No doubt the right way to proceed is to think of circumstances in which the two models give widely different predictions and to look around for real-life situations that offer the opportunity to discriminate between them. But that may not be possible. (Chemists can do experiments. There is a movement that does experimental economics, but I cannot guess how far it can go.) So naturally the temptation becomes irresistible to compete by adding variables, making slight changes in formulation, looking around for especially favorable data, and otherwise using the tricks of the trade. It can become very difficult ever to displace an entrenched model by a better one. Clever and motivated—including ideologically motivated—people can fight a rearguard battle that would make Robert E. Lee look like an amateur. (And, of course, they may turn out to be right.) Old models never die; they just fade away. So the model-building approach to economics has its problems. But it is what we have: not formalism, and not the more discursive approach that began to break up in the 1940s and is now long gone.

As this description suggests, model-building economists tend to be natural-born, loose-fitting positivists. Progress will come from weeding out empirically unsuccessful models and improving and extending those that survive empirical tests. This is not to say that mainstream economists think explicitly about method. Philosophical tendencies may come and go. They are attended to only by a tiny fringe of economists who care about formal methodology. Their arguments make no dent in the mainstream, which goes on making and testing models.

It may be useful if I tuck in here a brief commentary on recent and current controversy within academic macroeconomics, as seen from the point of view advanced in this essay. (David Kreps's discussion is similar, but not identical.) This was not part of my original plan, but the controversy is highly visible. The conference held at the Huntington Library in March of 1995 seemed to have a lively interest in the details. Most intriguingly, however, the controversy is often presented as a dispute between formalists and informalists. It would not damage the argument I have been making if there were an element of truth in that characterization. Maybe there is, a little. But in fact I think the story is ultimately a strong confirmation of the thesis of this essay.

In the mid-1970s, the standard textbook treatment of macroeconomics was recognizably "Keynesian" or "American Keynesian." It aimed specifically to provide an aggregative model of the whole economy that could give some sort of analytical account of unemployment, excess capacity, and recession (and their opposites) as pathologies of the market economy. Opposition comes from a school of thought that did in fact invoke the equally standard formal theory of a capitalist economy (the theory of general competitive equilibrium). This school pointed out that this (microeconomic) model had no room for unemployment, excess capacity, and recession, and made the (somewhat) formalist appeal that mainstream economists were in the position of teaching on Tuesday and Thursday a macroeconomics that was fundamentally incompatible with the microeconomics taught on Monday and Wednesday. I do not think that the appeal to "microfoundations" amounted to much. Macroeconomic hypotheses had always been justified by some sort of appeal to microeconomic reasoning.

Nevertheless it was in part an appeal to formal criteria, and there was considerable force to this logic. But the "New Classical Macroeconomics" then faced the problem of explaining, or explaining away, the fluctuations in aggregate income and employment that constitute the everyday history of prosperity and recession. And this task had to be performed within the framework of a formal theory that seemed to exclude even the possibility of the events to be explained. I will not recount the ingenious proposals that were invented to perform this feat because they were ultimately felt to be implausible. No empirical successes were forthcoming. This approach languished.

The original New Classical Macroeconomics evolved into, or was superseded by, a related style of modeling called "Real Business Cycle Theory" ("real" means "nonmonetary"). And now we cut to what I take to be the chase in this narrative. The goal of Real Business Cycle Theory was the same: to show that the everyday experience of economic fluctuations could indeed be accounted for within the framework of formal general equilibrium theory, without the "impure," "ad hoc," "Keynesian" violations of standard principles. In doing so it proceeded to abandon formalism in all but name by canonizing one very simple, very special, and very maneuverable version of competitive general equilibrium—in fact, by adopting a highly specific model. It is a model of an economy populated by a single immortal family with perfect foresight. The industrial and market structure of the economy is such that it carries out, step by step, the infinite-horizon optimal plan of the single "representative consumer." The generality that is the hallmark of formalism is gone.

The gimmick is that the economy is disturbed by irregular, unforeseeable changes in the preferences of the representative consumer and/or in the technology available to the industrial sector. Economic fluctuations are thus not pathological at all; they are the best that can be done by way of adapting to these pleasant and unpleasant surprises. The model itself was already there to be used. The bulk of the intellectual effort goes into the ways of showing that the data of observed fluctuations are compatible with the demands of the model. This is not easy because the key driving forces—irregular changes in tastes and technology—are not directly observable.

So this is formalism, in more or less a window-dressing sense. In practice it is a little bit of model-building and a lot of fairly sophisticated data analysis. It is not a revolution or transformation in the way macroeconomics is done.

To be sure, there has been a dramatic change in doctrine. One genealogy of models has replaced another. One set of implications has replaced another. This was a genuine shift of ideas, perhaps related to events of the 1970s that were, at least temporarily, hard to explain with older models, perhaps related to the general mood of conservatism and suspicion of government action that affected economists as well as others. Such shifts occur from time to time, in macroeconomics and elsewhere. This one did not amount to a significant move toward formalism. The new doctrine does try to appropriate an air of "rigor"—a standard ploy—but this is mostly advertising.

* * *

My reading of the current state of affairs is much like Kreps's. In the course of massaging the model to make it conform to the facts, the more adventuresome advocates of Real Business Cycle Theory have found it necessary to modify many of the clean but extreme assumptions that give formal general equilibrium theory its artificial vanilla flavor. As the representative-consumer-with-perfect-foresight model has been extended to allow for elements of imperfect information, imperfect competition, imperfect flexibility of prices, incomplete markets, and a teeny bit of heterogeneity among the inhabitants, it has come closer and closer to the more or less "Keynesian" model it was supposed to discredit. It is possible—though surely not inevitable—that in another decade all that will be left are some purely technical differences in modeling strategies plus an underlying difference in spirit, with one side regarding all those imperfections as (removable?) flaws in the system and the other side regarding them as the essence of the system itself.

Seen this way, the macroeconomic controversy (made more intense by ideological freight) only makes the model-building tradition seem pretty irrevocable. But then what about a historical approach to economics? Is such a thing viable? The issue is worth discussing, and it will shed some further light on the main argument. In one sense, economics *is* history. I have been insisting that the modern approach to economics is mostly about accounting for data. It is hard to imagine where else data can come from but the past. So economics is about accounting for the past. Most of the time it is the recent past, but there is no reason why the more distant past cannot be treated in the same way, if only the relevant data are available or can be reconstructed.

When I studied economic history as a graduate student at the end of the 1940s, my teacher was A. P. Usher. I read his *History of Mechanical Inventions*,[6] Clapham on British economic history, and sections of various works on monetary history. They were long on narrative and short on analysis, a lot like the elementary textbooks of a decade earlier. It did not occur to me then, as it has since, that the more distant past provides something potentially valuable to the model-building economist. A good model embodies *accurately* a representation of the institutions, norms, and attitudes that govern economic behavior in a particular time and place. There is no reason to presuppose that a successful model of the supply of labor in the second half of the twentieth century will apply unchanged to the nineteenth century when institutions, norms, and attitudes were different. Long runs of history offer the economist or historian or economic historian the chance to figure out how changes in the "noneconomic" background factors have an influence on behavior in the narrowly economic realm. It is a little like being able to extend the range of temperatures or pressures available in a laboratory.

I am not sure that is how it has worked in practice. One thing is certain: the same progression from discursiveness to model-building has happened in economic history as in economics. Economic historians have become a lot more like economists than economists have become like economic historians. Today's economic historians are very likely to be model-builders. I have the disappointing impression that they are far too willing to accept the models devised by late twentieth-century economists and apply them uncritically to the data of other times and places. There are certainly some sterling exceptions who do properly exploit the advantages offered by exotic data; my insider informant says they are few and far between. There are a few who use the study of the evolution of institutions as a laboratory for economic analysis under unconventional assumptions. There are even some who continue to do narrative economic history. On the whole one has to report that the historical approach to economics has lost most of its distinctiveness and is losing the rest. This seems to be a case of not being able to lick 'em, or not wanting to.

The case is much the same with respect to the other social sciences. I am tempted to guess that economics has drawn further away from the other social sciences in the past half-century. But the truth is that there was little or no interchange even in 1940 or 1950. Despite the existence of the occasional sport like Richard Thaler or George Akerlof, who learned from the other social sciences, most of the flow of ideas is in the other direction. There are subcultures in political science and sociology that seem to want to adopt the methods, the terminology, and sometimes the assumptions of economics. Those *Wahlverwandtschaften* are best discussed from within the other disciplines. Richard Swedberg's *Economics and Sociology* is full of interesting material,[7] but I am less optimistic than he is about any systematic development.

Some sociologists and political scientists are drawn to the way economics uses rationality—in effect, constrained maximization—as an organizing principle and as a source of ideas for model-building. You could do a lot worse. But there is an irony tucked away in that remark. Some economists, though not many, would like to look to sociology as a way of escaping from the narrow idea of rationality. Actually, that way of putting it is not quite right, so I shall try again. The program of constrained maximization has to rest on a careful statement of what is being maximized and what the constraints are. Mainstream economics takes a narrow view of both; some hardy souls would like to try out a wider range of assumptions. They look to sociology and social psychology as a source of alternative ideas. On the whole they do not find what they are looking for, though again there are notable exceptions.

This is not anybody's fault. The writings of people like Jon Elster, Mark Granovetter, Arthur Stinchcombe, and Aage Sørensen— just to take those who are closest to the economists' wavelength— are full of interest to those all too few economists who read them. But they do not provide the usable raw material (or intermediate product) that is being sought. Even a book like Elster's *The Cement of Society*,[8] intelligent as it is and on exactly the right subject, does not send an economist racing to the drawing board. I suppose, though without much confidence, that this failure to connect may arise because the other social sciences have not adopted the model-building philosophy that motivates and guides economists. Experience has taught me that I should say explicitly that I have no neocolonialist designs: sociology may be right to stay away from model-building as a mode of thought. Adjacent territories may adopt different track gauges for good and sufficient reasons, but their railroads will have problems at the border crossings.

It might be useful for me to say some fairly informal things about the analogies between economics and the natural sciences. It is an uncomfortable task. I have read the usual quota of layman books and, after forty-seven years on the faculty at MIT, I have a lot of friends who are physicists, chemists, and biologists, not to mention engineers. But it is perfectly clear to me that I have no real sense of what goes on in a physicist's or biologist's mind. Still, it is a topic that often comes up in cross-disciplinary discussion.

There is no doubt that economists are attracted to the style of explanation they see (or think they see) in physics. This is at least clear in the externals. Economists feel at home with equilibrium conditions deduced from first principles or from reliable empirical statements. Similarly, they are used to deducing dynamics from local assumptions or generalizations; economics is full of differential or finite-difference equations. All this seems fairly harmless, as long as it works. It will occasionally turn out that some piece of economics is mathematically identical to some piece of utterly unrelated physics. (This has actually happened to me, although I know absolutely nothing about physics.) I think this has no methodological significance but arises merely because everyone playing this sort of game tends to follow the line of least mathematical resistance. I know that Philip Mirowski believes that deeper aspects of mainstream economic theory are the product of a profound imitation of nineteenth-century physical theory. That thesis strikes me as false, but I would not claim expert knowledge.

To the extent that economists have the ambition to behave like physicists, they face two dangerous pitfalls. The first is the temptation to believe that the laws of economics are like the laws of physics: exactly the same everywhere on earth and at every moment since Hector was a pup. That is certainly true about the behavior of heat and light. But the part of economics that is independent of history and social context is not only small but dull.

I want to suggest that a second pitfall comes with the imitation of theoretical physics: there is a tendency to undervalue keen observation and shrewd generalization, virtues that I think are more usually practiced by biologists. There has long been a tendency in economics to promote biology as an analogy. Even a genuinely great man like Marshall took this line. Most of what is said on this subject is a hopelessly vague use of unexamined analogy, uninformed by biological theory. I am making a much weaker point, that there is a lot to be said in favor of staring at the piece of reality you are studying and asking, just what is going on here? Economists who are enamored of the physics style seem to bypass that stage, to their disadvantage.

There is another respect in which a broader biological analogy might be relevant. Many economists have noted that the evolutionary paradigm ought to be a useful way of doing business. In isolated instances it has already been valuable in economics, but perhaps a little less so than might have been expected. I attribute this to the absence of any close parallel to the quantitatively analyzable transmission mechanism provided in biology by population genetics. Now, with the rapid development of evolutionary game theory, there may be an opening for real progress. The loop closes, because what is now needed is a body of data to be exploited by the evolutionary game-modeler.

* * *

Nothing that has been said in this essay is complicated enough to require summary. Since part of my aim has been to dispel a misperception, I should conclude by making another pass at explaining how the misperception has come to be so widely accepted. Many observers in the other social sciences and in the wide, wide world perceive that economics has become formalistic, abstract, negligent of the real world. The truth is, I think, that economics has become technical, which is quite different. (Nobody regards computer-aided tomography as formalistic.) Far from being unworldly, modern model-builders are obsessed with data.

How could this confusion arise? I have already suggested that it may be the trappings of mathematical model-building that gives the wrong impression to outsiders. Now I will try out another thought. There is a tendency for theory to outrun data. (This includes statistical theory as well as economic theory.) Theory is cheap, and data are expensive. Much the same thing seems to happen in high-energy physics. I am told that the very latest ideas in particle theory could not come close to being tested with any current accelerator or even with the superconducting supercollider if it were to be built. No one even knows how enough energy could be mobilized to do the experiments that might confirm today's most advanced speculations.

In economics, model-builders' busywork is to refine their ideas to ask questions to which the available data cannot give the answer. Econometric theorists invent methods to estimate parameters about which the data have no information. And, of course, people are recruited whose talent is for just these activities, whose interest is more in method than in substance. As the models become more refined, the signal-to-noise ratio in the data becomes very attenuated. Since no empirical verdict is forthcoming, the student goes back to the drawing board—and refines the idea even more. Oscar Wilde described a fox hunt as the unspeakable in pursuit of the inedible. Perhaps here we have the overeducated in pursuit of the unknowable. But it sure beats the alternatives.

ENDNOTES

[1]John Maynard Keynes, *The General Theory of Employment, Interest and Money* (London: Macmillan, 1936).

[2]Sumner H. Slichter, *Modern Economic Society* (New York: H. Holt and Company, 1935).

[3]Simon Smith Kuznets, *National Income and Capital Formation, 1919–1935* (New York: National Bureau of Economic Research, 1938).

[4]Sir John Richard Hicks, *Value and Capital: An Inquiry into Some Fundamental Principles of Economic Theory* (Oxford: Clarendon Press, 1939).

[5]Paul Anthony Samuelson, *Foundations of Economic Analysis* (Cambridge, Mass.: Harvard University Press, 1947).

[6]Abbott Payson Usher, *A History of Mechanical Inventions* (New York: McGraw-Hill, Inc., 1929).

[7]Richard Swedberg, *Economics and Sociology: Redefining Their Boundaries* (Princeton, N.J.: Princeton University Press, 1990).

[8]Jon Elster, *The Cement of Society: A Study of Social Order* (Cambridge: Cambridge University Press, 1989).

David M. Kreps

Economics—The Current Position

I N THE FIFTY-ODD YEARS SINCE World War II, economics has undergone a substantial transformation. Before the war the discipline was defined by the subject matter it encompassed, i.e., things connected with prices and markets. But the tools and theories used to study, say, international trade bore only scant resemblance to those used to study labor markets. In the two decades that followed the war, this largely changed. Mathematical modeling rose to preeminence in economics, and a sparse set of canonical hypotheses—Robert Solow has characterized them as *greed, rationality,* and *equilibrium*—became the maintained hypotheses in almost all branches of the subject. At first, this process was accompanied by a narrowing of the issues economists were willing to address; the detailed study of economic institutions (beyond prices and anonymous markets) fell out of favor. But beginning in the mid-1960s, technical innovations and increased access to data broadened the scope of greed, rationality, and equilibrium. The issues addressed by mainstream economists broadened, and continues to broaden, in consequence.

Economists do not form a monolithic army. There have been and continue to be those who decry mainstream tendencies. Greed, rationality, and equilibrium have each been the target of well-shot arrows by well-regarded scholars. But economists by and large have steered clear of what Jim March has affectionately termed the "saloons of sociology," both fearing the anarchy that (doubtless) reigns there and cherishing how much has been learned by pushing

David M. Kreps is Paul Holden Professor of Economics at the Graduate School of Business at Stanford University.

ahead with the canonical principles.[1] Indeed, what trade in ideas there has been between economics and the other social sciences has largely been one way, through missions established to sociology, political science, and the academic discipline of law. (Previously established missions to the fields of academic finance and accounting have led to an almost total conversion of the native populations.) Economists may scoff when unconverted scholars in the other social sciences attribute to us many of the aspects of a religious imperium, but this has been a pretty accurate analogy.

While the missions to new contexts continue, however, strange things are happening at the core. As a result of increasing access to both experimental and field-based data, pressure from important constituencies, and the desire to have something new to work on, the canonical principles are under attack in our nearest approximation of high temples—journals such as *Econometrica*, the *Journal of Political Economy*, and the *American Economic Review*. These attacks have been resisted to some extent by the faithful, but they have increasingly come from previously conformist supporters of the canon. To date, no one has been anathemized. Indeed, some of those who previously were viewed as heretics have been welcomed back into the congregation.

It is not clear where this internal revolution is leading. It could end in schism, with a number of powerful surviving factions and a breakup of the old imperium. The old monolith could arise to expel the apostates. Economics might finish stronger, as overly restrictive canons are replaced by weaker but still workable principles that are fitted empirically to specific contexts and situations. While I do not have the crystal ball needed to predict what will happen, I will close with some hopeful speculations.

QUALIFICATIONS AND METHODOLOGY

Before fleshing out this thesis, let me be clear about its subjective nature. Economics is a broad and diverse discipline, and I occupy the fringe of a wing of the subject: To most people, economics means the (mis)behavior of the macroeconomy, both national and global; I am a microeconomist, whose concerns are much more the (mis)behavior of single consumers, firms, or industries. Economics, at least at its best, is empirical; I am a theorist, who has never run a regression or systematically collected data. Finally, economics is driven by a core of ideas that are typically taught to first-year graduate students. I missed all that; my undergraduate training was primarily in mathematics, and I studied applied math as a graduate student. And I continue to miss this inculturating experience from the other side; I am employed by a business school and spend my time teaching aspiring managers. Indeed, my place of employment probably warps my view of the discipline considerably.

Thus for me to address the current state of the discipline of economics requires me either to report on what (I think) is the mainstream view—and probably get it wrong—or to provide a much more personal view of the matter, and thereby give a misleading picture of what most economists think about these things.

Believing that the latter is better but still unsatisfactory, I have consulted approximately twenty colleagues worldwide. (Acknowledgments come at the end; let me apologize here for my bastardization of their opinions.) Of course, my contacts in the profession tend to be, like me, microeconomists and theorists, although I did include a few macroeconomists and others whose focus is more empirical.

From the perspective of this essay, the results were helpful primarily in a negative fashion. It is an understatement to say that there is no consensus; those queried gave diametrically opposed responses, both in general and to specific questions. The exercise did help me refine my own opinions, which I proceed to give. But the reader should be clear that *1)* my report will be skewed towards the experiences and perceptions of a microeconomic theorist who works at a business school; *2)* the opinions expressed are my personal opinions; and *3)* I am aware of widespread disagreement in the field both as to the substance of the assertions I will make and about the current state of economics.

Indeed, an important weakness of this essay and in its author's qualifications is that I have virtually no training or background in macroeconomics, which most laypersons (and many economists) regard as the main branch of the discipline. I will write primarily about the state of microeconomics today; while I have and will briefly offer some opinions about the recent intellectual history of macroeconomics, they are formed largely out of prejudice and hearsay.

THE MATHEMATIZATION OF ECONOMICS

There is no question that economics underwent a revolutionary change around a half-century ago; mathematical modeling, a small piece of the subject until the 1940s and 1950s, became the all-encompassing (some would say suffocating) language of the discipline. Mathematical modeling and formal deductive logic have been a part of economic theory for much longer than that, but their embrace by the mainstream of the profession came in this period. For very persuasive evidence on this point, consult Gerard Debreu's 1989 Presidential Address to the American Economic Association.[2]

The embrace was so complete that, as a neophyte economist in the mid-1970s, I had little exposure to less mathematical, more verbal treatments of economic questions. "Little" does not mean "none"; in the one macroeconomics course I took, we read both Marx and Keynes's *General Theory,* neither of which is exactly overrun with equations or symbols. But the teacher in this course assumed without the slightest hesitation that to understand these books, it would be extremely helpful to reduce the theories to systems of equations (which he provided, and which did help, at least me).

No single book had canonical authority in 1975, but from my perspective, Debreu's *Theory of Value* came the closest.[3] Debreu's classic develops the general theory of (market) value—what determines how much each item costs in the marketplace, including an analysis of why markets are efficient[4] in the setting of general equilibrium (all markets considered simultaneously)—in 114 pages. To read this, one needs a fairly high level of mathematical sophistication—although Debreu begins by defining the notion of a set, it would be hard to learn the requisite mathematics for the first time from his synopsis—but the economic development is self-contained.

The book was and remains a powerful advertisement for deductive reasoning in economics. Beginning with assumptions about what drives the market behavior of individuals and firms, one proves formally that an overall market equilibrium exists and is "nice" in certain very precisely defined ways. The book contains important extensions of the basic model; while the analysis is conducted statically, as if all economic activity took place in a single instant, it points out how this can be extended to economic activity that involves time, uncertainty, or both. Further, because of its resolutely deductive nature, it allows the reader who objects to the conclusions reached to trace her objections back to basic assumptions made. For example, the efficiency of an economic outcome depends crucially on the assumption that each consumer derives satisfaction entirely from his own private consumption; he does not compare himself to his neighbors, nor does the activity of his neighbor disturb or improve his own well-being.

I should be clear that *Theory of Value* was canonical in terms of basic principles or laws. Its formal setting and its reliance on pure deduction was not embraced as a workaday methodology by the majority of the profession; most economic analysis relied more heavily on special assumptions drawn from something between careful and casual empiricism. (For a description of how most economists use mathematics and models, see Solow's essay in this volume.) Also, because of its very abstract and general level, *Theory of Value* lacks some techniques—e.g., methods of comparative statics—used to study more specific contexts. But the principle of rigorous deduction within the framework of a mathematical model, as well as the basic tenets of *Theory of Value*—purposeful behavior by firms and consumers, and price-mediated market equilibration of those behaviors—were widely embraced as economic canon law.

The allure of mathematical modeling and reasoning in economics comes first and perhaps foremost from the power it gives us to define our terms (say, "efficiency") precisely and unambiguously and to show that certain precise assumptions lead to other precise conclusions. It also allows us to stretch our analyses and to unify them; once we have worked our way through the logic that assumptions A imply conclusion X, we may see how assumptions A' lead to conclusion X' by the "same basic argument." It allows us to appreciate how critical are certain (often implicit) assumptions: If A leads to X, but a slight change in A to A' leads to not X, then we can appreciate that X or not X depends on the seemingly slight differences between A and A'; hence X is not a very robust conclusion. Taking these logical deductions back to the real world, where the satisfaction of assumptions A or A' is a matter of some controversy, our developed intuition concerning what assumptions lead to which conclusions, together with a sense of how closely the real world conforms to A or A', gives us the courage to assert that X will or will not pertain with very high probability.[5]

Debreu points to another explanation for why deductive reasoning has allure to economists. This concerns our (relative) lack of controlled data. In the absence of data with which to test our theories, if we allow logical inconsistencies or lacunae, we let in too many possible conclusions. The test of logical coherence is a poor substitute for data when one is trying to understand the real world, but it gives some discipline and sharpness to theorizing.

Of course, the rise of mathematics in economics and its powerful hold on economic theory in 1975 (and today) does not trace solely to these advantages. The use of a powerful and somewhat obscure tool confers power on the user. As economists became convinced of the value of mathematical rigor, the reward system (based on peer review) reinforced this tendency.

THE RISE OF STATISTICAL METHODS

Allied with the rise of formal mathematical models was the rise of statistical methodology in economics. Formal statistical techniques— hypothesis testing, inference, regression, and the like—certainly existed prior to this, but their embrace by mainstream economists also came during the postwar period. Of course, these techniques require mathematical specification of a hypothesis or model to be estimated, so the development of mathematical skills among economists was reinforcing. And those relatively more skilled at understanding statistical methods tended to be those relatively more skilled at deduction; as a social phenomenon, the rise of one reinforced the rise of the other. Indeed, one of the most important forces for the development of both in economics was the Cowles Commission, which was formed to advance both branches simultaneously, given how natural was the (seeming) connection between them.

For much of the postwar period, most empirical work was substantially more difficult than theory-building for two reasons: data were hard to gather and relatively expensive to process. In cases in which the government paid for data collection and was willing to subsidize its processing—national income accounting and the like—careful statistical modeling was relatively more prevalent. But the real proliferation of empirical work in economics trailed the proliferation of formal modeling by a bit.

ROMER'S HOURGLASS

The rise of mathematical modeling and statistical methods in economics meant a change in the way economists reasoned and communicated. But it had two further effects that are crucial to my history. Both are captured broadly by the image of an hourglass, suggested by Paul Romer. Within economics, there are many different topical concerns, such as international trade, development, economic history, labor markets, public finance (and, more broadly, the interplay of economic and political institutions). Before the mathematicization of economics, these fields maintained significant intellectual autonomy. Things a student would learn in, say, development economics would not resemble all that closely what was taught in public finance. Emphasis was placed on typologies and on the institutions that pertained to the subject in question. There were, if you will, a number of regional dialects of "Economese," dialects that were close to being distinct languages.

As economics was mathematicized, the power of formal deductive modeling and statistical methods, and the status their use conferred, resulted in their acceptance by the more applied fields. This was not a matter of the applied fields recognizing the power of these new techniques and, thus persuaded, welcoming them with open arms. Acceptance was often grudging. Moreover, the process often involved imperialism, with an economist trained in mathematical technique in one area invading the topical domain of one of the applied fields. But however it happened, in most cases it did happen. The dialect of international trade today is very close to the dialects of industrial organization, development, and labor economics. Nowadays the languages used by different branches of economics sound a lot more like branches of a single methodological (rather than topical) tongue.

The process of unification meant something of a reduction in, or consolidation of, what was studied in economics. The mathematical techniques were developed first and most powerfully in the context of so-called competitive market exchange.[6] The adoption of mathematical techniques, often imported from price theory (the theory of competitive market exchange), meant a concomitant adoption of the modeling choices and concerns of price theory. In particular, the study of economic institutions—a big portion of mainstream economics before World War II—dwindled in importance. The newly dominant dialect of mathematical modeling lacked some topically important vocabulary; rather than speak in an unfashionable dialect, some things were just not discussed.

This contraction of topical concerns had its positive points. The unification of dialects, for example, means that insights obtained in one context can be easily transferred to another. Insofar as a graduate student in economics is meant to master several applied fields, having a unified language promotes the educational process. And, for reasons given above, I assert that the dominant dialect of mathematical deduction possesses some powerful grammatical advantages.

Nonetheless, the loss of certain topical concerns represented a real loss. Price theory for competitive markets is empirically very useful, but there are economically important matters that it simply misses. From 1975 to the present, what we have seen in economics is *1)* the development of further techniques that play by the basic rules of established (mathematical) economics but that broaden its scope and *2)* the application of those techniques to specific contextual questions, with the result that the field now seems to be returning to something like the breadth of the discipline before World War II.

Hence the image of an hourglass: The vertical axis represents time, and the horizontal axis the scope or topical breadth of economics. As time passes, we see first a narrowing of topical concerns as the language is unified and then a widening of concerns as the language develops. Throughout, it is important to note, the discipline of economics did not entirely abandon subjects such as institutional economics. Pockets of resistance to the revolution persisted; in some overseas locations and in some domestic departments, they dominated. The hourglass describes roughly the development of orthodox or mainstream economics, and (at that) primarily in the United States.

ENVIRONMENTAL INFLUENCES ON SUBJECT MATTER

As mainstream economics has broadened again, there has been something of a shift in the center of gravity of concerns, and new topics—for example, an increased emphasis on nonmarket exchange—have come to the fore. This shift in topical concerns may be seen as a response to an array of environmental influences.

As economic activity has become more global, demand for and interest in comparative economic systems has increased. There has always been an interest in comparing broadly different systems, such as socialism and capitalism. But recently interest has become more microeconomic. These days we discuss the merits of Japanese production techniques, the German system of (employee-employer) codetermination, and the impact of venture capital on newly created American firms.

At the same time, economic ideas have permeated a number of applied and professional fields, such as business, law, finance, accounting, and medicine. Practitioners in these fields have increasingly sought the advice of economists; and economists, seeing an increased demand for their services in these domains, have responded by shifting toward them.

As economic ideas have permeated such fields, academic economists are increasingly found outside of arts and sciences economics departments—in business, law, engineering, and even medical schools. Both the quantity and quality of professional-school economists has risen, and with them the influence of professional-school subjects within the larger community of academic economists. Within arts and sciences departments, a steep increase in the number of undergraduate majors with professional and professional-school aspirations has led to an increased demand for courses that serve their needs; in consequence, the field has seen an increase in courses that emphasize the normative applications of economic reasoning in the private sector while de-emphasizing abstraction for its own sake and downplaying economics as descriptive social science.

One should not overstate this shift in the center of gravity of the discipline.[7] Economists have not flocked en masse to new subjects, nor have they abandoned the old. But, on the margin, changes in topical emphasis have occurred. And the increased interest in nonmarket economic exchange—i.e., exchange within firms and other nonmarket institutions—represents more than a marginal change.

METHODOLOGICAL INNOVATIONS

Together with these environmental influences, the current portfolio of economic concerns and techniques has been influenced by some significant methodological innovations.

Our ability to process data has been increased enormously. This is not to say that empirical testing has only recently arrived, but the quantities of data we can process, and the ease with which the data can be manipulated, have increased enormously. Statistical tests are no longer limited to a small number of theoretically manageable parametric specifications; Monte Carlo methods have dramatically increased what can be tested and how.

The information age has given us a bounty of empirical data to study, including data at a microscopic level of aggregation. Financial market theory and accounting have been virtually revolutionized by the general availability of transaction-by-transaction trading data. Data on purchasing activities of individual households are increasingly available. We are close to the day when economists will easily access the Census Bureau's data base.

Where data do not exist, economists are increasingly willing to create them using controlled experimentation. Experiments in economics include testing choice behavior by individuals, behavior in competitive/cooperative situations, and behavior in marketlike settings. The growth in the computing power at our disposal has also made it possible to solve increasingly large and complex problems and to uncover via simulation the properties of heuristic decision rules. Standard economics places great stress on the idea that economic actors optimize their actions; we are increasingly able to compute what optimization means and to evaluate how short of this goal economic actors fall in complex settings.

SMALL NUMBERS, INFORMATION, AND DYNAMICS

These have been important methodological innovations; but the innovation that has had the greatest impact on economic thought has been the enrichment of the language of the field with the vocabulary and grammatical forms of information economics and noncooperative game theory. This enrichment has been crucial to the rewidening of the subject because it has allowed us to tackle with mathematical models three important classes of issues: small numbers interactions, privately held information, and true dynamics. Textbook microeconomics in the 1960s and early 1970s was largely about markets with large numbers of buyers and sellers who interacted anonymously. Markets were entirely driven by the prices of things; the theory of markets was, for all intents and purposes, the theory of prices—hence the name price theory. There was a theory of monopoly (one seller and many buyers), and there were simple theories of oligopoly (a few sellers with many buyers); but the abbreviated models that existed tended to be fairly wooden, with sheeplike buyers and artificially imposed conjectures. Buyers and sellers were assumed to operate on the same informational basis; the idea that, say, the seller of a used car knew more about the car than did the buyer did not enter the story. And it was held to be a great virtue of the theory that any sort of dynamic interaction could be reformulated as an equivalent static, one-time interaction, without any loss of generality. That is, when planning what to buy at the corner grocery store for the coming week, the consumer in an economic model would solve the problem of what to consume this week, the next, and for the rest of his life— contingent on uncertainties concerning his future income, the dividends his investments might pay, and so on. He would find the optimal lifetime *strategy* for consumption and then proceed today to implement its first step.

Today, the first theory course for acolytes (first-year Ph.D. students) begins with these basic models and assumptions, but then moves on. We consider with a limited amount of success how bargaining transpires between the single buyer and seller, when each has only limited alternatives in trading partners. We discuss with more success how terms of trade are set in specific institutions for price-setting, such as in auctions and highly organized exchanges. A large part of the second half of the typical first theory course concerns information economics, an innovation dating from 1970 or so. This concerns, for example, how markets in used cars and health insurance operate when sellers know more about their cars than do buyers, and insurees know more about their state of health than do insurers, or how the market in managerial talent will be affected when managers pursue agendas that do not automatically accord with those of the boards of directors and shareholders for whom they work. And a good deal more emphasis is put on how the dynamic character of an economic interaction can affect its outcome, e.g., what it takes for large industrial firms to collude, or how a monopoly firm might successfully deter entry into the markets it controls.

These factors become most interesting when they interact. To take a topic near and dear to my own concerns, organization theorists have for a long time remarked that many large firms operate so-called internal labor markets (ILMs): new hires enter the firm in entry-level positions and conduct their entire career within the firm, advancing up the hierarchy. This is a far cry from the perfectly competitive labor market that is implicit in *Theory of Value* (implicit because *Theory of Value* does not distinguish labor from any other economic commodity), where labor is a commodity that sells at a given equilibrium price. But a student leaving the first-year theory course today would be prepared to discuss such matters as how ILMs weaken the bargaining power of workers, because of inferences alternative employers will draw if a worker leaves an ILM prematurely (small numbers and private information); how a firm's desire to maintain its reputation among its other employees might protect the individual worker from exploitation (small numbers and dynamics); how an ILM might offer the firm a superior monitoring capability (and hence more efficient incentives), because of such factors as a delay in the realization of output measures, group-measurement effects, and/or risk-sharing through time (private information, dynamics, and small numbers); and what all these things mean for the worker's allocation of effort through time (private information and dynamics).

EVOLUTION OR REVOLUTION? THE THREE CANONICAL PRINCIPLES

Moreover, the student will discuss all these issues according to some fundamental principles that are basic in *Theory of Value*. These are:

1. *Far-sighted rationality.* On deciding to join firm A, worker X anticipates the contingent future of his employment relationship. This is not to say that worker X can foresee the future; but he has a detailed probabilistic picture of the future in mind, as does the firm (or its managers), and he uses this picture in forming his own actions.

2. *Behavior is purposeful.* Employees (and the firm employing them) act purposefully, to achieve a well-defined goal. This goal is put into the model as a numerical index of the individual's well-being, for example, utility for consumers and (usually) profits for firms.[8]

Combining (1) and (2), we have individual firms, employees, and consumers whose behavior is modeled as optimizing some numerical index in (generally) fantastically complex decision problems involving vast stretches of time and substantial uncertainty. Moreover, the solutions they arrive at fit together extremely well in an—

3. *Equilibrium.* Workers correctly anticipate how their colleagues will act and how the firm will act, now and in the future. The firm correctly anticipates the actions of workers. Given these correct anticipations of current and future actions, each party is doing as well for itself as it can, within the constraints of actions available to it.

While the contextual market assumptions of *Theory of Value*—large numbers and anonymity, all information is shared, all analysis is static—have lost canonical status, these three basic principles have not. Of course, the loss of the contextual assumptions makes a difference. Nowadays we speak of promises firm A might make to its workers, yet the only promises that are made are those that are credible in the sense that it will be in the interest of the firm to keep them when the time comes. We speak of information held by one party and withheld by that party from others, yet if employee X withholds information from her employer, the employer knows that X has information and correctly anticipates what X would do if that information were other than what it is. Considerations like this add enormously to what we can discuss and model. But the rules of these models have remained (1), (2), and (3). Note well: These three canonical principles were not born in the *Theory of Value*, nor with the general mathematization of economics. In less formal terms, they go back more than a century. But with the general mathematization of (micro)economics, they became the bedrock of the discipline; *Theory of Value* had something akin to canonical status because it was a particularly powerful formulation of these three principles, and an equally powerful derivation of some of their consequences, for a particular set of contextual assumptions about the economy.

In this sense, while the mathematization of economics was certainly a revolution, the subsequent expansion from the base of 1970 until today has been evolutionary. Most graduate students spend their first few months of microeconomics learning demand theory more or less as it was taught in the 1970s, and at some point in the first year they tackle general equilibrium theory, the basic subject of *Theory of Value*. They do less of this than did their predecessors, to make time for newer contextual assumptions. But they do it, because it is generally believed that such an understanding remains the essential starting point for more modern developments.

CONTINUING EVOLUTION

There continue to be developments of this evolutionary type. Now that economists speak a more or less common dialect, topical fads are common. For a year or so, everyone is doing industrial organization. Then international trade becomes hot. At the moment, microeconomic theorists are by and large chasing organization theory, the closely related subject of corporate finance, and/or growth theory (and, in particular, its connection to the human capital of a region). These fads do not appear entirely unbidden—the recent airwave spectrum auction created a boomlet in auction theory, and events in Eastern Europe and the Far East have prompted more activity in the topic of restructuring economies, with spin-offs into certain aspects of the theory of contracts, law and economics, and growth theory. But from wherever they come, these forays are part of the ongoing evolutionary development of the subject. Attacks on the context-of-the-year are made according to the three principles identified in the previous section, albeit enlivened with some specific contextual novelties, such as increasing returns to industrial production, or complementarities in various activities, or an assumption that no deal will go un-renegotiated (as long as both parties to the deal can profit from a renegotiation).

To put it briefly, the theoretical tools we have are pretty good, and many of my colleagues are happily engaged in their employment.[9] At the same time, the increasing availability of data, the now universal availability of computing power (used to compute solutions to optimization and equilibrium problems, to simulate suboptimal but reasonable behavior, and to process the data), and increased levels of laboratory experimentation have led to substantial increases in the empirical testing of economic theories. I am not enough of a statistician to be able to relate intelligently the latest innovations in these fields. But as an observer, I am impressed with the increasing level, quality, and scope of these endeavors.[10]

A COMING REVOLUTION

Many of my colleagues will consider this assessment delusionally upbeat. A question we often ask (as do, I suspect, all academics) is: "Read any exciting papers lately?" With some of my theory colleagues, the answer recently has often been "No." Theory development in economics seems fairly moribund, at least when compared with the late 1970s and early 1980s.[11]

Put it this way: the Econometric Society—the leading international professional society for economic theorists (and others)—holds a World Congress every five years. The most recent was held in Tokyo, in August of 1995. As part of the program, a number of plenary sessions are held on topics chosen by the program committee to summarize activity over the previous five years and to anticipate (or try to) future developments. These sessions concern relatively more applied topics (industrial organization, finance, and so on), the development of statistical methodology (time series, nonparametric methods, and similar approaches), and—because the Society has a large constituency of tool creators—sessions on recent developments in the tool-fashioning subindustry of theory. For the Tokyo Congress, there was no dearth of interesting sessions in the first two categories. Indeed, there were plenary sessions on topics that twenty years ago one would not have expected at this society's World Congress—economic history, political economy, organization theory, and restructuring socialist economies—reflecting the widening of topics and unification of language described above. But suggestions for session topics in tool-creation were few and somewhat forced; this sort of activity seems to have died back.

I say "seems to" because I do not actually believe this is so. Instead, a somewhat revolutionary shift in the economic paradigm has begun—one that mostly missed being on the program of the Econometric Society's 1995 World Congress because its pieces were and are not yet sufficiently advanced for plenary reviews. The shift involves a partial abandonment of the three canonical principles of rationality, purpose (or greed), and equilibrium.

First and foremost, the assumption that economic entities are hyper-rational and hyper-perspicacious is under renewed attack. The assumption of hyper-rationality has been under attack since it began to be taken hyper-seriously; Herbert Simon has been a strong and convincing critic for at least forty years. But until recently mainstream economists mostly shrugged their shoulders at such attacks and claimed that the alternative was theoretical anarchy—ad hockery run amok. Nowadays we see more measured attempts to find alternatives, and while no widely accepted standard alternative has emerged (and may never do so), mainstream economists are increasingly willing to try the alternatives that do arise. In particular, the study of adaptive learning and behavior by the individual has been an area of significant activity recently.

Second, the economic entities of *Theory of Value*—the firm and the consumer—are no longer purposeful monoliths. The attack on the firm has been going on in the guise of organization theory for quite some time. But increasingly one sees papers about consumers whose behavior, tastes, and expectations are socially determined or affected by psychological processes of perception and cognition. We also see papers that pursue a biological metaphor, where behavior is "instinctive," given exogenously, with the population of behavioral types determined through some sort of selection dynamics (whether seriously modeled in processes of imitation or just specified exogenously as part of the model).

Third, non-equilibrium states are discussed and sometimes even modeled. Interactive models of adaptive learning, in which individuals struggle to understand an environment that changes with the state of their struggle, are in vogue. Evolutionary models of behavior are, of course, also interactive. Whether one calls them temporary equilibrium or disequilibrium systems, they are certainly a step away from the full-equilibrium (and fully-rational, optimizing) assumptions of the current standard economic theory.[12]

This suite of changes responds to the maturation of the previous wave of developments and is a continued response to the environmental and methodological factors that helped shape the previous wave.

These changes respond in the first place to the limits the standard canon places upon us, especially when it comes to economic exchange involving a small number of parties and long stretches of time. For example, it takes very little empirical power to see that in the real world of exchange between employee and employer or between supplier and purchaser the relationship is ongoing and the "contract" between the two is seriously incomplete, in that what is exchanged, when, how, and at what price are determined as contingencies arise. Transaction cost economics[13] is based on this observation and on the notion that in such contracts one must focus on the governance structure implicit or explicit in the contract, i.e., how contractual adaptations will be made. As mainstream economists have become increasingly interested in the dynamics of exchange in general, and in non-market, non-anonymous markets in particular, they have recognized that an understanding of this contractual incompleteness and the relative efficiency of different forms of governance is crucial. Some very insightful models have been built to study contract incompleteness and governance that play within the confines of the three canons, wherein one restricts exogenously the terms upon which a contract can be based.[14] But in this context, the three canons, especially the canons of full (hyper-)rationality and equilibrium, imply that the individuals involved fully and correctly anticipate what contingent adaptations will take place. Hence explanations and investigations based on the three canons are somewhat tortured and miss the mark. Interest in this sort of exchange pushes theorists to explore revolutionary alternatives.

These changes respond as well to the increased availability of data, both collected in the field and produced in the laboratory. Debreu's *Theory of Value* correctly identifies the need for formal reasoning (and, I assert, canonical assumptions) as arising in part from the economist's relative lack of data. Compared to physical and biological scientists, economists are still relatively poor in controlled data. But our relative poverty is lessening, and we can (and are increasingly able to) afford a degree of theoretical ad hockery—if we can justify our modeling assumptions with data.

Recent trends in experimental economics are salutary in this regard. Most experiments are tests of the canonical models, either of how individuals choose in relatively controlled settings (usually, not as economic theory would have us believe) or testing equilibrium predictions of the theory. (Market equilibrium theory has tended to fare a bit better.) Recently, though, there has been an increase in tests outside the canonical models, both trying to refine our understanding of real choice (going from the observation that the frame of a choice matters to an investigation of *how* systematically the frame matters) and the processes of learning in multiperson settings that might get us to an equilibrium.

This oncoming revolution has also meant increased contacts with other scholarly fields, contacts that will surely increase. To put it on a purely personal level, I am currently engaged in writing a book on employment and human resource management with a card-carrying sociologist. Ten years ago, had I admitted the profession of my coauthor to my colleagues in economics, most would have said that my business school experiences had corrupted me irreparably. Today they may still think this, but they express substantial interest both in the project and what I am learning from it. Specifically, they recognize that standard economic models of long-term interaction suffer enormously from two lacunae: the standard models leave unexplained and unmodeled the idea that the interaction will change what individuals value; and while the standard model makes clear that what individuals expect of their trading partners is crucial, it does not have much to say about where those expectations come from. In the language of economics, sociological considerations help us understand how the social context of exchange affects both the preferences of the individual and what the individual expects of others. For example, sociological considerations offer explanations for how the symbolic character of employee benefits—presented as a gift, or as just another form of market compensation—might spill over into the day-to-day relationship between employee and employer.

To put it less personally, the interest in evolution means connections with biologists, the interest in the social formation of expectations and preferences means connections with sociologists, and the interest in the processes of perception and cognition means connections with psychologists. This is not missionary work, where economists issue epistles for others to follow, but is more like two-way trade (and, to judge by the testimony of some of my colleagues from these other lands, it may have become missionary work the other way around).

This probably sounds like a substantial and exciting amount of activity. So why, one may ask, does the question "Read any good papers lately?" draw "No" as the answer? The reason, and the best sense in which this is a revolution, is that this activity seems to imply a decrease in the importance of deduction in economics. For people like myself who were raised with *Theory of Value* as canonical authority, a good paper is one with an innovative new model that concludes with an interesting theorem (or, at least, proposition). A paper that reports provocative experimental data or even just a provocative simulation of some dynamic system does not pass the test. If I am right about the coming revolution, though, these standards will change, as will our willingness to report simulations along with the provocative experiments and empirical papers that we increasingly see.

WILL THE REVOLUTION THREATEN THE EVOLUTION?

Most of my colleagues agree that this potentially revolutionary activity is taking place. Some have decried its existence, claiming that the three canons are essential to economics. Perhaps a larger fraction, with empirical instincts, note that the cry "Bounded Rationality!" has been with us nearly as long as the three canons, and predict no lasting impact from the current flurry of activity along these lines.

But suppose that the revolution does come, and we learn how to reason fruitfully without the three canonical principles. Will this revolution threaten the accomplishments of the past twenty or thirty or even fifty years? I do not believe so. The advent of private information, small numbers, and nontrivial dynamics has not routed models that live (nearly) fully within the contextual and modeling assumptions of *Theory of Value*. One of the most productive fields of microeconomic study since 1970 has been the study of financial market valuation, which plays largely by the full set of assumptions. This field continues to thrive. These models can and do tell us a lot about what determines the market value of a share of AT&T or an option to buy a share of AT&T. But even so they do not tell us everything; this form of modeling financial market value has been enriched by developments in the study of market micro-structure (how stock markets operate transaction by transaction) and of corporate finance (what determines the level of debt as-sumed by public corporations)—developments that rely on the three canons but depart from the contextual assumptions of large anonymous markets, shared information, and essentially static optimization.

Similarly, the three canonical principles, while limited, have their sphere of relevance. Indeed, some of the models that step outside the three canons do so with the explicit intention of testing them, e.g., when do we derive (even approximately) an economic notion of equilibrium from a biological process of natural selec-tion? Within that sphere, the three canons will continue to guide informative study of specific questions. Perhaps needless to say, some of the sharpest debates to come will be over the boundaries of that sphere of relevance.

So is this a revolution after all? Some readers of early drafts of this essay assert that a revolution, by definition, must overthrow all of the old system. (*Webster's* supports this assertion.) So per-haps what I call a revolution is more like the earlier introduction of information economics and the language of game theory into economic discussions; that is, a burst of increased diversity that is evolutionary rather than revolutionary in character.

WILL THE ESTABLISHED PARADIGM IMPEDE THE REVOLUTION?

Conversely, will the established paradigm impede these new developments? There are good reasons to think that it will.

First, economists have an unfortunate tendency to believe that *rational behavior* by individuals means behavior that accords with the basic axioms of revealed preference enriched, in the case of choice under uncertainty, by Savage's axioms or, in the case of dynamic choice, by the principle of full dynamic consistency. These economists believe that behavior that does not accord with the standard model is irrational, unpredictable, and even somewhat unsavory—not a fit subject for serious discussion. I recall a conference on organization theory at which a prominent labor economist, within the space of fifteen minutes, decried models in which employees were concerned with their compensation relative to that of fellow workers and then related that his experience as department chair had taught him that his colleagues behaved in just this fashion. The second, though, was dismissed as "just an anecdote"; the first was "something serious."

Second, economics, at least as practiced by mainstream economists, is a field that values tradition. If phenomenon X can be explained within the standard canon, such an explanation is usually preferred to another explanation that ventures outside the canon because, given our relative paucity of data, adherence to canonical assumptions provides us with a measure of discipline. And, turning this seeming virtue into a vice, we have become adept at tweaking our true-to-the-canon models to produce almost anything we desire. We can empirically reject specific models that employ the canon, but our inventiveness with models has gotten us to the point where rejecting the canon is well-nigh impossible.

Finally, economists, or at least economic theorists, have a strong and developed taste for answering the question, "How efficient (in the precise economic sense) is this or that outcome?" Efficiency, in the precise economic sense, needs consumers with well-anchored preferences. To relax the first and second assumptions of the canon (far-sighted rationality and purposeful behavior) means at least a reformulation of the notion of efficiency, and perhaps something more dramatic—not a price most theorists will be happy to pay.

For these reasons and others besides, the very success of the continuing evolution—the playing out of the second wave of developments since World War II—may act to impede the third wave. Why abandon a seemingly winning hand? But, to give a purely personal opinion, I think the third wave will only be a little impeded: the empirical deficiencies of the canon, *where it is deficient,* are too glaring. The rich array of things to learn from other disciplines is too rich. And not least of all, the need for economic theorists to work on something new and different is too impelling.

MACROECONOMICS (AS VIEWED BY AN OUTSIDER)

I am quite content with the assertions in this essay insofar as microeconomics is concerned. But there remains the subject of macroeconomics. As already noted, I am very poorly qualified to talk about the recent history and current position of macroeconomics. At the same time, no essay on the current state of economics could possibly be complete without addressing those topics. So with the strong caveat that my opinions on the matter compound ignorance and prejudice, I proceed to give my impressions.

To begin with the "facts" concerning recent history (the scare quotes are intended to recognize that others will dispute these facts): Macroeconomics over the period from 1970 until 1990 or so was split into two camps, so-called saltwater and freshwater approaches. The names are derived from the geographic locations of the institutions that practiced these contending views. Thus, the temples of saltwater macroeconomics were MIT, Harvard, Pennsylvania, Princeton, Stanford, and Yale, while freshwater macroeconomics was developed at Carnegie, Chicago, Minnesota, and Rochester.[15] Saltwater macroeconomics is (by descent) the macroeconomics of Keynes. In terms of the models constructed, it is more behaviorist; consumers act in mathematically modeled ways but do not have quite the foresighted rationality of consumers who are making microeconomic decisions. Markets can fail. When we see workers on the dole, they are there involuntarily because, say, firms will not lower wages to clear markets. Freshwater macroeconomics, in contrast, begins with microeconomic-style consumers, who are not fooled by government attempts to manipulate them through fiscal or monetary policy (hence freshwater's alternative name, rational expectations macroeconomics). And markets in freshwater macroeconomics do work; any unemployment we observe is voluntary in a real sense.

The saltwater brand of macroeconomics was the establishment brand; freshwater was the revolutionary challenge to the status quo. The challenge was based on something akin to canonical purity: Saltwater macroeconomists accept (and accepted) the power of mathematical, formal models—they certainly accepted the relevance of statistical modeling and fitting—but they were skeptical about the canon of farsighted rationality and, as a reduced form, were willing to live with a bit of "disequilibrium" in their models. Greed, rationality, and equilibrium had their place in the saltwater pantheon, but that place was not above all other considerations. The freshwater challenge, then, was to take as paramount greed (or purpose), rationality, and equilibrium.

Battles between the two camps were common; as an outsider, I was privileged (if that is the right word) to observe these battles on various selection and review panels. Saltwater types would argue that they were being pragmatic, using the canons to guide their models as far as common sense and the data indicated was appropriate. (Macroeconomics is one field in which data have been fairly readily available, supplied by the government whose practical interests in the subject are obvious.) Freshwater types would argue that an edifice could only be as strong as its foundations; if you did not play by the rules of the discipline, you could not be sure what you had. In support of this argument, the freshwater types could cite evidence; during this period one of the fundamental empirical regularities of establishment macroeconomics, the Phillips curve (which said that governments could trade off unemployment for inflation), was badly mauled by stagflation.

The battlegrounds were grants, publications, positions, and the minds and souls of the next generation—otherwise known as graduate students. Both sides had victories and defeats. My sense, as an observer, was that the freshwater types had victories especially in the arena of graduate students; better graduate students can excel more quickly when excellence depends on the mastery of mathematics and logical purity rather than on an experience-based sense of how far to push on canonical principles, hence better graduate students are strongly drawn to topics and approaches that stress technical expertise and novelty. I can recall an archdeacon (at least) of the saltwater church sitting on a selection panel for fellowships for younger faculty members and complaining about how all the bright young macroeconomists, including his own students, were reading, believing, and (according to him, worst of all) doing freshwater-style work.

Today the war has largely abated. In part, interest among macroeconomists has moved on to questions about the determinants of long-term growth, which run orthogonal to the saltwater/ freshwater debate. And in part, having built and studied the simple models, freshwater macroeconomics has proceeded to more complex models, with richer information, strategic and dynamic effects (the evolution in microeconomics), and, very recently, models in which the individual consumers are not hyper-rational (the revolution). The models that emerge may not take us all the way back to saltwater macroeconomics as it was in the 1960s. But saltwater types maintain that once these real-world complications are added to freshwater models, what emerges is just a somewhat more detailed version of what they (the saltwaters) have been chasing all along. Hence both sides claim a brackish victory. The saltwater types insist that the freshwater folks have begun to abandon the ivory tower for more realistic models of individual behavior. And the freshwater types insist that, at last, the saltwater types are taking seriously what impels individual behavior, which is just what the freshwaters wanted.

From the perspective of the basic thesis of this essay, the story of macroeconomics (if I have it right) is interesting on two related grounds. First, it gives an example of the tension in economics between treating the canonical principles as ironclad precepts or as loose guidelines. In his essay in this volume, Solow argues that serious economists (i.e., everyone except perhaps the high theorists) use mathematical models opportunistically, constructed to shed the most light on the phenomenon under consideration, without doing violence to empirical observations. It should not go unnoted that Solow is a high priest of the saltwater school of macroeconomics. This is not to say that Robert Lucas—a high priest of freshwater—would disagree in principle with Solow's description of how economists should use mathematics and canonical principles. But they would disagree on how ready one should be to bend canons to perceived circumstances.

Second, the story may give some guidance for what will happen as the third wave of bounded rationality and disequilibrium breaks on mainstream, more doctrinally pure, microeconomics. At the conference for which these essays were prepared, it was commonly observed that economics was different in an important way from the other three fields discussed—English, philosophy, and political science. Economists by and large agree on what they are doing and how to do it. The discipline has not been the scene of major methodological conflict, based on different generations or anything else. The freshwater/saltwater wars were as close to this as we have come. And in those wars, the common heritage and shared respect for the canon (even if some economists are less observant than others) led to an armistice with both sides feeling victorious. In the third-wave story there are important differences; most importantly, the revolutionaries are seeking to weaken the canonical assumptions instead of increasing adherence to them. But notwithstanding the differences, as one of the new revolutionaries, I can hope that if the wars to come will not be friendly, neither will they be internecine.

ACKNOWLEDGMENTS

I am grateful to Kenneth Arrow, James Baron, Ken Binmore, Tim Bresnahan, Don Brown, Mike Hannan, Jim March, John McMillan, John Roberts, Paul Romer, Alvin Roth, Tom Sargent, Eytan Sheshinski, Robert Solow, Manuel Trachtenberg, Robert Wilson, Mark Wolfson, Michael Woodford, and Jeff Zwiebel for helpful comments and insights.

ENDNOTES

[1] Jim March was contrasting economics and sociology; his counterpose to the "saloons of sociology" was the "well-ordered Methodist Church of economics." As evidence that economists are well-ordered Methodists, unacquainted with saloons, I can report that an economist friend, reading this line in an earlier draft, was concerned that my spell checker had converted "salons" into "saloons."

[2] Reprinted as "The Mathematization of Economic Theory," *American Economic Review* 81 (1991): 1–7.

[3]Gerard Debreu, *Theory of Value* (New Haven, Conn.: Yale University Press, 1959). While Debreu's work (and that of his colleagues in general equilibrium theory) played a role in the mathematicization of economics, I do not mean to assert that they were solely or even principally responsible for this revolution. To attribute credit (or blame) for this revolution is outside both my charge and my expertise, although I would be remiss not to mention in this regard Paul Anthony Samuelson's vastly influential *Foundations of Economic Analysis* (Cambridge, Mass.: Harvard University Press, 1947). I am only asserting here that in 1975, when the revolution was (largely) over, *Theory of Value* was as close to canonical as anything, at least for microeconomists.

[4]The term "efficient" here does not conform to the normal-usage meaning of the word. Roughly, a market outcome is efficient if there is no way to reorder economic activity that would be unanimously preferred by all the individuals in the economy. Needless to say, this is subject to conditions and qualifications.

[5]For further development of these points, together with some examples, see Debreu, *Theory of Value,* or David M. Kreps, *Game Theory and Economic Modeling* (London: Oxford University Press, 1990), chap. 3.

[6]"Competitive" here means that no economic entity has so much power as to be able to affect any market price.

[7]Because I work at a business school, I may see more of this than there actually is.

[8]In Robert Solow's trinity of "greed, rationality, and equilibrium," greed is a code word for purposeful behavior. Most economists populate their models with greedy individuals—those whose purpose is self-interest, very narrowly defined. In this sense, Solow's code word is entirely appropriate. But the formal canon is that individuals act purposefully, and in theory (if not in many models) the goals pursued could be an equitable distribution of resources or a "just" outcome somehow defined.

[9]To add a darker note here: Economists are often accused of trying to force the world to fit their modeling forms. Within economics, the context-of-the-year phenomenon gives rise to a related accusation, viz., the theory community will descend upon a particular context and write a bunch of papers that are motivated in large measure by their theoretical appeal and only in small measure by empirical observation. Then the theory steamroller moves on, leaving scholars whose careers are in the context-of-last-year to deal with the litter left behind, viz., papers that may have been fashionable but that too often miss the contextual mark. Context specialists need to have a healthy skepticism concerning what they can learn from general-purpose theorists. Happily, their skepticism is usually in robust good health.

[10]And to add a darker note here: It is universally appreciated, I think, that theorists are able to tweak their assumptions in order to reach any conclusion they wish. The believability of the conclusion depends not only on the fact that it was reached but on how hard the theorist had to tweak the model to get there. On the other hand, it is less clear how much we appreciate that with increased availability of data and computational power, and with journals that naturally select papers that are novel, we collectively face a data-mining problem, at least as far as claims of statistical significance are concerned.

[11]Another piece of data, perhaps a bit more objective, is the large number of textbooks being produced on the subjects developed over the past two decades.

[12]There has been enough work on these topics so that a plenary symposium was held at the Tokyo Congress on adaptive learning and evolutionary models of behavior.

[13]See, for example, Oliver E. Williamson, *The Economic Institutions of Capitalism* (New York: Free Press, 1985).

[14]For a recent survey, see Jean Tirole, "The Current State of Incomplete Contract Theory" (University of Toulouse, 1995, mimeographed).

[15]The past tense in this sentence is intentional. Most saltwater temples have at least one practicing priest of freshwater in residence nowadays, and at least one of the saltwater temples has been largely taken over by the other side. Moreover, the distinctions are no longer so severe, although that gets a bit ahead of the story.

William J. Barber

Reconfigurations in American Academic Economics: A General Practitioner's Perspective

L ET US PROCEED FROM Jacob Viner's oft-quoted dictum: "Economics is what economists do." A fair number of those who are paid to "do economics" do so by representing the discipline to students in liberal arts colleges. I write from the vantage point of a teacher-scholar at one of the nation's well-regarded liberal arts institutions from 1957 to 1993. I like to think that this account of changes in the way economics has been presented in that environment over the past four decades or so captures the essentials of what has happened in liberal arts colleges at large. But the reader needs to be reminded that this narrative may be seasoned by a local flavor. Institutional differentiation on points of curricular detail is altogether healthy. Certainly, liberal arts colleges cherish their idiosyncrasies.

The essays in this volume by Professors Solow and Kreps effectively convey the character of change in the way economics is "done" where the specialist scholars are trained.[1] The transformation wrought by the emphasis on mathematization and by the increased technical sophistication expected of aspiring professionals has been dramatic and undeniable. In the culture of the general practitioners, economics has also changed—but in a manner that is both qualitatively and quantitatively different. As employers of products of Ph.D. programs, economics departments in liberal arts colleges are affected by what happens in the major graduate schools, albeit with a time lag. Given the academic tenure system, the

William J. Barber is Andrews Professor of Economics Emeritus at Wesleyan University.

waves generated by specialists in the first instance are more like ripples in the world of general practitioners. There is a constraint as well on the extent to which particular types of emphases in the graduate schools can be replicated in liberal arts colleges: undergraduates who are being initiated to the discipline cannot be expected to command comparable mastery of mathematical technique, even though their departments have steadily escalated the technical skills required to qualify as a Bachelor of Arts with a major in economics.

Over the post-World War II decades, formidable pressures for substantive revision in what the discipline's general practitioners offer has come from another direction—i.e., from changes in tastes in their student populations. These years have been marked by periods of considerable turbulence in American society that in turn have stimulated noteworthy challenges to the manner in which the academy had become accustomed to going about its business. As far as the content of an economics program is concerned, it is at least arguable that the general practitioners have been more immediately exposed to contemporary societal currents than their colleagues specializing in graduate instruction have been. Directors of graduate programs, of course, must pay some heed to what is going on in the worlds of business and government when they shape their curricula: nonacademic employers now hire a substantial fraction of the new Ph.D.'s. Nonetheless, a distinction can be drawn between general practitioners and specialists with respect to the nature of their engagement with their respective student audiences as it affects what they put on offer. The specialists expect to serve a pre-professional clientele that is receptive to focusing primarily on analytic innovations emerging from the discipline's internal intellectual dynamics. Instructors of undergraduates face a different problem. If they are to find a market for their services, they need to meet students where they are. Undergraduate concerns—initially, at least—are usually very much linked to their perception of issues in the "real world."

The discussion below begins with a broad-brush characterization of reconfigurations in a standard liberal arts economics curriculum since the late 1950s. (This account, it should be noted, draws heavily on my personal experience as a participant-observer.) Various approaches to the discipline in this setting have gained favor or fallen from it over this span of time. Some tentative considerations concerning factors that might explain these outcomes will be advanced. Particular attention will then be directed to the divergent fates of various subdisciplines—some of which have been revitalized in a new guise, while at least one has become a candidate for the endangered species list. Finally, the question of whether or not a stable equilibrium (circa the mid-1990s) has been achieved in the relationships between the specialists and the general practitioners will be addressed.

CENTRAL TENDENCIES IN CURRICULAR REDESIGN

When illustrating shifts in the curricular "mix," it will be useful to distinguish between two components of the economics major program in the typical liberal arts college. The first is a core of courses required of all students; the second consists of elective field courses, a specified number of which must be completed to satisfy the stipulations for graduation. There has been remarkably little change in this aspect of the programmatic pattern. But this element of continuity should not mask the fact that what counts as core—as well as what is available on the list of electives—has undergone substantial transformation.

The core, as prescribed by the undergraduate faculty I joined in 1957, consisted of a year-long sequence in intermediate economic theory (macro and micro) and a year-long course in the history of economic thought (which included attention to selected topics in economic history).[2] Change was already underway in what was packaged as intermediate economic theory. Unlike their elders, the "young Turks" entering the profession in the 1950s had been schooled in Keynesianism, and this doctrine soon approached—for a season—the standing of an orthodoxy. It was no accident that Paul Samuelson's *Economics,* with its Keynesian orientation, quickly dominated the liberal arts segment of the undergraduate textbook market. As the faculty guard changed, the menu of electives was modified as well. Members of the professoriate reaching *emeritus* status in the mid- to late 1950s frequently offered courses in such fields as "Public Utilities" or "Transportation." These topics were dropped from the course catalogs when they left the payroll. There was continuity, however, in elective offerings such as money and banking, labor economics, industrial organization, public finance, and international trade. Elective space opened up and was filled by a newcomer: "Economic Development." The expression "Third World" had not yet been coined, but the beginnings of the postcolonial era brought excitement to this field.

In the graduate schools in the mid-1950s, an "econometric revolution" was occurring simultaneously with the "Keynesian revolution." In the undergraduate curriculum, a Keynesian penetration tended to take precedence, but a curricular assimilation of quantitative technique was not far behind. By the mid-1960s, the "History of Economic Thought" had dropped out of the core at Wesleyan (though it remained as an elective, as did "Economic History"). A required course in "Quantitative Methods" occupied most of that vacated space. Meanwhile, the authority of Keynesian macroeconomics seemed to have been validated in the Kennedy-Johnson demand-side tax cut of 1964. Among the electives, undergraduate enthusiasm for President Kennedy's Peace Corps enhanced the popularity of the course in "Economic Development." Economics faculties on liberal arts campuses basked in reflected glory with the liberally-oriented undergraduate body at a moment when it appeared that the discipline had found a way both to "fine-tune" the economy to a full-employment growth track with price stability and to uplift the underdeveloped world.

This mood of heady self-confidence was abruptly shattered by events in the late 1960s. Student culture took a radical turn with both the demonstrations protesting American involvement in Vietnam and the sit-ins demanding changes in the ethnic composition of the student body and faculty. On most campuses—large as well as small—academic regulations of long standing were drastically modified. The anti-establishmentarianism of the time typically produced a major rewrite of the specifications for a Bachelor of Arts degree. Few of the former institutionwide requirements for its completion survived. In most instances, however, the authority of individual departments to set requirements for their majors remained in place. Certainly at Wesleyan (and I suspect at sister institutions as well), the economics department subsequently lost ground in the competition for the ablest undergraduates.

Some of the most articulate campus "activists" of the late 1960s and early 1970s have subsequently become captains of corporate finance—and, along the way, have come to regard economics as a discipline worthy of serious study. In an earlier incarnation, many of them spurned it. Enrollments in economics tumbled, as all too many students perceived the subject—incorrectly—to be nothing more than an apologia for *status quo* capitalism. Various measures were available to counter their misperceptions; I recount ones taken in my own department. In the first instance, the catalog description of the course in introductory microeconomics was modified. The revised language emphasized that the course would treat cases of market failure (as well as instances of market success) and that the issue of environmental pollution would receive particular attention. An upper-level course on the "Economics of the Environment" was added to the list of electives. Especially noteworthy was the addition of a course in "Comparative Economics," which focused on the problems of resource allocation facing centrally-planned economies and those organized on worker-cooperative principles. These were not the easiest years, however, for instructors in courses dealing with "Third World" development. Student attitudes toward this subject matter were conditioned, in part, by fallout from Vietnam that generated a predisposition to the view that any contact between rich countries and poor ones was self-evidently an offensive form of "neo-imperialism." The changing ethnic composition of the student body left a mark as well. It was not unknown for some of its more militant members to challenge the competence of the instructor (if white) to present material on economic development problems in Africa. At this time, the "History of Economic Thought" enlarged its audience. This gave students who wanted to read Marx an opportunity to do so. Indeed, a number of institutions then engaged untenured faculty members to present the perspective of "radical political economy." Meanwhile, some institutions (e.g., the New School for Social Research and the University of Massachusetts at Amherst) chose to specialize in this material.

In light of the experience of the 1970s, what was taught as intermediate macroeconomic theory also underwent a sea change. The realities of "stagflation" stripped the Keynesian doctrine of much of its earlier luster; the standard model lost a lot of its previous explanatory power. These years witnessed considerable professional soul-searching—the "crisis" facing the profession became a familiar theme for presidential addresses to the American Economic Association (AEA). Whether or not they agreed with the monetarist critique of the Keynesian doctrine, instructors in macroeconomics felt honor-bound to familiarize their students with the properties of Chicago-style thinking. The latter perspective has had a continuing influence (though not necessarily a dominating one) on the way macroeconomics is presented.

Since roughly 1980, shifts in the style and content of the liberal arts curriculum have been driven primarily (although not exclusively) by the changing makeup of economics faculties. The B.C. (Before Computer) economists of an earlier era have left the scene. Their chairs have been filled by members of a younger generation whose approach to the discipline has been shaped by specialized graduate training, with its heavy dosages of mathematical and statistical technique. For economists in this generation, it comes naturally to insist on higher levels of technical competence from their students, and they gear their teaching accordingly. Courses in "Mathematical Economics" and "Econometrics" have taken on increased prominence in the menu of electives. Indeed, at Wesleyan a new major program has been spawned—the Mathematics-Economics Program. Students electing to join this interdepartmental venture can satisfy its requirements for a degree by completing twelve upper-level courses offered by the two departments (with a minimum of five courses in advanced mathematics). In addition, one post-core research seminar treating advanced topics in economic theory is offered each semester. This innovation—which places Wesleyan ahead of most peer institutions—is designed for students intending to pursue graduate studies in economics.

Revisions of this sort in the curricular mix are in keeping with the trends set by the specialists in the major graduate programs. Departmental old-timers sensed that something else was also at work in the reconfigurations of the past decade or so. Undergraduates were far from totally insulated from features of the predominant national mood of Ronald Reagan's America. In increasing numbers, students approached the economics major with vocational aspirations—and, in particular, looked to it as a step toward a successful career in the world of business, with or without an M.B.A. For many, the most sought-after postgraduation affiliation was with an investment banking house. This trend was accompanied by a perceptible decline in the enrollment in upper-level economics courses of students with keen interests in public policy issues. It appeared that this segment of the undergraduate population found its tastes better catered to in Wesleyan's department of government. Courses styled as "political economy," with a focus on policy analysis, had been added to its curriculum, and they enjoyed strong demand.

DIVERGENT FATES OF VARIOUS SUBDISCIPLINES

There can be no ambiguity about the main thrust of the reconfigurations of the recent past: the priority enjoyed by the mathematical emphases has meant that much of the earlier attention accorded to a historical perspective on the discipline has been displaced. (At Wesleyan, a course in "The History of Economic Thought" is no longer on the regular menu of departmental electives.) Part of the explanation for this turn of events can be traced back to the graduate schools. With but a few exceptions, the study of this subdiscipline is no longer a live option for Ph.D. candidates in the major programs. Mastery of refined mathematical technique is unquestionably a time-intensive activity and, if the lives of graduate students are to be made more liveable, something has to give. But the systematic study of dead economists has been vulnerable for another reason. One suspects that directors of most Ph.D. programs could readily identify with a view expressed by a prominent French economist in the early nineteenth century. J.-B. Say, one of the pioneers of classical political economy who aspired to see the discipline recognized as solidly scientific, remarked: "The more perfect the science, the shorter its history." If one is persuaded that the economics of the late twentieth century has approached scientific perfection, it follows that inquiry into its history is dispensable.[3] For those of this mind-set, a study of the past has nothing to contribute to an understanding of the present or of the future.

In the high-visibility graduate departments of economics, the subdiscipline of the history of economic thought has thus been marginalized to the point that it is threatened with extinction in that setting. It does not follow, however, that interest in this subject matter has vanished altogether. On the contrary, scholarly activity in this field, as measured by the mushrooming of specialized publications, has probably never been greater. The journal *History of Political Economy* (published at Duke University), now entering its second quarter century, has mobilized an enthusiastic international clientele of readers and contributors. In addition, a History of Economics Society, founded in 1972, has flourished. At its annual meetings, representatives from the major Ph.D.-producing departments are conspicuous for their absence. (In recent memory, the only member of the Harvard faculty to be an attendee held an appointment in its History of Science department.) The liberal arts colleges, by contrast, are well represented at these gatherings. It is also noteworthy that the History of Economics Society contains more than a sprinkling of members whose academic appointments are in departments of history or philosophy, rather than in economics.

The study of the history of economic thought thus continues to show strong vital signs by leading an existence outside the mainstream of the economics profession. Whether or not life on these terms is altogether satisfactory is a matter worthy of reflection. The reasons why the subdiscipline has been shunted to the sidings in the institutions where the bulk of the professionals are prepared are altogether comprehensible. Even so, the proposition that the younger professionals are intellectually poorer because of this disposition is at least entertainable. The subdiscipline may still have something useful to contribute to the education of economists. First, it has the potential to blunt excessive professional hubris with reminders that interesting analytic problems can be formulated in a variety of ways and that the paradigm in fashion today may be passé tomorrow. Second, to members of a profession with a high propensity to focus on matters that can be measured, it provides a reminder that the economist's agenda need not be bounded by the availability of numerical data and that not everything that counts can be counted.[4]

The fate of the subdiscipline of economic history has been altogether different. Traditionally, the standard approach in this field had been long on institutional description, though tending to be short on hard-core analysis. This situation changed dramatically with the advent of "cliometrics"—an innovation that amounted to a marriage between mathematical modeling and statistical analysis of historical data—in the late 1950s. In this incarnation, economic history has been revitalized and has maintained a strong curricular presence in both graduate and undergraduate economics programs. This success story has been made possible by the fact that the cliometricians could easily assimilate the profession's high techniques. This accommodation did not satisfy all comers. As Claudia Goldin, a "new" economic historian at Harvard, has noted, there was considerable resistance from the old-timers who viewed "those who were formalizing the field. . .as outsiders" and as "theorists with little knowledge of the facts and with no sense of history."[5] Without doubt, the cliometricians have carried the day. When surveying recent developments in the field, one of their number sounded a note of triumphalism. "My view," wrote Christina D. Romer of the University of California at Berkeley, "is that the war is over and the good guys won. More concretely, the field of economic history is no longer a separate, and perhaps marginal, subfield of economics, but rather, is an integral part of the entire discipline."[6]

A word is in order about the character of change in an applied field or two as it has been influenced by the world of events, by shifts in the makeup of the profession, or by both. The reformulation of issues addressed in labor economics is an interesting case in point. Well into the 1960s, the specialists in this field were preoccupied with investigations of the impact of trade unions on wages and employment. This is no longer so. The decline in organized labor's share of the work force has stripped the earlier agenda of much of its relevance. But another conditioning factor has also been at work, namely, changes in the gender and racial composition of the profession. As increasing numbers of women and minorities have become professionally credentialed, the central focus of labor economics has tended to shift toward research into the gender and racial dimensions of occupational categories and pay scales.

The collapse of the Communist order in the former Soviet Union and in Eastern Europe, it should be noted, has reenergized practitioners in another applied field. This turn of events has cut much of the ground out from under courses in "Comparative Economics" that were built around juxtapositions between centrally planned and private market-driven economies. Accumulated expertise in that subject matter is now being reallocated to the study of the "Economics of Transformation." Courses with this description currently have lively constituencies at both the undergraduate and graduate levels.

HAS EQUILIBRIUM BEEN ACHIEVED WITHIN THE DISCIPLINE?

In the recent past, considerable disquiet has been in evidence within the community of professional economists. Officers of the American Economic Association—as well as a number of the profession's senior establishment figures—have been at the forefront of some exercises in self-criticism. Economists teaching in liberal arts colleges have been catalytic agents in this process. On two principal grounds, they have found fault with the direction in which the major graduate schools have led the discipline: 1) that economics, as presented at the graduate level, has become increasingly ill-suited to the preparation of future members of economics faculties in the undergraduate liberal arts setting; and 2) that graduate economics programs in their current state are no longer attracting and retaining the ablest students from strong undergraduate institutions as they once did.

A significant stimulant to the current round of soul-searching was provided by an essay, which appeared in 1987 in a publication sponsored by the American Economic Association, that reported results of surveys of graduate students at six of the nation's leading doctoral programs.[7] One of its central findings was that "graduates are well-trained in problem-solving, but it is technical problem-solving which has more to do with formal modeling techniques than with real world problems. To do the problems, little real world knowledge of institutions is needed, and in many cases such knowledge would actually be a hindrance since the simplifying assumptions would be harder to accept." In addition, the survey data indicated that substantial majorities of the survey population perceived two skills as "very important" to professional success: "being smart in the sense of being good at problem-solving" and "excellence in mathematics." Some 68 percent of the respondents reported a belief that "having a thorough knowledge of the economy" was "unimportant."[8] Many of the general practitioners found these results to be consistent with conclusions they had arrived at from less systematic observations.

General practitioners were also disturbed for another reason. For the bulk of the twentieth century, the selective liberal arts colleges have nurtured notable recruits to the profession, on a scale disproportionate to their size. By the later 1980s, it was abundantly clear that that historic pattern no longer held. A study orchestrated at Oberlin College (in which nine of the country's most selective liberal arts colleges participated) indicated that the decade of the 1980s had witnessed a reduction in the flow of their graduates to Ph.D. programs in economics to merely 50 to 60 percent of the rate to which they had formerly been accustomed, despite the fact that the number of undergraduates majoring in economics at these institutions had grown considerably. In addition, the drop-out rate from graduate programs among the B.A.'s produced in nationally-known liberal arts colleges was abnormally high. Much of the explanation for these phenomena turned on cognitive dissonance concerning what the discipline was really all about. Even though mathematical expectations for an economics major had been expanding over time, most students came away from their experience in liberal arts colleges persuaded that economic analysis had payoffs in heightening the rationality of practical decision-making, that it had relevance for public policy, and that it offered useful insights into the workings of an economy's institutions. Indeed, these factors were usually responsible for attracting them to the discipline in the first instance. Those dimensions of "reality," however, were largely squeezed out of the standard first two years of graduate study in favor of concentration on the sophisticated techniques. The result was disaffection on the part of some promising talents.[9]

Stirrings such as these prompted the American Economic Association to create a Commission on Graduate Education in Economics that was charged to "take stock of what is being done [in graduate education] and, as far as possible, what results we are getting."[10] In its Report (which appeared in September 1991), the Commission noted that particular dissatisfaction with the output of economics Ph.D. programs had been expressed by two groups of potential employers. Department heads in liberal arts colleges were increasingly concerned about the mismatch between the technical skills acquired by new Ph.D.'s, on the one hand, and their capacity to meet the pedagogical expectations of undergraduates, on the other. Nonacademic employers (e.g., governments, banks, consulting firms, etc.)—who collectively absorb just over 40 percent of the annual flow of new Ph.D.'s—registered disquiet about the ability of the profession's recruits to conduct empirical research and to communicate their findings.[11] The Commission remarked on its "fear" that "graduate programs may be turning out a generation with too many *idiots savants,* skilled in technique but innocent of real economic issues." The Commission, however, did not propose any major departures from the *status quo.* On the contrary, it concluded that there was "*not* [emphasis in the original] an excessive use of mathematics," though it acknowledged that there was "considerable scope for improvement in ensuring that students' knowledge of economic problems and institutions enables them to use their tools and techniques on important problems." With respect to one of the grievances expressed by economists at liberal arts colleges, i.e., the attrition rate of their products in graduate programs, the Report suggested that members of these faculties might want to make some changes of their own. The Commission recommended that students be made aware "that undergraduate coursework offered by most economics departments is in itself insufficient preparation for graduate work" and of the "need to become adequately skilled in mathematics" before entering graduate programs.[12] With respect to a concern registered by nonacademic employers, the Commission recommended that graduate programs should assign higher priority to honing the communication skills of Ph.D. candidates.

QUO VADIS?

Contention among economists about the course their discipline ought properly to take is not new to the American scene. Indeed some of the current debate about the respective weights to be assigned to "rigor" versus "realism" is reminiscent of some rather bitter infighting that occurred roughly a century ago. In the *Methodenstreit* of the late 1880s and 1890s, swords were drawn between champions of two rival "schools." "New schoolers"— most of whom had been influenced by the teachings of German historicism—maintained that the discipline should eschew abstractions and concentrate on the study of the "realities." Representatives of the "old school" identified with formal theorizing as developed in the British tradition and typically regarded their American challengers as unscientific and soft-headed.[13] These were days when economists were still struggling to achieve a secure base for themselves in the academy. And, as leaders in each of the two "schools" came to realize, internecine intellectual warfare carried on in public compromised the image they were trying to cultivate as professionals with insights that deserved to be taken seriously. Both sides had a stake in reaching a balance in which curricular coexistence for both points of view would be tolerated.

In light of the concerns over the direction of the discipline that have become manifest in the recent past, how likely is a significant rebalancing in the late twentieth century? A number of considerations would suggest that a major reorientation is not on the immediate horizon. Unlike the situation a century ago, the discipline does not have to fight for an existence within the academy; the specialists are solidly established. This state of affairs provides an environment suited to permitting the discipline's substance to be shaped primarily by its internal intellectual momentum. And there is no lack of dynamism in the thrust toward ever higher levels of technical sophistication. After all, those who have invested heavily in mastering these skills have an obvious interest in reaping a payoff from their use. They have every incentive to do so: in the current professional reward system, prestige is accorded to those maximizing production of technical papers—an objective that is more readily reachable when the high techniques are deployed to treat narrowly circumscribed topics. Yet another factor contributes to the sustained weight of technique in the curricular configuration, namely, changes in the "mix" of the graduate student population. Though the aggregate number of Ph.D.'s produced has been fairly stable over the past two decades, the number of Americans in the group has declined. United States citizens accounted for about two-thirds of the economics doctorates in 1977, but they represented less than half of the total by 1989. This shift toward a rising number of graduate students for whom English is not a first language can reasonably be presumed to have had some programmatic implications. As one informed observer has commented, "It is conceivable. . . .that the content of graduate economics shifted somewhat to accommodate the changing mix of students by emphasizing quantitative rather than verbal skills and theoretical rather than institutional knowledge."[14]

It is at least thinkable that a few steps toward rebalancing might be taken as a by-product of dissatisfaction with the *status quo* that continues to be expressed by some general practitioners. In 1993, for example, 463 members of economics faculties committed to undergraduate teaching signed a "Petition to Reform Graduate Education," which specified the competences they expected candidates for appointment at their institutions to demonstrate. In particular, attention was drawn to: *1)* a background in the economic debates and literature of the past twenty years and how those debates have shaped what we as a profession believe; *2)* a solid training in the models that they will be teaching to undergraduates; *3)* knowledge of economic institutions and the role institutions play in the economy; *4)* an ability to communicate orally, and in prose, the central ideas conveyed in introductory and intermediate micro- and macroeconomics; *5)* knowledge of the alternative approaches in economics and an ability to compare and contrast different approaches; and *6)* knowledge of econometrics, but also of the limits of econometric testing.[15] If this initiative has had any impact on pedagogy in graduate programs, it has thus far been well concealed.

But it is also possible that the next wave of curricular adaptations might move liberal arts colleges (or at least some of them) closer to what graduate programs expect, as opposed to movement the other way around. As has long been the case, new entrants to the faculty ranks—for at least their first decade or so—typically bring to undergraduate classrooms what they have absorbed from graduate studies. There is thus a natural gravitational pull that tends to bring what is presented to undergraduates closer to the prevailing orientation of Ph.D. programs of the recent past. In addition, many in academic life aspire to recruit their best students to follow in their professional footsteps and derive considerable job satisfaction when they are successful in doing so. Such considerations are reflected in the Report of the Oberlin Group that focused on measures to enlarge the numbers of their graduates who would earn a doctorate in economics. Taking a cue from the AEA's Commission on Graduate Education, the authors of the Oberlin document called for greater attention to advanced mathematically-oriented economic theory in the undergraduate curriculum. They recognized "that the increased regularity of such courses may lessen the ability of the colleges to offer basic courses in economic history and history of thought, and that, consequently, professional economists may never be exposed to an overall view of the field." Given the intensity of their concerns about the flow and fate of their graduates in Ph.D. programs, they regarded this outcome as "a necessary price to pay."[16]

This assessment amounted, in effect, to a statement that the primary objectives of the economics program in liberal arts colleges should be reconsidered. The old-fashioned general practitioners usually construed their functions to be multi-faceted. In their understanding of the job, the undergraduate course menu should aim to provide students with an economic literacy that would equip them to be more thoughtful citizens and voters as well as better informed managers of their personal business affairs. Additionally, most general practitioners aspired to sharpen their students' capacity to think analytically by acquainting them with various ways in which analytic problems have been formulated. Along the way, some of their students would elect to pursue careers as professional economists, but it was expected that the overwhelming majority would not. By contrast, the authors of the Oberlin Report recommend that a high priority in the allocation of pedagogical resources should be assigned to the needs of a small cadre of "semi-professionals" in order to strengthen their survival skills in the world of the specialists.

Those who do economics in the setting of the liberal arts colleges do not, however, speak with one voice. Indeed, the extent to which the views articulated in the Oberlin Report are representative of that population at large is not clear. To many, it remains far from self-evident that the course menu should be guided by the interests of the 5 percent of the national pool of economics majors who anticipate entering graduate programs in economics, rather than by those of the 95 percent who do not. Moreover, on the strength of the evidence, a plausible case can certainly be made in support of an altogether different conclusion, namely, that the narrowed focus of the discipline at the graduate level should mean that breadth and variety in the undergraduate economics curriculum should be promoted and treasured all the more.[17] One would be ill-advised, however, to bet the family farm on the prospects of that course being adopted.

ENDNOTES

[1]See Robert M. Solow, "How Did Economics Get That Way and What Way Did It Get?" and David M. Kreps, "Economics—The Current Position" in this volume.

[2]Wesleyan was probably atypical when requiring that this amount of time—two semesters—be allocated to historical aspects of the discipline. Nonetheless, courses in the history of economic thought and in economic history were then usually a part of the basic menu for economics students in liberal arts colleges. In addition, these were still the days when university regulations required freshmen to take a two-semester course in Western Civilization.

[3]This is not, however, a unanimous view among leading professionals. Two examples will serve by way of illustration. George Stigler and James Tobin—both Nobel Laureates, though of differing analytic persuasion—share a commitment to economics as a science and have also enriched the literature of the history of economic thought.

[4]There may be something suboptimal as well about the creation of specialized journals and societies devoted to the history of economic thought. It would be unfortunate if these developments should produce a cult whose members talked only to one another.

[5]Claudia Goldin, "Cliometrics and the Nobel," *Journal of Economic Perspectives* 9 (2) (Spring 1995): 194.

[6]Christina D. Romer, "The End of Economic History?" *The Journal of Economic Education* 25 (1) (Winter 1994): 9.

[7]See David Colander and Arjo Klamer, "The Making of an Economist," *Journal of Economic Perspectives* I (2) (Fall 1987): 95–111. Graduate students at Chicago, Columbia, Harvard, MIT, Stanford, and Yale participated in the inquiry.

[8]Ibid., 100, 108.

[9]See Hirschel Kasper et al., "The Education of Economists: From Undergraduate to Graduate Study," *Journal of Economic Literature* XXIX (3) (September 1991): 1088–1109. In addition to Oberlin, the institutions participating in this study were Amherst, Haverford, Middlebury, Smith, Swarthmore, Wellesley, Wesleyan, and Williams.

[10]The Commission had a distinguished membership: Anne O. Krueger (Duke) as Chair, Kenneth J. Arrow (Stanford), Olivier Jean Blanchard (MIT), Alan S. Blinder (Princeton), Claudia Goldin (Harvard), Edward E. Leamer (UCLA), Robert E. Lucas (Chicago), Rudolph G. Penner (Urban Institute), T. Paul Schultz (Yale), Joseph E. Stiglitz (Stanford), and Lawrence H. Summers (Harvard).

[11]A report on a survey of the attitudes of nonacademic employers enlarged on this theme as follows: "New Ph.D.'s were viewed as less well trained in the fundamentals of economics, less able to carry out empirical research, not much interested in conducting policy-relevant research, and unable to communicate effectively their knowledge of economics and particularly the nature and results of their research. Employers expressed dismay that new Ph.D.'s possessed so little institutional knowledge of the economy. They also commented on their weak knowledge of economic data, its quality, and its interpretation." W. Lee Hansen, "The Education and Training of Economics Doctorates: Major Findings of the Executive Secretary of the American Economic Association's Commission on Graduate Education in Economics," *Journal of Economic Literature* XXIX (3) (September 1991): 1085.

[12]Anne O. Krueger et al., "Report of the Commission on Graduate Education in Economics," *Journal of Economic Literature* XXIX (3) (September 1991): 1035–1053.

[13]It should be noted as well that antagonisms between the two "schools" involved more than just disputes about method. There was an underlying political agenda as well: "old schoolers" were typically staunch defenders of laissez-faire, whereas "new schoolers" were sympathetic to state intervention to correct what they perceived to be social abuses arising from unbridled market power.

[14]Hansen, "The Education and Training of Economics Doctorates," 1057–1058.

[15]"Petition to Reform Graduate Education," as reproduced in the *American Economic Review* 83 (5) (December 1993): ii-iii. The "Petition" and the names of its signatories appeared as a paid advertisement.

[16]Kasper et al., "The Education of Economists," 1106.

[17]This point of view has been well articulated by Bradley W. Bateman (of Grinnell College) in "The Education of Economists: A Different Perspective," *Journal of Economic Literature* XXX (3) (September 1992): 1491–1495.

M. H. Abrams

The Transformation of English Studies: 1930–1995

I BEGIN WITH A CONFESSION. I began studying English literature as a freshman at Harvard as long ago as 1930. I later discovered that, as a systematic field of study consigned to a college department, English was then only some fifty years old. Now, in 1997, I am startled to realize that my life as a student and teacher of English spans a good deal more than half its existence as an established academic discipline.[1]

Within its span of a half-century, the English department at Harvard had by 1930 achieved a highly developed and durable institutional form, with numbered courses taught by teachers who ranked from instructor to full professor, set requirements for an undergraduate major (in Harvard parlance, a "concentration"), and a distinction between those participating in the program for a pass and those aspiring to an honors degree. The offerings included courses in English composition (an enterprise that English departments had acquired by historical accident) as well as a few courses in public speaking (the remnants of a curriculum in rhetoric and elocution to which occasional readings in English literature had, before the 1880s, been ancillary). The lectures in literature—some primarily for undergraduates and some specifically for graduate students—included an initial survey of the "History and Development of English Literature"; a series of period courses from the Old English era to "Contemporary English Literature (1890 to the Present Time)"; courses devoted to single authors—Chaucer, Spenser, Shakespeare, Milton; courses on literary genres—poetry, the novel,

M. H. Abrams is Class of 1916 Professor of English Emeritus at Cornell University.

drama, the essay; and a miscellany of topical and thematic offerings such as "The Tradition of King Arthur" and "The Historical and Intellectual Background of English Literature." Some five or six courses were devoted to American literature, a field of study that had been introduced at Harvard in the 1890s. There was also a harbinger of things to come: I. A. Richards, as a visiting professor from Cambridge University in 1930, lectured on "Practical Criticism"; his book of that title, published the same year, analyzed students' commentaries on poems that were presented without identification of author or era. This book, together with *Seven Types of Ambiguity* by Richards's student William Empson, became a prime model for the detailed explication of poems that was advocated a decade or so later by the New Critics.

When I began graduate study at Harvard in 1935, the central requirements for a doctorate in English still accorded with the model established in the 1890s, in which a training in linguistics and historical philology was judged necessary to give literary studies a subject-matter and methodological rigor that qualified them as a discipline equivalent to the natural sciences. After preliminary examinations in the reading of German, French, and Latin, there were programs for the Ph.D. candidate that combined English and the classics or focused on medieval language and literature; but the plan that almost all students elected to follow required at least six semester courses in the Old and Middle English languages, Old French, Gothic, and "historical Germanic linguistics." The remaining half of one's studies, as the *Register* of 1935–1936 described it, had the grandiose aim of covering "English literature of all periods, though some acquaintance with American literature and relevant foreign literatures is also expected." And, of course, one's training culminated in a dissertation that, in the words of the *Register,* "must give evidence of research or of original treatment of a fitting subject."

The philological parts of the graduate curriculum, however rigorous, were distinctly unexciting. For example, there were the lectures on Old French texts, in which the professor of Romance Literature, in a detailed linguistic analysis of the *Chanson de Roland,* only once uttered a comment that approximated literary criticism. We had come to the climactic moment at Roncevaux in which Roland, his rear guard of twenty thousand men besieged by four hundred thousand Saracens, refuses to sound his horn in order to call up reinforcements. The lecturer looked up from the page. "Gentlemen"—in those days, he could assume that graduate students were male—"some say that Roland's refusal to blow his horn was an ultimate act of chivalry. But to my mind, Roland was nothing but a dumb athlete." The distinguished medievalist with whom I studied Chaucer spent a number of hours in his seminar simply dictating bibliographical references. In much the same spirit, for the final examination in historical German linguistics, we exploited a device that had no doubt been covertly handed down through student generations: For each type of historical sound change, each of us chose a word that exemplified the change, then converted the long series of exemplary words into nonsense sentences, which were duly memorized. As the need arose, one silently recited the appropriate sentence, retrieved the verbal example, and used this to identify, triumphantly, the sound change in question.

Looking back, I do not regret the drudgery I spent on these required philological and historical studies; they turned out, later, to be useful in unexpected ways. The truth is, however, that the required regimen of graduate study had little relation to what we were taught on the undergraduate level and to what we ourselves were expected to teach undergraduates after receiving our doctoral degree. A number of the offerings that I attended as an undergraduate were lively and rewarding and as diverse as the interests, temperament, and pedagogic talent of the individual teacher. Chester Noyes Greenough, who taught the literature of the Restoration and the early eighteenth century, assigned almost as much reading in documents of social, political, and religious history as in the literary texts that he related to these historical contexts. George Lyman Kittredge, in courses focused on only two Shakespeare plays, insisted on a meticulous familiarity with the details of Shakespeare's text; his final examination, I recall, included a large selection of fragmentary phrases—"patience on a monument," or "unhous'led, disappointed, unanel'd"—that we were asked to attribute to the speaker and situation, to interpret, and then to add a comment on its function in the drama.

I remember most gratefully John Livingston Lowes, a small man with a big, resonant voice that communicated most effectively his passion for poetry. He was a learned man who had a zest for painstaking research in recondite texts. His *Road to Xanadu*,[2] detailing how Coleridge's imagination transformed his immense reading into the substance and shape of "The Ancient Mariner," is the high monument of the old scholarly sport of source hunting, but it is also a work of literary criticism in its own right and propaedeutic to all later criticism of Coleridge's poem. And in his lecture series of 1918, published as *Convention and Revolt in Poetry*,[3] Lowes's acute critical discussions extended from Chaucer to poets who were then, in his words, "the most modern of the modern," Ezra Pound and Amy Lowell, as well as to the debate then raging about the merits of free verse.

REDEFINITIONS OF ENGLISH STUDIES AT MID-CENTURY

During the first two decades of my career as a teacher, the most prominent and most debated innovation in literary studies was the New Criticism. This movement began in 1938 with the first edition of Cleanth Brooks's and R. P. Warren's enormously successful textbook *Understanding Poetry*; was christened in 1941 by John Crowe Ransom's little book *The New Criticism*; was provided with a systematic theoretical foundation in 1942 by René Wellek and Austin Warren in their influential handbook for graduate study, *The Theory of Literature*; reached its apogee of critical application at the time of Cleanth Brooks's *The Well Wrought Urn* in 1947; and maintained its position in the teaching of literature through the 1950s.[4]

The central claim of the New Critics was that the concern of literary study proper was with the individual literary work in itself, conceived as a self-sufficient entity whose borders and "autonomy" were guarded against critical transgressions by quasi-theological prohibitions against "the personal heresy," "the heresy of paraphrase," "the intentional fallacy," or "the affective fallacy." In *The Theory of Literature,* Wellek and Warren identified "intrinsic criticism" with the treatment of a poem as an object in itself and delegated all studies of the biographical, social, and historical conditions and aspects of the poem to marginality as an "extrinsic approach to the study of literature." To analyze the constitution of a poem as such, the New Critics developed their distinctive critical practice of "close reading." This consisted of a detailed analysis of the "ambiguities," or multiple meanings, that in all good poems (it was claimed) interacted to compose a poetic structure of irony and paradox. That is, the poem was said to be constituted by a "tension" of discordant significations and feelings that are organized around a central "theme" into an inclusive unity of opponent attitudes that is the mark of a mature and realistic stance toward reality.

In our current climate of critical opinion, the New Criticism is often derogated as the prime example of mid-century "formalism"; that is, of the approach to a literary text as a purely verbal entity that is to be analyzed independently of the historical conditions of its production, and as subject to universal and unchanging criteria of value. In its time, however, it was a useful corrective to the tendency of many earlier literary studies to confine themselves, in dealing with a literary text, to a consideration of the life or the temperament or the historical and intellectual situation of its author. And it seems to me an injustice to depreciate what the New Critics largely invented—the close analysis of the semantic constitution of a literary passage or work. It is easy in hindsight to recognize both the narrowness of a critical method that applied to all literary genres criteria relevant to only one kind of lyric poem and also its inherent tendency towards explicative overload. But we are in fact all heirs of the technique for close reading developed by the New Critics—including the American deconstructive critics, whose "closer reading" (in Paul de Man's term) shared the ahistorical formalism of their predecessors but replaced their predisposition to discover coherence and a paradoxical unity of opposing meanings with the predisposition to discover incoherencies, "ruptures," and the undecidable gridlock of opposing meanings called "aporias."

That being said, it should be added that it is an error to suppose, as a number of commentators now do, that literary study in the mid-century was dominated by the New Criticism. What the New Criticism dominated was the pedagogy of courses designed to introduce undergraduates to the reading of poems, plays, and novels. But the era of the New Criticism was also the era of a great variety of enduringly important critical works that made frequent and diverse uses of the biographical, psychological, social, economic, and historical matrix of imaginative literature, without supposing that such references either displaced or were in conflict with a consideration of literature as its own kind of human accomplishment. The free-ranging critical practices of many of these writers is in conformity with Kenneth Burke's declaration, in opposition to the exclusionary formalism of the New Critics, that "the main ideal of criticism. . .is to use all that there is to use."

The 1930s opened, most auspiciously, with I. A. Richards's *Practical Criticism,* William Empson's *Seven Types of Ambiguity* (1930), Edmund Wilson's *Axel's Castle* (1931), and T. S. Eliot's *Selected Essays* (1932).[5] The year 1936 alone, at the dawn of the New Criticism, saw the publication of three major contributions: F. R. Leavis's *Revaluations* of the standard classification and hierarchy of English poets; A. O. Lovejoy's *Great Chain of Being,* a remarkable narrative of the interchange and alteration of ideas and conceptual patterns in literary as well as philosophical, historical, and other texts; and C. S. Lewis's revision of the way to read medieval and Renaissance narrative poems, *The Allegory of Love.*[6]

Even a cursory survey reveals the range and vigor of the modes of literary scholarship and criticism that replaced the curriculum of my student days, from the publications of Richards and Empson in 1930 until, say, 1961, when Wayne Booth's *The Rhetoric of Fiction* redefined the critical approach to the art of prose narratives.[7] During that span the Chicago neo-Aristotelians, under the mentorship of Ronald Crane, concurred with the New Critics in focusing on a literary work as such while insisting on what the New Critics ignored—the great multiplicity of literary kinds, of their modes of artistic organization, and of their effects on the reader. And although they themselves preferred to deal with a work as an artistic entity, the Chicago critics espoused a theoretical pluralism, which proposed that alternative approaches by way of biographical, intellectual, and social history were not only valid but indispensable for a broad understanding of literature in its many aspects and relations to other human activities and interests.

Simultaneously but antithetically, the myth and archetypal critics—including Maud Bodkin, Francis Ferguson, and most impressively Northrop Frye—replaced the focus on a work as an independent entity by a concern with recurrent plot patterns and character types. These they regarded as the imaginative productions of universal human needs, occurring not only in the literature of all times and places but also in mythology and in the type patterns of religious and social rituals. That same quarter-century saw the publication of Erich Auerbach's *Mimesis* (1946),[8] an extraordinary survey of diverse stylistic modes of representing reality from the literature of the Old Testament and Homer's *Odyssey* to the novels of Proust and Virginia Woolf; the analyses by G. Wilson Knight and Caroline Spurgeon of literary works in terms of their distinctive images and image patterns; the downright moral criticism of Yvor Winters and the much more nuanced moral and aesthetic criticism of R. P. Blackmur; the brilliant, if sometimes erratic, treatments by Kenneth Burke of literary works as symbolic modes for encompassing and coping with experience; the impressionist essays in literary appreciation by Virginia Woolf; and the fusion of social, moral, psychoanalytic, and artistic concerns that distinguishes the critical contributions of Lionel Trilling. This was the era also in which books such as Perry Miller's *The New England Mind* (1939), F. O. Matthiessen's *American Renaissance* (1941), and Alfred Kazin's *On Native Grounds* (1942) changed for many of us the ways we envision the literary, intellectual, and cultural history of America.[9]

Everyone familiar with the mid-century will want to augment this list, but it suffices to support the judgment that, for inventiveness, variety, and vitality, the literary studies of that time had no parallel in any earlier period. Almost all the American writers on the list were full-time or part-time members of a faculty, and their writings were rapidly assimilated by many other teachers, especially in upper-class and graduate courses. How far the New Criticism was from primacy during its heyday is indicated by the fact that this era, beginning in the latter 1930s, was precisely that of the inauguration and rapid spread of the cross-disciplinary program called "American Studies" or "American Civilization," an investigation of the interinvolvement of American literature, thought, and life.[10]

This vigorous, often mutually combative, diversity in literary enterprises continued until the great divide of the late 1960s and early 1970s, when the poststructural movement, by its radical challenges, brought to light the foundational assumptions that the earlier scholars and critics, under their differences, had implicitly shared.[11]

THE CURRENT CURRICULUM IN ENGLISH

Harvard's *Register of Courses* for 1994–1995 serves as a convenient index to the transformation in English studies since my time as a student. Immediately striking is the fact that whereas in the 1930s there were no women in the Harvard department, they now constitute almost 40 percent of the faculty, and there is every indication that this proportion will increase. The department continues to offer courses in English composition, now expanded to include "creative writing" in poetry and prose fiction. We find also a continuation, nominally, of the types of subjects available to me as an undergraduate—an initial survey of "major British writers," followed by period courses from the earliest literature to the present, as well as offerings on individual authors, in the various literary genres, and in special themes or topics. Within these traditional groups there is a multiplication of courses in American literature (the department has in fact been renamed "English and American Literature and Language"), as well as a large increase of courses in contemporary writers and writings.

The conspicuous difference in the present curriculum is the proliferation of categories and subject areas that had no precedent before the late 1960s. There are courses in literature by and about women, in gender studies (that is, gay, lesbian, and bisexual studies), in Afro-American, Asian American, Native American, and postcolonial literature, as well as offerings in such topics as race and ethnicity, modes of "representations," politics in literature, and "cultural studies." Prominent in a number of course titles is the stress on what is called "theory," thus: "Postmodernism: Theories and Fictions"; "Current Questions in Feminist Theory"; and "Contemporary Feminist and Gender Theory." Even in courses that by their titles seem to be traditional offerings in periods, authors, and genres, the accompanying descriptions often indicate a decisive change in what they teach and the way they are taught, suggesting that this change has something to do with theory; a course in Restoration drama, for example, describes its subject as "the major male and female playwrights. . .read through the lens of recent psychoanalytic, economic, and performance theories."

This wide spread of offerings at Harvard is representative of what is happening in colleges and universities throughout the

United States, especially in the larger departments. For example, at Cornell, my home university, the English curriculum of 1994–1995 lists an even larger proportion of courses than at Harvard in what are called "Minority Discourses" (expanded here to include "US Latino" and "Chicano/Chicana" writings), as well as offerings in film and other public media and studies of "culture" in general. And in the 774 lectures and discussion groups listed for the 1994 convention of the Modern Language Association of America (MLA)—an organization that through the mid-century had been the bastion of academic conservatism—the diversity of the categories, and the sprawl of literary studies to incorporate broad-gauge inquiries into gender, sexuality, race, ethnicity, class, colonialism, and a large miscellany of culture studies, is even more conspicuous. In the MLA, as in the universities, the new approaches and subject areas have not displaced, but are simply superadded to, traditional offerings.

But the distinction between what is traditional and what is innovative is itself deceptive, because increasingly the subject matters of once-standard courses are taught in accordance with criteria for the choice of texts, with modes of reasoning about the interpretation and evaluation of these texts and with assumptions about the political genesis, reception, and present uses of literary texts, which constitute nothing less than a new intellectual and cultural ethos in the faculties of English and other literatures. So drastic is the change that a representative of once-normative modes of scholarly investigation and criticism is often at a loss to discover enough common ground in assumptions and vocabulary, and in the standards for what counts as evidence for an assertion, to support profitable—or sometimes even mutually intelligible—discussion with an all-out exponent of the new dispensation.

POSTSTRUCTURAL THEORY AND ITS VARIETIES

One can point to a number of factors that help account for both the extremity and rapidity of changes in the cultural climate of departments of literature. One is demographic: A substantial part of the population in faculties of literature consists of members, now middle-aged, of the radical generation of the Vietnam era, many of whom have imported an anti-establishment and counter-traditional stance into their pedagogic concerns. There has been at the same time a steep increase in the student population of women and of racial and ethnic minorities who believe—and are prompted by some of their teachers to believe—that their group has been victimized, and its literary and other contributions marginalized or ignored, by the power structure that has dominated the inherited culture. Another factor is institutional: In the profession of literature, the system of appointment, promotion, awards, and academic status depends in large part on publication, and this fact fosters in younger scholars an understandable avidity for viewpoints that promise breakthroughs in research or generate new, and hence publishable, things to say about old and oft-discussed texts. A third factor is psychological: the phenomenon of boredom. When the exciting novelties of New Critical explication settled into a routine quest for the ironic tension of opposed attitudes, it gave way to a succession of other innovations that promised to transform literary studies; however, each of these in turn, and with increasing acceleration, also dwindled into a standard procedure for making predictable discoveries.

The distinctive component in each of these recent innovations is denominated, in the current vocabulary, by the cover-all term "theory." In the last three decades there has been an explosion of competing theories, each claiming to reconstitute totally our understanding of literary and other texts. In 1993, for example, a list of writings in the book *Contemporary Critical Theory,* which described itself as only "A Selected Bibliography," occupied 201 pages. In that same year there appeared an *Encyclopedia of Contemporary Literary Theory* that devoted 656 pages to articles ranging the alphabet from "Archetypal Criticism" to Derrida's essay, "White Mythology."[12] Among the theoretical modes that succeeded the New Criticism and its near contemporary, archetypal theory, are phenomenological theory, structuralist theory, reader-response theory, reception theory, semiotic theory, speechact theory, and Bakhtinian dialogic theory. However, most deeply influential in fostering the radical character of literary studies in America have been the works (often grouped as "postmodern" or "poststructural") of four French writers—the deconstructive theory of Jacques Derrida, the "power/knowledge" theory of Michel Foucault, the revised Freudian theory of Jacques-Marie Lacan, and the neo-Marxist ideological theory of Louis Althusser.

Critical theory—in the sense of a set of concepts, principles, and procedures for identifying, classifying, analyzing, and evaluating works of literature—is as old as Aristotle's *Poetics*. What makes poststructural theories genuinely revolutionary is that they alter drastically the enduring Western paradigm—the tacit intellectual site and frame of reference—for dealing with literature. Whatever their conspicuous divergencies, the major commentators on literature, from Aristotle and Horace to the scholars and critics listed earlier in this essay, all took for granted a humanistic paradigm: the site of literature is the human world, and a work of literature is the product of a purposive human author addressing human recipients in an environing reality.[13] Poststructural theories on the other hand, whatever their disagreements, coincide in abstracting literary texts from the human world and relocating them in a nonhuman site—specifically, in the play of language-as-such, or else in the forces that operate within a discourse already-in-being. The first-order result of this shift of intellectual vantage is a radical transformation of the elementary components in the humanistic frame of reference. That is, the human agents who produce and interpret a literary work, as well as the world that the work is said (directly or in a qualified way) to refer to or represent, are all translated into the products, effects, or constructs of language or discourse; at the same time, the functions of human agency are transferred to the immanent dynamics of the signifying system. Many of the salient novelties in present-day literary studies derive from this shift of intellectual vantage from a world of human activities to the systemic economies of language and discourse.

It should be noted, however, that none of the poststructural theories I have mentioned was formulated with specific reference to literature. Instead, each was presented as a *grande idée* that would revolutionize our understanding of all human activities and productions, of which literature was only a small part. But these theories were especially welcomed in literature departments, where their critiques of language and other modes of "representation" were perceived to be readily adaptable to literary studies, in which the way had been prepared by the New Critical emphasis on the language of poetry, its essentially figurative nature, and the multiplicity of its meanings. The theory that Derrida named "deconstruction," for example, was in various ways reformulated and applied to the criticism of literature by such writers as Paul de Man, J. Hillis Miller, and Barbara Johnson. And it was largely under the aegis of English and comparative literature departments that the basic concepts of Foucault, Althusser, and others, usually fused in some way with deconstructive concepts, were shaped into various forms of the New Historicism or adapted to the intellectual bases—and often, the political agendas—of feminist, gender, ethnic, and cultural studies. The result has been that literary departments, which had hitherto represented themselves as the chief conservators, interpreters, and propagators of the humanistic tradition and of the writings that Matthew Arnold represented as "the best that has been thought and said," have become the major source of radical challenges both to the tradition and to the inherited literary canon.

I want to take note also of the utility for literary studies that has been demonstrated by the shift in intellectual vantage inaugurated by poststructural theorists, especially Derrida and Foucault. They have infused energy into literary pursuits, made them exciting and attractive to a number of bright young students, and by their critiques have impelled a reexamination of the premises and procedures of an underlying consensus that had been taken for granted. Their altered perspectives have been able, in some applications, to effect what Coleridge called "freshness of sensation among old and familiar subjects"; when applied heuristically as discovery procedures, they have also proved capable of generating insights that survive testing by the criteria of traditional critical procedures.

One needs, however, to distinguish two modes and applications of poststructural theories. The endemic disease is a hardening of categories that transforms a lower-case theory into an upper-case Grand Theory. A lower-case theory is tentative, hypothetical, and fosters assertions that are subject to an appropriate type of empirical disconfirmation. A Grand Theory, on the other hand, is grounded on an *a priori* proposition of the form "all X is Y." Despite their animadversions against the universal claims they call "totalizations," the proponents of diverse poststructuralisms are prone to highly dramatic assertions of universal scope: "In language, the conditions of its possibility are what make it impossible." "All readings are necessarily misreadings." "All literary texts are allegories of their own unreadability." Or in politically-oriented theories: "All discourse is political." "All postcapitalist discourse is ideologically subservient to the interests of the dominant class." "All modes of Western representation are racist (or sexist, or phallocentric)." What defines a full-fledged Grand Theory is, first, that it is grounded on a premise predetermining what, upon investigation, one will find; and second, that it generates procedures guaranteeing one will find it. As the revolving history of recent innovations demonstrates, however, this advantage is gained at the price of rapid obsolescence, as the initial sense of exhilarating discovery gives way to a repetition of the kinds of conclusions that have been built into the premises.

As indicators of the foundational shift in literary studies, it may be useful to specify a set of views so widely shared that they constitute the commonplaces of poststructural ways of thinking. Many of these, like the *topoi* or commonplaces in ancient rhetoric, function as positions from which one argues but for which one feels no need to argue. I describe some of these views in ways favored by deconstructive theorists, who (until the last decade or so) were essentially apolitical: they propounded a linguistic skepticism without limit, based on the absence of any "presence" for establishing determinacy of meaning, truth, or value—a skepticism that applies just as much to the truth claims and value claims of radical as of conservative political thinkers. Other commonplaces I describe in forms favored by political critics—both the neutralist critics (who largely confine themselves to interpreting texts as the field of play for political forces of domination, revolt, and containment) and the activist critics (who put their literary criticism explicitly in the service of their political agenda, as a way of "intervening" in order to "transform" the existing social order, by means of a transformation in the way we read literature). Taken together, these poststructural commonplaces make up an intellectual landscape that seems alien, and in some instances outrageous, to adherents of the tacit consensus that underlay the manifold enterprises of earlier historians, scholars, and critics of literature.

The Adversarial Stance

Prominent in the poststructural climate of opinion is an explicit opposition to the established grounds, standards, and procedures in all provinces of Western intellection. Sometimes the adversarial stance is qualified as aiming merely to "challenge," "interrogate," "problematize," or "unsettle" a standard way of thinking. Derrida, for example, often asserts that "to deconstruct" is not "to destroy" but merely to "resituate" or "reinscribe" any matter that is put to question. But in many instances the undertaking is explicitly to "undermine," "subvert," "dismantle," or "undo"; and what the theorists propose to undo is not merely literary humanism but, as John Searle has pointed out, "the Western Rationalistic Tradition" and its core concepts of reality, truth, rationality, and objective knowledge.[14] At the deconstructive end of the spectrum, these ideas and ideals are dismantled as illusory "effects" that are engendered by the processes internal to our logocentric language; at the political end of the spectrum, they are subverted as ideological constructs whose actual function is to mask the realities of coercion, domination, and exploitation and to inhibit any attempts to transform these social inequities.

An interesting feature of poststructural writings is the widespread acknowledgment that such a critique-without-limit of Western language and the Western tradition of rationality rounds back upon and subverts the subverter. A theory that unmasks all discursive formations as constructs of ideological forces and historical circumstances is itself, since it is discourse, an ideological and historical construct; it is a matter of frequent note in poststructural writings that the critic is inescapably involved, hence involuntarily "complicit," with the system that he or she sets out to undermine. In a parallel way, deconstructive thinkers acknowledge that they have no option except to use logocentric language to undo logocentric texts, so that, as Derrida puts it, "borrowing all the strategic and economic resources of subversion from the old structure. . .the enterprise of deconstruction always in a certain way falls prey to its own work."[15] Some critics cope with this and other dilemmas generated by the premise that all texts are an unresolvable conflict of self-opposing forces by exploiting an ethic and aesthetics of vertigo. That is, they represent the act of deconstructive reading as a courageous and heady engagement in the "double-binds," "aporias," or regressions *en abîme* of what Paul de Man called the "vertiginous possibilities of referential aberration."[16]

Writing, Reading, and the Universalized Text

The humanistic literary paradigm, as noted, is that of a transaction in an environing world with a human being at each end. In contrast, a poststructural theorist, by transferring the site of vantage to the system of language or discourse, converts the human being from the effector into an effect of linguistic and discursive processes. This poststructural undertaking remains in accord with what was voiced by Lévi-Strauss in 1962, that "the ultimate goal of the human sciences is not to constitute man but to dissolve him."[17] Foucault especially has conducted what strikes the traditionalist as a vendetta against assigning any initiating or operative role to human beings. He found it, he said, "a source of profound relief to think that man is. . .a new wrinkle in our knowledge, and that he will disappear again as soon as that knowledge has discovered a new form." He remarked later that, to "the warped and twisted forms of reflection" that take man "as their starting point in their attempts to reach the truth," we "can answer only with a philosophical laugh."[18]

In literary theory, the dissolution of human agency (usually identified as "a critique of the subject") has focused especially on the concept of authorship. Both Foucault and Roland Barthes famously proclaimed, in almost simultaneous essays, that the author is dead.[19] The operative roles of purpose and design, however, are not simply canceled but reassigned from the human agent to the grammatical and rhetorical dynamics of language, or to the ideological forces and configurations of power that constitute discourse.[20] The traditional author is reconceived as a space traversed by linguistic and discursive forces; or, in an alternative formulation derived from Althusser, the author is represented as endowed with a "subjectivity," and occupying a "subject position," that is generated and assigned by the ideology specific to a time, place, and particular institutional apparatus. From inside poststructural ranks, the occasional remonstrances against too unqualified a surrender of authorial agency are voiced mainly by political activists—not, however, in order to account for differences in the constitution and quality of literary and other human achievements, but in order to salvage the possibility that an individual may retain enough initiative to conceive and inaugurate a transformation of the power structure of which his subjectivity is itself a product.[21]

What had hitherto been the literary "work" is depersonalized into a text, or into *écriture,* in order to erase any suggestion that it is the product of an intentional human agent; the text itself is often represented as a field within which there circulate forces, energies, or warring components that function as a purposiveness without purpose, so as to generate effects not only of design but also of reference. To a radical deconstructionist, textual representations impose their own constructions on what they posit; all uses of language, accordingly, are said by de Man to be "performative," in that they perform the reality that they purport to describe. In deconstructive usage, the term "text" itself undergoes a spectacular spread in signification. In the absence of unmediated access to any "presence" or reality, the reasoning goes, not only linguistic utterances but all human perceptions and concepts are modes of representation; and all representations, since they require interpretation, function as texts. "There is nothing outside of the text" (*il n'y a pas de hors-texte*), in Derrida's notable formulation.[22] The universe thus dissolves into the *acqua regia* of textuality. Assertions, history, people, experience, material reality—all need to be interpreted, but the subjects who perform the interpretation are themselves textual constructs. At the same time, every textual particular, in order to be interpreted, requires a context; but every context, when called into play, is itself a text needing to be interpreted. *En abîme....*

Poststructural New Reading

Poststructural theories converge on another commonplace, namely, that all texts are constitutionally duplicitous, so that they cannot mean what their writers undertook to say, or thought they had said, or have been agreed by earlier readers to have said. The cause of the duplicity is variously assigned to self-opposing forces internal to language, or to conflicting compulsions in the writer's unconscious, or (by political theorists) to the workings of a class- or gender-effected ideology or of "the historical unconscious." In any case, the consequence for reading is a universalized form of what Paul Ricoeur, with reference to the interpretive practices of Nietzsche, Marx, and Freud, called "the hermeneutics of suspicion." J. Hillis Miller, adapting Derrida's grammatology into a theory and practice of literary criticism, defined a deconstructive reading as one that "seeks to find. . .the element in the system studied which is alogical, the thread in the text in question which will unravel it all, or the loose stone which will pull down the whole building."[23] The closer reading of poststructural analytics is a suspicious reading, in which one is called on to proceed "against the text" in order to detect its uncanny dissemination into an undecidability of warring significations, or in order to unmask one or another kind of subversive subtext in accordance with what a theory has established as the cause-of-causes, or the motive-of-motives, in all forms of discourse.

Dissolving Boundaries

In the poststructural terrain, there is something that does not love a boundary. In 1992 the Modern Language Association published *Redrawing the Boundaries,* edited by Stephen Greenblatt and Giles Gunn, in which twenty-one distinguished contributors surveyed, in the words of the subtitle, "The Transformation of English and American Studies" in the last quarter-century. The essays expound, and many of them also exemplify, the theoretical positions and topics that I describe in this essay. Moreover, they make it evident that, in the course of the last two decades, deconstruction has yielded its place in the vanguard of literary theory to the spectrum of pursuits known as "the New Historicism." The essays reveal also that the critical interrogation and dismantling of the inherited concepts, subdivisions, and procedures in literary studies continues unabated.

In their introduction to *Redrawing the Boundaries,* the editors indicate that by "boundaries" they mean the areas of signification delineated by concepts, distinctions, classifications, and criteria— that is, by all the components of traditional reasoning and knowledge. A particular concern, however, is with the boundaries that define departments of literary studies in the academy, and even more with the boundaries imposed by the traditional concept of what literature is, in contradistinction to history and other nonliterary forms of discourse. The claim is that, with the emergence of recent theories and orientations, the earlier belief in "the possibility of a unifying, totalizing grasp of our subject" has receded and also that the old notion of "the interdisciplinary"—defined as "the desire to see from different sides of the same border" but without recognizing that all borders are cultural and discursive impositions—is being replaced by the genuine interdisciplinarity of current historical enterprises.[24]

I find it hard to recognize literary studies as I knew them in these representations of the tradition. For example, I do not know what it would be like to have the "unifying, totalizing grasp" of English studies that we are purported to have assumed or sought, although I do recall that some of us, sometimes, worried about the seeming gap between the enterprise of literary criticism and that of researches in literary biography and history. Occasionally one of us, following the example of the New Critics, would hazard a definition of what is properly literary that served to privilege his own pursuit and derogate someone else's. As for "interdisciplinarity"— well, the notion that extensive inquiry into works of literature involves history, philosophy, rhetoric, and morality is as old as literary and rhetorical studies of the Greek and Roman era.

A quarter-century ago I wrote a book, *Natural Supernaturalism,* that may stand as an example of the interdisciplinary enterprise before the emergence of poststructural critiques.[25] In that book I identified the occurrence, from the 1790s to the 1930s, of a highly distinctive set of ideas and patterns of reasoning, narrative forms, and sentiments that had been fostered by the political, intellectual, and emotional ambiance of the French Revolution. I described the origins of this constellation in theological exegeses of the Biblical narrative from Genesis to Apocalypse and its prevalence in secular schemes of the history of mankind, in the grand systems of contemporary metaphysics, in political and social essays, and in autobiographies, as well as in a wide variety of poems, dramas, and prose fiction. It did not occur to me, nor I am sure to many of my readers, that I was transgressing boundaries that were inscribed in the nature of these things. Like many of my colleagues, I took for granted that established disciplinary limits were the result of historical developments and that they served, in Coleridge's terms, as distinctions but not divisions; I considered that, for some scholarly purposes, working within established distinctions was greatly convenient, even indispensable, but that in undertakings such as my own, one was free to follow wherever the evidence led.

There are nonetheless, as the editors of *Redrawing the Boundaries* suggest, important differences between the conduct of older interdisciplinary studies and that which is proposed and exemplified by committed New Historicists. Traditional scholars, in telling their interdisciplinary stories, deployed terms such as "communication," "influence," "adoption," and "transmission"; the matters communicated were ideas, conceptual schemes, plot forms, sentiments, and evaluations; and these were communicated from human beings to human beings. On the other hand, the distinctive operative terms of the New Historicists are "circulation," "negotiation," "exchange," and "commerce." These metaphors from the marketplace are intended to suggest the importance of economic factors in intellection. Of greater consequence, however, is that the materials that are said to circulate are usually high-level abstractions such as "power" or "energies"; the vehicle of circulation is discourse; and the circulation is not between human beings but between texts, or else between a text and a historical context that is itself claimed to be a text.[26] In short, the intellectual site of a thoroughgoing New Historicism is not the traditional human world but a discursive theory world.

The editors of *Redrawing the Boundaries* recognize that although conceptual borders can be "revised. . .or replaced," they "cannot be in literary studies. . .entirely abolished"[27]—or else, of course, we would lack the linguistic purchase even to begin to talk about literature or anything else. But since they are cultural constructs, inherited discursive boundaries are, by widespread theoretical prepossession, attributed to the ideological power play of bourgeois individualism or of Western humanism; hence, especially by left-wing Historicists, they are grievously suspect as a covert apparatus for oppression and exclusion. Some Historicists undertake, by discursive legerdemain, to dissolve, even as they employ, the conceptual discriminations with which they cannot dispense. As one contributor to *Redrawing the Boundaries* observes, "The boundaries have been redrawn, although in disappearing ink."[28]

There is an anomaly in the present state of English studies in the American university. To the extent that all intellectual products are reduced to a common condition as texts to be interpreted, they are viewed as the natural province of the putative experts in texts and interpretation who inhabit departments of literature. The literary discipline has, in consequence, become the imperialist province of the academy, invading and incorporating the subject areas of other disciplines. It has been remarked that, these days, if one wants to study Nietzsche, Marx, Freud, Derrida, or Foucault, one must apply not to departments of philosophy, psychology, or sociology, but to departments of English or comparative literature. At the same time, however, the theorists most responsible for this territorial expansion assiduously dissolve the category of literature, which has served to establish the identity of literature departments, the basic subject matter of their teaching, and the rationale for their training of graduate students.

In this decade of its ascendancy, it sometimes seems as though the New Historicism in all its varieties aspires to the condition called "cultural studies." Exponents of this rapidly expanding field dismantle the standard boundaries that distinguish cultural institutions, productions, and artifacts; a number of them also delete the distinctions—attributed to the "elitism" of a dominant group—between high culture and popular culture and between major and lesser cultural products. Comic strips, film, television advertisements, pornography, and industrial manufactures thus become equal candidates for scholarly attention—a literary work, when it figures at all, is simply one among innumerable cultural products—and all these products are analyzed mainly by reference to the social structures and power processes that have brought them into being and endowed them with their meanings, their values, and their relative social status.

BUT WHAT ABOUT LITERATURE?

For the survivor from an earlier era, the question is inescapable: "But where in this array of theory-generated and theory-oriented enterprises is the literature that, nominally, is the concern of English and other literary departments?" Or in T. S. Eliot's formulation, what has happened to the study of literature primarily as literature and not as another thing—not, for example, as a branch of sociology, psychology, political and economic history, or cultural anthropology?

In an enlightening institutional history entitled *Professing Literature,* Gerald Graff makes the point that in the course of the last century there has been a recurrent appeal to the "literary work itself" and to "literature read as literature" by critics and literary generalists who felt threatened by the incursion of philological and historical specialists. Now, however, these former opponents join together in appealing to the concept of literature as literature, as a defense against the threat posed to both of them by the new theorists. The persistence of the concept need not mark it, however, as an empty counter in the game of institutional one-upmanship; instead, its indefeasibility may be taken as evidence that the concept has valid application. It applies to the often attested experience of being captivated and engrossed by a text and of taking delight in following the imagined human actions that it signifies, from its beginning to its satisfying end. This pleasure in the sheer engagement with the matters that a text represents, in just the way that it articulates and orders what it represents, as many critics have affirmed, is the distinctive experience of reading literature as literature.

The New Historicists discount the advocacy of reading literature for itself as a maneuver to seal the text off from context and from recourse to history. But to set oneself to read and analyze a work as literature need in no way exclude an alternative analysis of the same work as historically and biographically conditioned, as one's critical interest shifts from the work itself to any of the multiple circumstances that may plausibly be claimed to have affected its composition or reception; and the writings of many scholars and the experience of many readers demonstrate that such inquiries can be not only consonant but concurrent with the awareness that one is dealing with literature and not another thing. More than that: the activity of reading literature as such, far from excluding, necessitates that the reader bring to the text a broad range of contextual knowledge. In a view common to many Historicists, to propose reading a literary text as such commits one to the illusory belief that the text is invested with a transcendent, transhistorical essence. Quite to the contrary; a text does not captivate and move the reader by appealing to an insulated aesthetic sense adapted to a timeless aesthetic quality. It can only do so by engaging our overall intellectual and emotional economy, including the complex of beliefs, values, and moral propensities derived from our overall experience in the world. For a literary text to be even minimally intelligible requires that the reader share with the author not only a knowledge of the requisite linguistic and literary conventions, but also a huge body of knowledge, personal and historical. Bringing to bear a still broader range of contextual and historical knowledge, as the writings of literary scholars and critics demonstrate, can enhance the minimal meaning, making it more complex, nuanced, and dense. But the judgment as to how much and what kind of contextual knowledge is adequate for a minimal understanding; the judgment of the farther limit at which contextual knowledge ceases to enhance meanings and begins to distort and impose meanings; and above all, the judgment as to whether and at what point to resist and contest, rather than accede to the beliefs and norms with which a work invites our involvement—these are not judgments we can make by applying rules. Instead, we must bring to bear an intuition, informed by experience and intellection, that Coleridge called "tact." But such judgments of tact are essentially contestable; they have always been and always will be contested.

That is in fact the nature not only of judgments in literary interpretation, appreciation, and assessment, but of humanistic studies in general: They pose questions that are of prime human importance, for which no answers are uncontestably certain. As F. R. Leavis once put it, we learn in these areas of inquiry to expect that when a proponent asserts, "This is so, isn't it?" an interlocutor will at most reply, "Yes, but...." The necessity, vitality, and vexatiousness of literary and other humanistic studies lies in the fact that they raise and reraise questions about the concerns we live by, to which they offer and reoffer answers that, however strongly supported, turn out never to be the last word.

WHAT NEXT?

My essay and the others in this volume appear as we approach the end of both a century and a millennium, and by ancient ritual that is a time not only for retrospect but for prophecy. Some traditionalists, gazing bleakly at the current scene, swept with confused alarms of theory struggles and culture wars, foresee the end-time of literature in the academy. My one-time student Harold Bloom, in a passionate advocacy of the Western canon and of reading literature for the love of literature, writes that "I have very little confidence that literary education will survive its current malaise. . . . Finding myself now surrounded by professors of hip-hop; by clones of Gallic-Germanic theory; by ideologues of gender and of various sexual persuasions; by multiculturalists unlimited, I realize that the Balkanization of literary studies is irreversible."[29]

It is the subject of pleasantries by my colleagues that although I am a traditionalist, I am an uncommonly cheerful traditionalist. Let me try to live up to that reputation by proposing a counter-prophecy about the study of English and other literatures in the coming century. I am heartened by the assertion of the editors of *Redrawing the Boundaries* that, although their survey focuses on innovative theories and practices, they find that "exemplary traditional scholarship" continues to be "produced in virtually all the historical fields."[30] I am encouraged also by recalling how happily disparate, during my own student days, was the teaching of literature to undergraduates from the curriculum required in graduate studies, and by my strong impression now that what professing theorists teach in their classrooms is not nearly so joyless, impenetrable to nonspecialists, and immune to distinctively literary values as one might expect from what they say in conferences and publications directed to fellow initiates.

I am confident, first, that after all the current challenges and alternatives, the primary site of literary criticism and studies will again be, as it has been for twenty-five hundred years, the human world; that is, a world of purposive human beings communicating with each other in an environing reality. The reason for my confidence is that such a world is an indispensable precondition to account for the historical development of a common language, as well as for the way each individual in turn learns to understand and to use that language; it is also the indispensable presupposition of all linguistic interchanges in the conduct of everyday life. Even the most confirmed poststructuralist has no option but to abandon his theory world for the human world the moment he engages in ordinary and everyday linguistic transactions, including his disputes with other theorists. Accordingly, what will once again be considered normal criticism will conceive of literary texts, and deal with them, not as inscriptions produced by the play of linguistic forces and discursive configurations, but as works composed, within particular historical and personal circumstances, by, for, and about human beings. As always in their long history, however, humanistic studies will not remain static but will adapt to changing intellectual and cultural circumstances, and in the course of doing so will assimilate insights from alternative theoretical perspectives that have demonstrated their survival value when subjected to the traditional criteria governing scholarly and critical inquiries.

Among the surviving innovations, it seems certain, will be the study of writings by women and by racial, ethnic, and other groups that have been overlooked or marginalized by the limitations in perspective of scholars and shapers of culture, most of whom, as the proponents of these interests claim, were white European males. But such minority studies, having matured past the stage of militant advocacy, will be pursued more as an area to be studied and less as a political cause to be advanced. They will also become much more discriminating in what at present is their wholesale critique of the Western intellectual tradition, in the recognition that the standards to which they themselves appeal—standards such as evenhanded justice, human equality, and human rights—are ideals that have been developed within the highly diversified tradition that many proponents of the new studies indict as monolithically and irredeemably patriarchal, logocentric, Eurocentric, and sexist.

Within the humanistic frame of reference, the study of literature as literature will once again be a central, though far from exclusive, concern. A chief reason for this conviction is that a need to engage with artfully realized imaginative constructions, signaled by delight when the need is satisfied, seems innate in just about all of us, and ineradicable in most of us. But there are other reasons as well, of which I have time to mention only one. A commonplace in all varieties of poststructural theory is the privileging of difference and the valorizing of otherness; but this is typically of difference-as-such and of otherness-in-the-abstract. I think it will come to be seen as an anomaly that a poststructuralist reading undertakes to dissolve the differences of literature from other modes of discourse, while to read a literary work for itself is precisely to experience its particularity; that is, its differentness not only from other kinds of discourse, but from all other works of literature as well. I think it will be recognized also that a responsive reading of literature as such has an irreplaceable function in fostering sympathies with human differences-in-particular and otherness-in-the-concrete. A suspicious reading of a literary text in order to disseminate its meanings or to unmask its subtext is alienating. In a receptive reading of the text as literature, on the other hand, we participate from the inside with subjectivities very different from our own—the subjectivities both of the author and of the characters that the author has bodied forth—and so are enabled to see ourselves as others see us, to see others as they see themselves, and to acknowledge in others some part of ourselves.

I venture a concluding prophecy. Some fifty years from now the American Academy of Arts and Sciences will convene a conference on the transformation of American academic cultures, for which a scholar will be commissioned to review the history and condition of English and other literary studies. She will find the analysis and history of literature, both as literature and as inter-involved with other human activities and concerns, to be a prominent component of the academic curriculum. And looking back, she will conclude that literary studies, having undergone some such changes as I have sketched, are (in a favorite expression of my favorite literary theorist, S. T. Coleridge) *alter et idem*. The Latin may be translated freely as "transformed yet recognizable."

ENDNOTES

[1] See William Riley Parker, "Where Do English Departments Come From?" *College English* 28 (1967): 339–351; and Gerald Graff, *Professing Literature: An Institutional History* (Chicago, Ill. and London: University of Chicago Press, 1987).

[2] John Livingston Lowes, *The Road to Xanadu* (Boston, Mass.: Houghton Mifflin Company, 1927).

[3] John Livingston Lowes, *Convention and Revolt in Poetry* (Boston, Mass.: Houghton Mifflin Company, 1919).

[4] Cleanth Brooks and R. P. Warren, *Understanding Poetry* (New York: H. Holt and Company, 1938); John Crowe Ransom, *The New Criticism* (Norfolk, Conn.:

148   M. H. Abrams

New Directions, 1941); René Wellek and Austin Warren, *The Theory of Literature* (New York: Harcourt, Brace, 1942); and Cleanth Brooks, *The Well Wrought Urn* (New York: Harcourt, Brace, 1947).

[5]I. A. Richards, *Practical Criticism* (New York: Harcourt, Brace, 1930); William Empson, *Seven Types of Ambiguity* (London: Chatto and Windus, 1930); Edmund Wilson, *Axel's Castle* (New York: C. Scribner's Sons, 1931); and T. S. Eliot, *Selected Essays* (London: Faber and Faber, 1932).

[6]F. R. Leavis, *Revaluations* (London: Chatto and Windus, 1936); A. O. Lovejoy, *Great Chain of Being* (Cambridge, Mass.: Harvard University Press, 1936); and C. S. Lewis, *The Allegory of Love* (Oxford: The Clarendon Press, 1936).

[7]Wayne Booth, *The Rhetoric of Fiction* (Chicago, Ill.: University of Chicago Press, 1961).

[8]Erich Auerbach, *Mimesis* (Bern: A. Francke, 1946).

[9]Perry Miller, *The New England Mind* (New York: Macmillan, 1939); F. O. Matthiessen, *American Renaissance* (New York: Oxford University Press, 1941); and Alfred Kazin, *On Native Grounds* (New York: Harcourt, Brace and World, 1942).

[10]Tremaine McDowell, *American Studies* (Minneapolis, Minn.: University of Minnesota Press, 1948); and Kermit Vanderbilt, *American Literature and the Academy: The Roots, Growth, and Maturity of a Profession* (Philadelphia, Pa.: University of Pennsylvania Press, 1986), 489 ff.

[11]The great divide in American literary studies is conveniently dated as having begun in October 1966, when Barthes, Lacan, Derrida, Todorov, Lucien Goldman, and many others participated in a conference at Johns Hopkins that introduced both structural and poststructural thinking to a wide range of university teachers in America. The papers read at the conference, together with the lively debates they occasioned, were published as *The Languages of Criticism and the Sciences of Man* (Baltimore, Md. and London: Johns Hopkins University Press, 1970).

[12]Donald G. Marshall, *Contemporary Critical Theory: A Selected Bibliography* (New York: Modern Language Association of America, 1993); and Irena R. Makaryk, ed., *Encyclopedia of Contemporary Literary Theory: Approaches, Scholars, Terms* (Toronto: University of Toronto Press, 1993).

[13]The main theoretical divergences in the history of criticism before poststructuralism can be mapped as shifts in focus and orientation among the four elements that constitute the humanistic paradigm: the author, the environing world, the audience, and the internal requirements of the literary work itself. See M. H. Abrams, *The Mirror and the Lamp* (New York: Oxford University Press, 1953), chap. 1, "Orientation of Critical Theories."

[14]John R. Searle, "Rationality and Realism, What is at Stake?" *Dædalus* 122 (4) (Fall 1993): 55–83.

[15]Jacques Derrida, *Of Grammatology*, trans. Gayatri Chakravorty Spivak (Baltimore, Md. and London: Johns Hopkins University Press, 1976), 24.

[16]Paul de Man, *Allegories of Reading* (New Haven, Conn. and London: Yale University Press, 1979), 10.

[17]Claude Lévi-Strauss, *La pensée sauvage* (Paris: Plon, 1962), 326.

[18]Michel Foucault, *The Order of Things* (London: Pantheon Books, 1970), xxiii, 342–343.

[19]Roland Barthes, "The Death of the Author," in *Image/Music/Text*, trans. Stephen Heath (New York: Hill and Wang, 1977); and Michel Foucault, "What Is an Author?" *The Foucault Reader*, ed. Paul Rabinow (New York: Pantheon Books, 1984).

[20]As Kenneth Burke has remarked, "even schemes that make much show of discarding 'purpose' have plenty of words to replace it. They'll even tell you their purpose in throwing out the term." Reply to Wayne Booth, in Wayne Booth, *Critical Understanding: The Powers and Limits of Pluralism* (Chicago, Ill. and London: University of Chicago Press, 1979), 134.

[21]See, e.g., the attempt by Louis Montrose to keep open the possibility of individual initiative in *Redrawing the Boundaries: The Transformation of English and American Literary Studies*, ed. Stephen Greenblatt and Giles Gunn (New York: Modern Language Association of America, 1992), 412–415.

[22]Derrida, *Of Grammatology*, 158.

[23]J. Hillis Miller, *Theory Now and Then* (Durham, N.C.: Duke University Press, 1991), 126.

[24]*Redrawing the Boundaries*, 4–5.

[25]M. H. Abrams, *Natural Supernaturalism* (New York: Norton, 1971).

[26]In Louis Montrose's widely quoted definition of "the post-structuralist orientation to history," it is "a reciprocal concern with the historicity of texts and the textuality of history." "The Poetics and Politics of Culture," in *The New Historicism*, ed. H. Aram Veeser (New York and London: Routledge, 1989), 20; see also 23.

[27]*Redrawing the Boundaries*, 4.

[28]George Levine, "Victorian Studies," in *Redrawing the Boundaries*, 152.

[29]Harold Bloom, *The Western Canon* (New York: Harcourt Brace, 1994), 517–518.

[30]*Redrawing the Boundaries*, 9.

Catherine Gallagher

The History of Literary Criticism

URING THE LAST DECADE many academic literary critics have developed an intense interest in the history of their discipline. No longer content to know merely what previous critics wrote, they explore the institutional and broader political histories surrounding critical theories and practices. Such resorts to collective narrative are, of course, common reactions to intellectual crises, so it should not surprise us that the various histories now available come to the reassuring conclusion that literary studies have always been in crisis.[1] We have not created more chaos than earlier generations, they seem to say: literature professors have always disagreed over the fundamental principles of the profession, always engaged in theory wars, always been prompted by extra-literary political concerns, and even always been accused of posing a threat to the American way of life.

While one might take a certain rueful comfort in these reflections, one might still wonder why the period dominated by the New Criticism (1938–1965) continues to look, if only retrospectively and relatively, like a time when basic critical protocols commanded wide agreement. I will try to answer that question by describing the temporary stability the New Critics brought to English departments. I will also describe how the New Critics prepared their own supersession and how the ambient academic ecology depended on theoretical eclecticism in literature departments. The New Critics set a standard for the successful integration of professional tasks that was difficult to maintain after 1965, when questions about the ultimate good of literary criticism sparked

Catherine Gallagher is Professor of English at the University of California, Berkeley.

a debate over its very nature. Two kinds of inquiry—one asking what literary criticism is good for and the other asking what its unique form of knowledge is—have elicited largely incompatible or simply unrelated responses in the last two decades. The sense that there is something wrong with this state of affairs stems from a perception that the status quo ante, which was based on a confluence of justifying beliefs, was normal. Our histories may have demonstrated that such a confluence was not at all normal, but they have not convinced us that it would not be desirable.

* * *

The New Critics of the 1930s identified themselves with an international, aesthetic modernist reaction against certain aspects of modernization. Against the homogenizing tendencies of the marketplace, the merely formal individualism of democratic politics, and the standardized consciousness produced by industrial workplaces and urban living, they counterposed a deeper, truer, and more qualitative selfhood. Their subjects were not interchangeable units with identical rights, but unique entities, substantive persons, whose very existence was threatened by marketplace exchange and mass culture. Their sentiments about modern society were translated into a critical practice by letting the "integrity" of the literary work stand in for the "integrity" of all forms of endangered specificity. In this regard, they did not depart from the standard aesthetic doctrines of the nineteenth century. Rather, the founding New Critics placed a new, modernist emphasis on "particularity," on meanings that were inextricable from their expression. For example, they stressed ambiguity because they disapproved of language that was a medium of exchange. Fungibility and translatability were the enemy; an adequate paraphrase would be the sign of a bad poem. Hence, they made a new kind of problem out of meaning, one that was not amenable to the historical-philological methods then dominating the discipline.

But if the New Criticism opposed itself to modernization in terms that are recognizably modernist, it just as emphatically nominated itself as a movement for professional consolidation. Its stunning success probably owed more to the deftness with which the ideas were woven into a discourse of professionalism than to the ideas themselves. The New Criticism reinvented the discipline by unifying what had formerly seemed to be competing professional exigencies. Before the New Criticism, the two legs necessary to the forward stride of any profession—specialized learning and public service—were uncoordinated in English departments. Each leg had a separate institutional footing: the philological research activities of the faculty organized the graduate school, while the undergraduate curriculum was generally devoted to what one professor called "the diffusion of culture."[2] That institutional compromise allowed English undergraduate programs to grow, indeed to establish themselves at the center of the humanities in American universities, without either engaging or disturbing the research interests of the majority of the faculty, who concentrated on the history of the language and largely ignored both the explication and evaluation of literary works. Even in the 1930s, this compromise seemed eminently practical to most English professors, who were quite willing to fulfill the "collegiate" duties of undergraduate education while insisting that "these have nothing to do with learning."[3] English departments did not lose by this compromise; indeed, they expanded under it. Nor did the majority on the faculties seem to find it particularly onerous.

There was no widely-felt crisis in English departments when the New Critics began their campaign, but they exploited the existing compromise as a contradiction and fully capitalized—to a far greater extent than the philologists had—on the ethos of professionalism. In a protracted struggle, the New Critics, along with assorted allies, attacked and finally defeated the philological establishment. Only at this point did the discipline of English studies achieve its current intellectual (as opposed to institutional) outlines. The New Critics changed our subject matter from language to literature, and they changed our skill from scholarship to criticism. They effected these changes, moreover, in the name of increased professional consolidation: they promised to integrate English studies, overcoming the disjunction between graduate and undergraduate curricula, between specialized knowledge and general educational service; and they promised simultaneously to differentiate English even more sharply from its neighboring disciplines.

John Crowe Ransom's 1937 essay "Criticism, Inc." is an excellent example of new critical rhetoric that clearly displays the relations between the institutional, professional, methodological, and theoretical elements of the movement. I will describe it fully because it became a founding document of the postwar English department. First, it ingeniously combines its antimodernization campaign with an emphasis on disciplining and professionalizing literary-critical, as opposed to historical-linguistic, studies. Criticism, Ransom argues, must no longer be left to the amateurish writers of book reviews but must instead become the systematic business of English professors. There are clear rhetorical links between Ransom's argument and that of the earlier philological professionalizers, such as H. C. G. Brandt, for both invoke the need for a specialized knowledge: "It is not anybody who can do criticism,"[4] Ransom asserts, just as Brandt some fifty years earlier had insisted that "everybody cannot [teach English]."[5] But whereas Brandt had argued that English studies should be a "science" like any other, Ransom places English in a more highly differentiated intellectual environment. Stressing an increasingly complex university, he is far more specific than the philologists had been about the exact niche that English studies should carve out for itself in the academic ecology. Instead of following the lead of numerous earlier would-be reformers of English studies by attacking the overspecialization of philological scholarship, Ransom instead comes up with the brilliant stroke of accusing philology of *under*specialization: "English might almost as well announce that it does not regard itself as entirely autonomous, but as a branch of the department of history, with the option of declaring itself occasionally a branch of the department of ethics."[6]

Never before had the philologists been challenged on their own professional high ground—that of promulgating specialized knowledge. Underlying the charge was the New Critics' insistence that literature, and not the history of the language, should be the special object of the English professor's study. "It is true," wrote Ransom, "that the historical and ethical studies [of the unreformed English department] will cluster round objects which for some reason are called artistic objects. But the thing itself the professors do not have to contemplate."[7] The thing itself, or literature as *art*, could only be intelligently contemplated by one whose skills were critical rather than historical: "Criticism is the attempt to define and enjoy the aesthetic or characteristic values of literature."[8] It is not, however, to be confused with aesthetics as a branch of philosophy: "The philosopher is apt to see a lot of wood and no trees, for his theory is very general and his acquaintance with the particular works of art is not persistent and intimate, especially his acquaintance with their technical effects."[9] Ransom thus redefined both the object of study and the skill required for studying it in terms that fully satisfied the professional requirement of distinctive knowledge—knowledge carefully set off from that of all the adjoining academic disciplines.

Second, Ransom adeptly mobilized the service leg of the profession, creating two constituencies outside the university, both in need of the same skill, for literary criticism to serve: *1)* writers of contemporary literature and *2)* the reading public at large. He dexterously intertwined the threat of being outdone or absorbed by other departments with the accusation that the English department lacks "usefulness": "Here is contemporary literature, waiting for its criticism; where are the professors of literature? They are watering their own gardens; elucidating the literary histories of their respective periods. . . . This has gone far to nullify the *usefulness* of a department personnel larger, possibly, than any other. . . ."[10]

If the English departments replaced historical scholarship with criticism, they could maintain a separate identity, hold up their heads among other disciplines as experts on modern phenomena, and simultaneously fulfill the requirement of service. In the last sentence of this passage, Ransom manages to turn even the sign of the English department's success—its large size—into a source of shame: the more people in it, the more talents wasted "watering gardens" rather than overseeing the great endeavor of contemporary literature.

Ransom's essay waxes even more eloquent about what criticism can do for the general reader and the culture at large, once it has replaced the amateurish book reviewers and set about reforming the public's taste. Indeed, only in explaining what criticism is good for does Ransom reveal the anti-modernization impulses in his aesthetic modernism. His formulations of the value of literary criticism are strikingly difficult and untranslatable into the values of other disciplines. That is, once again the professional desiderata of difficulty and uniqueness are inextricably bound to those of usefulness and service, so that the two legs of the English department could not possibly become uncoordinated. According to Ransom,

> Studies in the technique of the art belong to criticism certainly. They cannot belong anywhere else, because the technique is not peculiar to any prose materials discoverable in the work of art, nor to anything else but the unique form of that art. . . . They would be technical studies of poetry, for instance. . .if they treated its metrics; its inversion, solecisms, lapses from the prose norm of language, and from close prose logic; its tropes, its fictions, or inventions, by which it secures "aesthetic distance" and removes itself from history. . . .[11]

This third innovation, the emphasis on technique, rather than theme, moral, or significance, was meant to differentiate literary from other kinds of language, to make a claim for the specialized nature of the critic's object, a nature his training alone could recognize. To explain the general value of such an elucidation of "peculiar" language uses, literary *technique* had to be defined as a good in and of itself, quite apart from any uplifting "prose" message that an art work might contain. The value of technique could not be explained in terms of any consideration outside of literature. But if technique was what sealed literature off from other kinds of language and history itself, if it was composed of "lapses" from conventional norms, how could it be said to be important to the culture at large? Only in such lapses, Ransom claimed, can true particularity find a refuge. Technique is what keeps literary language from becoming a utilitarian means of communication, and hence for Ransom it stands in for all forms of resistance to abstraction and exchangeability. The uniqueness and integrity of the poem preserve what he calls "the object, which is real, individual, and qualitatively infinite." I will later return to this substitution of "the object" for the poetic subject, but suffice it to say here that by valuing the particularity of the poem, by learning to talk about it without compromising it, one was supposed to be resisting a more general capitulation to abstract universalism.

The idea that literary studies should be a counterweight to the gravitational pull of competitive capitalism and utilitarian modernization was certainly not new. Popularized by Matthew Arnold in the English-speaking world, it was a sentiment shared by the philologists and their critics from the inception of the discipline. But the New Critics' claim that these values would arise out of seemingly neutral disciplinary procedures was new. The aesthetic modernism that they introduced into the curriculum and that formed their sensibilities had sternly expelled naive, nostalgic idealism from the province of literary value. Abandoning vague talk about the Anglo-Saxon spirit or the ineffable essence of the poet and pouring contempt on those innocents who thought that a work's values were explicitly stated in its paraphrasable meanings (its "prose core"), the New Critics promised to maintain ideological continuity in the profession while seeming to discipline the effusive enthusiasm of former critics and rise above ideology altogether—an extraordinary advantage in mid-twentieth-century America.

The New Critics fought hard to take over the discipline, founding academic journals, setting up summer institutes, working tirelessly in the Modern Language Association,[12] so we certainly cannot attribute their success simply to the fine mesh of institutional and intellectual rhetoric invented by John Crowe Ransom. Nevertheless, I would contend that the New Criticism carried the discipline through the fifties and early sixties because it continued to offer an elegant solution to the problem of the divided exigencies of academic professionalism. Its proponents gained and held power because they built their critical structure squarely on the institutional foundations that already existed; moreover, they articulated the institutional-intellectual connection so compellingly that most English departments are still working inside their formulations.

We might do well to pause here, before turning to the topic of how the New Critics prepared their own supersession, and take stock of their secure legacy. First, the primary object of our studies, despite recent expansions of our subject matter, is still literature. Before the New Criticism, the primary object of scholarship was language; now, literary works might yield knowledge about the history and structure of the language, but that knowledge is not the principal aim of most critics. Second, literature is still normally defined not by loftiness of sentiment, aptness of expression, or even the employment of certain genres, but by techniques that create linguistic difficulty and density, that therefore make meaning problematic. Third, the skill we teach and practice is criticism, even when mixed with other kinds of scholarship or analysis. Fourth, criticism is the elucidation of literary techniques and not the process of judging works according to some extrinsic set of values. Although these ideas have undergone at least twenty-five years of serious questioning, they continue to subtend the curriculum of most English departments.

*   *   *

It is hard to say just when the challenges began. By becoming the axioms of the discipline, the four assumptions I just enumerated ceased to be the exclusive property of any one group of English professors; they were not experienced as New Critical orthodoxy but as the defining features differentiating literary critics from other sorts of intellectuals. As such, they underlay a gradually expanding number of critical theories and practices in the forties, fifties, and most of the sixties. Neo-Aristotelian criticism, reader-response analyses, and intentionalist hermeneutics all challenged aspects of the New Criticism, but they did not question the above-named postulates. More surprisingly, Freudian and Jungian psychoanalysis, existentialism, archetypal analysis, Marxism, and structuralism all mixed well with what came to be thought of simply as techniques of "close reading" or "practical criticism," and the concentration on the opacity of literary language in turn gave something back to each of those theoretical orientations. In short, it cannot be the case that an influx of extrinsic theories was to blame for the breakdown of consensus, since the departments of the fifties and sixties were already awash in "isms" that left the foundations of the discipline intact.

In fact, the New Criticism's cosmopolitanism was largely responsible for making English departments hospitable to theoretical diversity. That cosmopolitanism, derived from modernist impulses, opened English departments not only to European literature in translation but also to other currents of European thought, which were sometimes reinforced by the migration of intellectuals from Europe. In turn, the cosmopolitanism of English departments encouraged the spread of comparative literature departments as well as world literature and literature-in-translation courses. In the humanities, literature departments became the busiest academic ports of entry for European postwar intellectual movements.

At the same time that English departments were defining their subject matter as what Matthew Arnold had called "the best" that was thought and said "in the world," many other academic disciplines were developing increasingly impermeable boundaries: philosophy was almost exclusively Anglo-American analytic philosophy, psychology was behaviorist psychology, and political science, after a brief interest in political theory, seemed to be consolidating an empirical consensus. Since one could not read Sartre in the philosophy department, Freud in the psychology department, or Lukacs in the political science department, one read them in literature departments. Literature departments (sometimes in conjunction with smaller pockets of faculty in sociology, anthropology, history, and religion) often took responsibility for contemporary thought primarily because other disciplines defaulted.

English professors, moreover, were primed to regard the seeming indifference of neighboring academics to current European thought as further evidence of an American tendency to deny the complexity of life. Lionel Trilling's influential argument that our liberal intellectual traditions were inadequate to the puzzles of human experience, and especially unequal to understanding all that might be categorized as "irrational," could easily be applied to academia. Writing in 1950, he described the reductive dynamic inherent in the liberalism of the time:

> As it carries out its active and positive ends it unconsciously limits its view of the world to what it can deal with, and it unconsciously tends to develop theories and principles, particularly in relation to the nature of the human mind, that justify its limitation. . . . And in the very interest of affirming its confidence in the power of the mind, it inclines to constrict and make mechanical its conception of the nature of mind.[13]

A quick look at other departments seemed to corroborate Trilling's view of the prevailing limitations. In the wake of World War II, it seemed that students were being offered courses in philosophy that confined themselves to analyses of sentences, psychology seminars that preferred to study the simplified behavior of rodents, and political science classes bent on refining opinion polls. Little wonder that students agitated by recent history flocked to literature departments or that their teachers turned not only to contemporary literature but also to continental philosophy, psychology, and political thought for a fuller understanding of the depth and breadth of human existence.

That turn, as I have been claiming, was partly the doing of the New Criticism itself; English departments were theoretically open and eclectic in the sixties and seventies, not despite the New Criticism but because of it. Its flexibility and its ability, as an analytic technique, to mix well with various theories provided the sense of a common enterprise that many English departments now seem to lack. The eclecticism, nevertheless, eventually came to include ideas that seemed corrosive to the bases of the program, ideas that discounted the foundational concepts of "the literary" as a particularly intricate and difficult kind of language and of "criticism" as the discipline of analyzing the literary.

Internal challenges to the idea of the literary came from various sources. The reader-response criticism of Stanley Fish, for example, with its roots in analytical philosophy, pragmatism, and linguistic theory, began breaking down the "object" status of the literary work in the late sixties and developed a strong critique of the special nature of literary language throughout the seventies.[14] His was an internal critique in the sense that it spoke mainly to literary professionals about the extent to which their methods created their objects. Fish did not attack the methods but merely called for a more sophisticated understanding of them. This stage of reader-response criticism attempted to adjust the profession's sense of its unique knowledge, to bring about change in what I have called the "specialization" function of the profession.

Another attempt to reformulate the profession's specialized knowledge came from phenomenologically-inspired hermeneutics, which, although not destructive of the idea of the "literary," did challenge the "objective" status of the text and prepare the way for the later, deconstructive version of literariness that many old-guard critics would find uncongenial. Paul de Man's "Form and Intent in the American New Criticism,"[15] which was written before he became a Derridean, defends the idea that "literature is an autonomous activity of the mind, a distinctive way of being in the world to be understood in terms of its own purposes and intentions."[16] But it defends the literary by attacking the New Critical understanding of its "objective" existence. By trying to get along without intentionality and concentrating on "the surface dimensions of language," de Man claimed, the New Critics had mistaken the nature of the literary object, confusing it with a natural object.

> Certain entities exist, the full meaning of which can be said to be equal to the totality of their sensory appearances. . . . [T]he "meaning" of "stone" could only refer to a totality of sensory appearances. The same applies to all natural objects. But even the most purely intuitive consciousness could never conceive of the significance of an object such as, for instance, a chair, without including in the description an allusion to the *use* to which it is put. . . . By asserting *a priori*. . .that, in literary language, the meaning is equal to the totality of sensory appearances, one postulates in fact that the language of literature is of the same order, ontologically speaking, as a natural object.[17]

There is a literary text, de Man argues, but it is an *intentional* entity, that is to say, one in which an intentional act forms part of the object's structure: "the concept of intentionality is neither physical nor psychological in its nature, but structural, involving the activity of a subject regardless of its empirical concerns, except as far as they relate to the intentionality of the structure."[18] De Man does not let intentionality move him back toward the historical, empirical author, however; instead, he uses it to explode the possibility of a self-enclosed work. Invoking the idea of the hermeneutic circle, he argues that the poem and its meaning are never simultaneously given.

> Literary "form" is the result of the dialectic interplay between the prefigurative structure of the foreknowledge and the intent at totality of the interpretative process. This dialectic is difficult to grasp. . . . The completed form never exists as a concrete aspect of the work that could coincide with a sensorial or semantic dimension of the language. It is constituted in the mind of the interpreter as the work discloses itself in response to his questioning. But this dialogue between work and interpreter is endless.[19]

This is still a far cry from deconstructive undecidability, but de Man takes an important step toward redefining the "literary" and discrediting the naive empiricism of the New Criticism.

In both Stanley Fish's reader-response criticism and Paul de Man's open-ended hermeneutics, we can discern attempts to reformulate the foundational ideas of the discipline, especially the idea of the literary, without sacrificing professional autonomy or distinctness. Both can be seen as efforts to make the primary claims of the profession more coherent and defensible. They therefore raise a question: what was the profession defending itself against in the late sixties and early seventies?

The answer is quite obvious as soon as we turn to the "service" function of the profession. When students, who had been attracted to the English department because of its intellectual openness and inclusiveness, became more politicized, the techniques of literary analysis seemed laughably inadequate for the phenomena they sought to understand. Moreover, the very idea that they should look to literary technique, the untranslatable particulars woven into a "tissue of irrelevancies" (to use Ransom's phrase), as the repository of personhood appeared a quietistic proposal for reconciling themselves with what was perceived as an oppressive bureaucratic state. If the intellectual Left of the thirties and even the forties could see aesthetic modernism as always potentially subversive in its very forms, many students of the sixties were impatient with the indirection of modernism and considered it intrinsically elitist. Modernism's social and political impetuses, it seemed, had dwindled to a fussy discontent, a mere fastidious disdain for bourgeois vulgarity. Furthermore, the fact that literary modernism was itself passé revealed the historical bias in the New Critical description of the literary. Analytical tools developed to explicate Eliot's *Wasteland* could not effectively grapple with Ginsburg's *Howl,* which seemed to demand a different level of response.

The challenges mounted. Did not the restrictiveness of the idea of the literary privilege an already privileged white, male, middle-class consciousness, primarily concerned with safeguarding its precious uniqueness? And did not that restrictiveness relegate the more urgent, unambiguous, and collectively-conscious writings of minorities, proletarians, and women to the category of the "non-literary"? Could it not also be said to have eradicated all signs of historical specificity and alterity from the works of past authors, creating a canon that narcissistically mirrored a narrow stratum of mid-twentieth-century American experience?

Versions of this political disaffection hit all of the humanities and social sciences departments simultaneously. But in a less overtly political vein, the literature students of the sixties were also irritated by the absence of the category of pleasure in most critical studies. Ransom's severe insistence that poetry was a "desperate," last-ditch maneuver to salvage a besieged singularity echoed throughout English departments. Literature seemed less a vital and robust activity than a chastened, disillusioned, middle-aged response to a constantly threatening world. The relentless pessimism of the works selected for analysis in Cleanth Brooks's and Robert Penn Warren's widely-used book, *Understanding Poetry* (1938),[20] for example, as well as the analyses themselves, could give the unpleasant sensation that one was being encouraged to adopt a coping strategy of mild depression. Although "emotion" received a fair amount of attention in the New Critical books, "pleasure" was almost always limited to the relatively tepid enjoyment of cognitive harmonies and dissonances. Any mention of the power of the text to create bodily sensation, to arouse erotically or to stimulate desire, was conspicuous by its absence. Susan Sontag spoke for her generation when, in *Against Interpretation* (1966),[21] she demanded a new "erotics of art." Sontag's emphasis not only prepared the reception of Roland Barthes's *The Pleasure of the Text* (1973)[22] but also brought into fashion a more playful and performative style of literary criticism. A critic should not simply register pleasure, she implied, but also relay it. In short, the question of what "the literary" was good for was emphatically reopened by a generation at once highly politicized, draftable, increasingly ethnically diverse, and dedicated to the resurrection of the body.

As these fundamental issues were being urgently pressed in English department classrooms and faculty meetings, the academic environment was also reorganizing. Programs that drew heavily on English department personnel—American studies, ethnic studies, women's studies, film studies—created interdepartmental contexts for reconsidering the canonical and noncanonical texts of the past as well as for receiving the increasingly disparate contemporary literatures written in English. Situated between the humanities and the social sciences, the new programs both alleviated pressures in the established departments and provided places for interdisciplinary experimentation, which in turn stimulated more contextualism inside the departments.

Few people in the new surrounding programs were interested in the nature of the literary, and the emphasis of many scholars inside English departments also began to shift toward what were often called "larger" issues. The professional requirement of a unique subject matter was experienced by younger critics as a restriction, preventing their participation in the grand, ambitious, synthetic projects of the period: Marxist humanism, structuralism, feminism, semiotics, cultural history. Hence, in giving up the claim to a unique subject matter, these younger critics were simultaneously laying claim to a vastly expanded field of inquiry and representing literary criticism as one mode, among others, of understanding systems of signification or cultures. The special analytical skills of the profession, it was argued, were applicable to all cultural phenomena, and only unadventurous critics would confine themselves to conventional literary texts.

The fundamental assumptions about the value of the literary and the usefulness of a criticism devoted to it, in short, were both directly attacked and cavalierly dismissed. Deprived of those unifying assumptions, which had always been more procedural and ethical than theoretical, the former theoretical diversity of English departments developed into a full-blown theoretical division. The dynamic might be described this way: because one segment of the profession claimed an expanded field of investigation within which literature was only one among many phenomena, another segment focused on the idea of the literary with renewed intensity. The "theory" practiced by Stanley Fish and Paul de Man, in other words, was partly a defensive reaction against the imminent loss of a unique subject matter. We might, indeed, think of what came to be called the "theory wars" of the seventies and eighties as the sound of alarm bells going off in the "specialized knowledge" wing of the profession in response to violations in the "service" wing's perimeter.

"Theory," then, was neither a foreign imposition nor a sudden, drastic departure from settled practice. As de Man's essay demonstrates, the theoretical debate began as an effort to protect the profession's integrity: "Contemporary French structuralism applies methodological patterns derived from the social sciences. . .to the study of literature; similar tendencies can be observed in the renewed interest of American critics in sociological, political, and psychological consideration that had never ceased to be present, but had been kept in the background."[23] For de Man, this blurring of the disciplinary outlines prompted "a long overdue re-examination of the assumptions on which the position of autonomy was founded."[24]

One of the great ironies of the recent history of the profession is that the attempt to shore up the foundational idea of literary autonomy was widely interpreted as an attack on the discipline's values. To understand why this happened, we should note that the specific terms in which de Man and other deconstructionists finally built their case for the uniqueness of literary language sheared off all the values that had clustered around the term "autonomy" for the New Critics. The hermeneutic open-endedness de Man advocated in his essay on the New Criticism had already called the "objectivity" of the text into question, thereby denying that poets could rescue imperiled experiences and preserve them as poetic objects. For Ransom, each great poem's form had been autonomous in the sense that it was complete unto itself and separated from all other instances of language by unique deviations from a prose norm. For the hermeneutically informed de Man, autonomy was an attribute of the *activity* of literature, something larger than the individual instances of its putatively complete products.

This redefinition of what was special about "the literary" disabled the substitutions inherent in the New Critical version of autonomy. There, it will be recalled, the poem's objective inviolability had stood in for the poet's unique experience, indeed, for the poet's uniqueness. And the critics' descriptions of the ways in which the poem frustrates the extraction of paraphrasable meaning represented our acts of homage to particularity in general, especially to our own intransigent singularity. All of this relied on a settled subject-object dichotomy: once the poet had completed his "desperate ontological act," his subjective experience was an objective thing, with all the independent solidity of a stone (to use de Man's metaphor), to be described and appreciated by another, distinct subject. From a hermeneutic point of view, however, the poetic act was not finished; the poem was not a completed object but a process requiring readers.

In the shift from the literary as a set of discrete, autonomous objects to the literary as an autonomous process, therefore, individual, autonomous *subjects* seemed at risk. When critics like de Man switched from hermeneutics to deconstruction in the late sixties and early seventies, the moral implications grew even more threatening. Derridean philosophy brought a version of the stony object back into literature, in the irreducible materiality of the signifier, all the while denying that the "irrelevancies" (to use Ransom's word) of the signifier stood for a bounded and supreme subjectivity. Language was certainly self-reliant, but not because its users were. Its independence rested on its very unsuitability to a writer's expressive purposes, on the fact that it is an internally riven, centerless system, incapable of producing either whole objects or distinct subjects.

"Language" thus returned as a master key to the plural phenomena of literature, as literary analyses aimed to display a rather limited set of putatively fundamental linguistic universals drawn from Ferdinand de Saussure's *Course in General Linguistics*: the arbitrariness of the signifier, the diacritical structure of signification, and the "systematicity" of that structure, from which Derrida derived the necessity of the deferral of meaning. This linguistic turn (a drastic turn away from academic linguistics) could hardly be called the philologists' revenge, however, since the aim of deconstructive literary critics was never to gain new knowledge about language. Literary texts exposed already-known linguistic properties; they were not tools for discovery. We might still, however, call deconstruction the return of the linguistic repressed, since it takes language to be the recalcitrant material always defeating the aesthetic subject's control, always producing the text's heteronomy.

Now the ethical core of the profession seemed undeniably under attack to New-Critically trained scholars, and they fought back with a moralistic fervor that surprised younger critics interested in the theoretical cogency of the arguments rather than their moral implications. Many of them were also busy arguing with deconstructionists, for the nature of "the literary" and the subjectivity it implied were under intense scrutiny from multiple perspectives. For example, it was analyzed by readers of Wittgenstein as a peculiarly referentless language game, by readers of Foucault as the historical production of a certain "subject effect," by readers of Althusser and Macherey as the internal distanciation of ideology through form, and by readers of Lacan as the undoing of the subject in the very acts of signification that constitute him.

Most of these "theoretical" positions seemed culpable to the critical old-guard, though, because they appeared to have conceded the very ground that the profession should have been guarding as its own: the defense of particular human subjects. M. H. Abrams's essay in this collection eloquently expresses that generation's sense of loss as it perceived its successors' apparent lack of interest in "the human agents who produce and receive a literary work." Abrams continues, "[T]he shaping and determinative functions of purpose and intentionality are translocated from the human agents to the impersonal dynamics inherent in the signifying-system, or to the impersonal operancy of the internal forces and power-configurations that constitute the discourse of a specific period."[25] Abrams rightly reminds us that, whether historicists like himself or "objectivists" like Ransom, critics before the seventies took what we might call their "methodological individualism" for granted. And the New Criticism, which had substituted the aesthetic subject for the historical or psychological subject in order to allow the work to stand in for the artist, revealed under pressure that its methodological habit was also its deepest commitment. Never having truly justified that habit, though, having merely inherited the idea of the aesthetic subject from a romantic tradition they often themselves spurned, the old-guard New Critics had little more than a defensive humanism to fall back upon. "Theory" became the enemy because it questioned the common sense of methodological individualism and thereby challenged the self-evident value of the humanistic subject. Thus, the theoretical attempts to limit the critical enterprise by redefining the nature of our special field of study resulted in further damage to professional cohesion. And, in a twist that the ironic gods of intellectual history no doubt relished, the previous professionalizers invoked common sense and discovered the virtues of reading like normal people, while the theorists often claimed the professional high ground of methodological rigor.

But the rigor of theory could not delimit a new professional identity for literary critics. The very axiomatic status of the claims that were made insured that they would always be partly extrinsic to the precincts of literary study narrowly conceived. Whether singularity is solidified or dispersed in literary language, whether "the literary" and its implied subject are universal realities or the discursive impositions of a specific historical period, whether literariness inheres in the language of texts or in readers' expectations—none of these disputes could be settled on the basis of literary evidence alone, since both how to read that evidence and exactly what constituted it were the very things at issue. The pressure of the theoretical discourse was, in other words, itself interdisciplinary. It was not only inspired by the synthetic zeal of structuralists and post-structuralists in several disciplines but also sustained by the corroborating work undertaken in other textually-based or interpretive fields: philosophy, psychoanalysis, linguistics, anthropology, art history, and so on. The very activity that de Man thought would preserve, through revision, our independence from other disciplines itself became an independent transdisciplinary enterprise carried on by "theorists" in numerous departments.

Where has all of this left literary criticism? From 1987—the year it was discovered that Paul de Man's early publications had appeared in a fascist journal—to the present, there has been a general lessening of theoretical polemical fervor. One might say that the most aggressive movements—ethnic studies, gender studies, feminism, New Historicism, and deconstruction especially—have been absorbed into the mainstream. Younger scholars seem more interested in carrying out research programs than in debating theories, and they seem capable of moving fluidly among available models of subjectivity and "literariness." It is now the norm to recognize the "constructedness" of such categories rather than to debate their objective existence. Critics often stipulate the "constructedness" of the categories, however, mainly in order to make their continued use uncontroversial. Critics no longer feel obliged to maintain an exclusive methodological focus on "text," "agent," or "system" (to use Abrams's terms) or to specify a theory that allows them to shift from one unit of analysis to another; those shifts have become routine. Indeed, the cordoning off of the units, based on the assumption of their discrete, noninterpenetrating modes of being, now seems counterintuitive. The nineties, one might say, resemble the fifties in that new kinds of "practical criticism" are once again gaining ground after a period of intense debate and reorganization.

Even a high level of comfort with the new eclecticism, though, entails a loss: critics of the nineties, unlike those of the fifties, can point to no underlying consensus about the general benefits that derive from their unique specialization. A widespread inattentiveness to the coordination of institutional and professional demands, the kind of coordination that the New Critics took so persuasively into account, has been characteristic of the last two decades. Deconstruction, for example, attracted many of the professorial elite by advocating a more difficult, recondite, and rigorous form of criticism along with (in its de Manian version) an even more technical definition of the literary. But it never caught on as a classroom practice for undergraduates because, unlike the New Criticism, it was difficult to convert into textual explication. Most novice students, who were as yet unable to explain any relation between meaning and technique, were not in a position to locate aporia and *mises en abîme*. The reading public, moreover, could not be talked out of the notion that deconstructionists were somehow disrespectful of the writer's art; that is, deconstruction could not be easily assimilated to appreciation. The New Criticism stressed how the poem, in its very ambiguity, cohered, whereas deconstruction seemed to explain the impossibility of coherence. Given that coherence seemed a self-evidently better thing than incoherence, the public, like most undergraduates, could not understand what deconstruction was good for. The service leg of the profession therefore appeared to some in danger of amputation.

Ethnic studies, feminism, New Historicism, and cultural studies have had the opposite problem: they have refused to assign a unique knowledge and function to the English department. Although often very popular with undergraduates and certain sections of the public, they have been hard put to explain why they draw their evidence from *literary* objects per se. Indeed, in many cases, they are not concerned with literature. "Cultural Studies," which sometimes bills itself as a new discipline, now both surrounds and radiates from English departments. Although it has the potential to encourage reflection on the processes by which cultural phenomena are set apart, in practice it often ignores the differentiations. The same tendency toward de-differentiation could be detected in other interdisciplinary approaches as well; although individual feminists or New Historicists may have full and elaborate accounts of the literary, the labels "feminism" and "New Historicism" do not automatically evoke those accounts. Indeed, all of these tendencies might claim to be meta-investigations into the social construction of the literary. But if so, what professional training or specialized knowledge would be required to carry on such an investigation? And how would that knowledge and training differ from that of intellectual or cultural historians or from cultural anthropologists, philosophers, or sociologists?

These are not unanswerable questions, but we have spent very little time seriously addressing them. Instead, those of us who favor one kind of interdisciplinary study or another have applied ourselves to the building of interdepartmental, rather than departmental, institutions: humanities institutes, interdisciplinary journals, women's studies programs, ethnic studies programs, film studies, team-teaching programs, and the like. While we attended to these institutional tasks, we avoided translating our ideas into coherent graduate programs. Ph.D.'s trained in today's English departments have widely dissimilar skills and knowledge; sometimes they possess knowledge that members of their own faculty refuse to recognize as such. Our students find it increasingly difficult to describe with one set of terms both the value of what they do and the reason they need a Ph.D. in English to do it. This fact may indicate that we are in the midst of an enormous institutional shift away from the traditional departments even though we continue to locate our professional training inside those structures. Perhaps our most difficult task now is to give our intellectual adventures the kind of secure institutional footing that would allow us to develop once again as a discipline.

ENDNOTES

[1]The most thorough and accomplished of these studies is Gerald Graff, *Professing Literature: An Institutional History* (Chicago, Ill.: University of Chicago Press,

1987). For the idea of academic professionalism drawn on in this essay, see Burton J. Bledstein, *The Culture of Professionalism: The Middle Class and the Development of Higher Education in America* (New York: W. W. Norton, 1976).

[2]Edwin Greenlaw, *The Province of Literary History* (Baltimore, Md.: The Johns Hopkins University Press, 1931), quoted in Graff, *Professing Literature*, 141.

[3]Greenlaw, *The Province of Literary History*.

[4]John Crowe Ransom, "Criticism, Inc.," reprinted in David Lodge, ed., *Twentieth-Century Literary Criticism: A Reader* (London: Longman, 1972), 232.

[5]Quoted in Graff, *Professing Literature*, 65.

[6]Ransom, "Criticism, Inc.," in Lodge, ed., *Twentieth-Century Literary Criticism*, 232.

[7]Ibid.

[8]Ibid., 231.

[9]Ibid., 228.

[10]Ibid., 233.

[11]Ibid., 237.

[12]See Graff, *Professing Literature*, 145–179.

[13]Lionel Trilling, *The Liberal Imagination; Essays on Literature and Society* (Garden City, N.Y.: Doubleday & Co., Inc., 1957), xi.

[14]See the essays collected in Stanley Fish, *Is There a Text in This Class? The Authority of Interpretive Communities* (Cambridge, Mass.: Harvard University Press, 1980).

[15]This essay was probably first delivered in 1966 or 1967; it was first published in Paul de Man, *Blindness and Insight; Essays in the Rhetoric of Contemporary Criticism* (New York: Oxford University Press, 1971), 20–35.

[16]Ibid., 21.

[17]Ibid., 24.

[18]Ibid., 25.

[19]Ibid., 31–32.

[20]Cleanth Brooks and Robert Penn Warren, *Understanding Poetry* (New York: H. Holt and Company, 1938).

[21]Susan Sontag, *Against Interpretation* (New York: Farrar, Straus, and Giroux, 1966).

[22]Roland Barthes, *The Pleasure of the Text* (New York: Hill and Wang, 1973).

[23]Ibid., 21.

[24]Ibid., 22.

[25]M. H. Abrams, "The Transformation of English Studies: 1930–1995," in this volume.

José David Saldívar

Tracking English and American Literary and Cultural Criticism

I
NTELLECTUAL HISTORIANS Richard Fox and James Kloppenberg
emphasize in *A Companion to American Thought* that many
innovations in American studies, such as the dismantling of
disciplinary boundaries and the focus on gender, class, and
ethnoracial formations, have given rise to a "militant" resistance
by academics associated with the National Association of Scholars, who have called for a return to "excellence" and a revival of
the teaching of self-evident "truths" contained in the classics of the
Western tradition.[1] Part of my task in this essay is to explain my
intellectual trajectory as a response to some of these larger issues.
At the outset, I do not hesitate to say that I come down on the side
of intellectual historians (like Fox and Kloppenberg) who convinc-
ingly argue that we cannot transcend our time anymore than our
predecessors could and that our judgments of writers, texts, and
contexts are themselves formed by historical contingencies.

THE BORDERLANDS OF AMERICAN STUDIES

When I first came to Yale to study American literature in 1973, I
knew very little about America. I was nurtured in the rhetoric of
the US-Mexico borderlands, what Américo Paredes called the limi-
nal spaces of "Greater Mexico."[2] I was absorbed, moreover, in
South Texas's attitudes toward "el norte"—a subalternity deep-

José David Saldívar is Professor of Comparative Ethnic Studies at the University of California, Berkeley.

ened by the pressures of economic, military, and cultural deterritorializations. This interpretation of America, however, was not given to me by my provincial, public school education in Brownsville, Texas, where history began and ended with the master periodizing narratives of the Alamo. I was taught all about regional hegemony and global colonialism's cultures, for culture, my teachers believed, always lived somewhere else—never in our own backyard. So I learned all the hard facts, which were, of course, pejorative. But the symbology of the two Americas that José Martí mapped out for us in his magisterial *Nuestra América*[3]— our America and the America that is not ours—remained largely hidden from me.

Nothing in my background prepared me for my initial encounter with the other America—a secular nation living like a dream on the back of a tiger. With the soundtrack of my adolescence running through my head (hybrid Tex-Mex *corrido* and *conjunto* sounds), I left South Texas to walk along the mean streets of New Haven and discover the rather different music of America—from Walt Whitman's "I Hear America Singing" to Funkadelic's "One Nation under a Groove" to Ruben Blades's transcultural salsa anthem "Buscando America." I was quickly immersed in the foundational myths of the Puritan fathers, evident everywhere around me at the Old Campus, from its neogothic buildings named after dissenters like Jonathan Edwards to the crunchy "literary criticism" practices taught to me in undergraduate tutorials and seminars. Beyond the walled-in panopticon of the Old Campus was something called the "New England way." To see this New England America as a fantasmatics was to historicize my own hybrid identifications.[4]

The point of these brief autobiographical remarks is not to demonstrate a Manichaean clash of identities but to begin mapping out the fantasmatics of the borderlands at our own complex *fin del siglo*. So what began in New England as a traditional American studies major became, years later, at a California university (founded by a prominent robber baron and member of the Gilded Age's "Big Four") a trail into the intricate symbologies of American cultural studies. In both New England and California, I encountered an imperial literary and cultural history: Perry Miller's garden-variety foray into the wilderness; R. W. B. Lewis's con-

structions of the American Adam; Harold Bloom's Western, ago-
nistic canon based on elite European and Euro-American male
isolates. Likewise, in California, I encountered Yvor Winters's and
Wallace Stegner's constructions of the Western American literary
frontier passages. The America they discovered (both the East and
West Coasts) seemingly appeared out of nowhere, out of some Old
Testament supernatural telos, respectively labeled as Nature, the
New England Mind, the Jeffersonian Way, and the American
Frontier thesis, culminating in Newt Gingrich's all too familiar
"Contract with America."

American literary and cultural studies had developed, as Amy
Kaplan brilliantly suggests in "Left Alone with America," with a
method designed not to explore their subjects of empire, for "the
study of American culture [had] traditionally been cut off from the
study of foreign relations."[5] This was a relatively simple lesson for
one such as myself, who was rooted in the cultural conflicts of the
US-Mexico borderlands, but it required time, comparative study,
and observation to absorb. My own ethnohistorical view of American
cultural studies (fully formed in 1987 when I studied with Sacvan
Bercovitch at the School of Criticism and Theory at Dartmouth
College) was that America was an "artifact" made text by imaginative writers, political scientists, anthropologists, and philosophers, among others, and by what Edward Said has called "traveling theorists."[6]

When I first arrived at Yale as an undergraduate in the early
1970s, the English department believed it was its business to teach
the canon of English and American literature. (As an aside, I
recently saw one of my former English professors, Harold Bloom,
mention on television that if multiculturalism only meant reading
Cervantes, he would be happy to include more multicultural writers in his book, *The Western Canon*.) As we know, this use of the
term "canon" traveled, as they say, from biblical studies, where it
originally meant a list of sacred or spiritualized texts accepted as
authentic.

The English and American literary texts I was assigned to read
as an undergraduate, from Shakespeare to Hawthorne to Toni
Morrison, were, of course, not God-given; they were produced by
men and women, and thereby understandable. Indeed, as the Welsh-
European literary and cultural materialist scholar Raymond Wil-

liams suggested in *Marxism and Literature* and "Crisis in English Studies," literature in its simplest form was historically established by the English departments themselves. "Literature," Williams writes, "had once meant, at least until the nineteenth century, a body of printed writings; indeed that neutral sense survives in such contexts as the 'literary supplement'. . . ."[7] Increasingly through the nineteenth century, however, there was a series of further specializations of the term "literature."

Literature came to mean "imaginative writing" of novels, plays, and poems, a distinction from discursive or factual writing. Additionally, Williams notes that "there was then a further specialization in which, so to speak, the category of Literature censored itself."[8] In other words, not all literature (novels, plays, and poems) was Literature in "that capital letter category."[9] And as I intensely felt it as an undergraduate and later as a graduate student in English, a majority of novels, plays, and poems were not seen by my professors as belonging to Literature. Moreover, the texts that made it into the "canon," or the selective tradition, were themselves established by both the old and new schools of criticism, including formalism, New Criticism, structuralism, poststructuralism, and deconstruction.

English and American Literature, in capital letters, at Yale and Stanford (and I presume at other major universities) thus came to be paired with "criticism." Since scholarship, in contrast to biblical studies, to paraphrase Williams, could not itself establish and script the literary canon, reading and rhetorical structures—as the title of my high-tech, senior "Literature Z" seminar co-taught by Paul de Man and Geoffrey Hartman put it—had to be taught as the condition of retaining the defining role of Literature.

Nowadays at the University of California, Berkeley, I hear some of my colleagues agitate that "literature is more important than any 'isms.'" These "isms" are not only the usual suspects, along with power-knowledge couplets of Marxism and poststructuralism, but also include the unholy family of feminism, postcolonialism, and critical multiculturalism. But one "ism" that goes unmentioned in my colleagues' list of "usual suspects" is the term "criticism." Criticism, as Williams noted in *Marxism and Literature,* was historically incorporated in the very establishment of the canon of Literature itself—it defines what we do as literature professors.[10]

To now retrace the sequence of transformations that I have all too quickly mapped out: first, literature meant all printed texts; then, it was narrowed to what are called "imaginative texts"; and finally there was a "circumscription" to a critically scripted minority of English and American canonical texts.

Simultaneously growing alongside this production of an English and American canon, there was, Williams notes, "another and more potent specialization: not just Literature, but English (and I would add American) Literature."[11] These constructions, English and American literatures, as Professor Abrams notes in his essay, were themselves historically late constructions. Is English the language or is it the country? In the English context, for instance, Williams reminds us that there were at least fifteen centuries of native writing in other languages: Latin, Welsh, Irish, Old English, Norse, and Norman French. And in the US context, what about the hundreds of Native American Indian languages and Spanish, French, or German? If it is not the language but the country, is that only England or the United States?

Let me end this initial section by turning to English departments and the issue of what Lauren Berlant calls the "space of the National Symbolic"[12]—how we are bound together by inhabiting the political space of the nation, a space tangling us up in a cluster of juridical, territorial, linguistic, and experiential issues. The term "national literature" dates from the 1780s in Germany, and histories of national literatures were written not only in Germany but also in England and France during the same period. Do not the very ideas of a literature and the space of the "National Symbolic" tell us something about the changing ideas of both "the nation" and of "cultural identity"? Is not the question of "Englishness" or "Americanness" full of sound and fury, full of emotional and irrational problems of identity and threat? Consider some postcontemporary attitudes that we have heard about recent work or graduate seminars as being too German, too French, or too Cuban. These are not just descriptive categories but are instead used, as Williams argues, "deliberately in a marking off sense."[13] What is being consciously defended is not just a canon of writing but a significant projection from this, in which an ethnoracial structure of feeling, a mood, a style, or a set of principles are, in Williams's words, "being celebrated, taught and—where possible—administratively imposed."[14]

This is a long way from where we originally started. English and American literatures, like other national literatures, are stands from which values and traditions are defended against all comers. Some twenty years after I first began my journey into the heart of the English department, I now believe that English and American literatures, historically, were not professions—in my opinion, they were callings and campaigns against illegally alienated intellectuals like myself. In saying this I do not wish to be misunderstood as being crudely "un-American." I only wish to suggest that I now see myself as belonging to a long history of ethnoracially minoritized "others" (primarily Jewish-Americans) in English departments in the United States who faced a general history of exclusions and quotas that institutions of higher education saw fit to impose on students and faculty. As one recent intellectual historian notes, Lionel Trilling "was just enough of a 'Jewish gentleman' to receive tenure in the English Department at Columbia University after a lengthy and demeaning battle, and thus also ended up serving tenure as the test case or thin edge of the wedge for other Jewish academics in the Ivy League."[15]

"ARE WE BEING HISTORICAL YET?"
                              —CAROLYN PORTER

I will now describe, briefly, the main and diverse tendencies in New (literary) Historicism and comparative cultural studies as they bear on what, by received habit, we in the United States call literary studies. To understand either of these properly requires much further elaboration, but I want to at least identify them as central to English departments on the West Coast.

In US English departments, Shakespeare always stands alone. Without a doubt, he is the preeminent "monumental" figure in the Western canon, what Rob Nixon calls the cultural gold standard of literature and literary value.[16] Typically, William Shakespeare is separated not only from his contemporary peers but from the most general historical ground. In my first undergraduate survey course on Shakespeare at Yale in 1974, my brilliant young professor,

Marjorie Garber, focused mainly on New Critical and poststructuralist readings of several plays, demanding that we allow the plays, like well-wrought poems, to speak for themselves. To be fair, Professor Garber consistently and persuasively argued that Shakespeare's plays were related to the world of dreams and the unconscious, and that psychoanalysis (Freud's and Lacan's) could provide us with a way of dealing with Shakespeare's overdetermined texts.

Today, much of what goes on in the New Historicist literary classroom argues against the New Critical, formalist idea of Shakespeare's plays as well-wrought poems, for literary works of art can no more transcend history than can real people. My colleague Stephen Greenblatt and my Stanford graduate school cohort Steven Mullaney, exemplars of the New Historicism, have radically changed the direction of Shakespeare criticism and pedagogy by setting his plays in the context of the social drama out of which theater in Elizabethan England arose. In Mullaney's *The Place of the Stage,* for example, the New Historicist critic begins his startling analysis of Elizabethan theater by turning to "the city itself and pursuing terms such as 'situation' and 'place' with as much literal-mindedness as can be mustered—more than might seem appropriate to readers trained, as I was, to regard plays as poems, and drama as primarily (if not entirely) a literary phenomenon."[17] What Mullaney contends is that "drama, unlike poetry, is a territorial art. It is an art of space as well as words, and it requires a place of its own, in or around a community, in which to mount its telling fictions and its eloquent spectacles."[18]

Mullaney's reading of Elizabethan drama as a spatial "territorial art" reflects the spatial turn in much postcontemporary theory, from Henri Lefevbre's *The Production of Space* to geographer Edward Soja's reading of Los Angeles in *Postmodern Geographies.* Intertextually speaking, Mullaney's work relies on Michel Foucault's writings about "heterotopias" and those devoted to madness and the prison to ground his New Historicist project. As with Foucault's reading of leprosy in the Middle Ages, Mullaney sees popular drama as taking place on "the margins of the city" where "forms of moral incontinence and pollution were granted license to exist beyond the bounds of a community they had, by their incontinence, already exceeded."[19] Mullaney's New Historicism thus overlaps with Foucault's analysis of the politics of social space and to the topology of contestatory power in civil society.

Stephen Greenblatt, however, is the real center of the New Historicist movement in US English departments. He alone was responsible for naming the school at the University of California, Berkeley, and guaranteeing the movement's dissemination by founding *Representations,* an interdisciplinary journal, bringing together many New Historicist scholars such as Catherine Gallagher, Eric Sundquist, Michael Rogin, and Walter Benn Michaels, among others. Although this is not the place for a complete critical review of Greenblatt's enormous contributions to Renaissance literary studies in particular, and to cultural studies in general, I want to focus briefly on his groundbreaking method of reading Shakespeare by looking at his now-famous riffs on *The Tempest* from his *Shakespearean Negotiations.*

As Brooke Thomas writes, "Greenblatt's exemplary status derives from the way in which he relates literature and history, particularly his challenge to the distinction traditionalists make between a text and its historical context."[20] Against traditionalist historicist work, say that of E. D. Hirsch, Greenblatt demolishes the assumption that literary texts and contexts have stable, unitary meanings.

Greenblatt's characteristic move is to begin from a colonialist episode and then proceed to the spiritualized Shakespearean text. For instance, in his graceful reading of *The Tempest,* the flow is from the cultural to the literary. He starts by discussing a story told during a sermon by Hugh Latimer, a Protestant martyr, that demonstrates the use of what Greenblatt symptomatically calls "salutary anxiety" to manipulate a condemned woman. Greenblatt shows how salutary anxiety is at work in *Measure for Measure* and in a fully developed manner in *The Tempest.* It is precisely in *The Tempest,* he asserts, "when. . .Shakespeare reflected upon his own art with still greater intensity and self-consciousness than in *Measure for Measure;* he once again conceived of the playwright as a princely creator of anxiety."[21]

Why is "salutary anxiety" important to Greenblatt, and how does it operate in *The Tempest?* In Latimer's narrative, anxiety is produced through his withholding of a royal pardon for the condemned woman until he can convince her to abandon her belief in the Catholic doctrine of purification for women after the birth of a child. Latimer thus created a state of anxiety for the woman who was convinced that she was doomed to execution. Greenblatt then tells us of another episode of salutary anxiety by James I following the execution of three men allegedly involved in a conspiracy against him. Three additional men were scheduled to die by hanging; at the last moment, however, the sheriff informed them of their pardon. To be sure, the first executions had created a real state of anxiety among the masses, although they were becoming resentful as executions appeared to be increasing. The king's pardoning of the last three prisoners thereby evoked a response from the populace—thus, according to Greenblatt, strengthening his power.

Here, Greenblatt uses these examples to demonstrate how the controlled management of anxiety will produce the desired effects in people—anxiety must be controlled to achieve its desired results. As Greenblatt puts it, "managed insecurity may have been reassuring not only to the managers themselves but to those whom the techniques were addressed."[22] Once the definition and practice of salutary anxiety is established, he proceeds to analyze it in theatrical and literary terms. In other words, Greenblatt analyzes controlled anxiety's place in *The Tempest* and then deals with the reciprocal nature of art and life by discussing, in detail, the influence on Shakespeare's play of William Strachey's famous letter regarding the shipwreck of the *Sea-Adventurer,* bound for the Jamestown colony. The pan-oceanic Atlantic as a whole cultural system thus stands behind Greenblatt's New Historicism. Shakespeare did not simply use Strachey's letter as a source grounded in the literature of voyaging; rather, for Greenblatt, an Atlantic phenomenon engaged both Strachey and Shakespeare, namely, the production of anxiety for managing a group of people or a situation. In Greenblatt's words, "the conjunction of Strachey's unpublished letter and Shakespeare's play signals an institutional circulation of culturally significant narratives. And as we shall see, the circulation has as its central concern the public management of anxiety."[23] Briefly, for Greenblatt, it is not simply that works of art borrow a situation from the "real" and fictionalize it; he sees the relationship between literature and history as more subtle. In his reading of Latimer's story of the condemned woman, he suggests that "if the practice he exemplifies helps to empower theatrical representations, fictive representations have themselves helped to empower his practice."[24]

Greenblatt ends his reading by telling the story of the explorer H. M. Stanley and his colonialist cultural contact with the Mowa people of Africa. Stanley claims he had to burn his copy of Shakespeare to appease "the natives" and to save the more important travel notes and mappings they had seen him writing in his tent. Because Stanley's notebook and fieldwork had survived with its essential information about the region and its people's way of life, the colony of the Belgian Congo could be established. Greenblatt notes that although other discourses (in this case Stanley's notes and maps) are more directly responsible for the imperial management of power, they might not survive without fictional discourse. Stanley's and Shakespeare's discourses, Greenblatt believes, are equally important in establishing and maintaining the state of power.

FRONTERA SOUNDINGS: REMAPPING THE NATIONAL SYMBOLIC

In the 1990s, an unkempt crowd of terms, interpretive metaphors, and metonymies jostle in cultural studies in an effort to map out the contact zones of regions, local spaces, and cultures: terms such as Paul Gilroy's "the Black Atlantic," James Clifford's "traveling cultural intellectual," Fernando Ortiz's "transculturation," Jonathan and Daniel Boyarin's "Jewish, generative, diaspora identity," and Gloria Anzaldúa's invocation of "borderlands." Important new journals, such as *Diaspora* and *Transition,* as well as new cultural studies centers, such as the University of California at Santa Cruz's Center for Cultural Studies (directed by James Clifford), are devoted to the history and current production of transnational cultures.

In my past work with the Center for Cultural Studies, where I sat on the center's steering committee, we attempted to link specific diasporas and borders as paradigms of intercultural crossings and mixings. While those who founded the Center were not consciously thinking about Richard Hoggart's Center for Contemporary Cultural Studies at Birmingham, England, (founded in 1964) when they established their center in 1988, they proposed, in the words of director James Clifford, "a center which would be visibly different from the many humanities centers around the country...." In other words, cultural studies, as Clifford defined it, "suggested a serious engagement with the social sciences and the political arts."[25] Fortunately, the Santa Cruz cultural studies center encouraged not only a Birmingham-like articulation of subcultural theory, feminism, and hegemony and its resistance, but also, as I felt it, a "homegrown" orientation for these interventions.

Briefly, cultural studies, in its multiple roots and routes from Britain to the Americas, is a counter-tradition conjured, syncretized, and customized. As Lawrence Grossberg suggested, "cultural studies is an alchemy; its methodology is one of bricolage; and its choice of practice...is pragmatic, strategic, and self-reflective."[26] The "rise of cultural studies," Latin Americanist Neil Larsen adds, "marks the disappearance of at least one component of the humanities/social science division of labor and 'knowledge.'"[27]

My work in comparative ethnic studies at the University of California, Berkeley, aligns itself with these international cultural studies movements, for it attempts to develop a new comparative area of what we now can confidently call "intercultural studies." This cultural conversation has not been sufficiently explored by either British or North American cultural studies because, as Paul Gilroy polemically argued in *There Ain't No Black in the Union Jack,* the central early focus of cultural studies in Britain (primarily under the intellectual leadership of Richard Hoggart and the *New Left Review*) was what he called "doggedly ethnocentric"[28]— concentrating on the formation of a nationalist, white male, working class.

Among other things, my work at Berkeley asks: How do US-Mexico border narratives strive for comparative theoretical scope while remaining located in specific histories of what Martí called "Our America"? What do such projections tell us about the cultures of empire and the cultures of displacement? Finally, it focuses on a variety of late nineteenth- and twentieth-century articulations of border contact—late *fin del siglo* quests for anti-imperialism, politics, and subaltern difference.

I want to conclude by illustrating some of the broad themes of my recently completed book *Border Matters* by considering the effects of shifting critical paradigms in American studies away from linear narratives of immigration, assimilation, and nation-hood. Is it possible to imagine new cultural affiliations and nego-tiations in American studies more dialogically or in terms of mul-tifaceted migrations across borders? How do musicians, writers, and artists communicate their dangerous‚crossroads to us? How do documented and undocumented migrants in the US-Mexico borderlands secure spaces of survival and self-respect in regions undergoing what social theorists call "deindustrialization," the decline of traditional manufacturing? What kinds of cultural for-mations are thematized by artists who sing about regions such as "El Valle de Silicon," in Northern California, where workers now produce computer chips instead of fruits and vegetables?

In the early 1970s, Los Tigres del Norte, together with their musical director, Enrique Franco, "illegally" migrated from north-ern Mexico to San Jose, California. Los Tigres del Norte have had a significant historical importance to *norteño* music in California (both Alta and Baja); they were one of the first undocumented bands to receive a Grammy Award for best regional Mexican-American recording, for their album *Gracias—America Sin Frontera* (Thanks—America Without Borders) in 1988. Los Tigres del Norte's use of what George Lipsitz calls "the circuits of commodity pro-duction and circulation"[29] allows us to bring forward one histori-cal, concrete instance in which the musical traditions of the US-Mexico border can be seen to have acquired a real historical valence. Franco's and Los Tigres del Norte's border *conjunto* music is simultaneously national, in that it has a direct impact on everyday life locally (Silicon Valley), and transnational, in that it tells us something about the limits of the national perspective in American studies.

In the story of Los Tigres del Norte's discrepant roots and routes, we can discover the shifting pattern of documented and undocumented border-crossing circulation. More importantly, the border migration of Los Tigres del Norte provides us with a little-known example of the problems that attended the passage of rural *norteño* musical forms to the mass cultural industries of the over-developed northern California region of Silicon Valley. Originally from Mocorito in the northern state of Sinaloa, Los Tigres del Norte migrated first to the border city of Mexicali before they were hired by a local musical promoter to reside in San Jose,

California. Since the early 1970s, they have lived and recorded their border music in Silicon Valley. Not until 1975, however, did their commercially successful "crossover" come, when they recorded the *corrido* "Contrabando y Tración." Los Tigres del Norte have now recorded over twenty-four albums, developed scores of musical anthologies, and even starred in and produced border movies and videos based on their popular songs, such as the international hit "Jaula de Oro" (The Gilded Cage).

I emphasize the band's undocumented migrations north from Mexico because, although Los Tigres are well-known in Mexico, Cuba, Latin America, and what Chicanos/Chicanas call "El Otro Mexico" (the other Mexico)—the Southwest, Midwest, and New York City—they are virtually unknown to cultural studies workers in our own backyard of Silicon Valley. As political scientist Jesús Martínez writes, "The musical styles and subject matters recorded by the group are alien to the values and life-styles of the rest of the population, reflective of the sharply segregated local order."[30]

It goes without saying, Martínez continues, that the real stars of Silicon Valley are the high-tech scientists, engineers, late capital managers, and multinational entrepreneurs such as the David Packards, William Hewletts, Steve Jobs, and Stephen Wozniaks. They are celebrated by the two hundred thousand Silicon Valley professionals who work at Apple, Hewlett-Packard, Borland, and IBM, among others.[31] At the low-tech end of the occupational spectrum are the scores of undocumented Mexican and Central American border-crossers who work in Silicon Valley mainly as janitors, assemblers, dishwashers, gardeners, secretaries, and so on. It is these undocumented workers who listen to, dance to, and consume the undocumented cultural soundings of Los Tigres del Norte. By posing the world as it is against the world as the socially subordinated would like it to be, the musical border culture of Los Tigres del Norte supplies what Paul Gilroy describes ethnoracial music in general as providing, "a great deal of the courage required to go on living in the present."[32]

In 1985, Los Tigres del Norte recorded the best-selling *corrido* "Jaula de Oro" (The Gilded Cage), a shattering portrait of an undocumented Mexican father and his family. The interlingual and accordion-driven ballad is an overflowing rush of lived feelings:

Aquí estoy establecido en los Estados Unidos. Diez años
pasaron ya en que crucé de mojado. Papeles no me he
arreglado. Sigo siendo ilegal.
(Here I am established in the United States. It has been
ten years since I crossed as a wetback. I never applied
for papers. I am still illegal.)

It focuses, like most *corridos,* on events of "particular relevance"
to the *conjunto* and *technobanda* communities:

Tengo mi esposa y mis hijos que me los traje muy
chicos, y se han olvidado ya de mi Mexico querido, del
nunca me olvido, y no puedo regresar.
(I have my wife and children whom I brought at a very
young age. They no longer remember my beloved
Mexico, that I never forget and to which I can never
return.)

¿De qué me sirve el dinero si yo soy como prisionero
dentro de esta gran nación? Cuando me acuerdo hasta
lloro aunque la jaula sea de oro, no deja de ser prisión.
(What good is money if I am like a prisoner in this great
nation? When I think about it, I cry. Even if the cage is
made of gold, it does not make it less a prison.)

"¿Escúchame hijo, te gustaría que regresáramos a vivir en
Mexico?" "What you talkin' about, Dad? I do not wanna go
back to Mexico. No way, Dad."
([Spoken] "Listen, son, would you like to return to live
in Mexico?" "What you talkin' about, Dad? I do not
wanna go back to Mexico. No way, Dad.")

Mis hijos no hablan conmigo. Otra idioma han
aprendido y olvidado el español. Piensan como
americanos niegan que son mexicanos aunque tengan mi
color.
(My children do not speak to me. They have learned
another language and forgotten Spanish. They think like
Americans. They deny that they are Mexican even
though they have my skin color.)

De mi trabajo a mi casa. Yo no sé lo que me pasa
aunque soy hombre de hogar. Casi no salgo a la calle
pues tengo miedo que me hallen y me pueden deportar.
(From my job to my home. I do not know what is
happening to me. I am a home-body. I almost never go
out to the street. I am afraid I will be found and de-
ported.)

—Profono Internacional, Los Angeles, 1985[33]

These lyrics dramatize, as anthropologist Leo Chávez suggests,
how the worker's and his family's undocumented status in the
United States "places limits on their incorporation into society."[34]
I hope they can serve as a pretext for my conclusion, a way of
exploring the hybrid and often recalcitrant quality of literary and
(mass) cultural forms in the extended US-Mexico borderlands:
linguistically hybrid because Los Tigres del Norte recorded an
interlingual (Tex-Mex accordion music and Spanish and English
lyrics) ballad setting the exemplary scene of hybridization; and
culturally recalcitrant because the *conjunto* band's hybrid verses
deconstruct what my colleague David Lloyd, in a different context, has called "the monologic desire of cultural nationalism."[35]
"Jaula de Oro" stands as a corrective to the xenophobic, nationalist, and racist "backlash" in the United States against the estimated four million undocumented workers in the United States,
with the great bulk of them (over two million) residing in California. To the undocumented troubadour-subject, the "jaula de oro"
is simultaneously the golden state of California and what used to
be called the American Dream. Looking at his family's incorporation into US society, the Mexican father feels tension everywhere
in California, imprisoning him both in his private and public
spheres. The street, his job, and even his home confine him, placing severe constraints on his movements. Everywhere "this great
nation" feels like a prison. A nightmarish culture of surveillance
and a profound sense of fear and anxiety pervade the undocumented worker's everyday life, north from Mexico.

This feeling in postmodern California of a proliferation of "new
repressions in space and movements"[36]—as Mike Davis finds in
City of Quartz—is doubly felt by the undocumented Mexican
worker and his family. In the 1990s, Davis asserts, an obsession

"with the architectural placing of social boundaries has become a zeitgeist of urban restructuring, a master narrative in the emerging built environment"[37] of our major cosmopolitan cities. While Los Tigres del Norte invoke this panopticon barrio-scape in "Jaula de Oro," the wild whirling fear the undocumented worker expresses is clearly something more than a response to the dizzying jolts of postmodern culture, for his anxiety speaks to the continuing desire in the United States for Anglocentric pure national spaces and for what Davis apocalyptically calls "a hoary but still viable. . .plan for a law and order Armageddon."[38]

In California and the rest of the United States, the idea that mostly brown undocumented workers and their children comprise a problem (or a set of problems) is part and parcel of what Bill Hing, a Stanford University law professor, sees as "the worst anti-immigrant hysteria in US history."[39] This is surely an exaggeration, for the ethnoracial history of California and the United States has been characterized by what multicultural historian Ronald Takaki calls rampant anti-immigrant "antagonisms."[40] Anti-immigrant racism assumes new forms and is articulated by both postliberal and neoconservative politicians alike. In crisis-bound California, for instance, anti-immigrant scapegoating (largely directed against undocumented Mexicans and Central Americans) endures and is created anew by draconian proposals to stop what the Republican governor of California describes as "the flood of illegal immigration."[41] Thus, Democratic Senator Dianne Feinstein calls for a $1 toll for border crossing with Mexico and Canada, Democratic Senator Barbara Boxer proposes a remilitarization of the US-Mexico border by assigning the National Guard to enforce border-crossing laws, and Governor Pete Wilson urges Congress to pass a constitutional amendment to deny legal citizenship to children born in the United States to undocumented workers.

Border Matters, like Los Tigres del Norte's "Jaula de Oro," proposes a different historical and (mass) cultural vision. We do not see the golden nation-state as being invaded by so-called illegal aliens, corrupting and polluting pure cultural spaces beyond the borderlands. We do not envision the border-crossing experience as racially pathological, requiring Senator Boxer's National Guard intervention. Nor do we understand the worker's and his family's undocumented status in the United States as separate from uneven global and hemispheric economic, political, and cultural factors. Rather, our projects make mass space for an alternative reading of what can now be called "the cultures of displacement"—a recognition hinted by the undocumented Mexican worker's vernacular assertion that he is irrevocably "established in the United States" by the simple fact that "it has been ten years since I crossed as a wetback." Ten years of laboring in California, paying taxes for Social Security, Medicare, and Medicaid, though denied the full services his taxes support—does this not count for legal and cultural citizenship?

Reading against the undocumented Mexican worker's deep and unreconstructed nostalgia for his *madre patria*—he laments that his children "no longer remember" his "beloved Mexico that [he can] never forget"—we are able to wonder how fully cognizant Los Tigres del Norte were in creating a mass cultural form that by its very hybridized form and content constantly transgresses the monology of cultural nationalism in the United States. "Jaula de Oro" is recalcitrant to the cultural and aesthetic politics of cultural nationalism. A significant challenge to nationalist monology occurs in the *corrido* when the son answers the question put to him in Spanish by the father, "¿Escúchame hijo, te gustaría que regresáramos a vivir en Mexico?" (Listen, son, would you like to return to live in Mexico?), in English, "What you talkin' about, Dad? I do not wanna go back to Mexico. No way, Dad." While the monolingual father despairs, the son's response in English hybridizes the *corrido's* cultural critique of anti-immigrant feelings; moreover, it points to Los Tigres del Norte's own hybrid formation in California, providing a renewed mass cultural ground for an alternative critique of the narrating of the nation.

Lastly, Los Tigres del Norte's "Jaula de Oro" functions as a highly danceable, musical structure. The group uses the well-known staccato riffs of the accordion as well as the tight three-part harmony and complex chord progressions of the polka to reach masses of documented and undocumented youth. The gliding movement of the dance itself, together with the accordion-driven tempo of the polka, forms what ethnomusicologist Manuel Peña calls "one symbolic structure."[42]

Los Tigres del Norte offer us an emblem of another America, eliciting both fear and wonder for them as undocumented border-

190 *José David Saldívar*

crossers. Their *corrido*, "Jaula de Oro," thematizes a critical method designed to shed light on the conflicts of boundary-crossings in the Americas (South to North and vice versa) and to draw out their unresolved hopes and sorrows about the Silicon Valley. My own hybrid New Historicist and cultural studies trackings have emphasized the processes of national hegemonies and the transnational circulation of capital. By juxtaposing earlier world systems (panoceanic and cultural) the New Historicism and cultural studies at our *fin del siglo* offer us alternate, discrepant diaspora and border networks that are redeemable as crucial political and aesthetic visions—worlds after "the West and the rest," after salutary anxiety and power, and after nativist Proposition 187s and so-called illegal aliens.

[1]Richard W. Fox and James T. Kloppenberg, *A Companion to American Thought* (Oxford: Blackwell, 1995), x.

[2]Américo Paredes, "On Ethnographic Work Among Minority Groups: A Folklorist's Perspective," in Richard Bauman, ed., *Folklore and Culture on the Texas-Mexican Border* (Austin, Tex.: University of Texas Press, 1993), 84.

[3]José Martí, *Nuestra América* (Habana: Imprenta y papeleria de Rambla y Bouza, 1891).

[4]I use the term "fantasmatics" to recall the use of that term by Jean Laplanche and J. B. Pontalis in which the identifiable locations of the subject are labile. See their "Fantasy and the Origins of Sexuality," in Victor Burgin, James Donald, and Cora Kaplan, eds., *Formations of Fantasy* (London: Methuen, 1986). The fantasmatic is to be understood not as an activity of an already formed subject but of the staging and dispersion of the subject into numerous identifiable positions.

[5]Amy Kaplan, "Left Alone with America: The Absence of Empire in the Study of American Culture," in Donald Pease and Amy Kaplan, eds., *Cultures of US Imperialism* (Durham, N.C.: Duke University Press, 1993), 11.

[6]Edward Said, "Traveling Theory," in Edward Said, *The World, the Text, and the Critic* (Cambridge, Mass.: Harvard University Press, 1983), 226–247.

[7]Raymond Williams, "Crisis in English Studies," in Raymond Williams, *Writing in Society* (London: Verso, 1981), 193.

[8]Ibid., 194.

[9]Ibid.

[10]Raymond Williams, *Marxism and Literature* (New York: Oxford University Press, 1977).

[11]Williams, "Crisis in English Studies," 194.

[12]Lauren Berlant, *The Anatomy of National Fantasy: Hawthorne, Utopia, and Everyday Life* (Chicago, Ill.: University of Chicago Press, 1991), 5.

[13]Williams, "Crisis in English Studies," 195.

[14]Ibid.

[15]Rael Meyerowitz, "Jewish Critics and American Literature: The Case of Sacvan Bercovitch," in Carol Colatrella and Joseph Alkana, eds., *Cohesion and Dissent in America* (Albany, N.Y.: State University of New York Press, 1994), 35.

[16]Rob Nixon, "Caribbean and African Appropriations of *The Tempest*," *Critical Inquiry* 13 (1987): 560.

[17]Steven Mullaney, *The Place of the Stage: License, Play, and Power in Renaissance England* (Chicago, Ill.: University of Chicago Press, 1987), vi–vii.

[18]Ibid., 7.

[19]Ibid., 9.

[20]Brooke Thomas, "On New Literary Historicism," in Richard W. Fox and James Kloppenberg, eds., *A Companion to American Thought* (London: Blackwell, 1995), 490.

[21]Stephen Greenblatt, *Shakespearean Negotiations: The Circulation of Social Energy in Renaissance England* (Berkeley, Calif.: University of California Press, 1988), 142.

[22]Ibid., 137.

[23]Ibid., 149.

[24]Ibid., 147.

[25]James Clifford, "The Transit Lounge of Culture," *Times Literary Supplement,* 5 May 1991, p. 1.

[26]Lawrence Grossberg, "Introduction," in Lawrence Grossberg, Cary Nelson, and Carla Treichler, eds., *Cultural Studies* (New York: Routledge, 1992), 2.

[27]Neil Larsen, *Reading North by South: On Latin American Literature, Culture, and Politics* (Minneapolis, Minn.: University of Minnesota Press, 1995), 191.

[28]Paul Gilroy, *There Ain't No Black in the Union Jack: The Cultural Politics of Race and Nation* (Chicago, Ill.: University of Chicago Press, 1991), 190.

[29]George Lipsitz, *Dangerous Crossroads: Popular Music, Postmodernism and the Poetics of Place* (London: Verso, 1994), 12.

[30]"Tigers in a Gold Cage: Songs of Mexican Immigrants in Silicon Valley," unpublished manuscript, 9.

[31]Ibid.

[32]Paul Gilroy, *The Black Atlantic: Modernity and Double Consciousness* (Cambridge, Mass.: Harvard University Press, 1993), 36.

[33]Lyrics to Los Tigres del Norte's "Jaula de Oro" can be found in Leo Chávez, *Shadowed Lives: Undocumented Immigrants in American Society* (San Diego, Calif.: Harcourt Brace Jovanovich, 1992), 158, 177.

[34]Ibid., 158.

[35]David Lloyd, "Adulteration in the Novel," in Alfred Arteaga, ed., *Another Tongue: Nation and Ethnicity in the Linguistic Borderlands* (Durham, N.C.: Duke University Press, 1994), 54.

[36]Mike Davis, *City of Quartz: Excavating the Future in Los Angeles* (London: Verso, 1990), 223.

[37]Ibid.

[38]Ibid.

[39]Bill Hing, quoted in Le Phung and L. A. Chung, "2.1 Million Illegals in California," *San Francisco Chronicle,* 7 August 1993, p. 1.

[40]Ronald Takaki, *A Different Mirror: A History of Multicultural America* (Boston, Mass.: Little, Brown, and Co., 1993), 7.

[41]Vlae Kershner, "Wilson's Plan to Curb Illegal Immigration," *San Francisco Chronicle,* 10 August 1993, pp. 1, A13.

[42]Manuel Peña, "The Emergence of Conjunto Music," in Richard Bauman and Roger D. Abrahams, eds., *And Other Neighborly Names: Social Processes and Cultural Images in Texas Folklore* (Austin, Tex.: University of Texas Press, 1981), 285.

Hilary Putnam

A Half Century of Philosophy, Viewed From Within

I N THIS COUNTRY, THE DEPARTMENTS THAT PRODUCE the majority of Ph.D.'s that will comprise the next generation of philosophy teachers are dominated by a single kind of philosophy, namely, "analytic philosophy." A typical graduate student might envision the history of the last fifty years as follows: until sometime in the 1930s American philosophy was without form and void. Then the logical positivists arrived, and about fifty years ago most American philosophers became positivists. This development had the merit of bringing "high standards of precision" into the subject; philosophy became "clear" and everyone had to learn some modern logic. However, it had other consequences as well. The (supposed) central tenets of the logical positivists[1] were false— according to the stereotype, the logical positivists held that all meaningful statements are either 1) verifiable statements about sense data or 2) "analytic" statements, such as the statements of logic and mathematics. They believed in a sharp distinction between synthetic claims (i.e., empirical claims, which they identified with claims about sense data[2]) and analytic statements; they did not understand that concepts are theory-laden[3] or that there are such things as scientific revolutions.[4] They thought that the philosophy of science could be done in a wholly unhistorical way. At the end of the 1940s, W. V. Quine showed that ontological questions, such as whether numbers really exist, make sense[5]—contrary to the logical positivist claim that all metaphysical questions

---

Hilary Putnam is Cogan University Professor at Harvard University.

are nonsense—and thereby contributed to the revival of realist metaphysics in the United States, even if he (regrettably) retained some positivist prejudices himself. Shortly thereafter, he determined that the analytic/synthetic distinction is untenable.[6] Later Quine showed that epistemology could become a part of natural science,[7] and I helped further demolish logical positivism by proving that the positivist dichotomy of "observational terms" and "theoretical terms"[8] was untenable. This paved the way for a robust metaphysical realism, which I (regrettably) gave up in the mid-1970s.

Although there are elements of truth here, one way in which this story is a distortion is in its account of what the logical positivists believed. The movement was diverse; the positivists did not think that philosophy could be done independently of the results of science.[9] Rudolf Carnap hailed Thomas Kuhn's book, *The Structure of Scientific Revolutions* (which presented a major case for the indispensability of the history of science to philosophy), and he is known to have been instrumental in getting it published.[10] These matters have been set right in the literature, even if the "oral tradition" has it otherwise. But there is a more subtle falsification in this account, namely, the claim that forty or fifty years ago logical positivism was dominant. It is true that if one is interested simply in the *internal* development of analytic philosophy, then the fact that the logical positivist professors were few in number is not important, since the views of many present-day analytic philosophers developed out of a criticism of the views of those few. Nevertheless, if we are not to rest content with a partly fictitious history of American philosophy, it is important to realize that *at the time* when logical positivism was supposed to have been dominant, logical positivists were extremely few and largely ignored. There was Rudolf Carnap (who did not produce a single Ph.D. student in the last ten years that he spent at the University of Chicago), Herbert Feigl in Minnesota, Hans Reichenbach at UCLA, and perhaps a few others. However, these people were quite isolated—Carnap had no intellectual allies at Chicago; Reichenbach had no intellectual allies at UCLA. Only at Minnesota, where Feigl created the Minnesota Center for the Philosophy of Science, was there a little bit of critical mass. Even Quine at Harvard had no permanent allies on the faculty until 1948, when Morton White[11] joined the department. Nor were these philosophers regarded as terribly important in the 1940s. At the end of the 1940s, most philosophers would have told their history in a way that few present-day analytic philosophers would be able to recognize. They would have recounted the rise and fall of pragmatism; they would have talked about the New Realists; they would have talked about Critical Realism (led by Roy Wood Sellars, whose son Wilfrid Sellars became one of the most distinguished American analytic philosophers); they would have talked about absolute idealism, which was waning but still had some distinguished representatives; but they would have regarded positivism as a matter of little consequence.

I do not mean to endorse this judgment: logical positivism was a movement that produced not only errors but also insights, and it richly deserved the attention that was later paid to it. But there were also real insights as well as errors in the writings of the American pragmatists, in the writings of idealists such as Josiah Royce, and in the writings of the New Realists and the Critical Realists.

In contrast to this fictitious history, let me cite my own experiences as an undergraduate and graduate student. At the University of Pennsylvania between 1944 and 1948 I know of no class (if we put aside a course taught by a graduate student, Sidney Morgenbesser) in which the writings of the logical positivists were so much as looked at. The department had one atypical pragmatist (West Churchman) but otherwise no one who was associated with a "movement" in philosophy. At Harvard between 1948 and 1949 I also cannot recall any courses in which the logical positivists were read, although I assume that Quine and White must have discussed them. At UCLA, from 1949 to 1951, Reichenbach was the only professor who either represented logical positivism (although he refused the label!) or discussed logical positivism. Harvard had one atypical pragmatist, C. I. Lewis, and UCLA had a Deweyan, Donald Piatt. American philosophy, not only in the 1940s but well into the 1950s, was decidedly unideological. If there were "movements" at individual departments, they were represented by one or two people. The present situation, in which American philosophy is dominated by a movement—a movement proud of how it differs both from what preceded it and from what it sees as the opposing tendency ("continental philosophy")—is utterly different from the situation that obtained in the field when I entered it.

1953–1960

Any account of a field over a fifty-year period must be based on an individual's perspective, and I shall continue to use my own experiences to draw a picture of the successive transformations. When I came to Princeton in 1953, the department had three full professors. Ledger Wood was the chairman, and within a few years he brought Gregory Vlastos and C. G. Hempel into the department. His first move towards transforming the department from a sleepy backwater was to hire four young men, myself and three recent graduate students from Harvard University.

Although five years earlier I had studied at Harvard for one year, these three Harvard men came from a milieu that was unknown to me. In a few short years, a group of graduate students at Harvard University had acquired something of a common philosophical orientation. The change appears to have been largely due to the influence of Morton White, who, in addition to assigning Austin and Strawson in his courses, had persuaded a number of the graduate students to spend a year at Oxford. The effect was that Oxford philosophy had reached Harvard, and these young teachers were wedded to something they called "ordinary-language philosophy." The point of that philosophy, as they understood it from reading Austin in particular, was that disaster occurs when philosophers—including philosophers who claim to be "scientific philosophers"—allow themselves to misuse ordinary language and especially to introduce what are in fact very unclearly explained "technical terms" into philosophical arguments. Questions of philosophic method had come to the fore and were the topic of most of our discussions.

At first my reaction was to scoff at "ordinary-language philosophy" and to defend what I called "rational reconstruction," that is, the idea that the proper method in philosophy was to construct formalized languages. Under the influence of Carnap, in particular, I maintained that philosophically interesting terms in ordinary language are too imprecise as they stand and that the task of philosophy is to "explicate" them, to find formal replacements for them. This is a view, however, that I quickly gave up because (to tell the truth) I found myself unable to give more than two or three examples of *successful* "rational reconstructions." I can almost remember the exact words that went through my head at that time: "If Carnap is right, then the proper task of philosophy is doing this thing called 'explication.' But what reason is there to think that 'explication' is *possible?* Moreover, even if we could come up with successful explications, *who* except Carnap thinks that scientists would really accept these explications, or adopt this artificial language to resolve controversies, and all that?"

In addition, I rejected the idea that one must *choose* between "rational reconstruction" and "ordinary-language philosophy." I felt that although one could learn a great deal from reading Reichenbach and Carnap on the one hand and Wittgenstein and Austin on the other, the totalistic philosophical methodologies that were being promulgated in their names were unrealistic.

My reasons for thinking that the version of ordinary-language philosophy that was being presented in the United States was unrealistic (when I visited Oxford as a Guggenheim Fellow in 1960, I came to appreciate how much richer the "real thing" was) were as short and simple as my reasons for thinking that "rational reconstruction" was also unrealistic. Reading Austin, I had appreciated the point I mentioned earlier, that confusion is often rampant when philosophers misuse ordinary language. That one should, as far as possible, try to do philosophy *in* ordinary language seemed indubitable. On the other hand, the idea that philosophy should be *about* ordinary language (or about the "ordinary use" of philosophically problematic expressions) was simply a non sequitur.[12] Indeed, I have never been able to believe that philosophy has a definitely delineated subject matter.

I have described a change in the mood of young philosophers, a change from *below*.[13] Older philosophers were, of course, necessarily involved. I have mentioned Austin, Strawson, and Wittgenstein, whose influence from afar had obviously reached Harvard, and Quine, who was going to be at the very center of all the developments in American philosophy for the next two decades and beyond. Indeed, Quine was partly responsible for creating the new climate. I do not mean to suggest that the particular wave of enthusiasm for ordinary-language philosophy that affected Harvard, and was later to affect other American institutions,[14] was due to Quine (Quine had no great admiration for ordinary-language philosophy), but Quine's attack on the analytic-synthetic distinction made issues in the philosophy of language central for young thinkers in the field.[15] At any rate, when C. G. Hempel joined the Princeton philosophy department (as I recall, this was in 1955 or 1956) he had already become convinced that Quine's attack on that distinction was certainly correct, and this became a hot topic of discussion among the graduate students. But thinkers of my own generation continued to play a role in this debate. For example, at the end of the decade, in 1959, Noam Chomsky and Paul Ziff both spent a year at Princeton—Chomsky at the Institute for Advanced Study and Ziff as a visitor in the Philosophy Department. Paul Ziff's seminar on the philosophy of language, which Chomsky attended, became a center for discussion of these issues. Chomsky's *Syntactic Structures* had also appeared in 1957,[16] and the Chomskian image of language as a "recursive" system (a system of structures that could, in principle, be listed by a computer[17]) entered all of our philosophical vocabularies, as did the Ziffian image of meanings as a recursive system of conditions associated with the sentences of the language.[18]

My own work also began to influence discussion outside of the Princeton department by the end of the decade. I was in the habit of explaining the idea of a "Turing machine"[19] in my mathematical logic courses in those days. It struck me that in Turing's work, as in the theory of computation today, the "states" of the imagined computer (the Turing machine) were described in a very different way than is customary in physical science. The state of a Turing machine—one may call such states *computational* states— is identified by its role in certain computational processes, *independently* of how it is physically realized. A human computer working with paper and pencil, a mechanical calculating engine of the kind that was built in the nineteenth century, and a modern electronic computer can be in the *same* computational state, with respect to a particular computation that all three carry out, without being in the same physical state. I began to apply images suggested by the theory of computation to the philosophy of mind, and in a lecture delivered in 1960[20] I suggested a hypothesis that was to become influential under the name *functionalism*: that the mental states of a human being are computational states of the brain. To understand them (e.g., in a scientific psychology) it is necessary to *abstract* from the details of neurology, as we regularly abstract from the details of the "hardware" when we program or employ computers, and describe mental states entirely in terms of the sorts of computations that they are involved in. Mental states are like *software*, so to speak. I later rejected this hypothesis, but it continues to be popular, and it certainly connected with what was to become a continuing effort of many philosophers to bring philosophy and science into closer touch with one another. At that time, I also decided that one of the positivists' favorite dichotomies, the dichotomy between observational and theoretical terms, was untenable, and I published a paper that was influential in totally rejecting the Carnapian view that in science only "observation terms" need to be "directly interpreted."[21] To explain why this paper was so well received, I must discuss the issue of "realism."

"SCIENTIFIC REALISM"

The prominence that the term "realism" later came to have was, perhaps, presaged by a remark in my essay "What Theories Are Not" to the effect that certain positivist views are "incompatible with a rather minimal scientific realism." At that point, to be a realist was simply to reject positivism. This was the way that I (and most of the analytic philosophers of my generation) thought about realism as late as when I wrote the introduction to *Mathematics, Matter and Method*. In that introduction, dated September 1974, there is a section titled "Realism," which begins: "These papers are all written from what is called a *realist* perspective. The statements of science are in my view either true or false. . .and their truth or falsity does not consist in their being highly derived ways of describing regularities in human experience." What was all this about?

According to most of the positivists, the claim that a scientific theory makes about the world was supposed to be expressible in a language that employed (in addition to logical vocabulary[22]) only such "observation terms" as "red" and "touches." In principle, it was claimed, one could use "sense-datum terms," terms referring to "subjective experiences" rather than to physical objects, and still state the entire content of science. The idea is that science is just a device for predicting regularities in the behavior of "observables." Unobservables such as microbes are simply, the positivists claimed, "constructs" we introduce to help predict how observables behave.

It was against this philosophy of science (which sounded, to my ears, a little like Berkeleyan idealism) that I reacted to in "What Theories Are Not" and in subsequent essays, and I was joined by many others, including J. J. C. Smart, with whom I had developed a friendship at Princeton in the late 1950s.

In addition to rejecting positivism, we also emphasized that statements of science are either true or false. The connection was as follows: Since in the positivist view it is only formalized science as a whole that has empirical content, it may well be that certain individual scientific statements S are, in themselves, empty of empirical content in the sense that it would make no difference to what we would predict (given the body of accepted statements) if we accepted S or accepted its negation. For example, it may well be that the scientific theory of a given time, say 1970, is such that if you conjoin to it either the statement that the temperature in a certain place inside the sun is A or the statement that the temperature in that place is B, where A and B are very different temperatures, no new observational prediction results. In that case, on the view that we were criticizing, both those statements would simply lack truth-value, that is, they would be neither true nor false. If a few years later, when scientific theory had changed, those statements had become testable, they would *now* have truth-values, that is, they would now become true or false, depending on what the new observations show. To the objection that the very same statement cannot both possess and lack a truth-value, the positivists would reply, "It is not really the same statement," that the change in theory changed the *meaning* of the term "temperature." (In "What Theories Are Not" and in later papers such as "Explanation and Reference,"[23] I excoriated the positivists for doing violence to all of the notions of sameness of meaning and change of meaning that we have, either in ordinary language or in linguistics, for the sake of protecting their doctrine.) Two things are especially disturbing about such a view. First, if each new theory of atoms, genes, or the AIDS virus changes the very meaning of the term "atom" or "gene" or "AIDS virus," then there can be no such thing as *learning more* about atoms, or genes, or AIDS; any discovery that purports to add to our knowledge about one of these things is actually a discovery about something we never talked or thought about before. The only thing that scientists can learn more about is *observables;* theoretical terms are nothing more than prediction devices according to such a view. (That is why in "Explanation and Reference" I characterized the view as a form of idealism.) Second, if we recognize that observational terms are themselves *theory-laden,* then it would follow that they too must change in meaning with every change in theory. This would lead to the Kuhnian conclusion that different scientific theories are *meaning incommensurable,* making it unintelligible that one can so much as *understand* earlier scientific theories.[24]

If what "scientific realism" meant to philosophers like myself at the beginning of the 1960s was simply the rejection of positivism and, more generally, of the idea that the statements of the natural sciences require *philosophical reinterpretation,* within a few years it was to develop into an elaborated metaphysical position, or rather a pair of positions (each of which has many versions). The first position, which I shall call "panscientism," holds that philosophical problems are fated, in the end, to be resolved by the progress of the natural sciences, and that the best the philosopher can do is to anticipate that progress and suggest how the sciences can solve them. The second position, for which I shall employ a term introduced by Simon Blackburn but which I will use in a wider sense, I call "quasi-realism." This position does not claim that all philosophical problems will be solved by natural science, but it does hold that the complete description of reality as it is "in itself" is given by natural science and, in most versions of the position, by *physics.* The idea that there is a sharp distinction between the way things are "in themselves" and how they appear to be, or how we speak of them as being, is characteristic of the position. What distinguishes the second position from the first is the idea that many of the ways we speak—and, indeed, *have* to speak—do not correspond to the way things are in themselves but represent "local perspectives." (As Bernard Williams, who introduced the notion of "local perspectives," uses the notion, a "local perspective" may be local in the sense of being the perspective of a particular culture—this is how he understands ethical language—or it may be "local" in the sense of depending on our particular human physiology—a "secondary quality," such as color, is supposed to be "local" in this sense.) To the extent that philosophy has to clarify and help us understand the status of these local perspectives, it has tasks over and above those of the natural sciences. The "local perspectives" do not, however, have any real metaphysical significance; only natural science has that. Paul and Patricia Churchland, Daniel Dennett, and Jerry Fodor, notwithstanding their substantial disagreements, are all representatives of the first position; as representatives of the second position, again notwithstanding substantial philosophical disagreements, I will cite Simon Blackburn and Bernard Williams. Of course, not all analytic philosophers are either panscientists or quasi-realists; but these two attitudes have very much come to dominate the scene in "analytic metaphysics." But I am getting ahead of myself.

OXFORD IN 1960

I spent the fall semester of 1960 at Oxford University. The four philosophers with whom I spent the most time were Elizabeth Anscombe, Philippa Foot, Paul Grice, and James Thomson, and not one of them fit the stereotype of a philosopher preoccupied with "the ordinary use of words." Anscombe was interested in just about every question in philosophy, and although she had been a student and close friend of Wittgenstein's, her own philosophical style is markedly different. At that time, she and Philippa Foot were developing a new approach to ethics, one that stresses the evaluation of character rather than the evaluation of actions (it has acquired the name "virtue ethics").[25] Other Oxford moralists (who mostly combined utilitarianism with noncognitivism in ethics) sneered at the new approach, but it continues to flourish today and has enormously enriched moral philosophy. James Thomson was becoming strongly interested in Chomskian linguistics, and, partly for this reason, I was able to persuade him to join me at MIT, where, from 1961 to 1965, I founded a graduate program in philosophy. And within three or four years, Paul Grice developed an approach to the theory of meaning that remains enormously influential to this day. It is sometimes said that "ordinary-language philosophy" began to decline about this time; it would be more accurate, I think, to say that the reality never fit the stereotype and that as time went by, the stereotype disappeared. But the individual *figures* at Oxford—one should, of course, add the names of Dummett, Hampshire, Ryle, Strawson, and still others to the list—not only did not disappear from the scene, but they continue to be discussed to the present day. It is just that, with the exception of Ryle (whose *Concept of Mind,* however, contains insights derived from his early interest in phenomenology!), they ceased to be thought of as "ordinary-language philosophers" and began to be treated as individual philosophers with distinctive contributions.

The later career of Paul Grice deserves a bit of description. When I met Grice, he was still grieving for Austin, who had died a few months before, and was, I believe, consciously trying to be a loyal Austinian; but within the next few years he was to break radically with Austin's way of doing philosophy (he would also leave Oxford for Berkeley). One aspect of that break is especially important. Austin's view represented a kind of *radical pragmaticism,* a view that is today represented by the brilliant work of Charles Travis.[26] According to Austin, the meanings of the words in a sentence do not by themselves determine exactly what is being said in a particular context; many different things may be said by using those same words with those meanings.[27] Grice, whose view is widely accepted today (although I myself agree with Austin's view), held that, on the contrary, there is such a thing as the standard meaning of a sentence and that the various "nonstandard" things we can use a sentence to say are all to be explained by what he called "conversational implicatures."[28] Pragmatics studies these conversational implicatures, while semantics, which is sharply distinguished from pragmatics, studies those "standard meanings."

THE RISE OF PANSCIENTISM

In 1961 I resigned from Princeton so that I could create a new graduate program in philosophy at MIT. If the scene (at least among the junior faculty) at Princeton in the 1950s represented the way in which a new generation of American philosophers was beginning to label itself as "analytic," the scene at MIT in the years I was there (1961–1965) represented how the content of that label was already changing. Although there were already philosophers at MIT, including Irving Singer and briefly John Rawls, the core of the new program consisted of myself, James Thomson, Judith Jarvis Thomson, and the two "Jerries": Jerry Fodor and Jerrold Katz. The five of us were close to Noam Chomsky, interested in the new "generative" linguistics, and attracted to the idea that computational modeling of the mind, generative grammar, and "semantics" were destined to solve the problems of the philosophy of mind and the philosophy of language (or at least to reformulate them as straightforward scientific problems[29]).

Quine's influence also played a huge role here, as it has continued to do to the present day. Although we thought that Quine's idea that psychology is the successor subject to epistemology was too simple, Quine's insistence that all philosophical problems are problems about the nature and content of science (because all knowledge is either science or aspires to be science) and the idea that philosophical problems about science are themselves to be solved *within* science appealed to us.[30]

Although I was aware of unresolved difficulties, for many years I too followed Quine in portraying logic (and mathematics) as empirical. For Quine, this does not have the same meaning as it does for a traditional empiricist—e.g., John Stuart Mill—that is, it does not mean that mathematics directly concerns the sensible or physical world. Quine is quite happy to posit a world of separately existing mathematical objects, e.g., sets, functions, and numbers. In this respect he is a Platonist of sorts. What it means, and here Quine parts company with more traditional Platonists like Gödel, is that positing the existence of a separate world of abstract entities is ultimately justified by the utility of the posit in *this* world. In line with this view, I defended Quine's "indispensability argument"[31] in the epistemology of mathematics—the argument that the justification for accepting mathematics is simply that it is indispensable in sciences that are unquestionably empirical, in particular in physics. As for the idea that even *logic* is empirical (in the sense of being revisable for empirical reasons), in 1960 the physicist David Finkelstein had persuaded me that the best interpretation of quantum mechanics involved abandoning a traditional logical law, the distributive law of propositional logic[32]—an idea first advanced by one of the greatest authorities on quantum mechanics, John von Neumann.[33] I thought that just as Euclidean geometry had been overturned (shown to be empirically false) by General Relativity, so Aristotelian logic had turned out to be empirically false and had similarly been overturned by quantum mechanics. (I eventually had to give up the idea of interpreting quantum mechanics with the aid of von Neumann logic because of insuperable technical difficulties, but that was three decades later.[34])

I left MIT and joined the Harvard philosophy department in 1965. Although every one of my colleagues at Harvard has influenced my thinking, I propose to focus exclusively on three tendencies that are still represented in the Harvard department and that I believe to be important for the development of philosophy (and not just "analytic" philosophy) as a whole. One of these tendencies is virtually identical with the philosophy of an individual, that is, W. V. Quine. The same is true for the second of these tendencies; it is essentially the philosophy of John Rawls. And the third, which has to do with the continuing interest in Wittgenstein's later philosophy at Harvard, was represented by at least three members of the department when I joined it: Rogers Albritton, Stanley Cavell, and Burton Dreben. I shall talk about these tendencies and figures in turn.

QUINE

I have already spoken of the impact of Quine's rejection of the analytic/synthetic distinction and of his "naturalization" of epistemology on the changing climate of American analytic philosophy. Also important was his famous doctrine of the "indeterminacy of translation," defended at book length in *Word and Object*.[35] In the radical form in which Quine defended it, the doctrine implies that there is no fact of the matter as to what any term in a language refers to.[36] At first the doctrine found few converts (most scientific realists, in fact, simply rejected it outright), but a version of it was later to be defended by Donald Davidson and to be (cautiously) endorsed by Bernard Williams.[37] A fourth Quinian doctrine, however, was enormously influential and introduced a significant change in the whole nature of analytic philosophy, especially in the United States. This was Quine's doctrine of "ontological commitment."

To explain this doctrine we have to explain Quine's use of "ontology." The ontology of a theory, in Quine's sense, is simply the objects that the theory postulates. But how are we to tell what objects a theory (or the science of a given time) postulates? (Scientists sometimes talk about "glitches"—is science thereby "committed to an ontology" of glitches?) For that matter, what is to count as an "object"? Quine's answer to these questions is straightforwardly in the tradition of the mathematical logician-philosophers, Frege and Russell: ordinary language, these philosophers claim, is too vagrant and idiosyncratic to reveal when scientists postulate objects and which objects they postulate. To answer such questions we must "regiment" our language, as Quine puts it; we must tidy it up (talk of "glitches" will be eliminated as inessential, for example), and we must standardize our idiom (thus "some particles are charged" will turn into something like "there exist some things such that they are particles and they are charged"). Ideally, we should write out the sentences of science (or of the particular theory whose "ontology" we wish to determine) in the notation of quantification theory, the logic of such expressions ("quantifiers") as "there exists an x such that" and "every x is such that." After this has been done, the "ontology" of a theory will be revealed by the use it makes of the existential quantifier ("There exists something such that"). Implicit in this way of thinking, of course, is the assumption that "exists"—or the existential quantifier that replaces it in "regimented notation"—is a completely univocal notion.

If we accept Quine's view, we have to say that modern science commits us to the thesis that *numbers, electrons,* and *microbes* "exist" in exactly the same sense and are "objects" in exactly the same sense.[38] (An "object" is anything that "exists.") Thus Quine has asserted that numbers are "intangible objects,"[39] his reason being that mathematics postulates these intangible objects, and mathematics is indispensable for the greater part of modern science.

Since the days of logical positivism, "metaphysics" had been pretty much a dirty word; even the new scientific realists, like myself, did not say that they were doing metaphysics. Nor did

Quine claim this in his essay "On What There Is." But what gradually sank in was that if Quine was right in "On What There Is," then one could not claim any longer that the questions "Do numbers really exist?" and "Do sets really exist?" were "pseudo-questions," as the positivists had. And once the question as to the real existence of numbers and sets had been rehabilitated (and Quine, as I mentioned above, had offered his "indispensability argument" for the answer, "Yes, they do"), it was not long before arguments (sometimes in the same style) were offered in connection with such questions as "Do fictional objects really exist?" "Do possible worlds really exist?"[40] and so on. People became comfortable describing themselves as "metaphysicians," something that would have been incompatible with being an "analytic philosopher" only a few years before, and the expression "analytic metaphysics" began to be heard. American analytic philosophy, and later British analytic philosophy, began to have an "ontological style." A curious reversal of roles took place, in which Anglo-American analytic philosophy, after having conceived of itself as anti-metaphysical during the positivist period, came to be the most proudly metaphysical movement on the world philosophical scene.

RAWLS

After the appearance of his monumental *A Theory of Justice* in 1970,[41] John Rawls began to have a highly significant impact on analytic philosophy. The logical positivists had not regarded ethics as a possible subject at all, although there was a subject called "metaethics" (devoted to showing *why* ethics is not a possible subject). Although a few brave analytic philosophers had continued to do ethics during the intervening years (I have already mentioned the "virtue ethics" of Elizabeth Anscombe and Philippa Foot), the field had been rather in the doldrums. With the publication of *A Theory of Justice,* however—which coincided with enormously important debates in American public life about the rightness or wrongness of the welfare state and over the requirements of social justice—ethics became extremely important, and once again large numbers of graduate students began to specialize in it. There is, however, a sense in which the Rawlsian revolution was quite contained. Insofar as *A Theory of Justice* presupposed an epistemology at all, that epistemology centered on the notion of "reflective equilibrium." Rawls credited this idea to Nelson Goodman's proposal that what we have to do in philosophy is to give up the futile search for necessary truths and—observing that the principles we in fact have are always in conflict with the ways in which we resolve some of the cases that we treat as clear in real life—engage in a process of "delicate mutual adjustment." In other words, by simultaneous reflection on both the principles and cases with which we start, we have to gradually (and experimentally) revise both the principles and the "intuitions" about the individual cases until we arrive at a stable equilibrium. As a sensible alternative to apriorism, it is hard to quarrel with this; but philosophers concerned with the questions raised by the logical positivists—"How do we know that ethical sentences are not just expressions of subjective attitudes? How do we know that they can have a truth-value (i.e., be either true or false) at all?"—will want a *philosophical argument,* which, in the nature of the case, would seem to have to come from metaphysics, epistemology, or the philosophy of language, against the positivist claim that such sentences are "cognitively meaningless." "Sure you might arrive at what you call 'reflective equilibrium,'" the positivist will say, "but that is just a fact about *you.* Someone else might arrive at a totally different equilibrium."

In subsequent publications, the most recent of which is *Political Liberalism* (1993) but starting already in his Presidential Address to the American Philosophical Association (1974),[42] Rawls denied the need for such a defense of his methodology from epistemology, metaphysics, or the philosophy of language; today the search is for a set of ethical claims whose "objectivity" consists simply in the fact that, in Western democracies with a certain political history, it is possible to find an "overlapping consensus" on their correctness, or on the correctness of ethical ideals and norms that presuppose them—at least, this is the most that the Rawlsian philosopher tries to demonstrate. (The idea being that if citizens agree to bracket their theological and metaphysical disagreements, they can still find a consensus on a number of specific principles of justice.) A normative ethics that disclaims from the outset any concern with metaphysics or epistemology, and which announces that what it is engaged in is "politics, not metaphysics," does not pose any kind of threat to the various self-understandings of analytic philosophy, and in particular not to what I earlier described as the "panscientistic" and the "quasi-realist" understandings of the task of philosophy.

It is not the case, however, that all the philosophers who believe that science delivers the whole truth about reality deny the possibility of true statements in ethics. *Some* of them do (e.g., John Mackie and Gilbert Harman argued in well-known books against the possibility of any such thing as ethical knowledge[43]); some tried to develop "in-between" positions—Bernard Williams has argued that while ethical statements can be "true," their "truth" is not absolute but only reflects the perspective of "some social world or other"[44]—but a group of scientific realists led by Richard Boyd, reviving the old naturalist tradition in ethics, have tried to argue that the predicate "good" does, in fact, pick out a "natural kind," concerning which it is possible in principle to build a scientific theory. However, the great majority of philosophers who interest themselves in normative ethics in Anglo-American philosophy departments today probably follow Rawls's lead in avoiding metaphysical controversy.

WITTGENSTEIN AT HARVARD

Three Harvard philosophers were interested in the philosophy of Wittgenstein when I arrived in 1965.[45] There were, naturally, certain differences in their interpretations, some of which I shall describe. But there were also large areas of agreement. In particular, they quickly convinced me that a version of Wittgenstein's later philosophy due to Norman Malcolm that I had criticized in several papers,[46] which made Wittgenstein little more than a disguised positivist, missed the real thrust of that philosophy. Under the influence of these readers I came eventually to see Wittgenstein as doing something quite different from offering a "philosophical position."

The easiest way for me to characterize the way I now understand what Wittgenstein was doing is by means of an example. For analytic philosophers who believe as Quine does that "exists" is a perfectly univocal notion, the questions "Do numbers really exist?" "How do we know that numbers really exist?" and "Is

Quine's indispensability argument really a good argument?" are all perfectly clear. We understand the meaning of "exist" when it is used in such mathematical statements as "There exist prime numbers greater than a thousand"; hence we must understand "There exist prime numbers" and "There exist numbers." We can ask whether we are justified in accepting mathematics with its "commitment" to "the existence of intangible objects" (the numbers). For Wittgensteinians, however, the idea that when a mathematician asserts that there is a prime number between ten and one hundred he has *asserted that there is an intangible object* with a certain relation to other *intangible objects* is a piece of confusion. While we use the same formal logical rules in operating with the existential quantifier "there exists" in mathematics as in empirical contexts, nevertheless, the use of "existence" statements in mathematics is *enormously* different from the use of empirical existence statements such as "There exist animals that can echo-locate." The idea that when we use "there exists" in mathematics we are talking about objects at all, albeit "intangible" ones, is a confusion.

This conclusion is one to which a logical positivist might also come, but his way of arriving at it would be very different. For the positivists, this conclusion is arrived at by applying the analytic/synthetic distinction and the "verifiability theory of meaning." According to the verifiability theory, there are two and only two (quite different) conditions for a statement being "cognitively meaningful," and hence there are two quite different sorts of cognitively meaningful statements. A statement is cognitively meaningful, according to the positivist's original verifiability theory, if either it can be empirically tested or it is decidable by purely logical and mathematical means.[47] For the positivist, it follows at once that mathematical existence statements belong to a wholly different class than empirical existence statements. The former are "analytic" and the latter are "synthetic" or "empirical" (the positivists treated the latter terms as synonyms). But in his later philosophy, Wittgenstein rejected the idea that there is such a thing as "the" criterion of meaningfulness. The Wittgensteinian has to begin with the sense most of us have that there is something extremely "fishy" about calling the number five an "intangible object" and getting worried about whether it "really exists," and explore very carefully and patiently why it is that we feel impelled to talk this way, and feel that unless we can talk this way, then mathematics totters. For the Wittgensteinian, the idea that the "indispensability argument" is *really* analogous to the experimental proofs a physicist offers for the existence of an unobserved particle is just an additional manifestation of the same confusion.[48]

This connects with the question of whether philosophical questions really are similar to questions in empirical science. Like Wittgenstein, I believe that the answer is "no," but after Quine's powerful attacks on the analytic/synthetic distinction, we who agree with this answer will have to show that it is not inconsistent to say that an investigation is conceptual *and* characterized by fallibility;[49] the claim that philosophy is able to arrive at *any* species of *infallible* knowledge is simply no longer credible.

Some interpreters of Wittgenstein, including Burton Dreben, tend to stress the moment in Wittgenstein's philosophy in which a question of traditional philosophy, or a "conclusion" of traditional philosophy, is revealed as a confusion. Their purpose is not, of course, to replace traditional philosophy with a new system, like the many systems of thought produced by logical positivism in the course of its development, but to free us of the illusion that we have here a set of important issues. In so doing, they are, I believe, making a point of fundamental importance, but one that is easy for present-day philosophers to misunderstand. I say "present-day philosophers" because the idea that some philosophical problems are illusory is not a new one in the history of philosophy; it plays a central role in as pivotal a work as Kant's *Critique of Pure Reason*. But for the most part the philosophers who find Wittgenstein's thought difficult to grasp are people who have little time for Immanuel Kant. In *their* memories, the idea that there are "pseudoproblems in philosophy" is inextricably linked to the name of Rudolf Carnap and to logical positivism. Thus, it is natural for them to suppose that the Wittgensteinians' denial of the intelligibility of certain philosophical issues *must* stem from a commitment to the positivist "verifiability theory of meaning," even if they deny that it does. That one can come to see that a philosophical issue is a pseudo-issue by *working through the considerations that seem to make it not only genuine but somehow obligatory,* and not by bringing a "criterion of cognitive significance" to bear on it from the outside, is something that can take someone with training in analytic philosophy a long time to see (it certainly took *me* a long time to see), and Dreben has the remarkable ability to convey this Wittgensteinian insight to students (including his colleagues).

Yet there is another, not incompatible but perhaps supplementary, way of seeing the upshot of Wittgenstein's later philosophy. For Stanley Cavell's Wittgenstein, philosophical confusions are not just matters of language gone wrong, but an expression of deep human issues that also express themselves in a variety of other ways—political, theological, and literary.[50]

In this connection, I would remark that many of the problems Wittgenstein discusses have to do with our uneasy relation to the normative. By the "normative" I do not mean just *ethics*. Consider the normativity involved in the notion of following a rule. That there is a right and a wrong way to follow a rule is what Wittgenstein would call a "grammatical" truth; the notion of a rule goes with the notions of doing the right thing and doing the wrong thing, or giving the right answer and giving the wrong answer. But many philosophers feel that they have to reduce this normativity to something else; they seek, for example, to locate it in the brain, but then it turns out that if the structures in the brain lead us to follow rules correctly, some of the time they also lead us to follow them incorrectly. (One can, of course, say with the Chomskians that there is a difference between the brain's "competence" and its "performance," but this is just to say that even in describing the brain we have to employ normative distinctions; what it means to follow a rule *correctly* is not really *explained* by saying, "One follows a rule correctly when one's brain behaves according to its competence, and one follows it incorrectly when one's brain makes a performance error." One is just *restating* the fact that one started with—the fact of the normativity of rule following—in a special jargon.) In the past, philosophers who saw that reductive accounts of rule following did not work either posited mysterious mental powers or Platonic entities to which the mind was supposed to have a mysterious relation. Both in the case of the scientistic reductionist and the old-fashioned metaphysician, the impulse is the same: to treat normativity, that is, the rightness of going one way as opposed to another, as if it were a *phenomenon* standing in need of a *causal* explanation (either an ordinary scientific explanation or a, so to speak, "superscientific" explanation). Wittgenstein's response was to challenge the idea that normative talk needs to be "explained" in one of these ways, indeed, to challenge the idea that there is a problem of "explanation" here.

From the outset of *Philosophical Investigations,* comfort and discomfort with the normative are associated with comfort and discomfort with the messiness of language—with the fact that language that is perfectly useful in its context may utterly fail to satisfy the standards of "precision" and "clarity" imposed by philosophers and logicians; indeed, with our desire to deny all of this messiness, to force language and thought to fit one or another impossibly tidy representation. "Cognitive scientists" (or philosophers who think of themselves as such), in particular, often speak as if there were an *essence* of believing, as if, for example, believing something were a matter of "the brain's putting a sentence in its *belief box.*" (I kid you not.) At the beginning of *Philosophical Investigations,* Wittgenstein emphasizes that such words as "believe," "question," and "command" represent (practically speaking) many different things. The desire in contemporary scientific realism to represent all questions as of one kind, as, in effect, empirical questions, and all justifications as of one kind, as empirical justifications, is simply another manifestation of the tendency to force a single representation on what is in no sense one unified phenomenon. Wittgenstein wants not to clarify just our concepts, but to clarify *us;* and, paradoxically, to clarify us by teaching us to live, as we must live, with what is unclear. On such a reading, a concern with Wittgenstein and a concern with personal and social transformation are not only not incompatible, but they can reinforce one another.

"THE MEANING OF 'MEANING'"

The ideas that I have just described did not substantially affect my thinking until the 1980s. But in 1966–1967, first in a philosophy of language class and then in lectures given at an NEH Summer Institute on the Philosophy of Language, I began to develop some new ideas about meaning—ideas not at all inspired by a desire to see how natural science could solve philosophical problems but rather by a negative reaction to the views that I had held when I was at MIT. According to those views, speakers' knowledge of the meaning of their words amounted simply to the tacit knowledge of a battery of "semantical rules" stored "inside their heads." What I had come to realize by 1966 was that the whole image of language as something that is entirely "inside the head" of the individual speaker had to be wrong. A number of considerations, which I will not review here, convinced me that the familiar comparison of *words to tools* is wrong, if the "tools" one has in mind are tools that one person could in principle use in isolation, such as a hammer or a screwdriver. If language is a tool, it is a tool like an ocean liner, which requires many people cooperating (and participating in a complex division of labor) to use. What gives one's words the particular meanings they have is not just the state of one's brain, but the relations one has to both one's non-human environment and to other speakers.

While this idea at first fell on more or less deaf ears, when I presented it at much greater length in a paper I wrote at the end of 1972 entitled "The Meaning of 'Meaning,'"[51] it found a surprisingly warm reception (partly because of its consonance with ideas in Kripke's celebrated lectures on "Naming and Necessity,"[52] which had been given in 1970 at Princeton), and at least this much of it— the idea that any complete account of meaning must include factors outside the head of the speaker—may by now even have become "orthodoxy" in the philosophy of language. (Please note, however, that this particular view did not arise from the program of "scientific realism" to which I had previously felt such strong attraction.) Also, starting about 1972, I became preoccupied with a problem with which Quine had long been concerned: how (and Quine would say, *if*) words could have determinate reference at all.

REFERENCE AND MODEL THEORY

The way in which this came to be a problem for me was as follows: like most people who subscribed to the computational model of the mind, I believed that when we see or hear events in the world, what actually happens is that certain visual or auditory sense data are produced in our minds/brains. Those sense data are what the mind/brain processes *cognitively*. The relation between the tables and chairs we perceive and the sense data is, on this picture, simply a matter of causal impacts on the retina and on the eardrum, and of causal signals from the retina and the eardrum to processors in the brain; we have no direct *cognitive* relation to the objects of perception. Our sense data are, as it were, the *interface* between our cognitive processes and the world. (This is what Descartes's picture of the mind turns into when the mind is identified with the brain.) The possibility of holding that what we are immediately aware of in veridical perception is genuine properties of external things and not "representations" is one that I categorically rejected. On this neo-Cartesian picture of the mind, there seemed to be no problem as to how the mind (conceived of as a computer) could know the "subjective experiences" (the sense data) the person has, since these were supposed to be events inside the computer itself and thus "available" to the computer. But what does it mean to say that these experiences "represent" objects *outside* the mind/computer?

As we have seen, most analytic philosophers had repudiated the positivist view, according to which a scientific theory is basically a device for predicting subjective experiences. Yet on the philosophy of mind that I and other analytic philosophers found attractive, it was hard to see how the mind's understanding of a scientific theory could really go *beyond* what the positivists would allow. One can understand how the mind, conceived of as a computer, can "understand" a scientific theory in the sense of being able to use it as a prediction device; but how can it understand a scientific theory "realistically" (i.e., understand terms like "atom" and "microbe" as referring to real things) in the way I had been calling for ever since my essay "What Theories Are Not"?

At this point, certain results in mathematical logic occurred to me. Without going into technical details, it turns out that if there is a correspondence between terms in a language and things in the world at all (e.g., the relation of reference that we supposedly all have in mind), then there are infinitely many different ones that *make the same sentences true* (and not only in the actual world, but in all possible worlds!).[53] It at once follows that if there is a fact of the matter as to which correspondence is *the* relation of "reference" between words in my theory and items in the world, then that fact cannot be ascertained simply by making predictions and testing them. If A and B are two different correspondences such that it would make no difference to the truth of any sentence (in any possible world) whether A or B is *the* reference-relation, then, in particular, *no empirical test can possibly determine whether A or B is the "right" relation.* The very idea of a "right relation" threatens to become hopelessly metaphysical. Yet Quine's characteristically bold way of dealing with the problem, which is to deny that there is a "fact of the matter" about what our words refer to, has never been one I could accept.[54] On Quine's view, as he himself puts it, when I think I am referring to my cat Tabitha (or to my wife, or to my friend, or to myself) there is no fact of the matter as to whether my words designate Tabitha or "the whole cosmos minus the cat."[55] It has always seemed to me that a view that is so contrary to our whole sense of being in intellectual and perceptual contact with the world *cannot* be right.

Scientific realism seems only to exacerbate rather than resolve these deep problems, because for scientific realists there are only two possibilities: either reduce reference to notions employed in the physical sciences, which seems impossible, or say (with Quine) that it is an illusion that there is a determinate relation of reference. I began to move away from hard-core scientific realism partly for this reason and partly because I was discovering the important work of a philosopher who has always insisted that understanding the arts is as important as understanding science in understanding cognition. That philosopher is Nelson Goodman. I found myself agreeing with Goodman's insistence that the world does not have a "ready-made" or "built-in" description; many descriptions may "fit," depending on our interests and purposes. (This does not mean that anything we happen to like "fits." That more than one description may be right does not mean that every description is right, or that rightness is subjective.) While I could not agree when Goodman went so far as to say that there is not one "world" but many worlds and that these are of our own making,[56] I still find his work a continuing source of stimulation. At this time I also began to take seriously an idea that I had first heard from my pragmatist teachers at the University of Pennsylvania and UCLA: the idea that "value judgments," far from being devoid of "cognitive meaning," are actually presupposed in all cognition; fact and value interpenetrate.

This was the context in which I was led to put forward my first attempt at a middle way between antirealism and metaphysical realism ("internal realism") in the 1970s and 1980s.[57] While I still defend some of the ideas that were involved in that attempt (the denial that reality dictates one unique description and the conception of fact and value as interpenetrating rather than discrete are as central to my thinking now as they were then), the project as a whole now seems fatally flawed by its allegiance to the traditional conception of our sensations as an "interface" between us and the world.[58]

I was by no means the only philosopher who was beginning to be troubled by these problems. Michael Dummett was thinking about some of the same issues and attempting to develop a form of verificationism free of the phenomenalistic strain we saw in positivism. And in the same period Richard Rorty broke with scientific realism and moved in a direction that he associated first with Derrida's "deconstruction" and later with American pragmatism.[59] Like Quine, Rorty rejects the idea that there is any determinate reference relation between words and things, but (unlike Quine) he holds that statements of science have no greater right to be called "true" than statements that give us satisfaction in any one of a variety of other ways. "True," for Rorty, is simply an adjective we use to "commend" beliefs we like.

Although I could not accept Dummett's "verificationist semantics," and Rorty seemed to me perilously close to giving up the idea that there is a world out there at all, I was pleased that they saw some of the same difficulties with what had become the standard realist metaphysics in analytic philosophy that I was seeing.

THE HISTORY OF PHILOSOPHY RETURNS

I have described the way in which I came to see that philosophical difficulties about "how language hangs on to the world" are not going to be solved by further investigations in natural science, including computational models of the mind. This is something that the distinguished Canadian philosopher Charles Taylor had long argued, and Taylor, in particular, had insisted that those difficulties arise because certain ways of thinking seem obligatory to us. It is his contention that without an investigation into the *history* of that obligatoriness, an investigation that tries to uncover the genealogy of the conceptual changes that made Cartesianism (or Cartesianism *cum* materialism) seem the only *possible* way of thinking about the mind, we can never come to see how *contingent* some of the assumptions that generate our problems are; as long as we do not see *that,* we will remain stuck in those problems. This was, however, something that I was not yet ready to hear at the end of the 1970s when I was writing *Reason, Truth and History.* In 1980, however (influenced by Richard Rorty), I began to make a serious study of William James and was at once struck by James's insistence that the picture of our experiences as "inside" our minds (or our "heads") is an error. Earlier I had been aware of the possibility of denying the interface conception from a reading of Austin's *Sense and Sensibilia* but had rejected the idea. But when I rethought the issue in the 1980s, it became clear to me that (even if James's approach contained some untenable elements) James was right in thinking that the traditional conception must be given up.[60] In addition (with Ruth Anna Putnam) I began to study John Dewey's voluminous writings, which provide a way of thinking about ethical inquiry that avoids many of the standard dichotomies (absolute versus relative, instrumental versus categorical, and so on).[61]

About that time, I became aware that a philosopher I enormously respected, John McDowell, was urging the rejection both of the neo-Cartesian picture of the mind and of the fact/value dichotomy in which analytic philosophy seemed, for the most part, to be stuck. For many years, McDowell's views were available only in the forms of occasional articles and talks, but in 1991 he delivered the John Locke Lectures at Oxford (now published as *Mind and World*). My own Dewey Lectures on a number of related issues were delivered at Columbia University in 1994. In both sets of lectures a non-Cartesian view is spelled out with full reference to the history of philosophy (as urged by Charles Taylor). The long dominance of the idea that "philosophy is one thing and history of philosophy is another" is now visibly coming to an end. Or is this too optimistic an estimate?

THE (NON-)RECEPTION OF CONTINENTAL PHILOSOPHY

I cannot close without mentioning a feature of Anglo-American analytic philosophy that will not have escaped the notice of even a minimally-informed observer: the exclusion of "continental philosophy." (The leading Ph.D.-granting institutions rarely include texts by Foucault or Derrida in their courses, and the work of Jürgen Habermas has only begun to receive attention—and then usually only in ethics courses—fairly recently.) At first blush, this might seem astonishing; after all, philosophy is classified as one of the humanities, and French "theory" is taken very seriously indeed in the *other* humanities. This indifference of analytic philosophy departments to what interests the other humanities departments is not surprising, however, when one realizes that the self-image of analytic philosophy is scientific rather than humanistic. If one aspires to be a science (even if what one actually writes is closer to science fiction), then being different from the humanities will seem a positive virtue. Of course, not all philosophers in analytic departments are happy with this state of affairs. (A few respected figures, for instance, have studied and taught Husserl's phenomenology, or Habermas's philosophy, or even Heidegger's philosophy for years.) However, most analytic philosophers justify excluding texts by the authors just mentioned on the ground that these authors are "not clear" or that the texts (which they may not actually have read) "do not contain arguments." They do not admit that their own conception of philosophy is scientistic; usually, when analytic philosophy is criticized, its defenders equate their style of philosophy simply with "argument" and "clarity." But the Tractarian doctrine that "whatever can be said at all can be said clearly" has become dogma; since the demise of the notion of "logical form" on which the *Tractatus* was based, I have never heard anyone actually offer an argument for it. Good prose, whatever its subject, must communicate something worth communicating to a sensitive reader. If it seeks to persuade, the persuasion must not be irrational (which does not exclude the possibility that what is involved may be an appeal to *see* something one is refusing to see—say, the appeal of a way of life, or what actually goes on in our linguistic, or scientific, or ethical, or political practices, and not simply a deduction from already accepted premises, or the

presentation of evidence for an empirical hypothesis). The demand
that we only say what can be said in the sort of prose that Bertrand
Russell wrote, marvelous as that prose was, will, in fact, necessarily limit what one can talk about.

SHOULD ANALYTIC PHILOSOPHY CONTINUE?

This account of the changes in the character of American philosophy in the half century that I have been able to witness it is,
necessarily, from one perspective. I am aware that I have
underemphasized some brilliant contributions; the work of Donald
Davidson, Saul Kripke, David Lewis, Robert Nozick, and others
has, for example, received at best passing mention. In partial
exoneration, let me say that my concern has been to trace the rise
of what seem to be the currently dominant tendencies and the
beginning of a move away from what I see as the errors of those
tendencies. Davidson, Kripke, and Nozick have affected those
developments but in ways that it would not be easy to describe in
a narrative such as this. Because I have been largely critical of the
scientific realist tendency and its relatives (e.g., Bernard Williams's
materialism *cum* perspectivalism and Blackburn's "quasi-realism"),
it may also seem that I am calling for the end of analytic philosophy, and that is a matter about which I must say a word.

If "analytic philosophy" means, simply, philosophy that is informed by a knowledge of science, a knowledge of the achievements of modern logic, and a knowledge of the great works of past
analytic philosophers from Russell, Frege, Reichenbach, and Carnap
through the present, then I am most certainly *not* calling for an
end to it. I am concerned about certain tendencies in analytic
philosophy—by the tendency to scientism, the tendency to patronize the history of philosophy, the refusal to *hear* other sorts of
philosophy—but fighting those tendencies is not the same thing as
fighting analytic philosophy. As a philosopher whose own writing
is full of references to Frege, Russell, Wittgenstein, Quine, Davidson,
Kripke, David Lewis, and others, I count myself as an "analytic
philosopher" in that sense. But, to mention one last tendency of
which I disapprove, I see the tendency to think of analytic philosophy as a "movement" (a tendency that has led to the creation of
new—and exclusionary—associations of analytic philosophers in

several European countries) as a bad thing. From my point of view, the only legitimate function for "movements" in philosophy is to gain attention and recognition for ideas that are not yet being received or which have been neglected or marginalized. Analytic philosophy has been around a long time, and it is certainly one of the dominant currents in world philosophy. Making it into a "movement" is not necessary, and it only preserves the features I have deplored. Just as we can learn from Kant without calling ourselves Kantians, and from James and Dewey without calling ourselves pragmatists, and from Wittgenstein without calling ourselves Wittgensteinians, so we can learn from Frege and Russell and Carnap and Quine and Davidson without calling ourselves "analytic philosophers." Why can we not just be "philosophers" without an adjective?

ENDNOTES

[1]The views I describe as the *supposed* central tenets of the movement are defended in A. J. Ayer's famous popularization of logical positivism, *Language, Truth and Logic* (London: V. Gollancz, 1936). They have come to constitute the stereotype of what a logical positivist believed. This stereotype is accurate to this extent: the logical positivists believed that metaphysical statements are nonsense (although they did not agree on just which statements *are* "metaphysical") and that they can be distinguished from "cognitively meaningful" statements (the statements of science) by the fact that they are either empirically testable or decidable by appeal to logic (in which they included mathematics) and definitions (see endnote 47). Ethical statements, and value judgments generally, were also considered to be "nonsense" if they were thought of as expressing truths about the world, although they could be allowed a second-class sort of meaning if considered as "emotive" expressions, i.e., ways of expressing an attitude, appeals to others to share an attitude, and so on.

[2]That all positivists believed that all empirical truths are "about" sense data is perhaps the most persistent misconception. Even Rudolf Carnap's celebrated "Aufbau," in *Der Logische Aufbau der Welt* (Berlin: Weltkreis-Verlag, 1928), only claimed that sense data provide *one* possible way of reconstructing the statements of science, and Hans Reichenbach, *Experience and Prediction* (Chicago, Ill.: University of Chicago Press, 1938), was undisguisedly hostile to this sort of phenomenalism.

[3]In fact, the idea that all scientific concepts—in particular, observational ones—are theory laden figures significantly in papers by Neurath and Reichenbach from the early 1920s on.

[4]This is a misconception for which Thomas Kuhn's influential *The Structure of Scientific Revolutions,* 2d ed. (Chicago, Ill.: University of Chicago Press, 1970) is

perhaps chiefly to blame. Both Reichenbach and Carnap came into philosophy in the wake of a scientific revolution, the Einsteinian one, and the central question of Hans Reichenbach's *The Theory of Relativity and A Prior Knowledge* (Berlin: J. Springer, 1922; Berkeley, Calif.: University of California Press, 1965) was precisely how to account for scientific revolutions without being forced into the idea that theories before and after such a revolution are "incommensurable," which Kuhn was later to advocate.

⁵"On What There Is" (1948), collected in W. V. Quine, *From a Logical Point of View* (Cambridge, Mass.: Harvard University Press, 1953).

⁶"Two Dogmas" (1950), collected in Ibid. Because the positivist way of allowing some empirically untestable statements—the statements of pure mathematics—into the class of the "cognitively meaningful" while banning "metaphysics" depended on a sharp, analytic/synthetic distinction, Quine's critique of the distinction helped to make the "science/metaphysics" distinction suspect among philosophers.

⁷"The Scope and Language of Science" (1957), collected in W. V. Quine, *The Ways of Paradox* (Cambridge, Mass.: Harvard University Press, 1976); and "On Epistemology Naturalized," in W. V. Quine, *Ontological Relativity* (New York: Columbia University Press, 1969).

⁸This dichotomy figured in Carnap's work after about 1939. It was assumed that "observation terms" (e.g., "blue," "touches") referred only to observables, and that the distinction between statements that function as observation reports and statements that function as theoretical postulates could be drawn as follows: the former contain only observation terms, while the latter must contain at least one theoretical term. In Hilary Putnam, "What Theories Are Not" (1960), collected in Hilary Putnam, *Mathematics, Matter and Method* (Cambridge: Cambridge University Press, 1975), it was shown that both of these assumptions are untenable.

⁹Cf. Michael Friedman, "Logical Positivism Re-Evaluated," *Journal of Philosophy* LXXXVIII (10) (October 1991): 505–519.

¹⁰See G. A. Reisch, "Did Kuhn Kill Logical Empiricism?" *Philosophy of Science* 58 (1991): 264–277. My thanks to Gerald Holton and Jordi Cat for this reference.

¹¹Morton White was not a positivist, but he took positivism seriously, as well as Oxford philosophy and American pragmatism.

¹²I have not seen Wittgenstein as an "ordinary-language philosopher" in this sense for a very long time, and I regard Austin's real importance as quite transcending his allegiance to this idea.

¹³White, who played a role in the change at Harvard, was both the youngest and the most recent arrival in the department (see also endnote 11).

¹⁴Cornell University, in particular, had a "Wittgensteinian" philosophy department for a number of years.

¹⁵As mentioned in endnote 6, in the context of the debates over logical positivism, Quine's attack on the analytic/synthetic distinction also undermined the whole idea of a "science/metaphysics" distinction.

[16]Noam Chomsky, *Syntactic Structures* ('s Gravenhage: Mouton, 1957).

[17]The recursive functions are a class of functions that, according to a thesis ("Church's Thesis") argued for by Alonzo Church and Alan Turing in the 1930s, exactly comprises the functions that a computer can in principle compute. Chomsky's linguistic theory has retained two central contentions in all its various forms: *1)* that the grammatical structures of a natural language are much more complex than traditional grammars ("phrase structure grammars") allowed, but *2)* that these more complex structures can still be described by using a formalism for the theory of recursive functions (and computational processes in general) first devised by Emil Post, an American contemporary of Turing's.

[18]Paul Ziff, *Semantic Analysis* (Ithaca, N.Y.: Cornell University Press, 1960). Today, graduate students generally suppose that this idea originated with Donald Davidson, "Truth and Meaning," *Synthese* XVII (3) (1967), and Ziff's book is, sadly, seldom recalled.

[19]"Turing machines" are abstract devices (at least they existed only as mathematical abstractions when Alan Turing described them in the 1930s) that form the basis for the modern theory of computation.

[20]"Minds and Machines," collected in Hilary Putnam, *Mind, Language and Reality* (Cambridge: Cambridge University Press, 1975).

[21]Putnam, "What Theories Are Not." This influence was partly due to a certain confluence of attacks on the Carnapian view. As Frederick Suppe describes what happened, in the preface to *The Structure of Scientific Theories* (Urbana, Ill.: University of Illinois Press, 1974), there were attacks of two sorts: "First there were attacks on specific features of the received view. . .designed to show they were defective beyond repair [this is how he classifies my attack]. Second, there were alternative philosophies of science advanced [Hanson, Kuhn, and Toulmin] which rejected the received view out of hand and proceeded to argue for some other conception of science and of scientific knowledge." Ibid., 4.

[22]This logical vocabulary was sometimes allowed to include the resources of higher-order logic or, alternatively, set theory. Cf. Rudolf Carnap, "The Methodological Character of Theoretical Concepts," in H. Feigl and M. Scriven, *Minnesota Studies in the Philosophy of Science*, vol. I of *The Conceptual Foundations of Psychology and Psychoanalysis* (Minneapolis, Minn.: The University of Minnesota Press, 1956).

[23]Reprinted as Putnam, *Mind, Language and Reality*, chap. 11.

[24]Donald Davidson's "The Very Idea of a Conceptual Scheme," *Proceedings and Addresses of the American Philosophical Association* 67 (1973–1974), contains a powerful (and celebrated) argument against the coherence of the idea of meaning incommensurability.

[25]Anscombe's "Modern Moral Philosophy" (1958) represented a call for this new approach. This is collected in G. E. M. Anscombe, *Ethics, Religion, and Politics*, vol. 3 of *The Collected Philosophical Papers of G. E. M. Anscombe* (Oxford: Blackwell, 1981).

[26]Charles Travis, *The Uses of Sense: Wittgenstein's Philosophy of Language* (Oxford: Oxford University Press, 1989).

[27]Consider, for example, the sentence "The table is covered with coffee." This may, depending on the context, mean that there are cups of coffee on the table, or that coffee has been spilled on the table, or that there are bags of coffee on the table. Yet in all of these uses, "coffee," "table," and "covered" have their standard "meanings."

[28]For a powerful critique of Grice's view, see Charles Travis, "Annals of Analysis," *Mind* 100 (398) (April 1991): 237–264.

[29]For example, the traditional mind-body problem was supposed to become simply the problem of the relation of the brain's "software" to its "hardware."

[30]See Quine, "The Scope and Language of Science" and Quine, "On Epistemology Naturalized."

[31]Cf. Hilary Putnam, *Philosophy of Logic* (1971), reprinted as part of Putnam, *Mathematics, Matter and Method,* 2d ed.; and Quine, "On What There Is."

[32]In its simplest form, this says that "p(q or r)" is equivalent to "pq or pr."

[33]See Hilary Putnam, "Is Logic Empirical?" (1968), reprinted as "The Logic of Quantum Mechanics" in Putnam, *Mathematics, Matter and Method.*

[34]For an account of these difficulties, see Hilary Putnam, "Reply to Michael Redhead," in P. Clark and R. Hale, eds., *Reading Putnam* (Oxford: Blackwell, 1994).

[35]W. V. Quine, *Word and Object* (Cambridge, Mass.: Technology Press of the Massachusetts Institute of Technology, 1960).

[36]A famous Quinian thought experiment, often used to illustrate the doctrine, involves the idea of encountering natives who speak a hitherto unknown language and who appear to call rabbits *gavagai.* In *Word and Object,* Quine argued that we could translate all occurrences of *gavagai* in the "jungle language" as an "undetached rabbit part" and make "compensatory adjustments" elsewhere in our translation scheme, and the resulting translation scheme would still fit all possible behavioral data. If we assume that the reference of words is publicly accessible from behavioral data (otherwise how can language be learned?), Quine asked, does this not show that there is "no fact of the matter" as to whether *gavagai* means "rabbit" or "undetached rabbit part"?

[37]In particular, Bernard Williams, *Descartes: The Project of Pure Enquiry* (Harmondsworth: Penguin, 1978), 299.

[38]Since contemporary mathematicians would accept the sentence, "There exist numbers greater than twenty-five," and contemporary biologists would accept, "There exist microbes that cause diseases in humans," Quine's criterion of ontological commitment implies that these scientists are "committed to the existence of" numbers and microbes, and since existence is univocal, numbers and microbes exist (if contemporary science is right) in exactly the same sense.

[39]"Success and Limits of Mathematization," collected in Quine, *Theories and Things* (Cambridge, Mass.: Harvard University Press, 1981), 149.

[40]Cf. David Lewis, *Counterfactuals* (Cambridge, Mass.: Harvard University Press, 1973), 84–91.

[41]John Rawls, *A Theory of Justice* (Cambridge, Mass.: Belknap Press of Harvard University Press, 1970).

[42]John Rawls, *Political Liberalism* (New York: Columbia University Press, 1993); John Rawls, "The Independence of Moral Theory," Presidential Address to the American Philosophical Association, Eastern Division, 1974, in *Proceedings and Addresses of the American Philosophical Association* 48 (1974–1975): 5–22.

[43]J. L. Mackie, *Ethics: Inventing Right and Wrong* (Harmondsworth: Penguin, 1977); Gilbert Harman, *The Nature of Morality: An Introduction to Ethics* (Oxford: Oxford University Press, 1977).

[44]Bernard Williams, *Ethics and the Limits of Philosophy* (Cambridge, Mass.: Harvard University Press, 1985).

[45]The three are Rogers Albritton, Stanley Cavell, and Burton Dreben; having retired from Harvard, Dreben now teaches at Boston University, but my younger colleague Warren Goldfarb, in addition to doing distinguished work in logic and in the history of analytic philosophy, also helps to continue the Harvard tradition of Wittgenstein studies today.

[46]See Putnam, *Mind, Language and Reality,* chaps. 15, 16, 17.

[47]After the discovery (by Kurt Gödel) that there are undecidable sentences in all systems of pure mathematics, the positivists made various complicated adjustments in their criterion to avoid having to say that any sentences of pure mathematics are cognitively meaningless. However, it is not my purpose to go into those adjustments here.

[48]See "Rethinking Mathematical Necessity" in Hilary Putnam, *Words and Life* (Cambridge, Mass.: Harvard University Press, 1994).

[49]Quine's attacks on the analytic/synthetic distinction were attacks on the positivist idea that a certain class of statements (the analytic ones) is in principle immune to empirical refutation. Philosophers who suppose that Quine disproved the very possibility of a distinction between conceptual knowledge and empirical knowledge (e.g., Richard Rorty) are tacitly assuming that any workable notion of conceptual knowledge must resemble the positivist notion of analytic truth in being *unrevisable*. But in *On Certainty*, Wittgenstein remarked that the distinction between a river and its banks is an important one, even if in time the banks and the river change places and even if some banks are more friable than others. He meant that there is a difference between "grammatical" (conceptual) and empirical claims, even if the status of a given claim changes with time, and even if some "grammatical" claims turn out to be mistaken.

[50]Among Stanley Cavell's recent writings on this theme are *Conditions Handsome and Unhandsome: The Constitution of Emersonian Perfectionism* (Chicago, Ill.: University of Chicago Press, 1990); *In Quest of the Ordinary: Lines of Skepticism and Romanticism* (Chicago, Ill.: University of Chicago Press, 1988); and *Philosophical Passages: Wittgenstein, Emerson, Austin, Derrida* (Oxford: Blackwell, 1995).

[51]Collected in Putnam, *Mind, Language and Reality.*

226   Hilary Putnam

[52]Saul Kripke, *Naming and Necessity* (Cambridge, Mass.: Harvard University Press, 1972, 1980).

[53]See Hilary Putnam, *Reason, Truth and History* (Cambridge: Cambridge University Press, 1981).

[54]W. V. Quine, *Word and Object* (Cambridge, Mass.: MIT Press, 1960); W. V. Quine, *Ontological Relativity and Other Essays* (New York: Columbia University Press, 1969).

[55]W. V. Quine, *Pursuit of Truth* (Cambridge, Mass.: Harvard University Press, 1990), 33.

[56]Nelson Goodman, *Ways of Worldmaking* (Indianapolis, Ind.: Hackett, 1978). For a debate about this view among Goodman, Hempel, Scheffler, and myself, see Peter J. McCormick, ed., *Starmaking: Realism, Anti-Realism, and Irrealism* (Cambridge, Mass.: MIT Press, 1996).

[57]See Putnam, *Reason, Truth and History*; see also Hilary Putnam, *The Many Faces of Realism* (LaSalle, Ill.: Open Court, 1987).

[58]Cf. Hilary Putnam, "Reply to Simon Blackburn" in Clark and Hale, eds., *Reading Putnam*, and Hilary Putnam, "The Dewey Lecture 1994: Sense, Nonsense and the Senses: An Inquiry into the Powers of the Human Mind," *The Journal of Philosophy* XCI (2) (September 1994), for what I now think was right and wrong about "internal realism."

[59]Richard Rorty, *Consequences of Pragmatism: Essays, 1972–1980* (Minneapolis, Minn.: University of Minnesota Press, 1982); Richard Rorty, *Philosophy and the Mirror of Nature* (Princeton, N.J.: Princeton University Press, 1979).

[60]Cf. "James' Theory of Perception" (1988), collected in Hilary Putnam, *Realism with a Human Face* (Cambridge, Mass.: Harvard University Press, 1994).

[61]See Putnam, *Words and Life*, pt. III.

Alexander Nehamas

Trends in Recent American Philosophy

T
HE STORY OF AMERICAN PHILOSOPHY during the second half of
this century is by and large the story of analytical philosophy and its transformations. This is not to say that other
approaches to philosophy have not had their followers: Dewey
has always been read and sometimes even admired; Husserl's and
Heidegger's phenomenology has been studied and taught in a
number of departments, which are often associated with the Catholic
Church (these same departments have maintained a strong Thomist
tradition); there were always admirers of Whitehead's "process
philosophy"; many people have written on Hegel; and the late
Heidegger and the tradition he inspired in Europe were being read
long before the recent incursion of "continental" philosophy, which
some consider as the only real alternative to the analytic philosophers' manner of doing things. The fact remains, though, that
most of the major figures and accomplishments of American philosophy during this period belong to the analytical tradition. To
the extent that American philosophy is known at all beyond the
confines of its own disciplinary boundaries, in the United States
and abroad, it is because of the writings of the best analytical
philosophers.

In discussing analytical philosophy—even informally, as I am
attempting to do here—we must not define it in terms that are too
narrow to allow us to account for its recent interactions with
alternative approaches, which constitute a topic worth considering
in itself. Broadly speaking, analytical philosophy comprises two

*Alexander Nehamas is Edmund N. Carpenter II Class of 1943 Professor in the Humani-
ties at Princeton University.*

major wings. Logical positivism, which traces its ancestry to Gottlob Frege, Bertrand Russell, and, on a particular reading of the *Tractatus Logico-Philosophicus*, to the early Wittgenstein, was mainly practiced by the members of the Vienna Circle and their Berlin associates. Ordinary-language philosophy, whose emblematic figures are G. E. Moore, J. L. Austin, and, again on a particular reading of the *Philosophical Investigations*, the late Wittgenstein, was the approach taken by a large number of philosophers in the great English universities. These two wings were transplanted to the United States and supplied the major building blocks for analytical philosophy as we know it today. Of the two, positivism—despite the fact that a number of American philosophers have been deeply and productively influenced by Austin's work—has had, I believe, a much deeper hold and influence on American thought.

If that is so, then the story of what happened to American philosophy between the 1940s and today begins, like most of the stories contained in this issue of *Dædalus,* in the 1930s. That was the time when many of the positivists, including Rudolf Carnap, C. G. Hempel, Hans Reichenbach, and Herbert Feigl, were forced to leave Europe and emigrate to the United States. Their emigration had far-reaching consequences.

The most important (though by no means the only) philosophical voice in the United States at that time belonged to John Dewey. Dewey's pragmatism, as a theoretical approach, cannot be easily distinguished from his social, educational, and intellectual activism. For Dewey and his followers (Sidney Hook was notable among them), philosophy was essentially a public enterprise; it was directly involved in the formulation and solution of large-scale practical problems. To the extent that it shied away from the world at large, philosophy was an object of suspicion to the Deweyan pragmatists.

By the time he arrived in America, Rudolf Carnap, the most prominent member of the Vienna Circle, had already known and worked with W. V. Quine, who was then beginning his career at Harvard. Positivism had received a forceful, popular treatment by A. J. Ayer, whose *Language, Truth and Logic,*[1] published in England in 1936, had given voice to its radical program of reforming philosophy and clearing the debris left by traditional metaphysics and the vagaries of ordinary language. In America, Carnap and the other members of the positivist school had a very difficult time finding university positions and, hence, did not immediately have a direct influence on the discipline at large. But Quine—despite his considerable objections to the positivist program—gradually succeeded in attracting serious attention to the movement and the writings of its forerunners. Little by little, a number of ideas began to take hold.

Primary among these ideas was "the verifiability theory of meaning." According to that theory there were two kinds of meaningful utterances. The first consisted of "analytic statements," which were true simply by virtue of the meanings of those statements' words; in addition to the truths of logic and mathematics, the most classic example of an analytic sentence, infinitely repeated in the analytic literature, was "All bachelors are unmarried males." The second kind consisted of "synthetic statements," whose truth depended not only on the meanings of the words but also on the fact that they concerned the empirical world and that there were procedures for determining precisely what it was that they said about that world; the meaning of those statements was "the method of their verification."

According to this theory, the meaningful parts of our language, strictly speaking, were logic, mathematics, and empirical science. In particular, the verifiability theory excluded "metaphysics," which was roughly defined as that which most of the figures of the history of philosophy before Frege had been doing, in addition to all statements that concerned moral and aesthetic evaluation. In that way, philosophy, which now came to see itself as the analysis and clarification of our legitimate concepts by means of determining the "necessary and sufficient" conditions for their application, withdrew both from its own history and from the public issues— which almost always involved questions of value—with which Dewey's pragmatism had been so intimately concerned.

As I have already remarked, Quine—without doubt the most important philosopher of this period—never belonged to the positivist movement. In fact, his criticisms of Carnap's views of truth and, in particular, of the analytic-synthetic distinction, on which the positivist program depended, are among the most trenchant ever made and led to a partial reconception of the nature of analytic philosophy. But Quine did accept not only the view that formal work, which positivism valued so highly, was crucial to philosophy, but also the austere conception of the domain and the goals of the discipline that positivism had articulated. Philosophical issues could be seriously discussed only when formulated in the clear, formal language of logical calculi; and only a few issues, in a few fields, could be formulated in that manner.

By the late 1940s, a picture of philosophy as an essentially theoretical discipline had been established under the influence of Carnap, Quine, and Quine's students. Philosophy now had an indispensable formal component, and logic was one of its main concerns. In addition, philosophers ceased to think of themselves, as many had done up to that time, as part of the enterprise to which their colleagues in literature and history departments were devoted; they started thinking of themselves instead as participants in the enterprise of science. Common sense ("that repository of ancient nonsense," as Nelson Goodman, who influenced analytical philosophy broadly but also led it in new directions through his work in the philosophy of art, once put it) and ordinary language were distrusted. They were held to be fundamentally unclear; and lack of clarity, which was often considered to be the most obvious feature of the prose of the great philosophers of the past, was held responsible for the creation of insoluble pseudo-philosophical problems. Interest in the history of philosophy almost disappeared: Quine was quoted as saying that two kinds of people went into philosophy—those interested in the history of philosophy and those interested in philosophy. Part of the task of philosophy was to reformulate the problems raised by earlier thinkers in a way that showed either that they could in fact be solved (in which case, of course, they were not pseudo-problems after all) or that they could not even be meaningfully expressed.

By contrast, clear (ideally, formal) expression could formulate genuine questions and offer lasting solutions. But practical public issues—the issues that had occupied Dewey—could not be formulated in such terms. American philosophy retreated from the public domain. It no longer saw itself as bearing a direct relation to the world. Instead, it saw itself as the analysis of the claims made by the various practices and disciplines that did bear a direct relation to it. Many people understood the central purpose of philosophy to be to distinguish those practices whose results could be trusted from those that offered no conclusions that constituted knowledge. Philosophical research, accordingly, focused on epistemic reliability. Not surprisingly, mathematics and the natural sciences did considerably better on that score than the social sciences and incomparably better than morality, politics, and the arts. They therefore attracted the attention of many American philosophers during the fifties, sixties, and most of the seventies. "Philosophy of science is philosophy enough," Quine wrote at that time.

Mathematical logic, which made immense progress during the twentieth century, came to be seen as an integral part of philosophy. Some of the great logical results (for example, Gödel's incompleteness theorems and Tarski's semantic definition of the concept of truth) were held as paradigms of serious philosophical work. They provided the inspiration for a huge number of other, less formal but very important advances in the philosophy of mathematics and, most importantly, in the philosophy of language, which emerged as the single most important specialty within philosophy during that period.

As a result of this shift to the more formal and abstract fields and issues of philosophy, moral philosophy in particular was replaced by "metaethics." Instead of investigating the nature of the good life, or of the right political organization, moral philosophy became the investigation of the meaning of our evaluative terminology. Instead of determining what is good, moral philosophy tried to determine what people mean when they praise actions, lives, or people as good. It was often concluded that our evaluative vocabulary did not have much of a cognitive or descriptive component: a number of metaethical theories at the time concluded that terms of praise were mostly, in one way or another, covert expressions of desires and preferences and not descriptions of the objects to which they were attached. Actual, substantive moral issues were hardly ever discussed.

Such a conception of philosophy as a "second-order" discipline that addressed and evaluated the claims of other, "first-order" practices also fit well with the self-image of a number of ordinary-language philosophers. The philosophers who were influenced by positivism thought that their task was to "reconstruct" everyday language. That meant doing their work in a language that combined the clear structures of logic, mathematics, and the empirical sciences and prevented the formulation of any problems that were not genuine and did not admit of a clear solution. Ordinary-language philosophers did not share their reconstructionist colleagues' suspiciousness of informal, everyday communication and had no desire to reform ordinary language in order to avoid philosophical pseudo-problems. On the contrary, they held that close attention to the complexities and nuances of ordinary language shows that most traditional philosophical perplexities stem from a failure to appreciate those nuances. Philosophical problems arise, in particular, when the way some terms are used in one context is unwittingly taken as paradigmatic and made to apply to other contexts to which it is not appropriate. So, for example, the problem of "our knowledge of other minds"—the question of whether we can know that other people really have minds of their own and that they are not just cleverly designed automata, a question that had engaged modern philosophy since Descartes—could be resolved, according to Austin, if we paid sufficient attention to the many varieties of knowledge to which we appeal and that we use in everyday communication without a second thought. In both cases, however, philosophy was thought of as a discipline that addressed problems created by practices independent of it; that was what constituted it as a second-order discipline.

Despite their other major differences, both wings of analytical philosophy were concerned, as they saw the matter, with the analysis of the concepts and the language of various institutions and practices other than philosophy itself. The role of philosophy was to a great extent not that of a participant in a common intellectual enterprise but that of an overseer: it was not coordinate with the other disciplines but superordinate to them. Still, this statement needs to be qualified. Quine himself argued that philosophy was continuous with science, a more abstract and general version of the natural investigation of the world (he might have said, "Philosophy *as* science is philosophy enough"). Substantive results were reached in formal logic. And even though working natural scientists were never very interested in what their philosophical colleagues were telling them about their own disciplines, some of Gilbert Ryle's work on the philosophy of mind as well as Quine's own behaviorism, which he accepted under the influence of B. F. Skinner, were slowly finding their way into the work of various psychologists.

The sharp line that was supposed to distinguish philosophy from the disciplines whose standards it aimed to analyze and evaluate had actually begun to blur already in the early and mid-fifties, partly as a result of Quine's continuing disputes with Carnap over the analytic-synthetic distinction and partly because of Hilary Putnam's reconception of the nature of scientific theories. In 1967, the *Encyclopedia of Philosophy* claimed that "philosophical analysis" had ended with the end of positivism, which it placed as early as 1950, when C. G. Hempel published a paper, "Problems and Changes in the Empiricist Criterion of Meaning," that took Quine's views very seriously. Such a view, however, depends on the narrow conception of analysis against which I warned at the beginning of this essay. We cannot define analytical philosophy simply in terms of the technical enterprise involved in analyzing the meaning of terms that is underwritten by the analytic-synthetic distinction. Analytical philosophy, more broadly, depends crucially on an emphasis of dealing with relatively small-scale problems that are amenable to careful dissection and in regard to which the distinction between good and bad arguments can be readily made. Analytical philosophy is not unlike the legal profession (it is interesting, in fact, to observe the linguistic parallels between philosophical and legal prose—both the prose of legal briefs and the prose of legal opinions): both disciplines must define their issues in the clearest possible way so that the relevance of various considerations to their adjudication can be made as clear as possible. And, perhaps tellingly, both disciplines address extremely diverse issues—often issues of great interest to a broad audience—in extremely technical terms and are unable to explain their inner workings to outsiders.

In any case, Quine's view that philosophy and science are continuous, articulated in detail in his *Word and Object*,[2] was accepted quickly and broadly. *Word and Object,* in addition, sparked an extraordinary interest in the philosophy of language; this, especially when Donald Davidson's work started appearing in the mid-sixties, blurred yet another line, that between philosophy on the one hand and linguistics on the other. And insofar as linguistics was to some extent connected with psychology, a number of philosophers began to study particular developments in that discipline as well.

At about the time that *Word and Object* was published, P. F. Strawson's *Individuals*,[3] though much more in line with the approach of ordinary-language philosophy, rehabilitated the interest in metaphysics that had almost disappeared in England. Despite the fact that Strawson's view, that spatio-temporal individuals are absolutely basic to our thought, was not widely accepted in America, it was still seriously discussed. In particular, his theory of what persons are and how they fit within the framework of individuals provoked many discussions of that notion and once again (if only indirectly) prompted philosophers to start looking more closely at the writings of psychologists.

A crucially important event at about that time was the publication of Thomas S. Kuhn's *The Structure of Scientific Revolutions*.[4] Many philosophers were suspicious of the book's apparently relativist thesis that scientists who accept vastly different theories actually inhabit "different worlds." But whether Kuhn did or did not accept such a relativist thesis, his book had an immense influence in the longer run. It convinced philosophers, once and for all, that the philosophy of science could not be pursued independently of the history of science and that a detailed knowledge of the special sciences is necessary for the study of their methodology. Philosophers therefore turned to a more serious study of history than they would have considered desirable even a few years earlier. They also learned more about the internal workings of the sciences than their earlier, much more abstract epistemological approach would ever have justified or even tolerated.

Kuhn's work showed that the positivist distinction between the pure data of sensation on the one hand and the conceptual operations of the theoretical understanding on the other could not be maintained. Sensation does not supply us with a stock of information that requires no interpretation and on which we can all agree before we proceed to offer different explanations for it. There is no absolutely basic, shared ground that assures that all disputes can ultimately be decided by reference to it. A similar attack on the idea of pure sensory data, or "the given," was being waged by Wilfrid Sellars, a philosopher who, though deeply influenced by Carnap, maintained a serious interest in the history of philosophy throughout his career and who convinced a number of his students that philosophy cannot be done completely independently of its own history. Sellars's doubts about the given became doubts about the project of traditional epistemology, which had been to show how the grand total of our knowledge of the world is ultimately based on and justified by the elementary information given in the same manner to all of us by the senses. But Sellars showed that even though all our knowledge depends causally on such sensory input, it cannot be justified by it. The project of determining the "foundations of knowledge," another central issue that positivism had inherited from Descartes and his tradition, began to lose its hold on the philosophical imagination.

The net effect of all these developments was to suggest that philosophy was by no means as pure and autonomous a discipline as the originators of analytical philosophy may have sometimes thought. Two other events also contributed to that change of view.

The first was the emergence of artificial intelligence as a serious field in its own right. The possibility of modeling the human mind on the structure of a digital computer attracted the interest and imagination of a number of philosophers. People interested either in formal work or in the philosophy of mind (or both) found here an exhilarating new possibility to make a direct contribution to the work of other disciplines. "Cognitive science," which is one of the most clearly interdisciplinary specialties within philosophy, has since become one of its most active fields.

The second, and perhaps more important, development was the reentry of philosophy into the public, normative arena with the publication of John Rawls's *A Theory of Justice*.[5] Rawls turned away both from metaethics and from utilitarianism, which, very roughly, understands "good" as that which contributes to the maximization of happiness and which was the closest thing to a normative theory of "good" at the time. He offered, partially under the influence of Kant, a complex and controversial substantive account of the conditions that a just society must satisfy as well as a philosophical defense of political liberalism. Rawls's book had an immense impact and enabled moral and political philosophy to stop seeing themselves as purely (or at least primarily) descriptive approaches: they could now claim an active role in the discussion and resolution of public problems. Needless to say, it would be nót only an exaggeration but a gross error to say that moral, political, and social philosophy have returned to the activism Dewey had envisaged and encouraged. Much of the political philosophy now practiced in the United States does not engage in the serious criticism of particular social institutions but is satisfied with an abstract defense of liberal principles. Still, it now appears possible that, through a mixture of theoretical and practical work, philosophy can gradually reclaim a role in public discourse. The same is true of recent developments in jurisprudence and the philosophy of law: philosophical work in these fields is not easily distinguished from the writings of lawyers. And the number of philosophers who hold joint appointments in philosophy departments and law schools is constantly growing.

Philosophy also had an opportunity to reenter public discourse and connect itself with other disciplines through the proliferation of what has been called "applied philosophy"—particularly business and medical ethics. As things turned out, the people who entered those fields were, on the whole, quickly absorbed by business and medical schools. Their professional affiliation actually changed, and their contact with philosophy as a discipline has gradually eroded. At the same time, however, there has been a fruitful interaction between philosophers and social scientists who are interested in rational-choice theory.

In general, though, I would say that the branch of philosophy that has been most successful in entering public discourse has been feminism. Feminism by and large found its voice through a reading of continental philosophy and not through the much more distanced and less activist analytic literature. Feminism is often associated with the arrival of continental European philosophy on the American philosophical scene, which began in the early 1980s when we witnessed the gradually increasing influence of Nietzsche and continental philosophy not only on philosophy but on the American academy as a whole. This, of course, is a delicate subject because a number of analytical philosophers consider the writings of continental thinkers as paradigms of sloppy, disorganized, and pretentious thought. In turn, continental philosophers and their American advocates find analytical philosophy arid, petty, and narrowly technical. That debate has not been fruitful. But slowly more and more students (and departments) are beginning to include some of the work of authors such as Habermas (who until recently was mainly studied by political theorists) or Foucault and Derrida (whose intellectual homes in America were the various literature departments) among the subjects that belong to their own discipline.

A major difference between analytical and continental philosophy is the role that the history of philosophy plays in each. Though analytical philosophers have been studying that history much more than they used to twenty years ago, their approach tends to be rather narrowly focused, both in regard to issues and to philosophers. So, for example, a specialist in British empiricism may also be familiar with European rationalism but will know little if anything about Plato, St. Thomas, or Hegel. By contrast, philosophers on the continent write as if they are deeply knowledgeable about the whole history of Western thought (though often they are only familiar with Hegel's, Nietzsche's, or Heidegger's idiosyncratic versions of that history). Stanley Cavell once offered a definition of the contrast between analytical and continental philosophy that was only half tongue-in-cheek: Though neither side is absolutely true to its own self-image, he said, continental philosophers tend to write as if they have read every philosophical work produced thus far, while analytical philosophers write as if they have read nothing. But the point remains that to engage oneself in the work of continental thinkers requires a much deeper knowledge of the history of philosophy than most analytical departments are prepared to offer their students.

Nevertheless, analytical philosophy is now more interested in the history of the discipline, and some philosophers are beginning to look at analytical philosophy itself as a historically situated movement, not simply as the revolution that for the first time stood philosophy right side up. The writings of Stanley Cavell, who has been influenced both by Austin and by Wittgenstein, have shown that philosophy and literature can sometimes illuminate one another and that in many cases they are involved in similar enterprises. At the same time, we are seeing a renewal of interest in the thought of the American pragmatists (with whom the work of Quine already showed some deep affinities), and both William James and John Dewey are being studied and written about more than in the past fifty years.

One very interesting feature of American philosophy during this period is that unlike many other disciplines in the humanities, such as modern language and literature, it has not faced a generational, political, and ideological split. Nothing in philosophy resembles the violence of the change from the New Criticism to structuralism to post-structuralism to race, gender, and ethnic studies that we have witnessed, for example, in English departments. Despite the various developments I have been describing here, and despite some attempts by groups opposed to analytical philosophy to take over the offices of the American Philosophical Association, the atmosphere in the field is calm, peaceful, and rather detached. Frankly, I have no idea what that shows, or whether it is a good or a bad thing.

I believe that philosophers today have, as a group, a broader sense of their discipline than they did twenty or thirty years ago. But I also believe that the discipline is still too isolated from other academic fields (most scientists are still not interested in what we do, and most of us are not interested in what our literary colleagues are doing). Philosophical prose is not designed to be read by a large public, and even some of the best work in moral and political philosophy is still too abstract to attract the attention of people who are concerned with solutions to practical problems. That is not purely the fault of philosophy. The difficulty is twofold. On the one hand, intellectuals in general and philosophers in particular have—in America—tended to confuse the public with the popular. Writing for a broad public has been identified with popularizing one's discipline, lowering one's standards, and catering to the lowest common denominator among one's audience. On the other hand, the broad public (or, at least, those among them who could make use of what philosophers or intellectuals in general might say) have no patience for any position that is not virtually self-explanatory, refusing to take seriously any view that requires careful thought and that cannot receive practical application without serious and sometimes relatively long preparation. If anything, I would suggest that the desire for positions that can be explained quickly and easily to a large audience is one of the main reasons why it has been so difficult to develop reasonable answers to questions of great public importance.

Further, the fact that philosophy today sees itself in broader terms than it did a few decades ago is not an unmixed blessing. Even if philosophy as a whole is broader, that does not mean that individual philosophers agree that such breadth is a good thing— it does not even mean that many of us are willing to accept much of what our colleagues are doing as "real" philosophy in the first place. That has led to what I believe is a dangerous fragmentation in the field, with people who teach together in the same department having neither any idea of what their colleagues are doing nor any interest in ever finding out. To see this point, it will help to discuss for a moment the canon of analytical philosophy.

The problem is that no such canon exists today. But if, perhaps not inaccurately, we say that a canon consists of those works that members of a discipline would be ashamed to admit they have not read, such a thing certainly existed in philosophy during the sixties and seventies. It was not a canon that included many of the great historical books of the past; instead, it consisted of a set of much more contemporary works of more limited scope and function, consistent with the self-image of analytical philosophy itself.

At the major departments of philosophy of the time, the canon began with Frege's "On Sense and Reference" (which someone once only half-jokingly characterized as "ancient philosophy"). Russell's "On Denoting" was part of it as were his lectures on logical atomism. A number of Carnap's works, Ayer's *Language, Truth and Logic,* Ryle's *The Concept of Mind,*[6] Wittgenstein's still-mysterious *Tractatus*[7] and *Philosophical Investigations,*[8] perhaps Austin's *How to Do Things with Words,*[9] and Strawson's *Individuals* were also part of it. Absolutely central were Quine's "Two Dogmas of Empiricism," "On What There Is," and, above all, *Word and Object,* especially chapter 2 on "the indeterminacy of translation." The early articles of Donald Davidson, which brought Tarski's semantic definition of truth into the center of philosophical thought, Kripke's *Naming and Necessity,*[10] and Hilary Putnam's attacks on positivist semantics and the philosophy of science as well as his work on "functionalism," which provoked great interest in artificial intelligence, round out the list. Most graduate students and faculty either had read these works or had seriously tried to do so; they were expected to have a view about them, whether their own or that of some independent authority.

These were also works that undergraduates read and could sometimes become almost enthusiastic about. Compressed as it was in time and range of topics, this group of works provided a common background against which philosophical discussion took place. Even the few people who were interested in the history of philosophy, in moral, social, and political issues or in aesthetics, had to be familiar with them.

No such common ground exists today. The closest thing to a book that people are ashamed to admit they have not read is Rawls's *A Theory of Justice,* but shame no longer prevents them from admitting the truth. What philosophers read is by and large specific to their immediate interests, which are reflected in the proliferation of specialized societies, conferences, and journals. We seem to be lacking the most elementary lingua franca to discuss our field in general, the most rudimentary notion of a set of problems that are common to the discipline—problems that, even if not all philosophers consider them to be their own, they might believe will make *their* problems more tractable when they are resolved. That is an important development, almost as important as the fact that it has never itself been made the subject of philosophical attention.

Analytical philosophy, broadly defined, is still the dominant approach of the major American philosophy departments. Interesting work is being done in a number of subfields, even though it is seen as interesting, by and large, mostly by people who already belong to those subfields. Some philosophers, of course, are read widely within the discipline; some are interacting with scholars in other disciplines; and a few (like Richard Rorty and John Searle, who actually occupy vastly opposed positions on the nature and importance of analytical philosophy) can write well for a general audience. But there is a sense that philosophy is now in a holding pattern, lacking a clear overall direction and an explicit sense of unity and mission.

In my opinion, philosophy needs to take seriously the need to communicate its concerns more broadly and to a larger audience. Not all philosophical concerns are amenable to such treatment, but some are. And those that are not are often crucial to formulating and resolving those that are. That, at least, is the lesson of Plato's *Republic,* which addresses problems—problems as practical as censoring the books that children will read or the distribution of personal property—on the basis of the most abstract speculation about the nature of the world, the human soul, and knowledge. (Plato's *Republic* also shows, of course, why philosophy still cannot be done independently of its history.) A philosophy with a public—not a popular—voice can preserve some of the substantive concerns as well as some of the formal virtues of clarity and rigor that characterized analytical philosophy at its best. But it can also be an engaged and consequential enterprise of the sort envisaged by the American pragmatists as well as by most of the great figures in its history. Whether such a philosophy will still be "analytical philosophy" as we now know it is a less interesting question than whether talented people will actively participate in it, raise important questions, and once again attract the attention of the academic world as well as of the world at large.[11]

ENDNOTES

[1]A. J. Ayer, *Language, Truth and Logic* (London: V. Gollancz, Ltd., 1936).

[2]W. V. Quine, *Word and Object* (Cambridge, Mass.: Technology Press of the Massachusetts Institute of Technology, 1960).

[3]P. F. Strawson, *Individuals: An Essay in Descriptive Metaphysics* (London: Methuen, 1959).

[4]Thomas S. Kuhn, *The Structure of Scientific Revolutions* (Chicago, Ill.: University of Chicago Press, 1963).

[5]John Rawls, *A Theory of Justice* (Cambridge, Mass.: Belknap Press, 1970).

[6]Gilbert Ryle, *The Concept of Mind* (New York: Barnes and Noble, 1949).

[7]Ludwig Wittgenstein, *Tractatus Logico-Philosophicus* (New York: Humanities Press, 1951).

[8]Ludwig Wittgenstein, *Philosophical Investigations* (Oxford: B. Blackwell, 1953).

[9]J. L. Austin, *How To Do Things With Words* (Cambridge, Mass.: Harvard University Press, 1962).

[10]Saul A. Kripke, *Naming and Necessity* (Cambridge, Mass.: Harvard University Press, 1980).

[11]This essay is a slightly revised version of the notes I prepared at an early stage of the planning of the conference where most of the papers appearing in this issue of *Dædalus* were delivered. That accounts for its casual style and approach.

Charles E. Lindblom

Political Science in the 1940s and 1950s

I N THIS ESSAY I WILL EXAMINE the discipline of political science (and my experience with it) in the 1940s and 1950s. To get off to a running start, I can place the discipline within an overview of all of the social sciences in that same period that Daniel Bell put forward in his book, *The Social Sciences Since the Second World War*.[1] Although no one's account should be taken as gospel, Bell's is excellently done and permits us to see political science not in isolation from but in relation to its sister disciplines.

A COMPARATIVE OVERVIEW

On an opening point in Bell's book, I do want, however, to file a demurral. Just as I lean on Bell, so Bell leans—but only to begin his work—on the well-known (though I do not endorse it) list of sixty-two alleged "basic innovations in social science, 1900–1965," constructed by Karl Deutsch and others.[2] Bell accepts a conclusion that Deutsch and his colleagues draw from the list: namely, that up to about the year 1930 qualitative innovations dominated, and thereafter mathematical and quantitative innovations dominated. This proposition is true only if the list truly captures the major innovations and is not itself a product of a disposition to count as major innovations those studies that take a mathematical or quantitative form. I am reminded of a graduate student who, to offer evidence that Catholicism is the one true religion, pointed out to me that all the saints are Catholics. Recently in a seminar another

Charles E. Lindblom is Professor Emeritus of Political Science and Economics at Yale University.

graduate student similarly argued that mainstream economics was on the right track: almost all Nobel prizes in economics, he pointed out, had been won by mainstream theorists.

In the 1940s and 1950s, one might list the following as major gains in political science:

- The reconstruction of democratic theory at the hands of Joseph Schumpeter, David Truman, Robert A. Dahl, and Anthony Downs, among others.
- Kenneth Arrow on social choice.
- The study of third-world politics.
- Public-choice theory.

If so, qualitative analysis in political science effectively competes with more mathematical and quantitative approaches, for three of the four are predominantly nonmathematical. Yet that proposition might instead be taken as evidence that political science was not taking a strong role in the advances of mathematical and quantitative analysis in the social sciences, whatever their importance, and was in that sense lagging behind.

This is perhaps as good a juncture as any to note the familiar embarrassment of political science in the 1940s and 1950s (which still persists, for that matter). Advances in political science seemed to come predominantly from other disciplines or occupations— think of Schumpeter, Arrow, Walter Lippman, Gunnar Myrdal, Albert O. Hirschman, Paul Lazarsfeld, Theodore Adorno and colleagues, and James Buchanan, among others, to which Deutsch would add Mao and to which I would add Max Weber, whose work became available in English in the 1940s. Of those, none are political scientists. Or think of how political scientists themselves have reached to other disciplines: Harold Lasswell, Robert E. Lane, and Herbert Simon to psychology, for example; public-choice theorists to economics, and attitude surveys and public-opinion polling to psychology. Or think of pervasive new or refreshed currents of thought that embraced the political science of the 1940s and 1950s, for example, functionalism, systems analysis, game theory, information theory, structuralism, positivism, and post-positivism. For those currents, we owe little to political scientists. Instead the names are A. R. Radcliffe-Brown, Claude Lévi-Strauss, John von Neumann, Ludwig Bertalanffy, B. F. Skinner, C. E. Shannon, and Norbert Wiener, among others, as well as a number of philosophers of science. This dependency of political science on other disciplines is noteworthy. But I see no reason to regret it.

Back now to Bell. He goes on to claim for social science a growing prestige in the 1940s and 1950s, and I accept on the whole both the claim and his explanations for it. First, thanks to new techniques and the computer, the social sciences were perceived as becoming harder, that is, more like the hard sciences in their capacities for empirical verification. Second, social science was credited with a capacity for matching to some degree the impressive achievements of the physical sciences in World War II. Third, the expansion of the universities (i.e., with returning veterans and then the baby boomers) greatly increased the number of people engaged in research. Fourth, the Cold War created a research-and-development rivalry between the United States and the Soviet Union. Fifth and finally, postwar America turned—although on the whole not until the 1960s—to a variety of social problems that required the "expert advice" of social science. Note that each of these reasons is, for the period *after* the 1950s, either invalid or weakened, and the prestige of social science accordingly declines.

Bell then selects from the social sciences of that period what he takes to be their outstanding accomplishments. On selections of that kind, informed opinions differ; but his selections are defensible, illuminating, and excellent for our purposes. A conspicuous feature of his selection, which he does not explicitly note, is that political science is nearly invisible. Economics looms large—it is Bell's "first domain of promise"—with the Keynesian revolution, national-income accounting, input-output analysis, mathematical analysis and econometric models, growth models, and welfare economics. Most of us will probably agree that in those decades political science could not at all compete with economics in terms of innovation.

Bell's second domain of promise is "modeling the mind and society." This category specifically concerns a number of intertwined intellectual developments: "cybernetics, information theory, structural linguistics, artificial intelligence and automata theory, and general systems theory." I suspect that most would agree on the great importance of these developments (although each of us might want to make one deletion). Again, it is hard to find anything of comparable importance in political science, nor do political scientists other than Herbert A. Simon make much of a contribution to these developments, which are in the hands of a variety of other disciplines. About Simon, we might suggest that he made his several great contributions to the study of behavior and society by distancing himself from the dominant interests of the discipline of political science.

For this period, Bell also credits two movements in sociology and anthropology: studies of culture and personality, and structural-functionalism (especially Talcott Parsons). Among political scientists, only Nathan Leites appears to Bell as a contributor to the study of culture and personality. But on culture we can think of other political scientists, namely, David Riesman and Harold Lasswell, among others. And then in the very early 1960s—only technically outside our time period—come James Coleman, Seymour Lipset, Gabriel Almond, and Lucien Pye, among others. Either Bell has mistakenly overlooked them, or it is his judgment that in the larger picture of studies of personality and culture, their contributions do not match those of the sociologists and anthropologists.

To understand political science of the 1940s and 1950s, it is helpful to call to mind some specifics of what it did *not* do in that period by noting accomplishments that came only after 1960. Bell's account of 1960 to 1980 claims for the social sciences as a whole only four major developments:

- Sociobiology.
- New paradigms in macroeconomics.
- New schools of neo-Marxism.
- Structuralism.

Political science did not much participate in any of these developments, not even greatly to neo-Marxist thought, which remained largely in the hands of mostly European sociologists, historians, and philosophers.

For the 1960s Bell notes the conspicuous attempt of the social sciences to make a greater and an explicit contribution to social policy-making. A clear opportunity for political science, we might think; indeed the discipline had earlier made contributions to the study both of policy problems and of the policy-making process (for example, Harold Lasswell, Daniel Lerner, and their associates in their 1951 *The Policy Sciences*[3]). In the 1960s and thereafter, at least dozens of political scientists tackled many issues of public policy and continued to study the policy-making process itself. This marked something of a change in political science from the 1940s and 1950s to the 1960s, with policy studies perhaps replacing—and at least subordinating—an earlier tradition of studying public administration. Whether the change in political science was consequential is not obvious. As Bell sees it, the major gains in policy-oriented social science derived from the development of social indicators, social forecasting, and social evaluation in which, I think he means to say, economists and sociologists were most prominent.

For our purposes, that is about all we need to take from Bell. For the 1940s and 1950s his picture—or our inference from his lack of a picture—is of a weak discipline, hardly worth explicit comment in an account of the great and exciting issues in social science of that period. My own personal experience parallels his implicit evaluation of political science. As an undergraduate in the 1930s, I flip-flopped in my choice of a major between economics and political science, first choosing economics, then abandoning it because it seemed narrow, complacent, and formalistic. But the mushiness of political science, indeed its frequent emptiness— these were no easier to bear. So I returned to a major in economics along with political science and in 1937 chose graduate work in economics rather than political science, confident that my studies would have a solid content even if sometimes bordering on disciplinary arrogance.

But perhaps Bell has left out something important; perhaps the eyes of a sociologist do not see political science clearly. Hence I supplement sociologist Bell with political scientist Charles Merriam, whose credentials as a political scientist are of the highest order. Attentive to and concerned about the discipline as he was, in 1950 he specified what he took to be the outstanding characteristics of political science:

1. A very broad range of collection and clearance of political data.
2. A noticeable shift from emphasis on forms and institutions to processes and patterns of behavior.

3. Very great attention to the technological and practical application of political assumption and principles in such fields as public administration, personnel, management, planning, and urbanism, on all levels in all areas and in relation to all functions of government.
4. Increasing attention to the study of political parties, public opinion, and various types of social groupings.
5. The far larger role of international relations as a subject of inquiry.
6. Awakening of interest in and utilization of psychological and socio-psychological methods.
7. New interest in measurement.
8. A far more intimate relationship with the field of economics.
9. Renewed interest and concern with the problems of political philosophy.
10. At the same time, the beginning of a reexamination of the relations between values and scientific conclusions.[4]

This list strikes me as a highly plausible characterization of the period. And with Merriam we pick up an acknowledgment of what came to be known as the behavioral revolution in political science. I should think that many—perhaps most—empirical political scientists would say that the major development of the 1950s, carrying well into the 1960s, was the behavioral revolution in political science, to which Bell gives not a word. Ill-defined as the term is, I am not brave enough to attempt a brief summary description or evaluation of the movement; instead, I offer a few inconclusive points. Many political scientists tell me that their sense of participating in an important current of thought for some years brought a zest, a sense of direction, and a confidence in the consequentiality of their work that they did not enjoy earlier, and do not enjoy now. The movement's direction was toward a more scientific practice of political inquiry. That meant taking more care to use concepts that could in appropriate ways be firmly, even if not always directly, attached to the empirical phenomena that they allegedly mapped. Becoming more scientific also meant straining for a clear-cut formulation of hypotheses and consequent empirical testing of them. But testing, as we shall see, still largely evades political science; and in that sense the revolution failed. What is more, the move of political science toward science was in the main a move to a positivist model of science at the very time that the model was, in several other quarters, under attack. Retrospectively, the behavioral revolution in political science emptied the cupboards of some useless and dubious tools, threw out some good ones by mistake (they were later recovered—ethical evaluation and historical narrative, as examples), and left the discipline with an improved yet limited competence only subsequently again expanded. And in drawing practitioners' attention to a careful choice of methods of inquiry—that is, of *how* to study—it may have drawn their attention away (though it was already far away) from a careful choice of *what* to study.

A further qualification: If the behavioral revolution carried many political scientists toward a more scientific practice of their discipline, the discipline could already claim, as Almond has recently pointed out, a line of practitioners with scientific aspirations, as well as scientific accomplishments commendable for their times. Scientific aspiration was not new to political science, though it may have been new to many within the discipline.[5]

We may also note during this period the rise of policy studies. I think we can locate in the 1950s, if not the 1940s, the beginning of the substantial, though not complete, transubstantiation of the field of public administration into that of policy studies. Master of arts professional training in public administration has given much ground to masters' programs in policy analysis, as clearly evidenced by now in the new policy analysis schools of recent decades. It is a noteworthy change in that it seems to indicate a widespread belief that the analysis of policy is an administrative rather than political task and one requiring technically skilled rather than politically negotiated solutions, calling at an extreme for correct rather than politically preferred answers.

One might think that it is the politicians rather than the members of the bureaucracy who need training in policy analysis—and that the bureaucracy still needs its older training in public administration. But the politicians have no time for sustained analysis of policy; they need staff analysis, which the new M.A.'s in public policy are trained to provide for them. Fair enough; but in that case, the staff members perhaps need to be educated or trained better to understand just what character of problem it is that their politician-employers face. It is not wholly a technical problem and rarely one for which a solution is to everyone's advantage. It is a problem for which all possible solutions carry gains for some people and losses for others, and therefore a problem for which every possible solution is in a sense arbitrary.

My impression is that training in policy analysis in the 1950s had not—and probably still has not—faced up to the non-technical, political, and arbitrary elements in policy-making. It had no clarity of thought about how the field of policy analysis should cope with these elements.

One more note on what political science was not doing in the 1940s and 1950s. David Cohen has suggested that social science has increasingly become the language of discourse on public policy.[6] Debate, to be judged competent, has to be familiar with social science; it must also be comfortable with many of its formulations, irrespective of social science's ability to offer findings. If economics achieved such status many decades ago, it is a status only recently achieved, if achieved at all, in the other social sciences; and it seems reasonably clear that in the 1940s and 1950s political science had not yet achieved it.

A MORE PERSONAL INTERPRETATION

From this brief conventional account of social science and political science in the 1940s and 1950s—"conventional" in the sense of identifying major new directions and accomplishments—I now proceed to a different kind of account and appraisal, one both more subjective and more idiosyncratic. For this part of my essay, with the reader's indulgence, I shall include as germane some points made in my book *Inquiry and Change*.[7]

When asked to describe the most important features of a discipline in a specified time period, one is tempted to identify those features of the discipline that first appeared in that period or that are most distinctive to it. That is a trap I want to avoid. The most important features of the discipline (by whatever standard one chooses) might well be those held in common with the discipline at other times—commonalities, not differences. We might say, to illustrate, that the most important feature of Ptolemaic astronomy was its assumption that the earth was the center of the universe, but Ptolemy was not distinctive in so believing. Or we might acknowledge that the most noteworthy feature of the Titanic was not design innovation intended to make it unsinkable but its similarity to all other ships: it was sinkable.

Scientific Discomfort

A first observation I want to make about political science of the 1940s and 1950s is that it then was (and still is?) confused by discrepancy between widely accepted scientific ideals and actual feasible practice, a discrepancy that was not faced and intelligently dealt with but rather swept under the rug.

On scientific ideals in political science, several frequent theses stand in conflict. One is that political science was not then (and perhaps still is not) sufficiently scientific; that is to say, that it was and is not sufficiently given to the formulation and testing of hypotheses and models, as in conventional or traditional science. A contrary thesis is that it was and is excessively given to the practice of conventional scientific methods: specifically, it apes nineteenth- and early twentieth-century physics. Both theses allege a fact and make an adverse evaluation. The interpretation offered here is that both theses are mistaken. More correctly stated, political science has not much practiced the scientific method as conventionally described and cannot do so; yet it venerates conventional scientific method, and hence suffers from continuing self-reproach and consequent disorientation.

In our time, in which "the" scientific method is widely discredited in favor of more eclectic views on how professional inquiry is and ought to be pursued, it might seem that political scientists' attitudes toward the traditional scientific method are no longer important. I am suggesting, however, that in the 1940s and 1950s— and still today—the aspiration to be conventionally scientific remains strong in the discipline, so that discomfort over failure and consequent confusion in the discipline continue. It is a discipline that cannot do conventional science well but, because it venerates an old scientific ideal, cannot free itself to formulate appropriate criteria for research and to practice confidently under their guidance. Is the discipline less scientific than it ought to be? This is not the problem. Is it more scientific than it ought to be—scientistic, as it is sometimes said? This is not the problem either. The problem— to say it again—is that the discipline is snared, crippled to a degree, and unclear about appropriate aspirations because it does not resolve the contradiction between long-standing ideals about method on one hand and feasible productive methods on the other.

What weight can I put behind this interpretation of political science? Let me answer this question by first laying out the argument.

Discovery. A conventional view of science—perhaps the dominant conventional view—is that it is a venture in discovery. I think it can be shown that discovery is atypical in political science, a fact about the discipline that is simply to be observed, however, not lamented. One reason for the rarity of discovery is that political science studies phenomena already familiar to lay (that is, nonprofessional) thought; it does not explore, as do the physical sciences, a world largely hidden from lay thought. It is not only from a poor introductory course that students recoil with "I knew all that already!" From even the best course, there will be something of a recoil because in fact students are familiar with the phenomena examined in the course. We political scientists may hope to expand, refine, or correct their knowledge; but we offer little in the way of surprises, for their world and ours is the same familiar world.

Contrast that familiar world with a world of tectonic plates, mitochondria, cellular transcription, quantum indeterminacy, and bosons. For physicists and biologists especially, their world is not the layperson's. Look at Bernard Berelson and Gary Steiner's 1964 book-length inventory of social-science findings, *Human Behavior*.[8] The findings are about familiar phenomena. Then look at the first thirty pages of an elementary text on biology, in which the lay mind is introduced to beta radiation, covalent bonds, anions, micelles, peptide bonds—to more than one unfamiliar phenomenon on every page. Or, look at the illustrations in an elementary text on biology; they offer glimpses through an electronic microscope into an astonishing world. Then look at the banal photographs in a political-science text—a street demonstration or a candidate entering a voting booth!

Sooner or later, of course, many discoveries in the natural sciences are communicated to lay people, with the result that aspects of a world once hidden to lay people come to be familiar. But what is familiar about politics in lay thought is not what professional thought dug out and displayed so that it became familiar; it is what was already familiar in lay thought.

Nor can political science at least claim to discover unfamiliar relations among familiar phenomena. Political science did not discover, for example, the alternative possible ways of exercising authority (and, earlier, neither did Weber, despite his articulation and organization of already existing knowledge of such alternatives). We did not discover the difference between formal and informal organization, nor the political functions of parties, nor the influences bearing on public opinion, nor the requisites of democracy. I leave to each reader the task of finding the only few examples that probably do exist of a political-science "discovery."

If we incorporate into the concept of discovery the formulation of a plausible if yet-untested hypothesis, the search for examples is not much eased. Largely what we find are refinements of already familiar hypotheses or beliefs, often taking the form of attempts to specify more precisely than in lay thought the domain or conditions of a relationship among variables. Thus, although it is widely known than party preferences are influenced by parents, political scientists will offer hypotheses about the circumstances in which the influence is stronger or weaker. But even such refining hypotheses are themselves often taken from lay thought. Often the role of a political scientist is not to discover or formulate such a refinement but to select one of the ideas present in lay thought and give it prominence for putative testing.

Since we are asked to draw on our personal experience, let me report a personal one with respect to discovery. A collection of papers has been recently published on my work.[9] Asked to write a final chapter of comment on the collected papers, I listed all the insights, findings, and the other contributions that the papers in the collection had attributed to me. They totaled 110. I then classified them. A dozen of them I identified as in fact broad-based lay knowledge, that is to say, lay in origin. Another sixty-seven I identified as long familiar to highly educated lay thought (as well as familiar to social science), again lay in origin. The last thirty-one I identified as being widely, though not universally, circulated in social science and as having some limited lay circulation—both before my attention to them. Their origins are obscure; some may have come from social science. In short, I find that for none of the 110 can I claim confidently an origin in social science, and clearly I cannot claim that I am the origin, nor is any other identifiable social scientist. It is an illuminating even if inconclusive sample drawn from work done in the 1940s and 1950s, and on into the 1990s.

None of these comments on the degree to which political science differs from conventional notions of science is intended to express regret. I simply want to show that political science has rarely done and can only rarely do science as conventionally described. Its conventionally scientific aspirations are bound to be disappointed.

Testing. To these comments on familiarity and discovery, one might reply on behalf of political science: "Well, at least we test!" Lay knowledge is highly fallible; it needs testing, and this we do. Yet for the 1940s and 1950s (and, I think, still today), the claim can be granted only if substantially amended or qualified. For most of the propositions about the political world—propositions on which we depend in order to live our lives—political-science testing is unnecessary and would be foolishly wasteful: Congress is composed of two houses. Britain has a parliamentary system, the United States a presidential one. Bribery of government officials is more frequent than rare. World War II came later than World War I. One can write to his senator. Some nation-states are not democratic. There exist penalties for breaking the law, and they are frequently administered. In politics, money shouts.

The claim that political science or any other social science tests, then, has to be reduced to a claim that it tests a small proportion of propositions. To that a claim will be added that the small number it tests are those of theoretical significance. That supplementary claim must itself be qualified, for many scientifically untested lay propositions are also of theoretical significance—for example, the proposition that penalties for law-breaking are frequently administered. For theoretical propositions, consequently, we have to say that their testing is shared by both lay and professional or social scientific inquiry. I have never counted or sampled the possibilities; but I suggest that lay inquiry tests the more easily tested propositions, while social science, including political science, tries to do the more difficult testing.

One consequence is that propositions about the political or social world not scientifically tested are more conclusively established than are propositions that emerge from scientific testing. I doubt that I can locate any scientific finding of political science that is as conclusively established as the never scientifically tested proposition that the US Congress is composed of two houses or that some elected officials are not closely governed in their policy choices by the wishes of a majority of their constituents.

Clearly in the 1940s and 1950s political science produced almost no general scientific propositions of a high degree of conclusiveness. Its most systematically empirical wing—voting studies—produced highly conclusive propositions about voting behavior, but only by limiting them to specified dates and areas (thus yielding an example of the inverse relationship between theoretical significance and degree of conclusiveness).

Nor did political science in this period go far in the direction of replication, which is an elementary requirement for testing. Taking all this together, perhaps a fair summary statement on political-science testing is that it attempted little and succeeded even less, even though the air of the 1950s was full of expressed ambition to test. The failure was less to be attributed to mistakes in the practice of political science than to the innate difficulties of testing propositions about so complex a phenomenon as the social world. To indicate more specifically the magnitude of the failure, however, I suggest that it was sufficient to justify the presumption that many, perhaps most, of the political scientists who tried to test would have been more fruitfully employed had they given it up and turned to other tasks within their capacities, tasks to be commented on below.

Discovery and Testing Taken Together: The Findings of Political Science

Conventionally, we can say of any science that it has achieved a "finding" if it can demonstrate well, even if not conclusively—thus with high probability—the truth or falsity of a nomothetic proposition, irrespective of whether it is a proposition circulating in lay thought or a proposition discovered by scientists. Hence, if we look into the "findings" of political science in the 1940s and 1950s we can explore further the degree to which the discipline achieved either discovery or demonstration. I remind the reader that I am trying to identify certain characteristics of the discipline, not to deplore them. Whatever an ideal political science might be, it will not be a conventional science.

Deutsch and his colleagues constructed their list of major advances in social science by specifying topics or areas rather than findings. Thus, for example, the theory about a one-party organization is claimed as a major advance but not as a proposition, identifiable insight, discovery, or test. So also quantitative political science is claimed as a major advance, but no finding is identified.

Bell attributed no finding to political science. In 1950, Charles Merriam's overview of American political science (noted above) made no claims that political science had achieved any findings. Nor, in the same volume, did Benjamin Lippincott, writing on "Political Theory in the United States." Nor did Lasswell, writing on psychology and political science. Nor did Maurice Duverger or F. L. Schuman in the same book. Indeed, one has to search tediously through six hundred oversized pages of contributions from roughly fifty scholars to find less than a half dozen identifications of a finding—each itself dubious. A curious state of affairs in a discipline trying to be conventionally scientific.

But, one might reply, these fifty or so contributors had been asked to discuss method rather than substance. Yet this does not answer the question, for, I suggest, we can be confident that a searching discussion of method would mention findings if any existed. Methods seek results; the results we seek, or so we tell ourselves, are findings. One cannot achieve any quality in analyzing method without looking into connections between method and findings, using reference to findings in the exploration of what methods are useful for what kind of findings—and what methods fail to produce any. The near complete absence of reference to findings in the entire collection of papers is, for a discipline that claims to be a science, extraordinary and even eerie, as strange as Hamlet without the Danish prince. It is all the more curious that, findings aside, method is also discussed without reference even to *questions* for the discipline to search. Questions, like findings, are missing.

As late as the 1980s, in a review of the political science of political development,[10] Almond made his claims for the accomplishments of the field. Again, these claims were not posited by detailing findings but rather by alleging that political scientists had "illuminated," "were concerned with," "gave special emphasis to," "developed insights, hypotheses, and analytical categories," "codified," "stressed the importance of," "examined the significance of," "placed in the context of," "treated variables theoretically," "produced good work," "were fruitful," "applied concepts and models to," "vastly improved our understanding," "dealt with," and "increased the level of rigor." I do not doubt these claims, but the absence of findings is noteworthy. None, we must assume he thought, were worth mentioning even as late as the 1980s.

What then did political scientists do in the 1940s and 1950s? If they did not discover, did not test, did not make findings, what did they do? One answer is that they spent time trying, often wastefully trying. More interesting is a second answer: they turned, as always, to other tasks more manageable and productive, even if of lower repute in conventional accounts of scientific method. These various tasks can be described in a number of ways, any one of which is adequate for present purposes.

Reporting. Just short of establishing a scientific finding is a task that might be called reporting, a task not to be deprecated. As late as 1971, Alice Rivlin suggested that the principal contribution of social science to social policy was not theory-building or scientific finding but reporting—getting the facts straight and keeping us up-to-date on such questions as: Who are the poor? How many single-parent families are there? What are children learning in school?[11] Clearly, reporting of this kind was a practice of political science in the 1940s and 1950s. And this suggests how contextual and historical, rather than theoretical, political science may have been.

Checklists. Like the other social sciences, political science in this period (and still today) engaged in a great deal of specification of possible relations among variables in complex situations in which it remained impossible to ascertain which of the possible relations actually held or would hold in any specified situation. Again, this is a task not to be deprecated. Would democracy flourish or decline in postwar West Germany? What differences in outcome would obtain as between two-party and multiparty systems? What will determine the level of bureaucratic efficiency and efficacy in the developing world? Political scientists produced many possible scenarios, useful on many counts, even if they could not answer the questions. They gave us checklists.

Evaluation. And of course political scientists continued, as always, in their 2,500-year-old task of evaluating institutions and policies while debating endlessly the propriety of doing so. The behavioral revolution in political science posed some challenges to the propriety of evaluation; but it appears that, like other social scientists, political scientists inevitably pick up from their practice of the discipline some skills in evaluation that only an occasional critic would rather they simply throw away. They might as well be heard from.

Design. In this period, as always, some of the energies of the discipline were invested in design: an improved party system or administrative reform, for example.

Correcting the discipline's own errors. One curious task may be worth mentioning in order to beg the question of how often we were called upon to attend to it. That task was the laborious correction of errors peculiar to the scholarly mind, errors that lay thought had not been led into. Take my own writing on incrementalism, for example. It was significant only because there existed in the academic mind an idealized model of rational decision-making that had in theoretical circles become confused with a description of both actual and ideal decision-making, to neither of which it did in fact correspond. On the whole, lay thought, including the thought of practical decision-makers, was not afflicted with the confusion; the confusion was an artifact of scholarly energy. To a mind clear and hard-headed on the complexities and frustrations of attempts at intellectual mastery of a complex decision problem and never taught in the classroom to confuse idealized rationality with real-world complex problem-solving, incrementalist theory has nothing to say. It speaks only to academic minds that have to unlearn academic errors. What I do not know—but it is a question worth exploring—is how much of the 1940s and 1950s was given to correcting our own errors, undoing our own damage. Was this, perhaps, iatrogenic political science?

Methodology. Other energies went, as always, into methodological dispute, so familiar as to require no elaboration here.

In short, throughout the period, as ever since, no end of tasks called for political science—despite its incapacity to achieve scientific findings.

The Improbable But Possible Uselessness of Political Science

Looking back over what political science has and has not achieved, I call attention to a remarkable feature it shares with all the social sciences. Nothing that political science ever achieved was *unarguably* or *demonstrably* necessary to any major social venture. That is to say, whatever humankind achieved in the period, we cannot find an unmistakable dependence of that achievement on any contribution from political science. I intend this claim to be no more than a statement of fact, however, and, for reasons that will become clear, not a lament.

By "major social venture," though I cannot precisely define it, I mean such activities or functions as educating the young, fighting wars, exploring space, controlling disease, constructing an atomic bomb, administering justice, constructing and maintaining systems of communication and transportation, maintaining law and order, organizing the society's labor and other resources for production, or averting or coping with social catastrophes.

For space exploration, certain achievements in theoretical physics and in engineering were unarguably necessary; without them, no space exploration would have taken place. For the control of some communicable diseases, biomedical research was unarguably necessary; so also was research in chemistry. For political science, I suggest, we cannot find that it was ever in the 1940s and 1950s— or ever since—unarguably necessary in a comparable sense. Its achievements may have helped society maintain law and order, and may have made some contribution to transportation and communication, or to space exploration, or to justice, or to some other major social venture. But there is no clear, unmistakable, demonstrated connection between political-science accomplishments and society's achievements. Not even between the distinguished contributions of a whole history of political philosophy and any of society's major ventures can such a connection be found.

That proposition is in itself illuminating—telling us as it does that a certain quality or level of achievement was, in the 1940s and 1950s, simply beyond the capacities of the discipline—and probably remains so today. Whatever the level or quality of its achievements, they did not reach a high mark. In addition, the proposition opens up the possibility that political science was in those two decades (and is perhaps today) without value. Most of us would reject such an inference. We would say that, despite the impossibility of demonstrating a political-science contribution to, say, good public administration, or international peace, or human rights, we can make a sufficiently plausible argument as to be widely, though not universally, persuasive. Yes, I think that can be done: a widely persuasive argument can be made for the value of political science. But it is an argument without force for a skeptic, one who begins his thinking on the issue with profound doubts about the influence of scholarship on human affairs rather than with the supposition that sustained, careful thought is almost certain to pay off one way or another. I think we political scientists have to acknowledge that we are practicing skills and making inquiries of dubious, though possibly great, worth. We have to face, at one extreme, the *possibility* that the world of the 1940s and 1950s—and today's world, too—would look pretty much as it does had there never been a Plato or Aristotle or their equivalents; never a Hobbes, a Locke, a Weber, or their equivalents; and never a core of professional investigators into voting behavior, public administration, or international negotiation among nation-states.

I shall further argue below that in assessing its own value, political science had not yet developed by 1960 a very significant competence—and not even by 1995.

POLITICAL SCIENCE AS A DEBATE

Returning now to my general interpretation of political science in the 1940s and 1950s as short of scientific finding and engaged instead in a variety of investigatory and evaluational tasks, I want to suggest a further implication. It is that for those decades, as perhaps for the present, the term "political science" was a name given not to a field of conventional scientific inquiry but to a continuing debate.

Now naturally debate is essential to scientific inquiry. But in that context it is a part of the process of winnowing out competing propositions and moving toward a finding. Put another way, it is subordinated to the establishment of findings. In political science, debate rarely leads to findings. And on any given big issue of fact or value, debate in political science tends to be endless rather than declining (or terminating in a finding). It has a further characteristic not much noted, which is that the debaters, knowing they cannot demonstrate their allegations to skeptics, talk largely to the already persuaded and to a marginal group of the undecided. The debate goes on because no more is required for success in participating than that the participant find endorsement by some large segment of colleagues, however inadequate his proof or demonstration.

Schumpeter, for example, never constructed anything that could pass for testing, verification, demonstration, or proof of his interpretation of democracy as competition for leadership. But what he offered appealed to political scientists ready for various reasons to agree with him. I do not mean to say that he did not skillfully construct a case; that he did, a case both for the descriptive accuracy of his model and for his favorable evaluation. But he did so more as a debater than as a scientist. In the same light, consider, as other examples, the work of David Truman, David Easton, E. E. Schattschneider, Lasswell, Almond, Dahl, and Theodore Lowi; or consider forty long years of inconclusive debate, devoid of scientific finding, on incrementalism, or an even longer debate on pluralism, both endless debates on fact and value alike.

For another bit of evidence that political science is a continuing debate rather than conventional science, consider the character of evaluations of journal and book manuscripts by referees—or even book reviews. They rarely ask if the reviewed paper or book is true or false. For the kinds of issues discussed in the reviewed manuscripts, one rarely dares to hazard an answer to that question. The referee or reviewer asks instead whether the manuscript has something interesting and significant to say and whether it contains a well-constructed argument. This is a relevant question to ask about a contribution to a debate, but quite different from the question of truth-value that would be raised by a referee of a scientific paper in, say, the physical sciences.

Regrettable? One is tempted to think so. But political science as a debate might be political science at its best.

CHOOSING DIRECTIONS FOR RESEARCH

Amateur Project Choice

In the 1940s and 1950s political scientists, like other social scientists, practiced only a low level of competence in their choice of the direction or topic of research. I think it is reasonable to call it amateurish rather than professional. On the matter of how to do research on a given topic, political science and the other social sciences had even, by the period under consideration, produced a vast library of books and articles on, for example, statistics, survey research, content analysis, and mathematical modeling. On the question of how to do research, political science had reached even then a high level of professionalism; but on the question of what to research, no comparable library exists. We retain our amateur status.

To develop professional competence in the choice of a project, political scientists would have to examine their own history of successes and failures, examining at the same time what constitutes success and failure. This they rarely did in the 1940s and 1950s, and even today it is not part of the training of political scientists. The embarrassing level at which political science operates even today is revealed in the common structure of a research prospectus. As justification for the project, it is alleged that the proposed topic is important, as though important topics did not vastly exceed the number to which political science can attend; next, that the topic has been neglected, as though the number of neglected topics did not vastly exceed the number to which political science can attend; and, finally, that the topic is feasible, as though the number of feasible topics did not vastly exceed the number to which political science can attend.

Some years ago, many of us in political science at Yale held a weekly seminar to discuss research directions. We continued the effort for two years. Each of us profited from some illuminations, and some made some marginal changes in their own research directions. But no one ever could develop a highly persuasive case for any one choice of direction in the face of articulated objection to it. After two years, each of us returned to the same lines of research we were pursuing when we began the seminar—evidence, I take it, that our choices were not the product of highly informed and rational professional expertise.

No Canonical Authority

All that I have said about the relation of political science to conventional science may throw some light on why, when I began the study of political science, there were no canonical works to give me much guidance in the direction of my own research. The great philosophers, say, from Plato to Hegel, were canonical to some members of the discipline but deprecated, if not denounced, by many others (as continues to be the case today). In empirical political studies, no political scientist had achieved a canonical impact on the discipline like that of Adam Smith, Alfred Marshall, Leon Walras, or John Maynard Keynes in economics. Of course I became aware of "big names" in the discipline, like Charles E. Merriam and Harold Lasswell, and could identify the direction of their scholarly interest; but I could not attribute to them the scholarly authority granted to a long sequence of economists.

What then guided or inspired my own research? Thinking back to my collaboration with Robert A. Dahl on *Politics, Economics and Welfare*,[12] I suspect that for both of us the legacy of the Great Depression was more influential than scholarly leads. We thought of ourselves, if I remember correctly, as off on a new track. While in graduate school a few years earlier, I had been enormously impressed by a talk in which Arthur Holly Compton had shown (though that was not his main theme) that the path of accomplishment in physics pointed most emphatically at any time toward necessary next research projects. Certain next steps were necessary; there were identifiable bottlenecks that had to be broken. I could see almost nothing at all similar in the social sciences. In these fields, it seemed as though any of hundreds, probably thousands, of research projects were more or less equally worthy or equally urgent—or equally lacking in urgency. Dahl's and my research grew out of a graduate seminar we jointly taught; it represented an amateurish project selection. We may have taken some inspiration from Popper's *Open Society and Its Enemies*,[13] but I cannot recall whether our interest in that book preceded or followed our project, nor can I remember whether we much talked or thought about Popper. I was, as is still the case, struggling with my ambivalence about both political science, which attracted me with its big questions, and economics, which attracted me with its solid theoretical core.

In addition, there are always institutional factors that influence the direction of research in any field, and here I do not refer only to the availability of funds. When Dahl and I first asked for departmental clearance to teach jointly the graduate seminar in planning out of which grew *Politics, Economics and Welfare,* the economics department asked us to label it not "Planning" but "Critique of Planning," to make sure that it would not appear as implicitly accepting or endorsing the idea of planning. That was Yale as late as 1948 or 1949. More important to my incentives was my department's (I was then a member of the economics department only) deprecation of the sort of work I did. But if this represented an institutional adversity, the ease with which Yale opened up opportunities for me in the political science department represented institutional flexibility and encouragement.

Later I found the National Science Foundation unwilling to support the work that produced *Usable Knowledge* (with David K. Cohen)[14] and *Inquiry and Change.* The Foundation's staff told me that, despite unanimous endorsement of my proposal by referees, they would give me nothing unless I would specify in advance the specific research methods I intended to employ, which I was unable to do. I mention this episode because it may reveal one of the costs of the bureaucratization (possibly necessary) of research funding.

Professional Standards, Values, and Attitudes

Comfortable axioms. In the debate that constitutes political science, significant long-standing propositions were treated in the 1940s and 1950s by very large numbers of political scientists— sometimes almost all—as true, despite their never having been systematically tested. These included such propositions as: That stable government requires the consent of the governed; that some degree of agreement on values, at least among elites, is necessary for stability; that an illegitimate political system cannot survive.

To the extent that these axiomatic or dogmatic propositions circulate as though known to be true, the debate is not political science at its best. Yet this condition continues today.

Benign interpretations. A further characteristic of political science of the 1940s and 1950s was that, Marxists aside, it was strongly disposed to see the main outlines of putative democratic political systems as benign. Elsewhere I have offered chapter and verse in support of this hypothesis,[15] citing, among other examples, defining political parties by reference only to their useful functions, interpreting political socialization as educational rather than impairing, and finding, without explanation or argument on the point, common good more than conflict and exploitation in the governmental process.

The frequent Pollyannaism of mainstream political science of those decades was given a scientific sheen when it was derived from or supported by the structural-functionalism of that period. Functionalism fell into a habit of looking for consequences benign for a society somehow considered as homogeneous, rather than for consequences benign for a ruling, dominant, or disproportionately empowered group. Following functional analysis, political science could, for example, find in citizen apathy a source of political stability without considering that it might perhaps as well have found it to be a source of opportunities for elite exploitation of the masses.

Indeed, in its preoccupation with the benign—and in other ways, too—political science of the 1940s and 1950s often displayed a noteworthy naïveté. Research on public opinion, for example, liked to ask in their survey work about respondents' sources of information (not misinformation, but information—and not sources of obfuscation, or of disincentives to thought). A more explicit example of naïveté is the American Political Science Association's 1951 *Goals for Political Science*,[16] a committee report on teaching. Assigning to teachers of political science the primary task of training students for intelligent citizenship, the committee issued the opinion that the making of citizens is a complex task "calling for the cooperation of all elements in society."[17] Now here is a pious thought suitable, if to anything, to political oratory or some other venture in rhetoric or public relations. But in a society in which, as in all societies, some people want only docile citizens, some want only limited education for potential troublemakers, and in which, in any case, intelligent disagreements abound over the desirable character of education and the desirable character of citizens, it is a statement bordering on the inane. It ought to be seen as an embarrassment to the discipline, as expressing naive simplemindedness rather than scholarly competence.

Political science and democracy. One might suggest that a touch of naïveté has always marked the discipline's conception of its relation to democracy. That conception is not wholly stable; it has varied as much as the difference between skepticism regarding the very viability of democracy in mass society and affirmation of democracy as the end point of political development for the developing world. On the whole, however, I suggest that political scientists have accepted a commitment to democracy that is inconsistent with their commitment to unfettered inquiry, as well as inconsistent with commitments that some political scientists think they can make to scientific neutrality.

I do not see how a social scientist can achieve a very profound intelligence about the social world unless his studies are guided by values. But since informed and thoughtful minds must be expected to disagree on values, I look askance at a discipline as uniformly committed to democracy as political science tends to be. The case against such values as democracy and liberty is not without merit, and the argument needs to be kept open indefinitely. It is therefore not the function of political science to promote or defend democracy, although it may be your function or mine to do so, just as it may be your function or mine, in a competition of ideas, to attack it. It is such a line of argument, which I cannot pursue further here, that the discipline has not well explored.

The discipline's clients. If we follow, as I do, the explicit or implicit proposition of Plato, Machiavelli, Hobbes, Mosca, Michels, Lasswell, and countless others that there is a fundamental distinction in politics between the elite and the masses, it is appropriate to register here the familiar observation that, like all social sciences at all times, despite its democratic inclinations political science in the 1940s and 1950s gave its help more to the elite than to the masses. So familiar is this proposition that I shall not embellish it except to note that most political scientists, in accepting grants and contracts or choosing research topics, left no evidence of having reflected on the issue: I do not recall that I have ever read a research prospectus that did so, although I am confident that some research proposals coming from the Left do so. Some political scientists who worked in or for government or on government grants simply assumed, I would guess, that democratic governments serve the people, as though the mediating elites who set tasks or administered research funds could be counted on to pursue no interests of their own.

Impaired citizens and impaired scholars. If we look to Plato again—remembering his cave (following on the same point, also Bacon, Locke, Rousseau, Marx, and Mannheim, among many others)—we incorporate the familiar proposition that all of us suffer not only from biologically imposed limits on cognitive capacity but also from incapacities of the mind that we have learned— have been taught both inadvertently and deliberately. "All of us" includes professional intellectuals like political scientists, who suffer from two kinds of learned impaired capacity to think: first, those that we share with most other people, including those learned long before we became political scientists; and, second, those peculiar to our discipline. That we suffer from both has been persuasively and frequently argued in the history of thought, and some of the points about political science that I have been making carry this implication. I can think of no more important thing to say about political science in the 1940s and 1950s (and today) than that we are all impaired, crippled by learned incompetences.

For reasons laid out in detail in *Inquiry and Change,* our impairments have always been not random but patterned. The pattern reflects parents' desires to *control* rather than edify their children, an older generation's desire to *control* rather than edify the younger generation, clerics' desires to *control* rather than edify an errant mass, and political and economic elites' desire to *control rather than edify* the masses. It is a pattern that constantly recommends to political scientists, as well as to all of us, hierarchy, obedience, deference, faith, inequality, and stability. Political scientists, I suggest, have been half-blinded to contrary or even questioning perceptions.

The extent and significance of our professional impairment is of course disputable, and my argument on it in *Inquiry and Change* is of course not conclusive. It is not an argument that builds from the strength of a history of earlier work within the discipline, for our own impairment is not a subject that the discipline has wished to study; there exists almost no history of research on it. Impairment remains a major phenomenon for political science to investigate. A point, then, about the discipline in the 1940s and 1950s (and still today?) is that it hardly gave such questions much thought.

*   *   *

If these observations seem too severe, let me place them in perspective, both with respect to how I intend them and how they might be received. On the first, I do not intend them as an account of why political science ought to be abandoned. I have enjoyed practicing it, have made some headway in understanding the political world, and would not discourage a young mind from pursuing political science. In considering how to weigh my most adverse assertions, remember that, in so far as we can trust fallible impressions, political science has long competed with sociology for the bottom rung on the ladder of social sciences. That, I think, is our repute with other social sciences, and it is our own judgment of ourselves. If that much is already assumed, my remarks are more explanatory than deprecatory. Bear also in mind that my most adverse comments on political science in the 1940s and 1950s seem to hold, as I repeatedly paused to say, for other social sciences as well.

In retrospect, I see some conflicting—not inconsistent, but conflicting—career interests that throw some light on the themes in this essay. Entering college during the depth of the Great Depression of the 1930s, I urgently wanted to understand how a society could fall into such disorganization. From that followed a persistent radical critique of social institutions. But from graduate school on, I also found continuing intellectual pleasure in uncovering the hidden rationalities of complex, mutually adjustive, and disorderly (on superficial examination) social processes.[18] For all its grave faults and despite its breakdown in the 1930s, the market is such a process; and there are other such processes, though less well developed, in government and public policy-making. My own discovery of the market's accomplishments and potential came to me not as an economics major at Stanford but from Frank Knight in my graduate work at the University of Chicago. It led directly to my subsequent interest in incrementalism and mutual adjustment.

At this late date, I find myself both critical of all existing societies (as in *Inquiry and Change*) and yet fascinated by such feats of social organization as are achieved by unplanned and superficially untidy, even ugly, mutually adjustive social interaction. It is understandable—but something of a curiosity—that as a result I seem to be a radical critic but a cautious rather than radical reformer. Seeing our social institutions as grossly defective, I am nevertheless intimidated by the intricacies of social organization and the indirections that policies must take in order to make the most of the hidden rationalities of mutual adjustment.

Looking at political science, as well as the other social sciences, I find myself again critical. They are both part of the social order I find faulty, and they seem inadequate, despite their accomplishments, for the task of social criticism that I take to be one of their responsibilities and for the design of policies or reforms that fit a world of complex mutual adjustment.

The social sciences, I have just said, are part of the social order. In my pursuit of an understanding of both social disorganization and organization, I was repeatedly led to ask questions about human cognitive capacity to cope with social problems, as well as questions about the possibility that the social sciences could raise that cognitive capacity. That in turn led me to see that some forms of organization demand less of cognitive capacity than do other forms—mutual adjustment, for example, asking less than centrally managed organization. Hence if we ask, "What can the human mind achieve in better social organization?" we must proceed to complex questions about both ordinary and academic inquiry operating within and about particular social institutions. This line of inquiry was little pursued by political science in the 1940s and 1950s, and it remains weak today.

270   Charles E. Lindblom

ENDNOTES

[1]Daniel Bell, *The Social Sciences Since the Second World War* (New Brunswick, N.J.: Transaction Books, 1982).

[2]Karl Deutsch et al., "Conditions Favoring Major Advances in Social Science," *Science* 5 (February 1971).

[3]Harold Lasswell and Daniel Lerner et al., *The Policy Sciences* (Stanford, Calif.: Stanford University Press, 1951).

[4]Charles Merriam, "Political Science in the United States," in *Contemporary Political Science* (Paris: UNESCO, 1950), 247 f.

[5]Gabriel Almond, *A Discipline Divided* (Newbury Park, Calif.: Sage Publications, 1990), 23–29.

[6]David K. Cohen and Janet Weiss, "Social Science and Social Policy: Schools and Race," *The Educational Forum* 41 (May 1977).

[7]Charles E. Lindblom, *Inquiry and Change* (New Haven, Conn.: Yale University Press, 1990).

[8]Bernard Berelson and Gary Steiner, *Human Behavior* (New York: Harcourt, Brace and World, 1964).

[9]Harry Redner, ed., *An Heretical Heir of the Enlightenment* (Boulder, Colo.: Westview Press, 1993).

[10]Gabriel Almond, *A House Divided* (Newbury Park, Calif.: Sage Publications, 1990), chap. 9.

[11]Alice Rivlin, *Systematic Thinking for Social Action* (Washington, D.C.: Brookings Institution, 1971), 9.

[12]Robert A. Dahl, *Politics, Economics and Welfare* (New York: Harper, 1953).

[13]Sir Karl Raimund Popper, *Open Society and Its Enemies* (London: Routledge and Kegan Paul, 1949).

[14]Charles E. Lindblom and David K. Cohen, *Usable Knowledge* (New Haven, Conn.: Yale University Press, 1979).

[15]See Charles E. Lindblom, "Another State of Mind," *American Political Science Review* 76 (1982).

[16]American Political Science Association, *Goals for Political Science* (New York: Sloane, 1951).

[17]Ibid., ix.

[18]As in Dahl, *Politics, Economics and Welfare*, and Charles E. Lindblom, *The Intelligence of Democracy* (New York: Free Press, 1965).

Rogers M. Smith

Still Blowing in the Wind: The American Quest for a Democratic, Scientific Political Science

W̲HEN I ENTERED GRADUATE SCHOOL in 1975, unsure whether my combination of philosophic and political concerns really belonged in political science, it was not reassuring to read two of the profession's leaders, Fred Greenstein and Nelson Polsby, explaining that I was joining an "ill-defined, amorphous, and heterogeneous" discipline.[1] That description had force then, and it still does today. True, most of us concede that quasi-experimental empirical research, today symbolized by multiple-regression equations, is in some sense the most "sciencey" part of political science. But there is no agreement that such work is the most important thing we do, much less that it is all we should do. My own sense of feeling very much at home with parts of the profession and not very connected at all to others is probably shared, in quite different ways, by most political scientists.

Consistent with my peculiar professional proclivities, the discussion here will be structured historically, not quantitatively, and I will not eschew normative prescription in the end. I will suggest that American political science has always been shaped by two often conflicting desires: to serve American democracy and to be a true "science." The tensions between those desires have contributed to periodic debunkings of the prevailing forms of political science, followed by quests for a "new science of politics" that can

---

Rogers M. Smith is Professor of Political Science at Yale University.

fulfill both desires better. After an era characterized by the dominance of "scientific" rational-choice theory, we are now entering one of our periods of transition and heightened uncertainty. But certain possibilities for new convergences in our work and that of other disciplines are discernible—possibilities that, on the whole, seem promising to me.

It is likely that our discipline will continue to become more rigorously empirical and somewhat more responsive to current political problems. But it will probably do so in ways that are more self-consciously historical, with both deductivist formal theory and abstract normative theory playing less prominent roles than they have recently—a pattern with counterparts in economics, sociology, even the increasingly pragmatist field of philosophy. Such developments would be largely to the good; but even if they come, American political science will still seek to define itself more fully and distinctively. I doubt it will be able to do so by finding either a grand theory or special methods that can generate a unique "science of politics." Rather, its distinctive mission must be cast in terms of its subject matter. I will argue that the discipline's task should be to explore in the most rigorous ways all topics that are arguably politically fundamental, with special attention to those that are predictably neglected, for both intellectual and political reasons, by governmental and private-sector analysts, politicians, and the media. That, I will suggest, is about as scientific and as serviceable to democracy as we can honestly get.

THE TRAJECTORY OF POLITICAL SCIENCE AND THE ROLE OF POLITICAL THEORY

Because the myriad neighborhoods within the polis of political science are likely to be unfamiliar to most readers, I will first self-indulgently make it clear "where I am coming from"; but autobiography will end soon. Like many in modern academe, I turned to political science as a result of political alienation. Having been raised a proudly upper-middle-class, Midwestern, WASP Republican American male, I became disillusioned with much of that (and with American politics in general) in the turbulent late 1960s. Those disillusionments compelled me to search for better answers. In the congenially unconventional university program I chose, the people who talked about politics in ways that echoed my experiences and addressed the big questions that preoccupied me were political theorists who had political science degrees and were teaching the "greats." Those works fell under the rubric of political science partly because philosophy departments largely disdained the history of philosophy, political philosophy, and big questions in favor of a conceptual analysis of ordinary language. That analytical work bored me to tears.

American political science had emerged in part out of nineteenth-century college courses on the "greats" of political and moral philosophy, as well as on history and the political economy; people with those interests could still find a place in the discipline. The teachers I encountered tended to be either students of Leo Strauss, sharing his sense that modernity had dangerously rejected much of ancient wisdom, or soft Marxists and social democrats, who used the history of political theory to expose American ideological prejudices. I was intrigued by both, and my teachers guided me toward an academic career.

Thus I really chose to enter the field of political *theory*, not political *science*. My advisors stressed that political theorists occupied an odd position in the discipline, a position I later grasped more fully by studying the profession's history. Recently, work on that history has proliferated rapidly, providing evidence that we are indeed in a period of disciplinary introspection and redefinition.[2] These studies vary greatly, but one near-universal theme is the tale of how American political science originated in the late nineteenth century with aspirations to be both truly scientific and a servant of American democratic citizenship, aspirations abetted by a deep and abiding faith that these enterprises went hand in hand.[3] I wish now to discuss this disciplinary faith, for it will loom large in what I say about where the profession is currently and where it might go.

Political science was a relative latecomer among the new professions that emerged out of the American Social Science Association and other reform efforts of the Gilded Age, located in the new universities created in imitation of German institutions, with members who were generally hopeful that scientific disciplines could promote the progressive changes that the nation's leading political parties could not. As Judith Shklar and Dorothy Ross have argued, the young profession's "science" reflected the broader intellectual currents of the times but was distinctively preoccupied with problems of the nation's titularly democratic institutions and with efforts to understand and to vindicate what was special about America.[4]

It can rightly be objected that so seminal a disciplinary figure as Woodrow Wilson denied at times that political studies could amount to "science," although public administration could. He did so because he believed there was an ineradicable element of creativity in statesmanship (but not "neutral" bureaucratic work) that no science could capture. He also thought, accordingly, that political writings gained influence more from rhetorical stylistic power than from scientific substance. But Wilson still differed only in emphasis from many of his Progressive Era academic successors. Like them, he believed that scholars of politics could provide citizens and statesmen with the refined knowledge about institutions and issues that democracies needed.[5]

One can also question the early discipline's democratic commitments: John Burgess's pioneering comparative and historical approach to political science at Columbia in the 1880s and 1890s used Hegelian and Darwinian views of nationalistic and racial struggle to justify a sharply limited conception of democracy. Burgess's example shows that commitments to America can be in tension with commitments both to democracy and to good science, and although I will not explore those tensions here, they have mattered greatly in a discipline always centered on American politics. But as it burgeoned in the Progressive Era the profession took on a more Deweyan cast, with the quests to advance science and democracy evermore in the foreground. Racial themes of American, Anglo-Saxon, or Teutonic capacities for liberty receded in favor of efforts to expand both the democratic character and the scientific competence of modern institutions and citizens.[6]

One of the discipline's deepest problems is that this early faith in the joint destiny of science and democracy has proven hard to sustain. Repeatedly, successive schools in American political science have been caught between desires for research that affirms and assists meaningfully democratic self-governance and desires for research that develops full causal accounts of politics, usually on a model from the natural sciences. The tension arises in part because such causal accounts tend deterministically to deny any consciously self-directed agency to the phenomena they study. A science of human political behavior thus can seem to debunk the self-understandings of democratic participants and the meaningfulness of their conscious choices.[7] Much of the apparently most "scientific" work in political science has carried such a debunking message, intentionally or not. Sometimes democratic commitments have been made to appear foolish in light of the ignorance of voters, the apparently inescapable power of economic, military, and professional elites, and the decisive role of technological, economic, demographic, linguistic, geographic, and climatic forces largely beyond conscious human control. Political scientists have implied that effective governance, if possible at all, requires scientific skill and empirical knowledge beyond the grasp of most citizens. Hence the assignment of extensive governmental powers to experts (like social scientists) has been made to seem preferable. These positions have frequently been advanced in highly technical language impenetrable to most citizens, who may therefore decide that politics *is* beyond them.

From the Progressive Era on, the tensions between the discipline's commitments to science and democracy have repeatedly forged an ironic arc in the careers of leading political scientists, from Arthur Bentley and Charles Beard to Charles Merriam, Harold Lasswell, David Easton, Gabriel Almond, and Robert Dahl. Early in their careers, these scholars criticized previous forms of political science for being naive about democracy, primitive and inadequate as science, and consequently incapable of contributing greatly to the conduct or reform of American democratic institutions. Each helped promote new efforts to create a true science of politics, explicitly or implicitly confident that it would help make more sophisticated forms of democracy possible. Subsequently, however, each became dissatisfied with the results and methods of their intellectual progeny. Their followers' works often disparaged the feasibility of democracy, however construed, and did so in professional jargon inaccessible to ordinary citizens. Thus, late in their careers, each of these leading figures turned away from emphasizing the pursuit of a truly "scientific" political science and stressed the vindication and advancement of effective human political agency by means of a more truly democratic politics. Such later works frequently have been judged, in turn, naive and unscientific by younger proponents of yet another "new science of politics."

This cyclical pattern has, however, been significantly modified by a secular linear one. Whereas Beard (and, to a lesser degree, Merriam) came to attack excessive "scientism" in politics, indeed even the possibility of a political science altogether, later figures have not issued such denunciations. Instead, the self-understanding of political scientists as members of a disinterested profession pursuing scientific knowledge for its own sake has become more entrenched. Furthermore, from the time of Lasswell onwards, the concerns to aid democratic politics of political scientists like David Truman, V. O. Key, Jr., David Easton, and Robert Dahl in the 1950s increasingly came to center on the provisions of tools and insights to managerial "democratic" elites. To be sure, from the late 1960s on, Easton, Almond, Dahl, and Charles Lindblom (among others) reinstantiated the older pattern by moving from an early emphasis on scientific analyses (of systems, group politics, and incrementalist decision-making, respectively) to explicitly normative efforts to further democracy, often by criticizing the power of corporations and experts and promoting a better-informed democratic citizenry. Generally, however, such figures have neither been quite so dismissive of political *science* as Beard came to be nor so optimistic about the possibilities for democratic improvements as Merriam remained.[8]

William Riker's writings dramatize how in recent decades the cyclical pattern of political scientists moving from an emphasis on science to democracy has been tempered by an increased commitment overall to the study of politics as a scientific pursuit, as well as the inevitability of elite predominance even in democratic politics. Trained in traditional political philosophy and empirical political science at Harvard in the late 1940s, Riker turned early on to the new enterprise of rational-choice theory, which promised to make the discipline a deductive science guided by a unified general theory in imitation (or extension) of neoclassical economics. For Riker, rational choice also offered the hope of vindicating reliance on markets instead of governmental programs. The enterprise's professed aim, however, was to develop formal models depicting all politics as comprised of strategically rational, goal-maximizing individual behavior within specified structures of rules.

Though the emphasis was on formal theory-building, models were then to be subjected to empirical testing, in the manner of Newtonian physics. Under Riker's guidance, the political science department at the University of Rochester became a seedbed of rational choice within the discipline, training many now-prominent figures.

After turning to rational-choice theory, Riker never abandoned his confidence that it was the right choice to guide a truly scientific politics. However, Riker also tried to show that although traditional democratic ideals were unscientific and naive (and particularly blind to cycling problems he saw as inherent in systems of aggregating preferences), an admittedly more elite-dominated version of democratic theory could be defended.[9] Relatively late in his career, he wrote a more popular work edifying citizens about the "heresthetic art" of democratic statesmanship, an art that "free men use to control their surroundings." "Heresthetics" included creative elements that rational choice could explicate but not generate or predict.[10] Thus Riker to some degree retraced the intellectual arc of Beard and Merriam but with commitments to science and an explicitly elitist theory of democracy more firmly in command. Despite those commitments, Donald Freeman reasserted the old faith in a 1991 essay on the profession that applauded Riker and Rochester. He contended that today most political scientists still "find no professional value conflicts between a scientific orientation and sophisticated education for democratic citizenship."[11]

If this sketch suggests that efforts to assist American democracy via science have indeed played a large role in the discipline historically but have led the discipline to set an agenda that is often at war with itself, some examples from a life in the discipline might help to illustrate how this has occurred. Accordingly, let me now describe how this recurring problem stood when I entered political science in the 1970s and explain its relationship to the peculiar place of political theory in the profession. In brief, the profession was completing a transitional era of uncertainty much like the one we are now entering. It was in the midst of a movement away from the forms of "more scientific" political science that had reigned since the 1950s—aided by support from private foundations like Ford and governmental agencies like the National Science Foundation—and toward such concepts as the pluralist group theory of

David Truman and Robert Dahl, and the systems or structural-functionalism of David Easton and Gabriel Almond. These concepts had themselves been inspired by the sociology of Talcott Parsons and the anthropology of the 1920s, which were used to undergird models of political development culminating in "modernization." During their heyday, these forms of behavioralism had pushed normative political theory to the margins of the discipline. But the pluralist and functionalist "new sciences of politics" subsequently confronted blistering assaults, especially for their undemocratic character and their perceived scientific inadequacies, in the late 1960s and early 1970s.[12]

The race riots, the politics of poverty, the ferocious protests over Vietnam (and the sometimes violent repression that came in response), and the mushrooming of the "counterculture" in the 1960s, followed in the 1970s by Watergate and the relative decline of the US global economic and political status after OPEC's embargo and the Vietnam withdrawal—all these considerations fueled these challenges to prevailing disciplinary portraits of American and world politics. Pluralists were accused of minimizing inequalities in group power and neglecting the ways that groups such as blacks and the poor might be unfairly excluded from politics. Functionalist or systems analyses seemed biased in favor of what was "functional" for the status-quo distribution of power and resources. They were also either naive or imperialistic to assume "modernization" took similar stages to similar ends everywhere. Thus to critics like members of the Caucus for a New Political Science, pluralist and functionalist theories appeared to be dangerously complacent, ethnocentric, and (hence) undemocratic. Though many criticisms were overstated, scholarly specimens could be found that exemplified each charge.[13] In that conflict-ridden era, political science could persuasively be accused of offering models that failed to reveal and challenge unjust inequalities; to produce any behavioral laws; or to predict, explain, or provide effective social guidance concerning the startling events then occurring. And most damning of all, to an embarrassing extent, the political science literature failed even to discuss these topics.[14]

THEORY AND THE "POSTBEHAVIORAL ERA"

This period of upheaval allowed political theorists to regain a fraction of their past prominence in the profession, though not their erstwhile centrality. Theorists contributed visibly to the embattlement of the prevailing forms of behavioral political science. Straussians had long criticized the discipline's semi-official faith in egalitarian democracy and empirical science as unreflective modern prejudices, willfully blind to the variations in human nature the ancients had understood and to the dangers of rationalistic social engineering. They thought, however, that American-style liberal democracy was the best regime possible under modern circumstances, so they generally saw their task as leavening its egalitarian and Enlightenment rationalist excesses with ancient wisdom. Old and New Left political theorists instead debunked the undemocratic faith in expertise, the misleading liberal democratic mythology, and the neglect of structural inequalities they saw in much of "mainstream" political science, arguing that radical intellectual and political changes were needed for true democracy and social justice.[15]

Political theory was further rejuvenated in these years via the philosopher John Rawls's 1971 publication of the first real candidate for a "great" work of constructive political philosophy in decades.[16] By enlivening liberal political theory and strengthening its egalitarianism, Rawls inspired political theorists generally. Liberals thought they, too, could further this bolstering of the philosophical underpinnings of liberal democracy, especially since a lot of us believed Rawls overemphasized liberal notions of justice at the expense of liberal notions of the good.[17] But Rawls's success also gave new energy to Marxist and Straussian critics of liberal democracy, who had a large new target.

At the same time, in the study of great works of political philosophy—the trade most political theorists practiced—Quentin Skinner's attacks on traditional textualist methods, in favor of an emphasis on recovering writers' historical contexts, sparked intense methodological debates. And J. G. A. Pocock's related claims that a vital Western tradition of "civic republicanism" had been buried by liberal historiography began a set of historical and normative debates that would have a far-reaching impact on both political theory and American politics. Thus political theory was a lively part of the discipline in the mid-1970s.[18]

Yet none of this theory work provided what political scientists were seeking after the debunking phase of the late 1960s and early 1970s. There was still no alternative approach to studying politics that was genuinely more rigorous and produced more scientific knowledge than the prevailing versions of behavioralism. Political scientists thus began referring to the period from about 1970 on as the "postbehavioral era," a tag that defines the period by what it is not, rather than what it is.[19]

Such a label disguises how influential rational choice was becoming in the discipline. Even so, these scholars are right to say that after launching their critiques, most traditional political theorists in the 1970s again disengaged from much of the rest of political science, rather than helping define what "postbehavioralism" might be. Many theorists sensitively explored great texts but then made disturbingly loose claims about the connections between those readings and past and present political controversies, without attending carefully to the empirical work done on those topics. Straussians particularly displayed this tendency, and they tended to be unreceptive to those who failed to draw politically conservative lessons. Members of the Skinnerian school, in contrast, virtually denied that the "great" texts had any significance at all outside their own historical political contexts (a stance that may explain the subsequent decline of interest in this approach). Marxist theory connected with some interesting empirical work, but that work often revealed, rather than redeemed, the failings of the theoretical stance. Rawlsian liberal theory, though stimulating, proclaimed itself an "ideal" theory that could only be applied to less-than-ideal empirical reality after several ill-specified but intellectually arduous adjustments. Rather than extend it in these ways, most theorists analyzed and critiqued it on the abstract, "ideal" level, never reaching many of the issues occupying other parts of political science or the political world outside. In consequence, compared to his great predecessor Dewey and Dewey's followers, Rawls and the Rawlsians were much less likely to play the role of "public philosophers."[20]

But if political theory, however lively, was too abstract and insular, much of the rest of political science in the mid-1970s seemed quiescent, still working through the critical assaults of the late 1960s and looking for new directions. From my limited vantage point as a graduate student, the debate between elitists and pluralist theories of power in American politics seemed to have converged on Theodore Lowi's picture of a bleak interest-group politics that did not fit either the most pessimistic accounts of class domination or the most optimistic accounts of group equality. Even so, Lowi's call for "juridical democracy" as the cure for the inegalitarian, incompetent aspects of American "interest group liberalism" found few adherents. In terms of empirical research, nothing seemed larger in the subfield than ongoing debates over the determinants of voting behavior, with the occasional appearance of mild, apologetic efforts to vindicate democracy by rescuing voter knowledgeability. Urbanists started to incorporate race more fully into their pictures of city power structures, and public-opinion scholars began giving more attention to understanding racial attitudes. But the American field as a whole was still only starting to address race, a central issue political scientists had generally minimized once they gave up defending racial hierarchies. After the battering of structural-functionalism and modernization theory, many comparativists were absorbed in a debate over whether "corporatism"—some sort of alliance among governments and powerful organized economic and social groups more systematic than interest-group liberalism—was replacing both capitalism and socialism. That thesis did not, however, prove as fruitful as its proponents hoped.[21] International relations seemed dominated by theoretical and empirical strategic studies of "bombs and rockets" tied to the ongoing Cold War. Although that focus was a victory for hard-nosed "realists" over older "idealists," this work had few carryovers to other fields.[22]

Amidst this relative water-treading, the discipline was replaying its historic pattern. Political scientists were looking in particular for ways to achieve a more scientific study of politics as well as ways they could better serve democracy, especially in America. Both these quests were met largely by endeavors calling themselves forms of political theory.

The biggest development was the meteoric ascendancy of formal rational-choice theories in the 1970s and on through the 1980s. The rational-choice enterprise had developed to the point where many now accepted that it might be the path through which a troubled hodgepodge profession could achieve a true science of politics at last, just as the messianic Bill Riker had promised. From the mid-1970s on, virtually all the nation's leading departments competed vigorously to recruit the leading scholars in rational choice. Their work also evolved from the most abstract and simple early models of voting systems and competitive games through the emergence of a rational-choice form of "new institutionalism" or "neo-institutionalism" in the 1980s. These analyses involve efforts to model how institutional structures affect the expression and aggregation of preferences, empowering some actors and at times resolving cycling problems by inducing a single, stable equilibrium. Moreover, because many political actors realize that institutional structures have these features, the politics through which institutions come to be adopted or reshaped can also be made subject to more or less formal rational-choice modeling.[23] Although the most prominent rational-choice work has focused on the behavior of voters, political parties, legislatures, and the collective action problems of social movements in American and comparative politics, as well as on game-theoretical models of international relations, rational choice now seemed equipped to illuminate the behavior of virtually all political actors and institutions in all eras of history. Thus it bloomed.

The impact of rational-choice theory was felt on more traditional forms of political theory. Few Straussians, to be sure, showed much interest. But Rawls's argument about the principles of justice that would be chosen in his "original position" was analyzed by many as a theorem within general rational-choice theory, a view Rawls himself seems to have entertained for a time. Scholars like Jon Elster began recasting Marxism in rational-choice terms. Democratic theorists struggled to respond to the challenges that rational-choice concepts posed for the coherence of voting systems of aggregating preferences as opposed to market systems.[24]

For though rational-choice scholars had much to say about democratic processes, most of it was negative. Fittingly, the major developments in normative political theory in the 1980s responded to the side of the discipline's characteristic quest that rational choice was not fulfilling—its aim to vindicate and strengthen democracy. Several strains of political theory arose that in various ways stressed the "socially constructed" character of human identities in professed opposition to all forms of liberal individualism, including both Rawlsian neo-Kantianism and rational-choice models. These normative theories sparked the hope that something might fill the void left by increasingly discredited Marxist defenses of political and social equality as the means for realizing humanity's "species-being."

Most prominently, the dominance of Rawlsian liberalism in political philosophy was challenged by the communitarian critique of Charles Taylor, Michael Sandel, Alasdair MacIntyre, and others. Their works strongly reinforced the Pocockian challenge to liberal historiography in favor of a stress on America's allegedly distinct civic-republican traditions (though Pocock himself was no communitarian). Communitarianism and republicanism dovetailed in ways that excited critics of liberalism across the political spectrum, but especially the social-democratic Left. Sandel's elegant attack on Rawls argued that the prevailing neo-Kantian liberalism conceived of human beings incoherently, as individualistic entities somehow able to choose all aspects of their identities and commitments, instead of recognizing that our identities are inextricably constituted by the array of social communities out of which our personalities arise. Civic republicanism's emphasis on the common good, civic virtue, and community identity seemed to many a democratic philosophy based on such a communitarian view of human beings instead of the abstract, rights-obsessed individualism of liberalism.[25]

In a cognate development, those previously obscure defenders of ancient republics, the Straussians, became literary lions and gained greater political influence in the Reagan-Bush years. A much wider audience now responded to their longtime claims that such individualistic liberalism promoted a leveling licentiousness and harmed prospects for human virtue, thereby weakening modern democracy. Yet if Allan Bloom and Francis Fukuyama sold more books, the increasingly prominent "communitarian movement" chiefly included writers like Amitai Etzioni and Benjamin Barber, who saw themselves as much further to the left. Similarly, although some conservative historians and political scientists saw republican revisionism as a way to combat the egalitarian excesses of contemporary liberalism, many more followed writers like Sean

Wilentz in portraying populist republicanism as the legitimating ancestry of a communitarian democratic politics today.[26]

Certain communitarian arguments had counterparts in burgeoning feminist critiques of American institutions and liberal political theory. Despite their myriad differences, most feminist theorists argued for the socially constituted character of gender identities. They added that America's "individualistic" liberalism contained masked but essential commitments to patriarchy; these stood in the way of a more truly democratic society. Various versions of democratic postmodernist theory also began to emerge, challenging Enlightenment-style rationalist master narratives of political life in favor of acknowledging the many ways modern discourses and institutions represent constitutive forms of domination that must be resisted, usually piecemeal, if a freer and more democratic life is to be achieved.[27]

None of these varied new "democratizing" strains in political theory have become very central to the discipline. Some are more firmly "anti-science" than virtually any of their disciplinary predecessors, and the scientific promise of rational choice has far outweighed their appeal. But they all have helped shape not only political theory but also agendas of empirical research. In every subfield, political scientists have begun to pay somewhat more attention to gender, race, ethnicity, and also religion. Contemporary conflicts over the legacies of the 1960s movements for racial, gender, and immigration reforms have probably played a greater role in prompting this research than any theoretical developments. The shared emphasis on the social construction of identity in communitarianism, feminism, and postmodernism has, however, reinforced them.

BACK TO THE FUTURE? THE EMERGENCE OF HISTORICAL INSTITUTIONALISM

But if rational choice and various forms of egalitarian "social constructionist" normative theory were prominent yet sharply contrasting responses to the twin problems of the discipline in the late 1970s, they were not alone. A variety of other responses by scholars with different backgrounds and motivations in American, comparative, and international politics are notable for the ways they have converged over time, thereby expanding their collective impact on the discipline. The convergence, still far from total, is toward what is called the "historical/interpretive new institutionalism," in contrast to rational-choice forms of "new institutionalism." Historical institutionalists have been suggesting that the discipline somehow has to do a better job of grasping political change by becoming more historical instead of treating patterns visible today as timeless behavioral laws, as much empirical work is said to do implicitly. They (we) also argue that political scientists must recognize more fully the roles institutions play in politics; that they have to be as open to the possibility of robust human political agency as to deterministic explanations; and that they must be less reductionist in their treatment of political ideas.

The most influential development along these lines came when scholars with generally left-of-center orientations, deeply critical of group theories and individualistic rational-choice models but also disenchanted with traditional Marxism, began arguing for "bringing the state back in" to political analyses, especially analyses of historical change. Initially, in Theda Skocpol's landmark study of comparative revolutions, this framework meant grasping the institutional capacities of political actors running state organizations, in order to identify when states were confronting pressures they could not meet, thereby precipitating revolution. In Stephen Skowronek's influential analysis of American political development, it meant showing how existing state institutional arrangements shaped and constrained processes of political change, including state-building, spurred by broader economic and demographic factors. Though Skocpol initially downplayed both ideology and individual human agency in favor of state structures, such "historical institutionalism" soon broadened in many more-inclusive directions.[28]

A pattern nonetheless emerged. In the words of comparativist Terry Karl, analysts moved toward "an interactive approach that seeks explicitly to relate structural constraints to the shaping of contingent choice" by political actors. Such "structural constraints," usually viewed as constituting and empowering political actors in certain ways as well as restricting them, increasingly have not had to be strictly part of the "state." All sorts of relatively enduring "structural contexts" for political behavior, including economic arrangements and traditions of ideological discourse encoded in organizational rules and routines, can be considered. And in many cases, scholars argue that interpretive understandings of institutional rules and roles, as well as actors' ideologies and purposes, are needed to explain their conduct.[29]

Historical institutionalism's sense of the importance of institutionally embedded ideologies and of interpretive understandings of ideas and meaningful actions is the source of its appeal for many of us initially trained in political theory. Frustrated by the gaps between textual analyses of "greats" and the real world of political problems that had motivated us to study in the first place, many of us had already responded in the late 1970s and 1980s by trying more rigorously to connect the history of political thought with concrete political institutions. I did so through a critical study linking theoretical problems of early liberalism to evolving Supreme Court doctrines. Others found aspects of the "republicanism" revival, Straussian intellectual history, and reappraisals of Progressive pragmatist thought sources of insight into the development of such political institutions as the presidency. Such work meshed smoothly with that of a historical institutionalist like Skowronek, who argued that republican ideology helped to explain why Americans built institutions hostile to the development of a national standing army, among other topics.[30]

Even when more empirical scholars have not turned so directly to works in political theory, a number have begun to argue that political analyses need to give more weight to the role of ideas, and in ways that make connections with political theory less difficult. Major edited volumes, including works by scholars in American, comparative, and international politics, have made it clear that this quest is a widespread one.[31] And in a final "converging" development, since the mid-1970s many more political theorists have contended that normative arguments should be rooted in systematic historical analyses of the political role that the doctrines of political theorists have played, rather than taking troubling passages in great texts or philosophic hypotheticals as starting points. These efforts did not prevent political theory in the 1980s from being dominated by an increasingly abstract debate over conceptions of the "self," but it is an aspiration visible in much current work. If such historically rooted normative theory flourishes, it should strengthen connections between normative arguments and all empirical work that better incorporates the role of ideas.[32]

Thus there are signs that historical/interpretive institutional approaches in American, comparative, and international politics are beginning to promote greater unity among those subfields and with historical and normative political theory. Historical institutionalist research has also increasingly made good use of quantitative techniques in political science—for example, to illuminate shifting voting coalitions in different eras. Most recently, even rational-choice models have been incorporated to illuminate strategic behavior once the actors' institutional and historical contexts have been clarified.[33] Yet while there are genuine signs of a historical institutional turn that draws on rather than simply opposes quantitative analysis and rational-choice theories throughout the subfields, most in the profession would probably still find all talk of convergence wildly optimistic if not pernicious.

THE DISCIPLINE TODAY

The more common and undoubtedly accurate description of the discipline at present is that it remains highly fragmented, with members sitting at "separate tables," in Gabriel Almond's widely discussed 1988 depiction. Rational-choice scholars responded to that description by insisting they had offered a general, impeccably scientific approach to all politics that promised to create a universal explanatory theory. Although some rational-choice proponents are now building bridges to "historical institutionalists," many instead regard the latter as a disastrous retreat from truly scientific rational-choice analysis.[34] It remains possible that much of the discipline will come to agree.

It seems unlikely, however. My colleagues Donald Green and Ian Shapiro have been galvanizing the profession by arguing that the focus on building a universal theory has led rational-choice scholars either to ignore empirical testing or to do it poorly. They contend that the empirically supported contributions of rational choice to our understanding of important political subjects are thus virtually non-existent. Formal theory has many other critics, and even many rational-choice scholars are acknowledging that their models can only produce determinate equilibrium predictions with some real-world empirical bite by relying heavily on the results of other sorts of empirical and interpretive inquiries. Some also concede that rational choice fails to encompass preference formation and transformation, being limited only to the investigation of strategic shifts in preference expression and maximization. And as David Kreps's essay in this issue indicates, even the economists whom rational-choice scholars in political science emulate are now placing more stress on testing models empirically, rather than simply focusing on their logical coherence. Hence it is becoming more and more likely that rational-choice scholarship will continue to contribute tools and hypotheses to political science but not provide a grand unifying theory or displace many other sorts of work. Acceptance of that limited role will surely cost rational choice some of its magic for political scientists.[35]

Yet precisely because the historical and interpretive variety of "new institutionalism" does not offer any grand theory to guide a universal science of politics either, it is also unlikely to become hegemonic in the profession. The historical institutionalism with which the discipline began lost favor precisely because it never generated much in the way of falsifiable general theory, a deficiency of which practitioners of the historical "new institutionalism" today are highly conscious. Even so, many historical institutionalists respond with skepticism about the possibility of grand theory-building. Instead they call for the sorts of "middle-level" theory favored by many behavioralists.[36]

By "middle-level theory," traditional political science empiricists mean hypotheses that go beyond merely describing observed behavior to offer a testable causal explanation for a fairly broad range of it. Such explanations are, however, derived from inductive generalizing about empirical observations rather than deduced from a grand theory of all politics. The inductively-reached generalizations are then tested against conduct other than the behavior that inspired them. Examples include propositions such as "Because of differences in both saliency and perceived moral status, people's preferences for public goods are less responsive to price than their preferences for personal goods," or "Because of their limited powers and elite staffing, courts are rarely if ever initiators of major egalitarian reforms."

For two main reasons, the historical institutionalists also incline to "middle-level theory" (e.g., "Because of their ideologies and unique powers, American courts drove American labor to seek workplace gains rather than general political goals via legislation, as labor movements elsewhere did").[37] First, when scholars see political actors as socially constituted in ways that differ with different institutional arrangements in different historical eras, they are often suspicious about the prospects for non-trivial universal laws of human political behavior, despite some enduring features of human conduct. Second, new institutionalists tend to hold the belief, subject to investigation, that there is an ineradicable contingency in conscious human political agency, which renders political analysis at best a probabilistic and interpretive, not a deterministic or fully quantifiable, science. That belief militates against the possibility of any grand theory guiding a universal science of politics. To be sure, many rational-choice analysts share this belief, as Riker's discussion of "heresthetics" shows. But whereas Riker brooded that political study was thus the true "dismal science," many other scholars simply conclude that if political conduct can best be captured in terms of probabilistic tendencies of actors constituted in particular ways in specific historical contexts, then middle-level theorizing is likely to be more productive than questing for a "general field theory" of politics.

The most determined theory-builders among the "new institutionalists" are Karen Orren and Stephen Skowronek, the editors of their school's flagship journal. In two important essays, they have argued that a "new institutionalist" approach means showing how patterns of political behavior emerge from the interaction of multiple institutional orders—the partly unintended consequence of different institutional systems with relatively independent traits and tendencies interacting. Those dynamic institutional configurations structure the identities, interests, opportunities, and (hence) the strategic choices of political actors without fully determining them. By mapping the relevant multiple institutional dynamics confronting and constituting actors, Orren and Skowronek contend, we can discern the characteristic problems historically situated actors face, the types of responses they can be expected to display, and the probable consequences of those responses, even if we cannot fully predict behavior.[38]

This program, exemplified in Skowronek's recent analysis of how presidential behavior and success arise from the incumbent's relationship to the constitutional structuring of the office, the prevailing partisan ordering of the government, and the rise of the modern administrative state, is sure to stimulate further work.[39] These authors and others are also working creatively at further defining a "multiple orders" institutionalist political science. But it is at best debatable whether such "new institutionalism" represents a general theory of politics or an account of why only more limited "middle-level" analyses are possible, as well as a guide to how to conduct them.

Many political scientists clearly fear that it is the latter, that the "new institutionalism" fails to answer the discipline's never-ending search for a universal science of politics. Furthermore, many scholars dislike these new institutionalist guidelines for research, fearing that they take us away from rigorous empiricism and experimentation to historical conjecture, and from identifying a few variables with clear explanatory power to depicting endless complexity. I believe, on the contrary, that historical institutionalism represents a healthy direction for political analyses appropriate to the subject matter of politics, and that the methods of empirical testing and the formal clarity that behavioralism and rational-choice models offer can be incorporated within it. But I do not think that most political scientists will soon come to agree.

What then is likely in political science in the near future? Currently the absence of a popular candidate to provide the field with a universal, unifying theory is accompanied by a surge of confidence among quantitative political scientists in their steadily improving statistical tools, aided by the computer revolution. Hence it is probable that many political scientists will continue to focus on the use of advanced statistical methods to test "middle-level" hypotheses in quasi-experimental research, perhaps with a heightened sense that this work is appropriate as the cachet of formal theory diminishes.[40] Many others are doing somewhat more ethnographic interviewing and "soaking and poking," producing interpretively rich, though less quantitative, empirical studies that again promise to illuminate some contemporary political issues, even if they do not test any grand theory. In most such work, even by scholars who do not see themselves as historical institutionalists, there is also a heightened awareness that the patterns discerned may be products of specific historical arrangements that may change in predictable ways, rather than instances of timeless behavioral laws. Thus fewer political scientists are dismissing history and more are trying to grasp historical changes than in the past. And political theorists of various stripes seem to be trying to connect more with concrete legal and political controversies today rather than abstractly debating the characteristics of "the self" or "the other"—though, to be sure, those discussions continue and in their feminist and postmodernist variants appear still to be a rising tide. Hence I see a near future in which more empirically rigorous, historically sensitive "middle-level" testing becomes more prominent across the subfields. But that forecast is so highly speculative, not to say self-serving, that I will not elaborate or defend it further. Instead, let me be even more presumptuous and turn to some further thoughts about what political science should be.

PROPHESYING WITHOUT HONOR

It would be natural at this point to wonder whether political science should not somehow outgrow its long-standing but perennially unfulfilled longings to found a grand new science of politics that will also make American democracy flourish. Political scientists have, after all, always sought to do those things in part for crass material reasons. American universities did not seem likely to recognize and fund a special profession of "political science" unless it was a distinctive science. American governments, businesses, and citizens did not seem likely to support a body of inquiry that did not assist their political endeavors and their political system more broadly. Yet beyond those material incentives, most political scientists have genuinely believed it is right, good, and exciting to further true knowledge about politics by the best methods available to us, an enterprise it is natural to call a "science" of politics. And most have also genuinely wished to aid American democracy, however deep their reservations might run about its current form. These features of the discipline are so deeply rooted that I cannot see them changing.

In fact, I share them. Like many political scientists, I take particular pleasure in the fact that one of the (few) products of political science that has had wide-ranging influence on broader intellectual discussions in recent years is Robert Putnam's research on the importance of "social capital" for democratic governance. Nothing could be more expressive of the characteristic themes of American political science: based on a twenty-year study of different regions in Italy as well as a variety of quantitative indicators in America, Putnam argues that societies with extensive networks of "secondary associations," like churches, civic clubs, unions, and recreational leagues, build patterns of cooperation and trust that make for demonstrably more effective political self-government. Here, it appears, is solidly scientific empirical work in genuine service of the cause of democracy, the dream of American political science fulfilled.[41]

Yet despite such accomplishments, I doubt political science will ever justify itself as a distinctive professional enterprise by achieving a common paradigm of scientific inquiry, much less by discovering a "science" unique to the discipline. Putnam draws on research in the other social sciences as much as on political science; and his results do not begin to settle many normative, tactical, and policy questions that other political scientists, and probably Putnam himself, would insist must be addressed in part by other approaches.[42] To be sure, I think political scientists can and should use scientific methods of rigorous hypothesis testing and search for general theories as far as they can. I have also indicated that a historical institutional understanding of political action seems to me most intellectually defensible and most capable of providing a framework, if not a theory, applicable throughout the discipline and capable of incorporating most techniques. But though the work that would result from doing so may well be as scientific as the study of politics can get, the discipline will still not be able to boast a deductive general theory of politics like neoclassical economics. It will still be haunted by the fear that it is "but a collective name descriptive of a large number of interesting matters that no other social scientists claim as their special territory," without "a coherent central structure of its own," as Leonard White worried in 1950.[43] And worse, most of its methods today, including survey research, interviews, historical investigations, and formal modeling, are done as well or better by scholars in other disciplines, along with governmental and industry analysts, think-tank experts, media consultants, and journalists. The risk remains that political science as a profession will contribute little to knowledge that is not provided elsewhere.

In the end, we may conclude that there is in fact no real justification for a separate profession of political science, that it makes more sense for politics to be routinely and regularly studied throughout the human sciences. But simply posing that alternative raises doubts about its adequacy. Although sociologists, psychologists, economists, anthropologists, sociobiologists, philosophers, literary scholars, and many others often study governmental institutions, political movements and ideologies, and human power relationships, and although collectively they employ every method political scientists use, none of them are chiefly devoted to those topics, and none train scholars extensively in the range of preexisting research on them. Yet these political subjects are far too important to be dealt with piecemeal, incidentally, and with only partial mastery of relevant knowledge. That approach risks neglect of some vital human topics. Having a profession centrally concerned with preserving and extending the whole wide variety of knowledge on all topics arguably political thus makes sense, even if such a discipline is unlikely to have a "coherent central structure of its own."

But though the vision of political science as a disciplinary caretaker and cultivator of thorough knowledge about certain central human concerns may be defensible, it may well ring uninspiring in comparison to the vision of achieving a grand "new science of politics." Let me therefore extend this notion of a discipline distinguished by its aim of insuring that important political topics do not get neglected, in a way that seems to me appropriate and actually uplifting.

My colleague Charles Lindblom has pointed us in the right direction with his award-winning yet still largely unheeded book, *Inquiry and Change*. In it he argues that social scientists should take as their task the pursuit of the questions that lay people in society care about but lack the skills to explore. Moreover, social scientists should be particularly attentive, Lindblom insists, to topics of which lay inquiry and understanding may be impaired in various ways, most of which are political. Impairment can arise from discrepancies in power, wealth, and prestige among interested parties who shape opinion on the issues in question; from disproportionate control of education and communications systems by advocates of one viewpoint; and from traditions and customs that constitute a familiar status quo with which many feel all too comfortable, as well as other factors. Lindblom calls for a social science that largely takes its agenda not from theory but from what people are experiencing as problems in their lives, modified by informed identification of topics they would probably perceive as problems if not for specifiable impairing influences, especially systems of unequal power.[44]

I think all Lindblom says applies with special force to political science. It is the discipline that is and that must be most centrally concerned with structures of power that can dominate people's lives and consciousness in ways that are often neither necessary nor desirable. It is therefore also the discipline whose agenda is most likely to be shaped and distorted by the systems of belief and power that favor the status quo (even as the status quo evolves). The profession's aspirations to be a science and to serve democracy are themselves evidence of those facts, even if I think those hopes defensible, for they clearly reflect dominant values in America. Hence political scientists should be concerned, more so than other scholars, to define an intellectual agenda that does not simply maintain and extend the political understandings favored by the powerful. Such an agenda should accept special responsibility for subjecting those understandings to critical questioning, from every intellectually plausible point of view. It should be particularly concerned with discerning how far those understandings arise from and reinforce dominant power structures. For of all the many people researching political issues—some to sell newspapers or boost ratings, some to give politicians popular policy positions, some to fulfill a bureaucracy's mandated mission, some to win arguments in courts—we academic political scientists are best equipped institutionally to challenge prevailing wisdom and explore what may prove to be truths about politics that are neglected or unpopular because they go against the grain.

I am well aware that political scientists are only very partially insulated. We are all citizens of one society or another (mostly of the United States) and shaped by attendant social and political forces. Within the profession pressures to work on topics funded by governmental agencies and leading foundations are substantial. We have no special disciplinary X-ray to let us see through whatever our society's, and our own, leading "impairments" may be. Yet we are still *comparatively* well placed to conduct and reward "impolitic" research. We have all the protections of an academic profession; and all concede that asking hard questions about politics is our job (unlike, for example, literary scholars). And I cannot think of a different sense of disciplinary purpose that would be as likely to contribute important knowledge about politics that people would not get elsewhere, at least not in as careful or rigorous a form.

Again, my view in this regard results from my own experiences. Dissatisfied with the abstract and unsystematic quality of academic debates over "liberalism" and "republicanism" and more popular discussions of American values, I embarked a decade ago on a comprehensive study of US citizenship statutes and judicial rulings throughout the nation's history. I thought the ways officials defined citizenship in law would be a useful empirical indicator of the values American governments had actually embodied. This work has convinced me that the portraits dominant in post-World War II scholarship and popular discourse of America as a basically liberal democratic society are misleading. They have survived largely because they serve the interests of governing elites; they also comfort many politically centrist Americans; and they simultaneously fit with the view of many on the Left that liberal capitalism is the chief source of all American ills. But they do a poor job of making sense of the incredible variety of ways American citizenship laws have explicitly used racial, ethnic, gender, and religious criteria to deny full citizenship to most people within America's borders as well as outside them through most of the nation's history. They have also led people to underestimate the now-looming possibility that illiberal, undemocratic ideologies, such as belief in the biological inferiority of people of African descent, will resurge in our time, as such beliefs have before.[45]

The arguments I have been making have been extensively resisted in political science, sometimes denounced as ideological and un-American, sometimes as too protective of liberalism. But the structure of our professional life has allowed me to continue piling up evidence and answering criticisms, so that now some new issues about the nature of American political culture are at least being discussed. Whatever the merits of my particular arguments, that *kind* of challenge to conventional wisdom seems to me now the most worthwhile thing to pursue and the kind of distinctive contribution to political understanding that political science can best make.

So though I no longer work primarily in what the discipline terms political philosophy or theory, I have come to favor a Socratic view of our professional mission. I think we are at our best when we are intellectual gadflies, rigorously questioning and testing accepted political truths, exploring ignored possibilities, courting unpopularity by offering suggestions that markets are not likely to reward and that people in power are not likely to approve. We have some skills and insights that make us serviceable in other roles outside the academy, as bureaucratic experts and media consultants, and it is not wrong to undertake such labors. But self-consciously critical research and teaching, along with preserving and extending existing knowledge about politics, should always be the heart of our academic work.

But if political science were to become more a "gadfly" profession of critical political inquiry, would it then become more of a science and better serve democracy? There are reasons to answer no, but I think the answer is yes. By challenging all forms of complacent and self-serving thinking, including sloppy arguments and evidence within our own discipline, such a sense of professional mission would be likely to make our work as intellectually rigorous as the study of politics can be. That will mean our work is as scientific as it can be. To be sure, if we do our work well, the best-supported general propositions we can advance may not sit well with the governors or citizens of American democracy. If the truth, insofar as we can ascertain it, is not supportive of democracy, our work may even undermine faith in democracy itself. I trust that will not be the outcome. But if it is, we American political scientists, and all other democratic citizens, certainly need to know it.

ENDNOTES

[1]Fred I. Greenstein and Nelson Polsby, "Introduction," *Political Science: Scope and Theory*, vol. 1, *Handbook of Political Science* (Reading, Mass.: Addison-Wesley Publishing, 1975), v.

[2]Cf., e.g., Jean Blondel, *The Discipline of Politics* (London: Butterworths, 1981); John G. Gunnell, "Political Theory: The Evolution of a Sub-Field," in Ada W. Finifter, ed., *Political Science: The State of the Discipline* (Washington, D.C.: American Political Science Association, 1983); John G. Gunnell, *The Descent of Political Theory* (Chicago, Ill.: University of Chicago Press, 1993); Stefan Collini, Donald Winch, and John Burrow, *That Noble Science of Politics: A Study in Nineteenth-Century Intellectual History* (Cambridge: Cambridge University Press, 1983); Richard A. Higgot, *Political Development Theory* (London: Croom Helm, 1983); David M. Ricci, *The Tragedy of Political Science: Politics, Scholarship and Democracy* (New Haven, Conn.: Yale University Press, 1984); James F. Ward, *Language, Form, and Inquiry: Arthur F. Bentley's Philosophy of Social Science* (Amherst, Mass.: University of Massachusetts Press, 1984); Raymond Seidelman and Edward J. Harpham, *Disenchanted Realists: Political Science and the American Crisis, 1884–1984* (Albany, N.Y.: State University of New York Press, 1985); Raymond Seidelman, "Controversy: Can Political Science History Be Neutral?" *American Political Science Review* 84 (1990): 596–600; Peter B. Natchez, *Images of Voting/Visions of Democracy* (New York: Basic Books, 1985); Andrew C. Janos, *Politics and Paradigms: Changing Theories of Change in Social Science* (Stanford, Calif.: Stanford University Press, 1986); James Farr, "The History of Political Science," *American Journal of Political Science* 32 (1988): 1175–1195; James Farr, "Political Science and the Enlightenment of Enthusiasm," *American Political Science Review* 82 (1988): 51–69; James Farr, "Controversy: Can Political Science History Be Neutral?" *American Political Science Review* 84 (1990): 587–591; John S. Dryzek and Stephen T. Leonard, "History and Discipline in Political Science," *American Political Science Review* 82 (1988): 1245–1260; John S. Dryzek and Stephen T. Leonard, "Controversy: Can Political Science History Be Neutral?" *American Political Science Review* 84 (1990): 600–607; Gabriel A. Almond with Stephen Genco, "Clouds, Clocks, and the Study of Politics," in Gabriel A. Almond, *A Discipline Divided: Schools and Sects in Political Science* (Newbury Park, Calif.: Sage Publications, 1990); Donald M. Freeman, "The Making of a Discipline," in *The Theory and Practice of Political Science*, vol. 1, *Political Science: Looking to the Future*, ed. William Crotty (Evanston, Ill.: Northwestern University Press, 1991); Dorothy Ross, *The Origins of American Social Science* (New York: Cambridge University Press, 1991); Dorothy Ross, "An Historian's View of American Social Science," *Journal of the History of the Behavioral Sciences* 29 (1993): 99–112; Dorothy Ross, "Institutionalism: Ideas, Structures, Methods," presentation at the Annual Meeting of the Social Science History Association, Baltimore, Md., 6 November 1993; Judith N. Shklar, "Redeeming American Political Theory," *American Political Science Review* 85 (1991): 3–13; and James Farr and Raymond Seidelman, eds., *Discipline and History: Political Science in the United States* (Ann Arbor, Mich.: University of Michigan Press, 1993).

298   Rogers M. Smith

[3]In addition to the more recent works cited in endnote 2, see, e.g., Bernard Crick, *The American Science of Politics* (Berkeley, Calif.: University of California Press, 1959); Albert Somit and Joseph Tanenhaus, *The Development of American Political Science: From Burgess to Behavioralism* (Boston, Mass.: Allyn & Bacon, 1967; 2d ed., 1982); Paul F. Kress, *Social Science and the Idea of Progress: The Ambiguous Legacy of Arthur F. Bentley* (Urbana, Ill.: University of Illinois Press, 1973); and Barry D. Karl, *Charles E. Merriam and the Study of Politics* (Chicago, Ill.: University of Chicago Press, 1974). The major contributions to the disciplinary history of Gunnell, Farr, and Seidelman tend to cast this tension as between science and the discipline's commitment to "liberalism." I agree that political scientists have generally thought of American democratic institutions and citizenship in terms that we refer to as liberal. But at least until World War II most political scientists used "democratic" far more than "liberal" to describe the political arrangements and forms of citizenship they wished to assist. Substitution of the term "liberal" partly reflects these political scientists' own concern that the discipline has not been democratic enough. See, e.g., Farr and Seidelman, eds., *Discipline and History: Political Science in the United States,* 46, 57, 120, 154, 164; cf. Ross, "An Historian's View of American Social Science," 100, 106, 109–110.

[4]Shklar, "Redeeming American Political Theory"; Ross, *The Origins of American Social Science*; and Ross, "An Historian's View of American Social Science."

[5]Woodrow Wilson, "The Law and the Facts," *American Political Science Review* 5 (1911): 1–11; Somit and Tanenhaus, *The Development of American Political Science,* 78; Seidelman and Harpham, *Disenchanted Realists: Political Science and the American Crisis,* 41; and James W. Fesler and Donald F. Kettl, *The Politics of the Administrative Process* (Chatham, N.J.: Chatham House, 1991), 17–19.

[6]John W. Burgess, *Political Science and Comparative Constitutional Law* (Boston, Mass.: Ginn & Co., 1890), 4, 37–39; and Farr and Seidelman, eds., *Discipline and History: Political Science in the United States,* 10, 77–78, 120, 125, 129. Ross, in *The Origins of American Social Science* and "An Historian's View of American Social Science," most fully explores the implications of beliefs in "American exceptionalism" for the social sciences in America. Gunnell, *The Descent of Political Theory,* stresses the often unconscious "Americanism" of the discipline.

[7]I have previously suggested that this tension reflects a deeper one that haunts the social sciences generally: the tension between asserting the importance of human agency and providing scientific explanations for it. Rogers M. Smith, "If Politics Matters: Implications for a New Institutionalism," *Studies in American Political Development* 6 (1992): 1–36.

[8]The preceding three paragraphs are chiefly distilled from the overviews provided by Crick, *The American Science of Politics*; Edward A. Purcell, *The Crisis of Democratic Theory: Scientific Naturalism & the Problem of Value* (Lexington, Ky.: University Press of Kentucky, 1973); Somit and Tanenhaus, *The Development of American Political Science: From Burgess to Behavioralism*; Ricci, *The Tragedy of Political Science: Politics, Scholarship and Democracy*; Seidelman and Harpham, *Disenchanted Realists: Political Science and the American Crisis*; Farr, "The History of Political Science"; Farr and Seidelman, eds., *Discipline and History: Political Science in the United States*; and Gunnell, *The Descent of*

Political Theory. Easton's noted critique of the profession, which still defends its scientific character, is his presidential address. See David Easton, "The New Revolution in Political Science," *American Political Science Review* 63 (1969): 1051–1061. Almond's progression from early works outlining structural-functionalist social science to advocacy of a focus on purposive human choices while critiquing functionalist and other approaches as "deterministic" can be traced by comparing Gabriel A. Almond and James S. Coleman, *The Politics of the Developing Areas* (Princeton, N.J.: Princeton University Press, 1960); Gabriel A. Almond and G. Bingham Powell, *Comparative Politics: A Developmental Approach* (Boston, Mass.: Little, Brown, 1966); Gabriel A. Almond, "Approaches to Developmental Causation," in *Crisis, Choice, and Change: Historical Studies of Political Development,* ed. Gabriel A. Almond, Scott C. Flanagan, and Robert J. Mundt (Boston, Mass.: Little, Brown and Co., 1973); and Almond and Genco, "Clouds, Clocks, and the Study of Politics." The later works of Dahl and Lindblom, pursuing more elaborately aspirations to inform citizens and combat obstacles to democracy that have been visible throughout their careers, include Robert A. Dahl, *A Preface to Economic Democracy* (Berkeley, Calif.: University of California Press, 1985); Robert A. Dahl, *Controlling Nuclear Weapons: Democracy versus Guardianship* (Syracuse, N.Y.: Syracuse University Press, 1985); Robert A. Dahl, *Democracy and Its Critics* (New Haven, Conn.: Yale University Press, 1989); Charles E. Lindblom, *Politics and Markets* (New York: Basic Books, 1977); and Charles E. Lindblom, *Inquiry and Change: The Troubled Attempt to Understand and Shape Society* (New Haven, Conn.: Yale University Press, 1990).

[9]William H. Riker, *The Theory of Political Coalitions* (New Haven, Conn.: Yale University Press, 1962); and William H. Riker, *Liberalism Against Populism: A Confrontation Between the Theory of Democracy and the Theory of Social Choice* (San Francisco, Calif.: W. H. Freeman, 1982).

[10]William H. Riker, *The Art of Political Manipulation* (New Haven, Conn.: Yale University Press, 1986), ix–x.

[11]Freeman, "The Making of a Discipline," 29; cf. Farr and Seidelman, *Discipline and History: Political Science in the United States,* 288.

[12]Robert A. Dahl, "The Behavioral Approach in Political Science: Epitaph for a Monument to a Successful Protest," *American Political Science Review* 55 (1961): 765–766; Purcell, *The Crisis of Democratic Theory: Scientific Naturalism and the Problem of Value,* 237–240; Somit and Tanenhaus, *The Development of American Political Science: From Burgess to Behavioralism,* 145–147, 167–172, 183–194; Ricci, *The Tragedy of Political Science: Politics, Scholarship and Democracy,* 112–113, 126–127, 134–144; Seidelman and Harpham, *Disenchanted Realists: Political Science and the American Crisis,* 151–159; and Almond and Genco, "Clouds, Clocks, and the Study of Politics," 46. There are important differences between focusing on "groups" and "systems," but the two modes of analysis could be linked, as Almond did, by treating "interest articulation" as a systemic function performed by various sorts of interest groups. See Almond and Coleman, *The Politics of the Developing Areas,* 33; and Almond and Powell, *Comparative Politics: A Developmental Approach,* 73–127. Other influential work, such as the numerous analyses of voting behavior, could be read as identifying existing political groups and mapping their interests and electoral behavior, even when pluralist theory was not explicitly invoked.

[13]This section relies chiefly on V. O. Key, Jr., "A Theory of Critical Elections," *Journal of Politics* 17 (1955): 3–18; V. O. Key, Jr., *Politics, Parties, and Pressure Groups*, 3d ed. (New York: Crowell, 1958); Almond and Coleman, *The Politics of the Developing Areas*; Almond and Powell, *Comparative Politics: A Developmental Approach*, esp. 34–451; Almond, "Approaches to Developmental Causation," 13, 22–23; Robert A. Dahl, *Who Governs?* (New Haven, Conn.: Yale University Press, 1961), esp. 34–36, 59; Purcell, *The Crisis of Democratic Theory: Scientific Naturalism and the Problem of Value*, 242, 260–266; Somit and Tanenhaus, *The Development of American Political Science: From Burgess to Behavioralism*, 188–189; Ricci, *The Tragedy of Political Science: Politics, Scholarship and Democracy*, 124–125, 136, 149, 155–157, 169–171, 214–217, 282–283; Theda Skocpol, "Sociology's Historical Imagination," in *Vision and Method in Historical Sociology*, ed. Theda Skocpol (Cambridge: Cambridge University Press, 1984), 2–3; Theda Skocpol, "Bringing the State Back In: Strategies of Analysis in Current Research," in *Bringing the State Back In*, ed. Peter B. Evans, Dietrich Rueschemeyer, and Theda Skocpol (Cambridge: Cambridge University Press, 1985), 4–5; Stephen D. Krasner, "Approaches to the State: Alternative Conceptions and Historical Dynamics," *Comparative Politics* 16 (1984): 227–229; Seidelman and Harpham, *Disenchanted Realists: Political Science and the American Crisis*, 178–183, 193; Terrence J. McDonald, "The Burdens of Urban History: The Theory of the State in Recent American Social History," *Studies in American Political Development* 3 (1989): 19–22; and Freeman, "The Making of a Discipline," 24–25, 30.

[14]Easton, "The New Revolution in Political Science"; Purcell, *The Crisis of Democratic Theory: Scientific Naturalism and the Problem of Value*, 267; Somit and Tanenhaus, *The Development of American Political Science: From Burgess to Behavioralism*, 213–217; Ricci, *The Tragedy of Political Science: Politics, Scholarship and Democracy*, 175–178; Skocpol, "Sociology's Historical Imagination," 3–4; Skocpol, "Bringing the State Back In: Strategies of Analysis in Current Research," 6–7; and Seidelman and Harpham, *Disenchanted Realists: Political Science and the American Crisis*, 188–198.

[15]Herbert J. Storing, ed., *Essays on the Scientific Study of Politics* (New York: Holt, Rinehart, 1962); Sheldon Wolin, "Political Theory as a Vocation," *American Political Science Review* 63 (1969): 1062–1081; William E. Connolly, ed., *The Bias of Pluralism* (New York: Atherton Press, 1969); and Freeman, "The Making of a Discipline," 30–31. In his 1993 book, *The Descent of Political Theory*, John Gunnell culminates his long-standing and persuasive argument that, from World War II on, émigré scholars who came to define themselves as political theorists of the Right and Left criticized the faith in American liberal democratic institutions and empiricism of American political science. He sees the behavioralism of the 1950s as an effort to defend those long-standing values. And he contends that the result in the 1970s was a professional peace pact that turned "political theory" into an insular subfield, remote from both real politics and from the surviving behavioralist thrust of an increasingly fragmented discipline.

[16]John Rawls, *A Theory of Justice* (Cambridge, Mass.: Harvard University Press, 1971).

[17]The debate over liberal "neutrality" and the priority of the right over the good is now voluminous, but no political theorist has played a more prominent role than William Galston. See William A. Galston, "Defending Liberalism," *American Political Science Review* 76 (1982): 621–629 and William A. Galston, *Liberal Purposes* (Cambridge: Cambridge University Press, 1991). The impact of Rawls's work was greatly abetted by theory-minded lawyers, especially Ronald Dworkin, *Taking Rights Seriously* (Cambridge, Mass.: Harvard University Press, 1978), whose arguments for connecting contemporary political philosophy and legal doctrinal debates helped give new legitimacy to such efforts by many political scientists in political theory and public law.

[18]Quentin Skinner, "Meaning and Understanding in the History of Ideas," *History and Theory* 8 (1969): 3–33; J. G. A. Pocock, *The Machiavellian Moment* (Princeton, N.J.: Princeton University Press, 1975).

[19]E.g., Farr and Seidelman, eds., *Discipline and History: Political Science in the United States,* 11, 285.

[20]References for this paragraph are in a sealed envelope, to be opened if I experience a sudden demise.

[21]See, e.g., Theodore J. Lowi, *The End of Liberalism* (New York: W. W. Norton, 1969; 2d ed., 1979); Ira Katznelson, *Black Men, White Cities* (New York: Oxford University Press, 1973); Ira Katznelson, *City Trenches* (New York: Pantheon Books, 1981); Michael N. Danielson, *The Politics of Exclusion* (New York: Columbia University Press, 1976); Norman Nie, Sidney Verba, and John Petrocik, *The Changing American Voter* (Cambridge, Mass.: Harvard University Press, 1976); David O. Sears, Carl P. Hensler, and Leslie K. Speer, "Whites' Opposition to 'Busing': Self-Interest or Symbolic Politics?" *American Political Science Review* 73 (1979): 369–384; Donald R. Kinder and David O. Sears, "Prejudice and Politics: Symbolic Racism versus Racial Threats to the Good Life," *Journal of Personality and Social Psychology* 40 (1981): 414–431; and Gabriel A. Almond, *A Discipline Divided: Schools and Sects in Political Science* (Newbury Park, Calif.: Sage Publications, 1990), 175–178.

[22]But because a leading figure in those studies, Henry Kissinger, had risen in the early 1970s to the highest office held by a political scientist since Woodrow Wilson's presidency, and another, Zbigniew Brzezinski, was almost as prominent in the Carter administration, political science did not seem to most of us so inconsequential as Charles Lindblom's essay here suggests.

[23]See, e.g., Kenneth A. Shepsle, "Institutional Arrangements and Equilibrium in Multi-Dimensional Voting Models," *American Journal of Political Science* 23 (1979): 27–59; Kenneth A. Shepsle, "Institutional Equilibrium and Equilibrium Institutions," in *Political Science: The Science of Politics,* ed. Herbert F. Weisberg (New York: Agathon Press, 1986); William H. Riker, "Implications from the Disequilibrium of Majority Rule for the Study of Institutions," *American Political Science Review* 74 (1980): 432–446; Riker, *The Art of Political Manipulation*; Kenneth A. Shepsle and Barry R. Weingast, "Structure-Induced Equilibrium and Legislative Choice," *Public Choice* 37 (1981): 503–519; Kenneth A. Shepsle and Barry R. Weingast, "When Do Rules of Procedure Matter?" *Journal of Politics* 46 (1984): 206–221; Kenneth A. Shepsle and Barry R. Weingast, "The Institutional Foundations of Committee Power," *American Po-*

litical Science Review 81 (1987): 85–104; Gary W. Cox, *The Efficient Secret: The Cabinet and the Development of Political Parties in Victorian England* (Cambridge: Cambridge University Press, 1987); and Matthew D. McCubbins, Roger G. Noll, and Barry R. Weingast, "Structure and Process, Politics and Policy: Administrative Arrangements and the Political Control of Agencies," *Virginia Law Review* 75 (1989): 431–482. Writing less formally, Terry Moe has evaluated and contributed to this body of work in a number of significant essays. See, e.g., Terry M. Moe, "The Politics of Bureaucratic Structure," in John E. Chubb and Paul E. Peterson, eds., *Can the Government Govern?* (Washington, D.C.: The Brookings Institution, 1989); Terry M. Moe, "The Politics of Structural Choice: Toward a Theory of Public Bureaucracy," in Oliver E. Williamson, ed., *Organization Theory: From Chester Barnard to the Present and Beyond* (New York: Oxford University Press, 1990); and Terry M. Moe, "Political Institutions: The Neglected Side of the Story," paper prepared for a conference on "The Organization of Political Institutions," Yale Law School Program in Law and Organization, New Haven, Conn., 27–28 April 1990, and references therein.

[24]John C. Harsanyi, "Can the Maximum Principle Serve as a Basis for Morality? A Critique of John Rawls's Theory," *American Political Science Review* 69 (1975): 594–606; Robert Paul Wolff, *Understanding Rawls* (Princeton, N.J.: Princeton University Press, 1977); Bruce Ackerman, *Social Justice in the Liberal State* (New Haven, Conn.: Yale University Press, 1980), 275–293; and Jon Elster, *Making Sense of Marx* (Cambridge: Cambridge University Press, 1985).

[25]Michael J. Sandel, *Liberalism and the Limits of Justice* (Cambridge: Cambridge University Press, 1982); Michael J. Sandel, "Introduction," in Michael J. Sandel, ed., *Liberalism and Its Critics* (Oxford: Blackwell 1984); Alasdair MacIntyre, *After Virtue*, 2d ed. (Notre Dame, Ind.: University of Notre Dame Press, 1984); and Charles Taylor, *Human Agency and Language* (Cambridge: Cambridge University Press, 1985), 102–105.

[26]Sean Wilentz, *Chants Democratic* (New York: Oxford University Press, 1984); Benjamin R. Barber, *Strong Democracy: Participatory Politics for a New Age* (Berkeley, Calif.: University of California Press, 1984); Allan Bloom, *The Closing of the American Mind* (New York: Simon & Schuster, 1987); Francis Fukuyama, *The End of History and the Last Man* (New York: Free Press, 1992); Daniel T. Rodgers, "Republicanism: The Career of a Concept," *Journal of American History* 79 (1992): 12–38; Amitai Etzioni, *The Spirit of Community: Rights, Responsibilities, and the Communitarian Agenda* (New York: Crown Publishers, 1993); and Barry Alan Shain, *The Myth of American Individualism* (Princeton, N.J.: Princeton University Press, 1994), xiv–xvi.

[27]Susan Moller Okin, *Women in Western Political Thought* (Princeton, N.J.: Princeton University Press, 1979); Jean Bethke Elshtain, *Public Man, Private Woman* (Princeton, N.J.: Princeton University Press, 1981); Michael J. Shapiro, *Language and Political Understanding: The Politics of Discursive Practices* (New Haven, Conn.: Yale University Press, 1981); William E. Connolly, *The Terms of Political Discourse*, 2d ed. (Princeton, N.J.: Princeton University Press, 1983); William E. Connolly, *Identity/Difference: Democratic Negotiations of Political Paradox* (Ithaca, N.Y.: Cornell University Press, 1991); and Helene Silverberg, "Gender Studies and Political Science: The History of the

'Behavioralist Compromise,'" in James Farr and Raymond Seidelman, eds., *Discipline and History: Political Science in the United States* (Ann Arbor, Mich.: University of Michigan Press, 1993), 363–381.

[28]Theda Skocpol, *States and Social Revolutions* (Cambridge: Cambridge University Press, 1979); and Stephen Skowronek, *Building a New American State* (Cambridge: Cambridge University Press, 1982).

[29]Terry Lynn Karl, "Dilemmas of Democratization in Latin America," *Comparative Politics* 23 (1990): 1. Cf. Skocpol, "Sociology's Historical Imagination," 1; Skocpol, "Bringing the State Back In: Strategies of Analysis in Current Research"; Theda Skocpol, *Protecting Soldiers and Mothers* (Cambridge, Mass.: Harvard University Press, 1992), 371; Stephen D. Krasner, "Sovereignty: An Institutional Perspective," *Comparative Political Studies* 21 (1988): 66–94; James G. March and Johan P. Olsen, "The New Institutionalism: Organizational Factors in Political Life," *American Political Science Review* 78 (1984): 734–749; James G. March and Johan P. Olsen, *Rediscovering Institutions* (New York: The Free Press, 1989), 1–52; Karen Orren, *Belated Feudalism: Labor, the Law, and Liberal Development in the United States* (New York: Cambridge University Press, 1991); and Peter A. Hall, "The Movement from Keynesianism to Monetarism: Institutional Analysis and British Economic Policy in the 1970s," in Sven Steinmo, Kathleen Thelen, and Frank Longstreth, eds., *Historical Institutionalism: Politics, Society, Economy* (New York: Cambridge University Press, 1992).

[30]For example, James W. Ceaser, *Presidential Selection: Theory and Development* (Princeton, N.J.: Princeton University Press, 1979), analyzed presidential selection systems and Jeffrey K. Tulis, *The Rhetorical Presidency* (Princeton, N.J.: Princeton University Press, 1987), analyzed presidential leadership by stressing how the more elite-centered republicanism of the founding era had been democratized, especially in the Progressive and Great Society years, in ways that expressed what they saw as a problematic modern egalitarianism. Cf. Skowronek, *Building a New American State*; and Rogers M. Smith, *Liberalism and American Constitutional Law* (Cambridge, Mass.: Harvard University Press, 1985).

[31]Peter A. Hall, ed., *The Political Power of Economic Ideas* (Princeton, N.J.: Princeton University Press, 1989); Steinmo, Thelen, and Longstreth, eds., *Historical Institutionalism: Politics, Society, Economy*; and Judith Goldstein and Robert O. Keohane, *Ideas and Foreign Policy: Beliefs, Institutions, and Political Change* (Ithaca, N.Y.: Cornell University Press, 1993).

[32]Works making normative arguments through contextual readings of the historical roles of political theory doctrines include MacIntyre, *After Virtue*; Stephen Holmes, *Benjamin Constant and the Making of Modern Liberalism* (New Haven, Conn.: Yale University Press, 1984); Don Herzog, *Without Foundations: Justification in Political Theory* (Ithaca, N.Y.: Cornell University Press, 1985); Russell L. Hanson, *The Democratic Imagination in America: Conversations with Our Past* (Princeton, N.J.: Princeton University Press, 1985); Bernard Yack, *The Longing for Total Revolution* (Princeton, N.J.: Princeton University Press, 1986); and Ian Shapiro, *The Evolution of Rights in Liberal Theory* (Cambridge: Cambridge University Press, 1986).

[33]Excellent examples of historical institutional analyses that use quantitative data include Calvin C. Jillson, *Constitution Making: Conflict and Consensus in the Federal Convention of 1787* (New York: Agathon Press, 1988); and Richard M. Valelly, "Politics, Coercion, and Inclusion: The Two Reconstructions of the South's Electoral Politics," *Politics and Society* 21 (1993): 37–67. A signal blend of historical and rational-choice "new institutionalisms" is Charles Stewart III and Barry R. Weingast, "Stacking the Senate, Changing the Nation: Republican Rotten Boroughs, Statehood Politics, and American Political Development," *Studies in American Political Development* 6 (1992): 223–271.

[34]Gabriel A. Almond, "Separate Tables: Schools and Sects in Political Science," *PS: Political Science and Politics* 21 (1988): 828–842; Kenneth A. Shepsle, "The Nature of Contemporary Political Science: A Roundtable Discussion," *PS: Political Science and Politics* 23 (1990): 40–42; and John E. Chubb and Terry M. Moe, "Controversy: Should Market Forces Control Educational Decision Making?" *American Political Science Review* 84 (1990): 565.

[35]John Ferejohn, "Rationality and Interpretation: Parliamentary Elections in Early Stuart England," in Kristen Renwick Monroe, ed., *The Economic Approach to Politics: A Critical Reassessment of the Theory of Rational Action* (New York: HarperCollins, 1991); Morris Fiorina, "Institutionalism: Ideas, Structures, Methods," presentation at the Annual Meeting of the Social Science History Association, Baltimore, Md., 6 November 1993; and Donald P. Green and Ian Shapiro, *Pathologies of Rational Choice: A Critique of Applications in Political Science* (New Haven, Conn.: Yale University Press, 1994), 17–18, 26–27.

[36]Rogers M. Smith, "Political Jurisprudence, the 'New Institutionalism,' and the Future of Public Law," *American Political Science Review* 82 (1988): 104; and Smith, "If Politics Matters: Implications for a New Institutionalism," 4–5.

[37]For an empirically-oriented defense of middle-level theory, see Green and Shapiro, *Pathologies of Rational Choice*, 29, 184–185, 189–191. The examples of middle-level propositions are drawn from Gerald N. Rosenberg, *The Hollow Hope* (Chicago, Ill.: University of Chicago Press, 1991); Donald P. Green, "The Price Elasticity of Mass Preferences," *American Political Science Review* 86 (1992): 128–148; and Victoria C. Hattam, *Labor Visions and State Politics* (Princeton, N.J.: Princeton University Press, 1993).

[38]Karen Orren and Stephen Skowronek, "Beyond the Iconography of Order: Notes for a 'New Institutionalism,'" in Lawrence C. Dodd and Calvin Jillson, eds., *The Dynamics of American Politics: Approaches and Interpretations* (Boulder, Colo.: Westview Press, 1993); and Karen Orren and Stephen Skowronek, "Institutions and Intercurrence: Theory Building in the Fullness of Time," *Nomos* (forthcoming).

[39]Stephen Skowronek, *The Politics Presidents Make* (Cambridge, Mass.: Harvard University Press, 1993).

[40]For prescriptions to this effect see Green and Shapiro, *Pathologies of Rational Choice*, 253–254.

[41]Robert Putnam with Robert Leonardi and Raffaella Y. Nanetti, *Making Democracy Work: Civic Traditions in Modern Italy* (Princeton, N.J.: Princeton University Press, 1993); and Robert Putnam, "Bowling Alone," *Journal of Democracy*

6 (1995): 64–79. I am grateful to Stanley Katz for reminding me of the importance of Putnam's work in relation to the themes of this essay.

⁴²Putnam, "Bowling Alone," 66–70, 76–77.

⁴³Leonard D. White, "Political Science, Mid-Century," in James Farr and Raymond Seidelman, eds., *Discipline and History: Political Science in the United States* (Ann Arbor, Mich.: University of Michigan Press, 1993; orig. 1950), 226.

⁴⁴Lindblom, *Inquiry and Change: The Troubled Attempt to Understand and Shape Society.*

⁴⁵Rogers M. Smith, "Beyond Tocqueville, Myrdal, and Hartz: The Multiple Traditions in America," *American Political Science Review* 87 (1993): 549–566; and Rogers M. Smith, *Civic Ideals: Conflicting Visions of Citizenship in U.S. History* (Yale University Press, 1997). See also Rogers M. Smith, "Science, Non-Science, and Politics," in Terrence J. McDonald, ed., *The Historic Turn in the Human Sciences* (Ann Arbor, Mich.: University of Michigan Press, 1996), 119–159, on which the current essay draws.

PART III

INTER-DISCIPLINARY
COMPARISONS:
HISTORICAL PERSPECTIVES

Carl E. Schorske

The New Rigorism in the Human Sciences, 1940–1960

W E SOMETIMES FORGET THAT FOUNDING fathers were once sons themselves. The four authors associated with the movements that reestablished their respective disciplines in America's mid-century decades have in their essays for this collection defined themselves to some degree, as sons often do, against the world of their fathers. Their depictions of their fields as they encountered them as students reveal kindred filial discontents and, more strikingly, similar impulses to provide order, clarity, and rigor to an academic culture that seemed to them too sprawling in its scope, too flaccid in its grasp.

Robert Solow, in order to dramatize the break in the conception of economics that refounded his discipline for America after World War II, begins his essay in this volume with a quick, revealing look at the educational practices of his student days. He compares the textbooks of the elementary economics course that he took at Harvard in 1940 with those in use today. In the very makeup of the textbook pages, Solow captures the contrast that fifty years have wrought. In 1940, printed prose prevailed; in 1990, graphs, tables, and equations crowd the landscape. The prose of 1940 conveys descriptions—descriptions of our economic universe, its commodities, institutions, and social practices, accompanied by "judicious discussion" or "historical reflections" that would presumably help the student to confront the confusing textures of

Carl E. Schorske is Professor of History Emeritus at Princeton University.

modern economic life, along with some modest theoretical perspectives that had been devised to understand it. In the 1990 textbook, the panoramic description of economic life has given way to something that resembles some sort of discourse on method. Economics has become a technical subject, the textbook a collection of analytic tools to be applied to observable situations. The transformation of economics from a loose, pluralistic social study of economic life with a variety of critical perspectives into a sharply focused analytic discipline with a strong methodological consensus (not to say orthodoxy) centering on model-building and on the statistical-empirical verification of largely mathematical theoretical hypotheses—that has been the work of Robert Solow's generation.

At the other end of our disciplinary spectrum, in English literature, M. H. Abrams also recalls his prewar Harvard education and uses it as a baseline for charting the transformation of his discipline. In the eclectic undergraduate courses of the 1930s, a loose historicism prevailed, sometimes arid, sometimes rich and rewarding in individual perspectives. It was the graduate program, however, that left young Abrams most dissatisfied. It was freighted with two anachronistic legacies of the nineteenth century's aspirations to *Wissenschaftlichheit*: on the one hand, historical linguistics and positivistic philology ("distinctly unexciting"); on the other, a false comprehensiveness, an excessive demand for "coverage" of the history of English literature. Abrams directs our attention, however, to what was absent from the offerings in English literature: any focus on criticism. Only one lone voice at Harvard— that of an outsider to the university, I. A. Richards—raised the claims of critical analysis as the central task of literary study. Abrams never became an orthodox adherent of the New Criticism that came to power in English departments in the 1950s. Yet his pathbreaking work, though historical, was a history of *criticism*— the subject he felt to be most lacking in Harvard's English department in the 1930s. His book, *The Mirror and the Lamp,* mediated the passage from philological and positivistic historical scholarship to the primacy of criticism in literary study that marked the postwar years.

Our economist and our literary scholar seem to agree that the prewar conceptions of their disciplines suffered from a heavy burden of superannuated intellectual baggage that inhibited the more focused functions that they both made central to their fields in the 1950s: rigorous analysis through positivistic model-building in economics and critical self-consciousness in English literature.

In political science, as in economics and literary New Criticism, those who had instigated the tone-setting behavioralist revolution in the 1950s were uneasy about the incohesiveness that had marked their fields when they were students. As an undergraduate, Charles Lindblom fled what he calls the "mushiness" of political science and instead pursued a major and graduate study in economics, although it was the "big questions" of politics that basically attracted him. David Easton, another pioneer in behavioralism, reports finishing his graduate training at Harvard "with his head in a whirl. . . . No one had ever tried to help me understand why my interest in politics required me to be exposed to such a wide variety of subject matters. . . . I gained no sense of a basis upon which I could infer that political science formed a coherent body of knowledge." In the 1940s, Easton complains, theory was still taught historically, seeking to explain the development of political ideas. Such theory, he felt, did not perform the function of theory in economics, chemistry, or physics—namely, the conceptualization of the present discipline in part or as a whole. While the fathers had overcome the institutional formalism of the nineteenth century and "had enlarged the rich body of informal activities of which public policy was formed," their political science was still loosely descriptive and often confused description with value. "Method was so taken for granted that it was non-problematic."[1] It was in the area of method, then, that the behavioralists were to seek remedy for the theoretically lax historicism and uncohesive pluralism of the political science of the fathers.

Of the four disciplines examined in this study, none acquired a new identity more fully than philosophy, where the rupture with the past was most radical. "The present situation, in which American philosophy is dominated by a movement," Hilary Putnam writes, "is utterly different from the situation that prevailed in the field when I came into it [in the late 1940s]." Putnam offers a picture of the recent history of philosophy as a present-day graduate student might conceive it: "[U]ntil some time in the 1930s American philosophy was without form and void. Then the logical positivists arrived [from Austria and Germany], and around fifty years ago most American philosophers became positivists." In correcting this picture, Putnam fills the "void" conceived by the graduate student with adherents of many philosophic outlooks: realism, pragmatism, even surviving idealism. The pioneering logical positivists, before and during the war, were largely émigrés— few, scattered, and as yet of little widespread influence. Putnam's general picture of the philosophic culture of the fathers thus resembles strikingly the description given by his colleagues in the other disciplines mentioned—economics, literature, and political science—that of a loosely eclectic field without a clear sense of mission or method. It would be too much to say that before the creation of the new, rigorous analytic schools that acquired salience in the 1950s, darkness lay on the face of the deep; however, the lights that hovered above it were many-hued and scattered, lacking the power to illuminate the terrain with strong, focused beams.

Before considering the characteristics of the new disciplinary order established by the sons in the 1950s and what they shared, I should like to take one more backward glance to prewar academic culture, this time to my own educational experience as a Columbia College undergraduate. My picture of the academic past differs rather surprisingly from those of my colleagues in other fields. While they manifest divine discontent with the state of learning to which they were exposed, I seem to have received my undergraduate education like a happy camper. Two factors may account for my more positive assessment: 1) as a historian, I have a professional interest in the still-strong place of history in the academic culture of the time; and 2) Columbia probably had a more coherent collective intellectual ethos in the 1930s than did most American universities. Columbia provides a more integrated vision of the prewar academic culture than that recalled by my colleagues as a backdrop for the postwar development of their separate disciplines. It places in higher relief the emergence of autonomy and the primacy of analytic method as the salient, though not exclusive, common characteristics of our postwar disciplines.

We are inclined to forget today how recently history as a mode of understanding suffused the world of learning. In America especially, whose tradition of the Enlightenment was revitalized at the turn of the century with the development of Progressivism in both politics and academic culture, Clio was seen as the muse that presided over the transformation of the world through the application of mind to the problems of man and nature. The idea of progress is far from the only way that history can be conceived. But in optimistic America, especially in the Progressive movement in politics and culture, the modern itself seemed a projection and fulfillment of history, rather than a break from it. Within the curriculum, the disciplines presented themselves in a historical frame: the *history* of economic or political thought, the *history* of literature, the *history* of philosophy. This temporal organization governed both introductory and prestigious advanced courses within each discipline. It also implied a progress in understanding based on the ingestion of past achievements and their transcendence in each field of learning.

At Columbia, perhaps more than elsewhere, the educational offerings wore the mantle of Clio. In a required introductory course in history and the social sciences, the values and aspirations of the university's general culture were vigorously compressed. "The Rise of Contemporary Civilization in the West" became influential in other institutions in the era of the New Deal. All the words in the course's title counted. The first year charted the "rise" of modern civilization in Europe and was historical; the second year aimed to describe modern society's nature and to address its problems, especially in America. Of course, there was no multiculturalism; this was the West only. Although attentive to problems of class, the course shared the almost total neglect of issues of race, gender, and ethnicity that characterized American prewar culture generally and scholarship in particular. Social scientists, historians, and philosophers, mostly young, designed and manned the program, injecting into it their professional and civic concerns. It was not so much interdisciplinary as it was multidisciplinary. Its basic way of making meaning was, however, historical: synoptic and synchronically associative, although its particular narrative order in a trajectory of progress would seem naive, almost meta-historical, today. Despite its limitations, the course offered a rich vision of the multifaceted nature of historical and contemporary life that made Harvard's politically-centered

History 1 course, which I later taught as a graduate assistant, seem impoverished and narrow. What would Robert Solow have thought of our second year when economic life was examined? Focused on contemporary America, it was even broader and conceptually looser than his Harvard course, for it involved more sociology. The instructors, though from different social science specialties, shared a public intellectual's kind of vocation—to show us in a rudimentary way how their disciplines could identify and address economic and social problems. They had an interest in institutional description and social criticism, which they saw as constitutive of, rather than ancillary or irrelevant to, their disciplines.

I do not wish to create the impression that all advanced education at Columbia followed the pattern of the contemporary civilization course. Even in the humanistic general honors program in which I majored, which was intended in part as a more timeless exploration of values, team teaching by historians, literary scholars, and philosophers was normal. There too, however, a synoptic historical mentality and the self-conscious orientation of specialized learning to the public sphere were, by today's measure, surprisingly pervasive in the faculty. External historical factors conspired with a local intellectual tradition to produce this characteristic ethos. The depression at home and the threat of fascism abroad shook confidence in and exposed the vulnerability of the American social system. Crisis sharpened the will to criticize and to engage in finding remedy. The local intellectual factor that doubtless shaped this consciousness was the influence of John Dewey on Columbia's academic intelligentsia. In his thinking, philosophy, science, and history still went hand in hand as he called for both normative critical inquiry and confidence in the power of the scientific method to effectuate social amelioration under the ordinance of time. Hilary Putnam, Alexander Nehamas, Rogers Smith, and others in this volume point to Dewey's powerful presence in the prewar academy well beyond Columbia. His was the most comprehensive formulation of a widely diffused academic vocational ethos that acquired new persuasive power when depression engulfed the land.

The recollected picture of my 1930s educational experience, focusing as it does on the general cultural aim and import of undergraduate social study, clearly lacks congruence with the images of my colleagues. With the exception of M. H. Abrams in English, they are concerned less with the substance of their fields at the time of their entry into them than with the problem of their intellectual focus and coherence. The contrast between our respective recollections of the culture of learning in the house of our fathers—for the two social scientists and the philosopher, an uncohesive eclecticism; for the historian, a relatively cohesive interdisciplinary educational field imbued with civic import—reflects more than the differences between the perspectives of our respective disciplines. It bespeaks a moment in American academic culture when it was preparing to turn away from the nineteenth century primacy of a loose, historical conception of meaning-making to the privileging of a scientific one. The passage here is from range to rigor, from a loose engagement with a multifaceted reality historically perceived to the creation of sharp analytic tools that could promise certainty where description and speculative explanation had prevailed before. Each of the four disciplines—English, too—in their various ways embarked upon the road to rigorous analysis. In three of them, the pursuit of the analytic method resulted in the contraction of the discipline's traditional subject matter. Their salient common characteristics in the 1950s and their comparative success in establishing their new disciplinary order will be our next concern.

* * *

"My generation was drawn to economics," Robert Solow told the participants at a conference in Pasadena in the voice of his generational culture, "by the depression and to a lesser extent by the war; by the desire to fix things, to do good. Today economists are drawn more by the appeal of scientism; this contributes to the appeal of Gerard Debreu [the mathematical economic theorist]." Is there not a historical connection between these phases? The depression provided not merely a stimulus to critical social thought, but also, through the New Deal, an opportunity for action, a chance "to fix things." Paradoxically, the engagement of university social scientists in the reforming work of the New Deal—a logical extension of their previous academic roles as independent social analysts and critics—began their transformation into technical experts for whom mathematics and statistics were of the highest usefulness. The war, with its expanded demand for purely operational, applied scholarship in the service of relatively uncontested policy goals, likewise increased the imperative for scientific reliability. The original political motivation for the university's intellectuals entering public employment, born of social and international crisis, could easily be transmuted to a career motivation in which the neutral application of technical skills assumed primacy over some normative public-service imperative.

Further encouragement and support for the development of a more astringent and scientific scholarship came to economics from the business community. One of the most fertile research centers for the development of economic theory refined by mathematics and statistics was the Cowles Commission. Its founder, Alfred Cowles, was an investment counselor who, after the crash of 1929, sought ways to improve the sadly deficient means of economic forecasting. After the war, the Cowles Commission became a vital center for new approaches to general economic theory and econometrics. The perfection of forecasting techniques and the fine-tuning of economic policy decisions became the vehicle for a closer involvement of professional economists with business as well as government elites. Central to the pursuit of such expanded social roles was the concentration of the discipline on mathematical model-building and statistical-empirical analysis. The intellectual quest for scientific objectivity and the professional advantages of a value-free neutrality reinforced each other in the establishment of a new methodological consensus as the basis of the discipline. This in turn affected the character of graduate training and increased the mathematical qualifications in student selection. Thanks to a combination of rigorous standards and strict gate control, economics has, from the 1950s until the present, become the strongest of the four disciplines in its intellectual identity and internal cohesion. It has also become the most closely identified with the American elite in government and business.

In political science, the behavioralists, new protagonists of the scientific method, did not achieve as full a victory as did their colleagues in economics. Four subfields that have long characterized political science remained intact and resistant: political theory in the philosophic tradition, international politics, public administration, and American politics. The behavioralists swept only the last field, that of American politics. Charles Lindblom, building on Daniel Bell's book, *The Social Sciences Since the Second World War*,[2] has pointed to the quite specific historical conditions that made the scientific method of inquiry congenial to the Americanists. The tremendous successes and prestige of the natural sciences, both theoretical and in operations research, coincided with and was fueled by America's embattled reaction to the new Communist threat. The overwhelming response of the academic community was to affirm American political and social institutions. Louis Hartz, Richard Hofstadter, David Potter, and other historians developed their various versions of America's "consensus history" to support the idea of the nation's traditional immunity from the class and ideological struggles that had blighted European social experience. The "end of ideology" that was heralded in America's embattled moment of Cold War defensiveness can be seen in historical perspective as the virtually unchallengeable supremacy of the nation's liberal-democratic ideology of which the academic culture was deeply, and often uncritically, supportive.

For behavioralists, as both Charles Lindblom and Rogers Smith observe, a dual commitment to science as a method and to the democratic system created a problem. The very nature of the scientific method is to affirm the given, the reality it aims to analyze. As Sheldon Wolin has observed, the natural scientist does not criticize nature. If nature fails to conform to his theory, it is his theory that is at fault and must be changed. Traditional political theory, anchored in pre-analytic philosophy, posits a different relation between theory and reality. Such theory, including as it does norms of moral and political judgment, analyzes reality not only for its inner workings but also in its relation to those norms. In the dissonance between the political reality and the claims of the traditional theorist, it is the given reality that must be corrected, not necessarily—or, as in the case of science, not only—the theory by which it is understood.[3]

Charles Lindblom formulates the problem of the behavioralists' two loyalties—to the scientific method and to American institutional structures and processes—as a tension between the "how" and the "what." In his view, the scientific model for politics, while intellectually exemplary, failed to produce results commensurate with those in nature or in economics because the subject matter, the "what," was too narrowly defined as a consequence of the behavioralist investigator's ideological identification with the given.

In the late 1950s and early 1960s the emergence of new political agents, essentially unrepresented in the political structure and its normal electoral processes, triggered a crisis of particular gravity for the behavioralists. The civil rights movement, the anti-war protests, the student rebellion, the explosion of the cities—these historical upheavals of the alienated, all of which were unanticipated under the scientific method, revealed how much the new political science in the 1940s and 1950s had fallen victim to what Lindblom calls "Pollyannaism." It had given "benign interpretations" to democratic political systems, defining political parties by reference only to their useful functions, ignoring racial exclusions and exploitation in the governmental and institutional processes. While crediting the behavioralist movement with genuine achievements on how to do research, Lindblom concludes that value commitments in the end inhibited his discipline in achieving the purity and cognitive efficacy of natural science or economics.

The essays by Rogers Smith and Ira Katznelson in this volume delineate the new tendencies in political science that arose out of the 1960s. Traditional, normative political theory with new foci, such as those of Sheldon Wolin and Michael Walzer, strong in their relations to history and community ethics, gained new followings. Behavioralism, while it suffered a loss of the prestige (not to say the primacy) it enjoyed and the enthusiastic élan it generated in the 1960s, continued as a major strand in the discipline. Like economics, it was sustained by the expansion of policy studies in and outside the government, with their stress on technical analytic skills. It also found a new link to economics, whose psychological assumptions and analytic methods were put to work in rational-choice theory. For the pursuit of the increasingly pressing issues of domination, community dysfunction, and racism that had been marginalized by the behavioralists' agenda of systemic affirmation, other less value-neutral approaches to the discipline proved more useable.

Philosophy must share with economics the double distinction of having both recast its intellectual foundations and successfully unified itself as a professional discipline on the basis of that achievement. Epistemological reliability became a primary focus of philosophical work. Once again, as in our social disciplines, science provided the model for the redefinition of the mission and methods of a field of learning. The émigré logical positivists, whose intellectual antecedents in nineteenth-century Central Europe were as much philosophically concerned scientists and mathematicians as scientifically engaged philosophers, gave a powerful impulse to the new movement in America. They were largely Austrians who shared in the English empirical tradition that informed that country's liberal tradition. Their vigorous anti-metaphysical and anti-idealist orientations found ready echoes among American philosophers seeking an autonomous *locus standi* amid the value-laden and ideological forces that had characterized their field.

The same combination (sometimes accompanied by tension) of formal mathematical theory and empirical constituents of scientific thinking that informed and inspired the model-building culture of the new economics appeared in philosophy. The same consequence attended it: the subject matter was reduced to topics that were securely verifiable. The analytic philosophers purged or marginalized traditional areas of concern where values and feelings played a decisive role. Ethics, aesthetics, metaphysics, and politics were all for a time equally excluded as the source of pseudo-problems that could not be formulated or addressed with the rigorous canons of epistemological reliability developed by and out of science. W. V. O. Quine's oft-quoted statement, "Philosophy of science is philosophy enough," while representing a more radical contraction of the discipline than many analytic philosophers would have underwritten, reflects accurately the privileged position of science in the movement's table of values.

The second branch of the analytic movement, ordinary-language philosophy, did not center its concerns so completely on the language and logic of science. Yet it too pursued conceptual analysis as its basic aim. Like the logical positivists, its practitioners defined their task as analyzing not the nature of the world but the meanings and validity of the concepts that others used to explore or understand it. With respect to the realm of value that had been so prominent a constituent in traditional philosophy, they held that the philosopher could not tell us what "the good" or "the beautiful" was. Such terms are too emotion-laden to be meaningful. The philosopher could, however, analyze the consistency and logical relations of terms and concepts used in evaluative or "emotive" discourse.

This second-order function, when the historical challenges of the 1960s began to hit home, could provide a bridge back to the world of value and emotion, which analytic philosophy had in its strictest observance placed beyond the pale of its proper concerns. In its orientation toward science, philosophy, like economics, cut its ties to the humanistic disciplines, perhaps most importantly to history. History was a field in which the world of fact and value, truth and goodness, "hard" and "soft" necessarily remained confused and messily intertwined. Philosophy's own history too was understandably jettisoned as useless to the discipline's present mission. The synthetic heritage of philosophy, as we have seen, had found its last influential spokesman in John Dewey. His linkage of philosophy with the social sciences in the execution of a historically conceived mission disappeared swiftly, with little trace. Philosophy in the 1950s essentially withdrew from the public realm.

In its New Critical movement, English literature shared the quest for analytic precision with the other three fields examined here. But how different from them is its trajectory of transformation since the 1960s! When our economist Robert Solow looks upon the work of his academic grandchildren, he rightly sees them as faithful to the analytic methods established by his generation. For M. H. Abrams in literature, by contrast, the grandchildren have seriously undermined what was common in the intellectual mission of his generation—to build the discipline around scholarly literary criticism, broadly defined. They have also assaulted the very cultural system of European humanism that bound the 1950s scholars—whatever their differences in their critique of their fathers' scholarship—to the past, to each other, and to the academic culture as a whole. In view of the deep and radical break represented by the advent of deconstruction and the culture wars after the 1960s, their own critical turn of the 1940s and 1950s, so fundamental to the other fields, recedes into comparative insignificance.

Should one then speak at all of a turn in early postwar literary scholarship that is the intellectual and historical equivalent of the new centering of economics, political behavioralism, and philosophy on science and its empirical methods? Surely, the New Criticism had some similar characteristics. If so, why did the literary disciplines as redefined under its suzerainty not survive the shocks of the cultural revolutions of the 1960s and 1970s? Why, when economics and philosophy maintained their hegemonies of method by modest adaptations to meet the challenges of new value claims against the given, was the New Criticism, ahistorical though it was, swept away as a quintessential part of the history from which the postmodernists in literature were making a decisive break?

Of the new and varied tendencies that superseded prewar positivistic historical and philological scholarship in literature, the New Criticism achieved a clear institutional ascendancy by the 1950s. Catherine Gallagher stresses the role of John Crowe Ransom in defining an autonomous focus for literary study: the work of literature as art. At its most astringent, his object-centered, formalistic kind of criticism freed the literary object from its nonaesthetic context—historical, moral, and psychological. As the literary work of art was distinguished from other kinds of language use by the special techniques that removed it from everyday reality, so the critic's task became a technical one. He would devise formal and structural analytic procedures to illuminate the particularity and protect the autonomy of the literary work. Here *l'art pour l'art,* an originary premise of modernism in art itself when its avant-garde protagonists freed it from social relationships, found its scholarly analogue in a modernist criticism.

As the text was separated from its context in this extreme object-centered form of criticism, so could the critic separate himself from other fields with which literary study had been associated. In this respect, the New Critic pursued for literature the same purging function that the analytic philosopher accomplished by extruding metaphysics and other areas not susceptible to his logical method, or that the economic model builder achieved in shutting out sociological and historical approaches from his discipline. In all cases, the clarification of method brought with it the reduction of the discipline's agenda.

In its purest, formalist variety, the New Criticism also provided the profession with a timely methodological shield of neutrality against the danger of ideological contamination in the era of

McCarthy and the Cold War. Even though its genealogy included both English and southern American strains of anti-industrial and anti-democratic conservatism, the New Criticism found in its ahistorical and amoral analytic technique the equivalent to the value-freedom that the social sciences of the 1950s had justified by their adherence to the scientific method and its fidelity to the given.

In its narrow sense, the analytic of the New Criticism that sought to lift the literary artifact clear of all historical and moral imbrication did not succeed in achieving in English departments the clear dominance that was won by the new rigorist approaches in economics and philosophy. Like behavioralism in political science, it succeeded only partly. Within faculties of English the competing viewpoints were too strong for a methodological New Critical victory. The most critical of these countervailing tendencies was a new form of historicism, far richer than the historical scholarship that had caused such tedium to M. H. Abrams and his fellow students in the 1930s. A series of pathbreaking studies in the new historical vein, Abrams's included, combined critical analysis of literary works with the configurative perspective and interpretive techniques of the rapidly developing field of intellectual history. Such contextual literary study naturally ran counter to the solipsistic aesthetic practice of hard-core New Criticism. It also resisted the effort of the New Criticism to separate literature from the other disciplines.

Some of the ablest contextualist scholars, such as F. O. Matthieson, Perry Miller, and Henry Nash Smith, fueled the interdisciplinary American studies programs that emerged in the late New Deal era. They combined the traditional ethos of humanism with a socially critical historicism to foster an American democratic cultural consciousness. In its explorations, its synthetic impulse, and its affirmation of public purpose, the American studies movement showed itself to be an offspring of Progressivist academic culture. Unlike the Dewey-inspired American year of the integrated contemporary civilization course that I had experienced at Columbia, which excluded the arts, American studies involved few social scientists and placed literary scholars beside historians in a defining, formative role. One can see here an adumbration of the function of literary scholars as animators of today's many interdisciplinary programs in cultural studies—ethnic, feminist, gender, and others. The moral humanist tradition of Matthew Arnold also found new favor in the early postwar years. Humanities programs for undergraduates, originating in the prewar conservative New Humanism of the 1920s, were now expanded and redefined to provide a foundation of traditional Western values for all students as part of a common cultural consciousness against the antiliberal ideological threats from the Right and the Left. College administrators—James Bryant Conant among them—and foundations lent strong support to this effort to nurture a common, European-based cultural consciousness. Some humanities programs reinforced the historical orientation of literary study, as at Hobart and William Smith College; others, as at Chicago and Annapolis, emphasized the "timeless" values enshrined in canonical texts. In either case, the humanities movement comported ill with the literary autonomism of the New Criticism, even though the latter's analytic methods could be deployed there.

If the New Criticism challenged its two principal rival approaches—the historical and the humanistic-cultural—with its methods, it also drew them together. As Catherine Gallagher demonstrates, it was a paradoxical peculiarity of the New Criticism in its period of ascendancy that it acted as both a centripetal and centrifugal force. As a centripetal force, it imparted an institutional unity and a distinct autonomy to the profession by placing the literary text at the center of concern. This object-focus could serve literary scholars as a mark of identity and function even as they dispersed into the expanding interdisciplinary programs. The focus on the text, on "close reading," did not necessarily imply subscription to the New Critical techniques of formal analysis, free of all contextual impurities. This softer side of New Critical object-centeredness could tolerate many forms of interpretation of a text. Here was the common ground on which many flowers could bloom. And bloom they did, as M. H. Abrams makes clear.

Yet a powerful centrifugality was concealed under the New Critical consensual umbrella of "close reading." Frederick Crews punctures the deceptive unity in his witty, erudite spoof, *The Pooh Perplex* (1963).[4] Crews parodies the many critical positions of the profession of his day as each is deployed to reveal through close reading the meaning of that great classic, A. A. Milne's *Winnie the Pooh*: Chicago neo-Aristotelian, Marxist, Freudian, beatnik, Christian humanist, and so on. In every interpretation, we can descry scattered remains of the dismembered text that have been ingested by the critic as he produces nothing but a statement of his own analytic or ideological system. The text as a whole, if it ever had an identity or existence, disappears in the Babel of criticism. One is reminded of Archibald MacLeish's protesting poet's voice: "A poem should not mean but be."

Is Crews's spoof a comic lament for the centrifugal consequences of the New Criticism's centripetal project? Whatever the author's intent, his book suggests how vulnerable the discipline would be to the diverse cultural and ideational commitments of its participants should the shared belief in the text, the literary artifact, collapse. The cultural upheaval of the 1960s brought the decentering of the text, and with it the disintegration of the professional consensus on literature as subject matter that had held the intellectually fragmented discipline together.

*   *   *

The protest movements of America in the 1960s and 1970s struck hard in the universities. Academic culture as a whole had to confront the revolution in values in each of its three dimensions— social, political, and cultural. Within the university an activated and socially expanded student body became a conspicuous protagonist for moral and social claims raised outside it. As the society moved away from the defensive consensual passivity of the first two Cold War decades to open up divisive issues of racial justice, war, sexual freedom, and women's liberation, the university, as befitted its traditional if not usually intended social function of intellectualizing the tensions and conflicts of society, was called upon—not to say pressed—from within and without to address them.

Needless to say, the relevance of the new issues to our four disciplines varied with their subject matter and self-definition. Their responses varied accordingly, yet all had a common problem. All had rebuilt their foundations and postwar professional identities on analytic methods, if to differing degrees. To do so, they had shrunk, marginalized, or extruded some of the value concerns of their traditional subject matter. Now the world of value, an ancient concern of university culture, rose in a "return of the repressed" to raise in new forms normative claims against the expanded dominion of science (or, in English, aesthetic formalism) in the study of man and the fields of social power with which it had, to varying degrees, become associated.

The transformation of the disciplines since the 1970s lies beyond the scope of this essay. But let me offer a few comparative observations on the relation of the disciplines to each other and their adaptation of the shared intellectual platform of the 1950s to the new cultural situation.

The polarity in the human sciences as a whole reveals itself most drastically in the fields of economics and English. No discipline stood its ground more securely through the storm than economics; none was more totally fractured by it than English literature. Economics, in its prewar, descriptive aspect often a center of social criticism, had left that function behind in the analytic consolidation of the 1950s. In a strange reversal of roles, however, younger members of literature departments, abandoning their aesthetic detachment, took up social-critical functions when the New Critical umbrella was shredded by the storm.

The shift in the disciplinary locus of engaged criticism from economics to literature, however limited, was appropriate enough. In the 1930s the discontents were strongly social and economic; in the 1960s, they were social and cultural. In fact, none of the 1960s movements—minority, feminist, or sexual—challenged the economic system. Like the economists themselves, the protest movements recognized, however tacitly, the capitalist free market as part of the factual order of things. The new claimants—women and African-Americans, to name only two—wished not to reshape that order but to gain access to its positions and its bounty. Why should there be a critical economics when the protesters themselves had little interest in economic criticism?

The economists felt secondary effects of the radical storms in the part of their constituency that was closer to home, namely, the student body. William Barber addresses this problem in this volume. He shows how, as Keynesian macroeconomics and attention to international socioeconomic development problems yielded to

Chicago-style economic thinking and as diffuse social radicalism spread, students became disaffected from economics.

This problem flowed into a larger, more endemic one for college teachers of economics. The requirements of a general economics suited to a liberal undergraduate education and those for graduate training of technical specialists have pulled in different directions, leading to a conflict between colleges that cannot get the teachers they need and graduate institutions that cannot get the kind of mathematically prepared students they want. The marginalization of history and sociology within the discipline has aggravated the problem at the college end. A consortium of economists at undergraduate colleges and the American Economics Association have tangled with each other as they try to deal with it.

David Kreps makes clear that as economics has established ties to different sectors of the professions—law schools, business, government, etc.—it has broadened its methods to include other "softer" disciplines such as sociology or anthropology in order to address problems in new topical domains (e.g., corporate culture). He stresses, however, that there will be no return to the distinct methods and languages that once prevailed in specialized economic areas in the premathematical era. There are only topical dialects of a single mathematical lingua franca. Firmly rooted in the global economic system, economics as a scientific discipline continues to expand the intellectual forms and social functions it developed in the 1950s.

As the most technical of social-scientific disciplines, economics centers its educational function on graduate and professional training and its social function on instrumental service to the elite. English, perhaps the most value-sensitive of the humanistic disciplines, has its principal educational mission in undergraduate education. In the cultural revolution, it has assumed (along with history and anthropology) a new social function: to study and fortify the culture of previously excluded minorities, as until now it has studied and fortified the high culture of Europe and the United States. The university-encouraged demographic change in the student body has created constituencies to support, in effect, a professional diaspora of literary scholars into cultural studies programs. Whether defined by ethnicity, race, or gender, the mission to the underprivileged and excluded weakens the walls that the New Critics built to separate the literary profession from others. José David Saldívar shows how a new vocational identity emerges from the new assignment. At the same time, an internal implosion of deconstructive criticism of the literary object has destroyed the center of the 1950s New Critical consensus. The situation in the English departments can be viewed as replicating in their cultural divisions and group allegiances the nation's cultural fragmentation, if in altered proportions. What remains common is neither art nor method, neither high nor vernacular culture, but the commitment to the making and illumination of cultural identity itself through its imaginative expressions, often with moralistic emotions of righteousness that disrupt the process of finding a new, non-exclusionist commonality. It is a task in which, consciously or otherwise, all of America is engaged.

Why should literature departments be a principal locus of the university's attempt to absorb the problem? (History is another such locus, yet that discipline, defined by configurational thinking rather than subject matter or conceptual principles, can absorb value conflict readily.) Literature departments have remained, despite the efforts of aesthetic purists, guardians of cultural values *par excellence* in the age of analysis. The European humanism of M. H. Abrams and the humanity of José David Saldívar's Chicano pop culture are of the same stuff: values sustained by deep affect. The methods of literary analysis to vindicate this kinship have yet to be found across the barriers of social division.

Of all the humanistic disciplines, philosophy had, in its analytic incarnation, most systematically distanced itself from the problems of culture. A preoccupation with epistemological and conceptual problems had led it to abandon the synoptic position it still maintained, based on Dewey's pragmatism, for a place with science at the "hard" end of the spectrum of disciplines. Analytic philosophy had basically disarmed itself to respond to the culture challenges of the 1960s. It could, however, still draw on its Lockean liberal heritage to reactivate its concern for ethics and politics. Opening new relations with the social sciences, analytic philosophers addressed again marginalized areas of value germane to the new claims for political participation, equality, and social justice. John Rawls's pathbreaking *A Theory of Justice* appeared in 1971,[5] the same year that Marshall Cohen and his colleagues founded

Philosophy and Public Affairs, a significant vehicle for expanding philosophy's public mission. Analytic philosophy had come out of the epistemological closet to develop its liberal political identity. This brought it closer to the social sciences and to professional schools such as law, medicine, and management, where professional ethics have become a concern.

Hilary Putnam has reminded us, however—not without a hint of malaise—that the distance of analytic philosophy from the concerns of humanities departments has not been closed: "The self-image of analytic philosophy is scientific rather than humanistic. If one aspires to be a science...then being different from the humanities will seem a positive virtue." That is why continental philosophers, with their direct concerns for problems of culture, history, art, and affective values, are largely taught outside philosophy departments. They often play a major role in courses in the humanities, history, and social theory and cultural studies. Only rarely does analytic philosophy enter those precincts. Political science, however, is a notable exception.

The polarization of the human sciences today follows, however roughly, the line of division between Anglo-Saxon and continental philosophic cultures. Quite aside from the problems arising from the incorporation of new social groups and non-Western cultures, the legacy of the 1950s was to separate the Anglo-Saxon empirical-scientific strand in American intellectual culture from the continental, value-oriented, and existential strands that were also strong in it. The marginalization of historical and descriptive approaches in economics, of philosophic theory in political science, of historical and psychological interpretation in the New Criticism—all these were cognates of the extrusion of non-Lockean values and existential problems within analytic philosophy. Most of the academic culture in the disciplines we have considered, along with the liberalism in which it was embedded, fell back in the 1950s on its Anglo-Saxon heritage and built, almost unwittingly, a kind of Atlantic wall against continental thought.

In 1955, Morton White, a pioneer in bringing English ordinary-language philosophy to America, wrote a book entitled *Toward Reunion in Philosophy.*[6] It was an attempt to unite some aspects of Dewey's capacious pragmatism, in which White had been educated, with the intellectual achievements of the analytic school that he had joined and whose agenda he wished to enrich. His book sought to build a bridge from the synoptic American philosophical culture of the 1930s to the rigorous scientistic culture of the 1950s. In the same year, White published a second book, an anthology he entitled *The Age of Analysis*.[7] Its purpose was to contrapose contemporary Anglo-Saxon and continental philosophy. In his commentary White makes clear his partisanship for the Anglo-Saxons over the continentals—Sartre, Heidegger, and others. He made no plea for a "reunion in philosophy" across this deeper gulf. But by giving the continentals a voice in America, he presciently proclaimed the problem that now occupies many of us and that a few philosophers such as Richard Rorty address: the need to recognize the value of the other in the contrasting philosophical perspectives that have exacerbated the difficulties of the academy in dealing with the problems of our culturally and socially divided society. For the academy to address the problems of difference, both social and intellectual, that have entered its body, it will have to find some equivalent for the more capacious, less rigoristic disciplinary culture with which this account began.

ENDNOTES

[1]David Easton, "Political Science in the United States," in David Easton and Corinne S. Schelling, *Divided Knowledge: Across Disciplines, Across Cultures* (Newbury Park, Calif.: Sage Publications in cooperation with the American Academy of Arts and Sciences, 1991), 40–41.

[2]Daniel Bell, *The Social Sciences Since the Second World War* (New Brunswick, N.J.: Transaction Books, 1982).

[3]For the reemergence in force of the distinction between scientific and philosophic political theory under the impact of the crises of the 1960s, see the contrasting statements of David Easton, "The New Revolution in Political Science," and Sheldon Wolin, "Political Theory as a Vocation," *The American Political Science Review* LXIII (4) (December 1969): 1051–1061; 1062–1082.

[4]Frederick Crews, *The Pooh Perplex* (New York: Dutton, 1963).

[5]John Rawls, *A Theory of Justice* (Cambridge, Mass.: Belknap Press of Harvard University Press, 1971).

[6]Morton White, *Toward Reunion in Philosophy* (Cambridge, Mass.: Harvard University Press, 1955).

[7]Morton White, *The Age of Analysis* (Boston, Mass.: Houghton Mifflin, 1955).

Ira Katznelson

From the Street to the Lecture Hall: The 1960s

WHERE HAVE THE SIXTIES GONE? With scant exception, the erudite histories in this issue have rather little to say about this period of upheaval. Abrams, Gallagher, and Saldívar pivot their considerations of English and literary criticism on the divide between the New Criticism of the 1940s and 1950s, which transcended historical philology and linguistics, and the various poststructural, postcolonial, postmodern, and New Historicist approaches deployed in the past two decades. Solow, Kreps, and Barber describe a self-confident economics profession that modernized to become an effective technical discipline in the 1940s. It subsequently developed as a continuous, scientific, mathematicized, model-building enterprise aiming at pithy simplification and empirical validation. Barber does take note of the radical student culture, but less for its effect on economics than for a temporary drop-off in student interest. Putnam's engaging personal history maps analytic philosophy in the Oxbridge-Harvard axis without any particular reference to the sixties, an ironic omission in light of his own close identification with Harvard's student movements (though there are hints about the impact of the period's developments in the essay's discussions of his own rethinking about language, the growing influence of Wittgenstein, and the reemergence of political philosophy). Writing about my own subject, Lindblom and Smith rightly identify the 1940s and 1950s as formative de-

Ira Katznelson is Ruggles Professor of Political Science and History at Columbia University.

cades for modern political science, and they persuasively read the discipline's history as a tension-ridden scientific search for liberal democratic values and institutions. Alone amongst our authors, Smith (though very briefly) assesses the intellectual consequences of the disorderly convulsions of the sixties, if only to treat these as minor, believing that political science's "debunking phase" in the 1960s and early 1970s failed to produce effective alternatives to mainstream behaviorism.[1]

Competing with this collective tale of limited significance, a more popular vision of the lineage of these academic disciplines makes the sixties generation, now putatively ascendant, responsible for much-disliked scholarly trends. In this version, current culture wars derive from the 1960s and from the manner in which developments three decades ago reshaped the academy's ideas, organization, and culture. This is a sorrowful story about the loss of standards and moorings; a tale of growing unseriousness; an elegy for earnest, thoughtful inquiry. Indeed, one reason, if certainly not the main one, many scholars tend to downplay the meaningfulness of the sixties is their defensiveness in the face of this mostly tendentious assault.[2]

As someone whose undergraduate and graduate education took place in the 1960s (thus perhaps with both a vested interest in the significance of the moment and in a sympathetic account of its critical impulses), I find both stories not so much wrong as deeply distorted. To be sure, they possess the ring of plausibility. On the one side, the direct intellectual harvest of the sixties proved modest. With the nontrivial exceptions of Marxist and Marxisant scholarship at the level of theory and of attention to such previously neglected topics as racial inequality, cities, and social movements, the scholarly accomplishments of the period's rebels proved more important for opening up the possibilities the essayists in this volume have underscored than for their immediate impact on their disciplines. On the other side, current critics of the academy from the Right correctly understand the sixties as a volatile "moment of madness" when ordinary rules, civilities, limits, and expectations were suspended, with important effects inside the academy.[3] The politics of the street burst the bounds of the lecture hall. However inchoate and unfocused, there was indeed a powerful revolt against the silences, limits of method, smug confidence, and regime-enhancing functions of postwar scholarship in the humanities and the social sciences. Nevertheless, in spite of these grounds of verisimilitude, the main competing readings of the sixties miss two key points.

First, these accounts either significantly understate or exaggerate the challenges to the various scholarly disciplines during the period when the civil rights and student (soon antiwar) movements electrified America's campuses. In these hothouse environments, graduate students and younger faculty drawn primarily from the humanities and the social sciences achieved significant scholarly work produced in exasperation at the indifference of their teachers to the inequalities and tumult in the society, in anger at the entanglement of the disciplines and the universities as institutions with power and privilege, in revolt against particular standards of objectivity that relied too heavily on models inappropriately drawn from the natural and biological sciences, and in the quest of moving class, race, gender, the national security state, and other neglected subjects from the margins to the center of systematic inquiry.

Notwithstanding the collapse in comity, diversity of temperaments, and disputes about the assumptions and unity of the disciplines, the vast majority of these critical scholars never broke with their disciplines. Instead, they located their contributions in a wider flow of scholarly give and take within conjoint canons of evidence and demonstration. What happened inside the disciplines—as distinct from challenges within the larger university, and especially student, culture—was rebellious but not seditious. The disciplinary insurgencies did matter, but not in the nihilist mode the strongest retrospective faultfinders allege to have existed. The vast majority of scholars in the sixties whose worldviews and scholarly commitments were nourished by the rebellious politics of the street never departed from the academic cultures that authorized their work and grounded it even as they contested the content and character of these traditions. By and large, they shared in the wider "liberal commitment to intellectual freedom. . .a commitment to a process, not to a specific set of beliefs."[4] Further, this critical rationality did not deploy a simple or singular "opposition," but a diffuse community of sensibility whose members shared a tone and an orienting perspective but not an epistemological perspective either radically different from the targets of their criticism or sufficiently powerful to traverse boundaries dividing the disciplines. Intellectual plurality expanded but as a pluralism nourished by interconnected disagreement. As a result, insurgent political scientists continued to share more with other political scientists than with insurgent scholars of English, economics, or philosophy; each of the fields continued to enclose a self-referential intellectual conversation. Certainly, the battleground of the sixties did not produce the most radical scholarly revision of all, the kinds of syntheses that would have rendered separate disciplines obsolete. Our distinctive genealogies remained segregated.

Second, the two contrasting estimations fail to specify mechanisms to account either for the lack of or the overweening importance of scholarly developments in the 1960s. To be persuasive, such accounts require at least rudimentary theory and a sociology of knowledge encompassing such matters as the periodization of change, institutional incentives and disincentives, generational cohorts, disciplines as practices and as epistemic speech communities, and relative weights assigned to the practice and content of scholarly work as opposed to the surrounding environment. Though I do not develop anything like a full-blown approach to studies of social knowledge with these elements (I take on the more modest task of a course-correction), my review of the sixties is not theoretically innocent.

I draw its most important orienting premise from the work of Donald Winch. He argues that ideas, like those we are considering in this issue, are best considered neither as the products of a holistic *zeitgeist* nor as merely facilitating instruments for fundamental interests that exist prior to and outside their articulation. Ideas do not have to be treated as the derived products of nonautonomous processes or as strong, causal independent variables. Rather, in societies like our own that "regularly require reasons to be given or assigned for public actions affecting the lives of others" and that possess specialized institutions preeminently located in university settings, which provide forums and procedures for examining the cogency of ideas and reasons, the significance of the creation and deployment of social knowledge requires no particular justification. After all, such ideas furnish the only means we have to make action meaningful and legitimate. Social knowledge, from this perspective, is "no more (or less) than an extension of the rules of everyday conduct."[5]

This perspective contrasts with the view that the social and human sciences are products of social and institutional changes that instrumentally require particular kinds of ideas, and also with the position that ideas located in free-standing discourses develop along well-defined disciplinary paths via the rules of inquiry and dialogue. Instead, it looks simultaneously at how the institutionalization of social knowledge in university disciplines as loci of intellectual authority bridges a two-way flow between the discursive constitution of politics and society by scholarly products and the ways the organization, subject matter, and methodologies of the academic disciplines are shaped by factors of state, economy, and civil society located outside the universities.[6] It is important not to choose *a priori* between ideational, material, or institutional causes. What matters is the distinctive qualities of their constellation at given historical moments.

I focus mainly on the universities and their professionalized disciplines as hinges linking large-scale changes in American society—including, in the 1960s, racial rebellion and democratization, far-reaching technological advances, and shifts in sexuality and gender—to specific sets of ideas and scholarly currents. In the quarter-century before the 1960s, America's research universities had grown dramatically but had not yet democratized.[7] They were flush with cash, confidence, and privilege. On the side of the join connecting them to the wider society, the social movements and radical sensibilities of the sixties were not located outside the universities as simply contextual, exogenous causes. The democratization of university admissions, governance, and effects were central goals for these movements; and the university itself, alongside church institutions, proved the movements' most important organizational assets.

We can see this "inside the academy" quality even at the decade's outset. The Greensboro, North Carolina, sit-ins begun in February 1960 and the Port Huron, Michigan, gathering sixteen months later to adopt a platform for a new organization, Students for a Democratic Society (SDS), did more than galvanize vast and effective national social movements. By their actions, rhetoric, and strategy, they affirmed modern social knowledge and the intellectual class as constitutive components of social change, and they identified the university as an intellectual and institutional site of great significance. Greensboro was a college town, the home of North Carolina A & T, a historically black college. The four freshmen who had initiated the protests were motivated, we know, by their studies of ethics and of Gandhi and Indian nationalism (just the themes and texts that inspired Martin Luther King, Jr., a minister in possession of a Ph.D.). Within ten weeks of their request for service at a Woolworth's counter, more than fifty thousand students had participated in the sit-in movement. The fifty-nine people who came to Port Huron, energized by the emergent civil rights movement, also sought to build an intellectually-grounded capacity to mobilize their fellow students.

When Tom Hayden, then a twenty-two-year-old student at the University of Michigan, first drafted the platform statement for SDS, he began by lamenting the character of research in the university as too value free, too specialized, too uncommitted. Instead, he searched for an alternative stance in the ideas of two scholars who had become public intellectuals: C. Wright Mills (who died in March 1962, as Hayden was composing the document), the Columbia University sociologist who had written *The Power Elite* (1954) and *The Sociological Imagination* (1958) and who had penned a widely-read "Letter to the New Left" in 1960, identifying the intelligentsia as the most likely source of social change;[8] and Iris Murdoch, the Oxford University philosopher who had become a major novelist. Hayden's preliminary draft of the Port Huron Statement twinned Mills's language about the duties of scholars and intellectuals with Murdoch's call for a new approach to academic inquiry to fill the space between "our technical concepts [that] are highly esoteric and our moral concepts [that] are excessively simple." Cautioning that "there is nothing in between," she had asserted that "we need, and the Left should provide, some refuge from the cold, open field of Benthamite empiricism, a framework, a house of theory." Hayden picked up this imagery, coming to think of the SDS manifesto as an initial attempt to build this house. He worked from a bibliography of books on democracy written by social philosophers and social scientists he had read mainly in his classes at Michigan, including Robert Michels's *Political Parties,* John Dewey's *Democracy and*

Education, Reinhold Niebuhr's *Moral Man and Immoral Society,* Sheldon Wolin's *Politics and Vision,* William Kornhauser's *The Politics of Mass Society,* and Robert Dahl's *A Preface to Democratic Theory.*[9] As the decade progressed, the imbrication of the period's social movements with scholarly currents and university settings deepened. Most civil rights, black power, and antiwar movement leaders either had experienced or were situated in America's campuses or felt compelled to visit and mobilize university constituencies. Hayden's intellectuality proved a harbinger of a quest for scholarly as well as political legitimacy. A half-decade later, Carmichael and Hamilton's *Black Power* grounded its insurgent manifesto in references to mainstream scholarship.[10] Rebellion did not preclude scholarly engagement or regard for accepted canons of inquiry.

On the other side of the hinge, specific disciplines were connected to this constellation of the university and the society in diverse ways in part because the disciplines had been targeting different substantive objects of social knowledge, thus setting separate tables for the bounded scholarly rebellions of the 1960s. The orientation of economics to public life, for example, had shifted considerably during the forties. In its ambition to create an economic science based on the marginalist revolution after Marshall, economics had grown quite aloof from day-to-day public policy. The combination of New Deal and World War II mobilization changed all that.[11] After the war, economic knowledge was increasingly oriented to the provision of policy advice and prognostication that could be deployed by public officials. "Most economists hope that their work will have an impact on public policy," a recent review of the profession notes, presenting us with the paradox that the most enclosed of our disciplines with regard to inquiry is the most ambitious with regard to public affairs.[12] By surprising contrast, with important exceptions mainly in the subfield of international relations, the large majority of political science researchers in the 1940s and 1950s turned away from a public role to focus instead on the patterning of the links between civil society and the national state via the mechanisms of political parties, interest groups, and public opinion. Insurgent political scientists in the midst of the sixties primarily geared their work not toward policy influence but toward an incorporation of inequality and social movements into the mainstream story of interest representation. Radical economists, however, sought to provide alternative public policy prescriptions.

English and philosophy had had rather different pre-sixties histories. Their centers of gravity in the New Criticism and language philosophy had distanced both from the public realm. Disciplinary rebels in these fields sought to secure a reconnection, but with a difference. Much like political science, English oriented itself to civil society and to the mass movements underway. Philosophy, much like economics, sought to clarify choices amongst repertoires of public policy. These attempts, of course, had mixed and uneven success. English was transformed the most, if not all at once. Political science also evolved a good deal, extending the scope of its methods and subjects. Economics and philosophy changed less. The analytic, scientific cores of these disciplines remained largely intact, but even here, we will see, insurgency produced change.

If unevenly, the scholarship of the sixties inscribed each of our disciplines. The varieties of disappointment expressed by the period's skeptical and radical scholars and the types of broadly pragmatist knowledge they created have marked their fields in three main ways. By confronting a more senior generation, they forced revisions to existing approaches, deepening their reach and depth. By exploring new themes and new ways of working, they directly altered the character of their fields. By way of these extensions, they created intellectual space for subsequent insurgencies.

As my primary example, consider political science. From its founding as a constitutive part of Progressive thought at the turn of the century, its foci, as Lindblom and Smith underscore, have been both moral and empirical. Its various constitutional, institutional, behavioral, and theoretical aspects, even its internal organization and estrangements, have been geared to secure normative commitments. These may be broadly identified as liberal, in the doctrinal and institutional senses of the term. More particularly, political scientists have worked principally at the point of intersection of the modern state and civil society at a time of growing state capacity to make war, organize economies, and promote social welfare. The development of political science in the past century also has paralleled the long moment when liberalism thickened and became both more legitimate (swallowing some of its former conservative and socialist competitors) and more vulnerable to a wide array of tyrannies and mass movements, almost all of which have been defended as constituting better versions of democracy than liberalism can accommodate.[13]

Transactions linking citizens and the state have provided the main objects of analysis for political scientists. Their concern with law, representation, voting, public opinion, interest groups, and cognate subjects in studies of the United States; with classifications of other regimes by reference to their degree of distance from models of liberal democracy; with liberal theory; and with understanding of how international orders led first by liberal Britain and then by liberal America could secure desired ends add up to a remarkably coherent program of research and writing. Even critics of the discipline's mainstream, including the critics of the 1960s, have accepted these foci and premises. They have directed their ire at the complacence, insufficiency of inclusiveness, implicit concessions to hierarchies of class, race, gender, and power, and institutional limits to political participation both in American society and in their scholarly discipline without breaking with the central axis of political science: to understand and promote a broadly liberal political order against all comers.[14]

Because political science is so deeply imbricated with political practice, its history as an organized body of social knowledge has been tied more than any other social science to situational conditions. Its most important shifts and innovations have come at moments when anxiety about the fate of liberalism has been most pronounced: the period spanning the close of World War II to the Korean War, the heyday of the totalitarian challenge; the 1960s, when insurgencies concerned with race and foreign policy challenged the postwar settlement; and today, when a concatenation of changes, variously characterized as postmodern, post-Cold War, postindustrial, postfeminist, and so on, make once seemingly fixed arrangements appear fluid and uncertain.

It is impossible to read the key texts of the 1940s without sensing their remarkable apprehension about the capacity of liberal regimes to successfully join democracy and capitalism, liberty and prosperity. Following a long period of crisis that centered on two world wars, an unprecedented global economic slump, the ascension of fascist and communist alternatives, and an insistent politicization of class relations, political scientists sought to fashion a multidimensional "realist" science to meet the urgent requirements of the time. Its overarching substantive goals included making liberalism more social (by incorporating groups, especially labor, within its embrace) and more international (by grappling with the twin challenges of totalitarianism and decolonization).

This program, concentrated primarily at a small number of research universities—Chicago, Columbia, Harvard, and Yale—was defined by such lead figures as David Truman, Carl Friedrich, V. O. Key, Harold Lasswell, David Easton, Hans Morgenthau, and Robert Dahl[15] as a self-conscious attempt to respond to current events by developing new kinds of empirical theory and methods that drew on, yet were distinctive from, the political science practiced in the discipline's first half-century. These colleagues thought the traditional focus on law, institutions, and the state archaic, and prewar empirical scholarship factitious and lacking in direction. At the same time, they constructed a legitimating genealogy, some of whose key figures were Arthur Bentley, Stuart Rice, E. E. Schattschneider, Pendleton Herring, and Charles Merriam, who were held in regard for focusing on how government *actually* worked to link organized citizens to the state. A double intent marked this effort: the construction of a realizable, sober liberalism (in the spirit of Schumpeter's "another theory of democracy")[16] that could serve as a rallying point in a disenchanted world and the systematic study of its operations. These two goals were joined together as an alternative to grandiose ideological temptations, especially those that co-opted Mussolini's label, "totalitarian."[17]

Located within a larger intellectual milieu that understood liberalism to be a background condition in a United States under siege by its enemies, this new and increasingly behavioral political science presented itself as beyond ideology. Alongside tandem disciplines, it pioneered new methods, including large-scale surveys and roll call analysis. As before, the field divided into four: international relations, American politics, comparative politics, and political theory. But each area was now marked by important shifts. International studies took their cues from Morgenthau's power-centered realism rather than Quincy Wright's more humanistic approach tinged with utopian elements. American studies shifted to focus on matters of process and representation, with an emphasis on interest groups (now valorized as a barrier to the atomization characteristic of mass societies vulnerable to totalitarianism) and public opinion (with its welcome mix of apathy and activism, ignorance and knowledge).[18] Comparative politics studied party systems and political institutions to understand both the possibilities for postwar democracy and threats to it; for the non-Western world it developed an explicitly practical and political set of area studies that aimed to remedy American ignorance at a time of assertive US international leadership. Political theory also took a new tack. Before World War II, and after, there had been a growing estrangement between political science and political theory, which some theorists sought to address by revamping theory into an adjunct of behavioral research, with both embedded in liberal assumptions.[19] Concurrently, nourished by the wartime experience that had brought many social scientists, including leading political scientists, into government service, public policy studies of a systematic kind at the junction of economics and political science achieved a new prominence. Post-New Deal liberalism (principally, but not exclusively, identified with the Democratic Party) discovered new applied tools capable of creating change without paying the price of potentially destabilizing disorder.[20]

During the 1950s, a self-congratulatory and consensual tone set in. America was the successful liberal leader. Totalitarianism had been checked. Prosperity and liberty proved capable of mutual constitution. Methodological advances could be combined with enlarged university resources. Policy specialists found a welcome in and out of government. Objectivist approaches to interests—especially Marxist ones—were vitiated by a realist focus on subjective interests and their pursuit within well-defined domestic institutions capable of canalizing protest and discontent. Politics came to be treated as a marketplace, one governed by rules and limits, and protected by military power and a diplomacy of containment.[21] An increasingly successful western Europe, now internally at peace, was appended to this political and intellectual community, forming a larger, confidently liberal, epistemic community.

The unanticipated racial revolt, student movement, and antiwar protests of the 1960s proved wrenching for American political science. The tacit rules of the game of the liberal polity were called into question both in public life and by a new generation of political scientists who noted that post-David Truman pluralism elided such issues as the nondemocratic qualities of interest groups, inequality between groups, and structural biases against the unorganized.[22] A burgeoning, vibrant literature on urban America called attention to the virtual nonexistence of concern with race and racial inequalities in prior treatments of American politics.[23] The experience of war in Indochina starkly divided the realist community of international relations scholars[24] and proved the occasion for a more fundamental critique of American foreign policy, focusing on dependency, imperialism, and underdevelopment.[25] Students of the Third World increasingly understood that pluralist self-regulation could not easily be generalized beyond American confines and sought to develop a new approach to political development appropriate to this understanding.[26] Professional meetings by the late 1960s came to resemble a war zone.

Yet underneath the rhetoric and dissension a remarkably creative process advancing the discipline's capacity to ask and answer hard questions had gained ground. Arguably the most important instance lay in the domain of group theory. The work of the 1950s, especially by Truman and Dahl, had been directed to provide scientific answers to questions concerning how the economic and social bases of politics are translated into influence via mechanisms of political representation; and how, in the face of the diversity of interests in American society, the political system remains quite stable. The group theorists sought to show that the heterogeneous interest group system is sufficiently permeable to entice orderly and legitimate political participation. Successful collective action to influence policy thus produces a reinforcing virtuous circle.

The critics writing in the 1960s argued that this analysis composed a mix of science and wishful thinking. Interest groups vary in their degrees of democracy and representativeness. Group demands do not only come from below; they are shaped, even manipulated, from above, by political elites. The system of representation is biased, singing, as Schattschneider put it, with an upper-class accent.[27] Some groups and interests, notably those associated with the racial divide, were excluded altogether. By eliding the notion of objective interests, interest group pluralism had substituted a vision of an open process for the reality of a relatively fixed, steep hierarchy and had substituted the illusion of multiple interests for the relatively few dimensions of stratification that really matter. Social structure was absent. Disruption and protest were viewed as abnormal and threatening. Social movements were hard to fathom and impossible to insert into the pluralist story, as were the ways political participation reshapes identities, worldviews, and interests.[28] Taken together, the critics argued, these traits made group theory a license for repression.

This multifaceted assault had a very considerable effect on studies of American politics. Writing inside the ambit of group theory in the mid-1960s, Grant McConnell showed how the exercise of power by private groups had both inward and outward qualities: groups have power over their own members and "over matters affecting the larger community." Both inward and outward power, he argued, are shaped by the narrow scale of constituent organization, introducing the bias of concentration into the interest system. Theodore Lowi, in turn, sought at the end of the decade to come to grips with the period's "crisis of public authority," which, he thought, had been generated by the unplanned, undisciplined qualities of interest group liberalism. When too many interests bloom, he argued, the public interest disappears.[29] The critics, in short, succeeded in stimulating significant revisions inside the dominant paradigm. McConnell's text quickly became a minor classic and, textbooks aside, Lowi's became the best-selling late-twentieth-century book in the discipline.

The effects of the sixties cohort, however, reached beyond modification by focusing attention on new subjects and theories. The contentious politics of the period stimulated broad currents of work on social movements, revolution, industrial conflict, and other forms of (and constraints on) collective action that, previously, had stood outside the ken of the discipline. Macroscopic analysis of epochal changes in class relations and political regimes and a new political economy of advanced capitalism extended the range of political science. Studies of symbols, the formation of political identities, and the configuration of resistance also made their appearance. Each of these initiatives was conditioned by a renewed interest in political and social theory, especially Marxian historical materialism and Weberian power-centered realism.[30]

These substantive and theoretical enlargements also had a longer-term effect. They authorized a process of appropriation and incorporation that has further stretched the scope of the field. From the late 1960s to the mid-1980s, there was a remarkable proliferation of new subgroups working on international political economy, American political development, and feminist theory, amongst others, and, primarily via the feminist impulse with roots in the women's movement that had developed momentum in the 1960s, the introduction of postpositivist currents into political studies. On a basis far more inclusive and challenging than that which prevailed before the 1960s, the older issues of the character and security of liberalism returned to the agenda with considerable presence and force. Still self-consciously focused yet more heterogeneous, political science may finally be maturing as a coherent intellectual discipline and as a critical political project.[31] None of this would have been possible without the charged challenges of the sixties.

Of course, like political science, the disciplinary histories of economics, philosophy, and literary studies have their own distinctive qualities. Nevertheless, my strong impression is that in each field scholarship forged in the crucible of the sixties had nontrivial effects in broadening inquiry and legitimating, or at least opening possibilities for, fresh ways of working. Under the banner of relevance, each of the four fields redeployed the junction term "experience" (connecting objective experiences of the world to subjective learning), which had been a centerpiece of late nineteenth- and early twentieth-century pragmatism but which had gone out of fashion in the quest for objective, realist, scientific inquiry. The difference, however, was that in literary criticism and philosophy this return of an experimental, problem-solving alignment soon took a semiotic turn, curling the pragmatist legacy away from material concerns, whereas in political science and economics it forced attention to unequal resources and information, and to the making (and manipulation) of preferences.[32] The main extant ways of working in these fields—behaviorism, New Criticism, language philosophy, neoclassical economics—appeared to their critics as mechanisms to keep the disciplines insulated from, and thus not germane to, political currents inside and outside the university. In each, these orientations were confronted with sharp attacks on assumptions and methods. Many of the mooted alternatives only took hold as minor revisions; others became important new sources of knowledge; some proved pathways to something else.

In English, for example, as Gallagher observes, the New Criticism first was powerfully questioned during the 1960s by Stanley Fish's reader-response criticism grounded in pragmatism and linguistic theory, E. D. Hirsch's intentionalist hermeneutics, and Paul de Man's phenomenological hermeneutics. These efforts called into question the distinctive coherence of literary objects and discredited the unexamined positivism of the New Critics. These assaults from the inside, as it were, effectively began to delegitimate the enclosed qualities of the enterprise both by opening the way to later forms of deconstruction and interpretation and by making room for the introduction of society and politics into the house of theory. In the latter regard, a central inspiring figure was England's Raymond Williams, whose Gramscian Marxism hinged between Leavis and later trends in cultural studies. The publication of *Culture and Society* (1958) and *The Long Revolution* (1961) effectively marked the start of a more political, sociological, and historical genre of criticism.[33]

Younger scholars in philosophy in the sixties also were succored by cognate trends. In addition to Gramscian and other varieties of humanistic Marxism, their rebellion against what they saw as the arid and enclosed qualities of Anglo-American language philosophy was nourished by other variants of continental philosophy represented in the work of Nietzsche, Heidegger, Sartre, Habermas, Foucault, and Agnes Heller, and they cultivated the history of philosophy. Inside the dominant analytical camp, which remained hegemonic throughout, there was a growing interest in the methods and achievements of the social sciences and renewed interest in social and political prescription, which together gave rise to a revival in political philosophy. In their third edited series of essays on "philosophy, politics, and society" in 1967, Peter Laslett and W. G. Runciman (both then at Cambridge University) contrasted their claim that "Anglo-American political and social theory has indeed been revived" with the declaration they had issued in the first series, in 1956, to the effect that "for the moment, anyway, political philosophy is dead."[34]

By 1971, with the publication of Rawls's *A Theory of Justice* and the launching in Princeton of a new journal entitled *Philosophy & Public Affairs*, this reviviscence had altered the center of gravity within analytical philosophy toward politics and ethics, even to the analysis of public policy.[35] In tandem, the cognate turn toward other continental traditions connected visions of the self to moral life, fashioned new phenomenologies of images and identities, and created a multifaceted exploration of links between these subjects in the work of such scholars as Charles Taylor, Richard Wollheim, and Alasdair MacIntyre.[36]

Finally, there is economics, the most enclosed and scientific of our four disciplines. Even here, the effects of the sixties were not negligible. Some of the most talented members of this graduate student generation, including David Gordon, Samuel Bowles, and Herbert Gintis, shaped a Marxisant radical economics that spawned journals and graduate programs (especially at the New School for Social Research and at the University of Massachusetts, Amherst) and sought to connect the science directly to movements for change. In tandem with such historians of economics as Robert Heilbroner, they argued that the professional mainstream had paid too high a price in lost economic sweep and vision, as well as normative purpose, for gains in methodology. By leaving the distribution of wealth and income unattended, by taking preferences as givens, by considering the variables of the capitalist system rather than its parameters, and by treating the economy in timeless terms, the radical economists forced renewed attention within the discipline to the kinds of issues with which traditional classical political economy had wrestled.[37] Although mutual enlightenment never quite happened and this movement has remained more marginal to the neoclassical core than comparable insurgencies even in philosophy, it has had a double-barreled effect: it provided something of a quasi-loyal opposition inside the profession, and, by questioning the mainstream's anti-institutionalist, nonhistorical, and stylized deductive ways of working as well as its assumptions about human motivation, preferences, and conduct, it opened pathways for other forms of challenge. The most important has been the genre of behavioral economics, which has sought to open the study of economics to insights from adjacent social sciences, especially cognitive psychology and economic sociology. Focusing on rationality, networks, and institutional pressures, this body of scholarship has treated both human agents and situations as more complex and uncertain than the economic mainstream.[38] As a result, as A. W. Coats has argued, "the literature of economic methodology has become more tolerant, more eclectic, more pluralist, less self-confident."[39]

This, in fact, could serve as a larger judgment of the effect of the sixties. The decade's new house of theory left each of our disciplines and the broader academic culture in which they were embedded more tolerant (difficult as this may be to believe in the current climate), more eclectic, more pluralist, and, even in philosophy and economics, at least a tad less self-confident. Three decades on, a glint of satisfaction is not out of order.

ENDNOTES

[1]That development, he argues, awaited the rational-choice revolution based on the theoretical core of economics, which has helped recreate exactly the divide between science and democratic normativity that the critics of the 1960s had sought to overcome.

[2]The relevant literature is vast. For example, see Hilton Kramer and Roger Kimball, eds., *Against the Grain: The New Criterion on Art and Intellect at the End of the Twentieth Century* (Chicago, Ill.: I. R. Dee, 1995); Irving Kristol, *Neoconservatism: The Autobiography of an Idea* (New York: Free Press, 1995); Lynne V. Cheney, *Telling the Truth: Why Our Culture, Our Country, and Our Schools Have Stopped Making Sense and What We Can Do About It* (New York: Simon and Schuster, 1995); Robert Hughes, *Culture of Complaint: The Fraying of America* (New York: Oxford University Press, 1993); and Richard Bernstein, *Dictatorship of Virtue: Multiculturalism and the Battle for America's Future* (New York: Alfred A. Knopf, 1994).

[3]Aristide Zolberg, "Moments of Madness," *Politics and Society* 2 (Winter 1972). For a sense of this ferment and volatility, see Sohnya Sayres, Anders Stephanson, Stanley Aronowitz, and Frederic Jameson, eds., *The 60's Without Apology* (Minneapolis, Minn.: University of Minnesota Press, 1984).

[4]Barrington Moore, Jr., "On Rational Inquiry in Universities Today," *New York Review of Books*, 23 April 1970, p. 30. Moore upbraided the student movement for taking the university too seriously as an instrument of change: "American radical students," he wrote, "show signs of learning that the attempt to change society through the university is like trying to pry up a stump with a bamboo crowbar." Ibid., 33.

[5]Donald Winch, "Economic Knowledge and Government in Britain: Some Historical and Comparative Reflections," in Mary O. Furner and Barry Supple, eds.,

348   *Ira Katznelson*

The State and Economic Knowledge: The American and British Experiences (Cambridge: Cambridge University Press, 1990).

[6]For work along these lines, see Bjorn Wittrock and Peter Wagner, "Social Science and the Building of the Early Welfare State: Toward a Comparison of Statist and Non-Statist Western Societies," in Dietrich Rueschemeyer and Theda Skocpol, eds., *States, Social Knowledge, and the Origins of Modern Social Policies* (Princeton, N.J.: Princeton University Press, 1996).

[7]The best surveys of these developments are Robert L. Geiger, *To Advance Knowledge: The Growth of American Research Universities, 1900–1940* (New York: Oxford University Press, 1986); and Robert L. Geiger, *Research and Relevant Knowledge: American Research Universities Since World War II* (New York: Oxford University Press, 1993). Also see, for a treatment of the issues of growth and democratization, Colin B. Burke, "The Expansion of American Higher Education," in Konrad H. Jarausch, ed., *The Transformation of Higher Learning, 1860–1930: Expansion, Diversification, Social Opening, and Professionalization in England, Germany, Russia, and the United States* (Chicago, Ill.: University of Chicago Press, 1983).

[8]C. Wright Mills, *The Power Elite* (New York: Oxford University Press, 1954); C. Wright Mills, *The Sociological Imagination* (New York: Oxford University Press, 1958).

[9]For a discussion, the Murdoch citation, and the bibliography, see James Miller, *Democracy is in the Streets: From Port Huron to the Siege of Chicago* (New York: Simon and Schuster, 1987), 92–94. See also Elinor Langer, "Notes for Next Time: A Memoir of the 1960's," *Working Papers* (Fall 1973); Paul Buhle, "The Eclipse of the New Left: Some Notes," *Radical America* 6 (July-August 1972); Kirkpatrick Sale, *SDS* (New York: Random House, 1973); and Richard Flacks et al., "Port Huron: Agenda for a Generation," *Socialist Review* 17 (May-August 1987). An interesting attempt to link the movements of the sixties to the character of public policy-making, with implications for our understanding of ties between the movements and the universities, is Hugh Heclo, "The Sixties' False Dawn: Awakenings, Movements, and Postmodern Policy-Making," *Journal of Policy History* 8 (1) (1996).

[10]Stokely Carmichael and Charles V. Hamilton, *Black Power: The Politics of Liberation in America* (New York: Alfred A. Knopf, 1967).

[11]As a baseline discussion of this shift, see Wesley C. Mitchell, "Empirical Research and the Development of Economic Science," in Arthur A. Burns, ed., *Economic Research and the Development of Economic Science and Public Policy* (New York: National Bureau of Economic Research, 1946).

[12]Robert Nelson, "The Economics Profession and the Making of Public Policy," *Journal of Economic Literature* 25 (March 1987). Also see Alice Rivlin, "Economics and the Political Process," *American Economics Review* 77 (March 1987).

[13]For relevant suggestive discussions, see Samuel P. Huntington, "One Soul at a Time: Political Science and Political Reform," *American Political Science Review* 83 (March 1988); John G. Gunnell, "American Political Science, Liberalism, and the Invention of Political Theory," *American Political Science Review*

83 (March 1988); and Theodore J. Lowi, "The State in Political Science: How We Became What We Study," *American Political Science Review* 86 (March 1992). For a discussion of the relationship of professional knowledge producers and modern liberalism in the late nineteenth and twentieth centuries, see Ira Katznelson, "Knowledge about What? Policy Intellectuals and the New Liberalism," in Rueschemeyer and Skocpol, eds., *States, Social Knowledge, and the Origins of Modern Social Policies.*

[14]This observation should not be taken to imply a unitary political science. The discipline is committed to diverse epistemologies that nestle uneasily in the space between the humanities and the sciences, and it is nourished by a wide array of imports from other fields. Nonetheless, the subject matter, goals, and value orientations of political science have been remarkably coherent in spite of this variety.

[15]Key works include David Truman, *The Governmental Process* (New York: Knopf, 1951); David Easton, *The Political System* (New York: Knopf, 1953); V. O. Key, Jr., *Politics, Parties, and Pressure Groups* (New York: Thomas Crowell, 1947); Harold Lasswell, "The Policy Orientation," in Daniel Lerner and Harold Lasswell, eds., *The Policy Sciences: Recent Developments in Scope and Method* (Stanford, Calif.: Stanford University Press, 1951); and Hans J. Morgenthau, *Politics Among Nations* (New York: Knopf, 1948).

[16]Joseph A. Schumpeter, *Capitalism, Socialism and Democracy* (New York: Harper and Row, 1942), chap. 12.

[17]Hannah Arendt, *The Origins of Totalitarianism* (London: Allen and Unwin, 1951); and Carl J. Friedrich and Zbigniew K. Brzezinski, *Totalitarian Dictatorship and Autocracy* (Cambridge, Mass.: Harvard University Press, 1956). A useful discussion of the historical lineage is provided by Abbott Gleason, *Totalitarianism: The Inner History of the Cold War* (New York: Oxford University Press, 1995).

[18]Earl Latham, "The Group Basis of Politics: Notes for a Theory," *American Political Science Review* 48 (June 1952); and V. O. Key, Jr., *Public Opinion and American Democracy* (New York: Knopf, 1961).

[19]Robert A. Dahl, *A Preface to Democratic Theory* (Chicago, Ill.: University of Chicago Press, 1956); and David Easton, *The Political System: An Inquiry into the State of Political Science* (New York: Knopf, 1963).

[20]Robert A. Dahl and Charles E. Lindblom, *Politics, Economics, and Welfare* (New York: Harper and Brothers, 1953).

[21]This version of political science as well as its tensions is well captured in Albert Somit and Joseph Tanenhaus, *American Political Science: A Profile of a Discipline* (Chicago, Ill.: Atherton, 1964), which defined a divide between the "haves," who adopted this program, and the nonbehavioral "have-nots," who were composed of a heterogeneous group of political theorists, including followers of Leo Strauss, scholars dedicated to older themes of public administration and constitutionalism, and still others who worked in a qualitative, case study mode, often drawing on history rather than on the newer behavioral trends in sociology or post-Keynesian economics. Within Europe, the emblematic figure was Raymond Aron, a liberal committed to power politics, anti-communism, and democratic institutions.

[22]Such critical works included Peter Bachrach and Morton Baratz, "Two Faces of Power," *American Political Science Review* 56 (December 1962); Henry Kariel, *The Decline of Pluralism* (Stanford, Calif.: Stanford University Press, 1961); and Jack L. Walker, "The Elitist Theory of Democracy," *American Political Science Review* 60 (June 1966).

[23]See Michael Lipsky, *Protest in City Politics* (Chicago, Ill.: Rand McNally, 1960); James Q. Wilson, *Negro Politics* (Glencoe, Ill.: Free Press, 1960); Edward Banfield and James Q. Wilson, *City Politics* (Cambridge, Mass.: Harvard University Press, 1963); Robert Crain, *The Politics of Desegregation* (Chicago, Ill.: Aldine, 1968); Gary Orfield, *The Reconstruction of Southern Education* (New York: Wiley, 1969); Ira Katznelson, *Black Men, White Cities* (New York: Oxford University Press, 1973); and J. David Greenstone and Paul E. Peterson, *Race and Authority in Urban Politics: Community Participation and the War on Poverty* (New York: Russell Sage, 1973).

[24]Some, as in the case of Hans Morgenthau, defected from the Cold War consensus; others looked to develop more effective counter-insurgency strategies. For the latter, see Nathan Leites and Charles Wolf, Jr., *Rebellion and Authority* (Santa Monica, Calif.: Rand Corporation, 1966).

[25]For an overview, see J. Samuel Valenzuela and Arturo Valenzuela, "Modernization and Dependency: Alternative Perspectives in the Study of Latin American Development," *Comparative Politics* 10 (July 1978).

[26]S. N. Eisenstadt, "Breakdowns of Modernization," *Economic Development and Social Change* 12 (July 1964); and Samuel P. Huntington, *Political Order in Changing Societies* (New Haven, Conn.: Yale University Press, 1968).

[27]"The flaw in the pluralist heaven," he wrote, "is that the heavenly chorus sings with a strong upper-class accent. Probably about 90 per cent of the people cannot get into the pressure system." E. E. Schattschneider, *The Semi-Sovereign People: A Realist's View of Democracy in America* (New York: Holt Rinehart, 1960), 35.

[28]For discussions, see J. David Greenstone, "Group Theories," in Fred I. Greenstein and Nelson W. Polsby, eds., *Handbook of Political Science* (Reading, Mass.: Addison-Wesley, 1975); and Mark Kesselman, "The Conflictual Evolution of American Political Science: From Apologetic Pluralism to Trilateralism and Marxism," in J. David Greenstone, ed., *Public Values and Private Power in American Politics* (Chicago, Ill.: University of Chicago Press, 1982).

[29]Grant McConnell, *Private Power and American Democracy* (New York: Knopf, 1966), 6; Theodore J. Lowi, *The End of Liberalism: Ideology, Policy, and the Crisis of Public Authority* (New York: Norton, 1969).

[30]For examples, see Isaac Balbus, *The Dialectics of Legal Repression: Black Rebels Before the American Criminal Courts* (New York: Russell Sage Foundation, 1973); Murray Edelman, *The Symbolic Uses of Politics* (Urbana, Ill.: University of Illinois Press, 1964); Murray Edelman, *Politics as Symbolic Action* (Chicago, Ill.: Markland, 1971); William Gamson, *Power and Discontent* (Homewood, Ill.: Dorsey, 1968); Bob Jessop, *Social Order: Reform and Revolution* (London: Macmillan, 1972); J. P. Nettl, "The State as a Conceptual Variable," *World Politics* 20 (July 1968); Mancur Olson, Jr., *The Logic of Collective Action*

(Cambridge, Mass.: Harvard University Press, 1965); Andrew Shonfield, *Modern Capitalism* (New York: Oxford University Press, 1991); and Frances Fox Piven and Richard A. Cloward, *Regulating the Poor: The Functions of Public Welfare* (New York: Pantheon Books, 1971).

[31]For a sense of these possibilities, see the work of Rogers Smith and Robert Keohane. For Smith: "The American Creed and American Identity: The Limits of Liberal Citizenship in the United States," *Western Political Quarterly* 41 (2) (1988); "One United People: Second Class Female Citizenship and the American Quest for Community," *Yale Journal of Law and the Humanities* 1 (May 1989); and "If Politics Matters: Implications for a New Institutionalism," *Studies in American Political Development* 6 (Spring 1992). For Keohane: "The World Political Economy and the Crisis of Embedded Liberalism," in John H. Goldthorpe, ed., *Order and Conflict in Contemporary Capitalism* (Oxford: Oxford University Press, 1984); "International Institutions: Two Approaches," *International Studies Quarterly* 32 (December 1988); "International Liberalism Reconsidered," in John Dunn, ed., *The Economic Limits to Modern Politics* (Cambridge: Cambridge University Press, 1990); and "International Relations Theory: Contributions of a Feminist Standpoint," *Millennium* 18 (Summer 1989). A useful overview of one key trend is provided by David Brian Robertson, "The Return to History and the New Institutionalism in American Political Science," *Social Science History* 17 (Spring 1993).

[32]An excellent treatment of the lineage of pragmatism can be found in James T. Kloppneberg, "Pragmatism: An Old Name for Some New Ways of Thinking?" *The Journal of American History* 83 (June 1996).

[33]Raymond Williams, *Culture and Society, 1780–1950* (London: Chatto and Windus, 1958); and Raymond Williams, *The Long Revolution* (London: Chatto and Windus, 1961).

[34]Peter Laslett and W. G. Runciman, eds., *Philosophy, Politics and Society* (Oxford: Basil Blackwell, 1967), 5, 1.

[35]Not just *Philosophy & Public Affairs*, edited by Marshall Cohen, but other journals in the field, notably including *Ethics* when it came under the editorship of Brian Barry in the 1970s, turned increasingly from regime to policy questions. For examples, see Marshall Cohen, Thomas Nagel, and Thomas Scanlon, eds., *The Rights and Wrongs of Abortion* (Princeton, N.J.: Princeton University Press, 1974); and Marshall Cohen, Thomas Nagel, and Thomas Scanlon, eds., *Equality and Preferential Treatment* (Princeton, N.J.: Princeton University Press, 1977).

[36]I am indebted here to the spirited discussion in Perry Anderson, "A Culture in Contraflow—II," *New Left Review* (182) (July/August 1990).

[37]For summaries of these lines of criticism, see Robert Heilbroner, "Radical Economics: A Review Essay," *American Political Science Review* 66 (September 1972); and Robert Heilbroner, "Analysis and Vision in the History of Modern Economic Thought," *Journal of Economic Literature* 28 (September 1990). A very useful overview of the character of the discipline is provided in Daniel M. Hausman, ed., *The Philosophy of Economics: An Anthology* (Cambridge: Cambridge University Press, 1984).

[38]Leading figures have included Daniel Kahneman, Amos Tversky, Jon Elster, Richard Thaler, Richard Nisbett, and Mark Granovetter, by no means all economists. See Daniel Kahneman, Paul Slovic, and Amos Tversky, eds., *Judgment Under Uncertainty: Heuristics and Biases* (Cambridge: Cambridge University Press, 1982); Leonard Green and John Kagel, *Advances in Behavioral Economics* (Norwood, N.J.: Ablex Publishers, 1987); Mark Granovetter, "Economic Institutions as Social Constructions: A Framework for Analysis," *Acta Sociologica* 35 (1) (1992); and James Allison, *Behavioral Economics* (New York: Praeger, 1983).

[39]A. W. Coats, "Explanations in History and Economics," *Social Research* 56 (Summer 1989).

David A. Hollinger

The Disciplines and the Identity Debates, 1970–1995

I N 1992 *CRITICAL INQUIRY* PUBLISHED a special issue on "Identities." In that same year another transdisciplinary journal, *October,* ran a special issue on "The Identity Question." The simultaneous appearance of these special issues is an emblem for two prominent features of American academic history of the last quarter-century. One is the emergence of a robust discourse about "theory" that focused increasingly on the problem of "identity." The second is the proliferation of transdisciplinary forums designed to facilitate and institutionalize this discourse across the lines separating the various social scientific and humanistic disciplines whose members were eager to talk "theory" and "identity." Social scientists and humanists managed to bring the theory wars and identity debates into their disciplinary forums, too, and they continued to perform work that was remote from these wars and debates. But anyone scrutinizing the social sciences and the humanities as a whole during the period from 1970 to 1995 will not get far without confronting these two, closely related developments.

Critical Inquiry is perhaps the most complete embodiment of the basic type of transdisciplinary "professional" journal that has proliferated in the last generation. This Chicago-based quarterly, founded in 1974, draws contributions from philosophers, historians, art historians, musicologists, and film critics as well as from the literary scholars at the journal's center. It is heavily footnoted and is decidedly not afraid of "jargon." *Raritan,* begun at Rutgers in 1980, represents a slightly different variation. It breaks the

David A. Hollinger is Professor of History at the University of California, Berkeley.

standard pattern by eschewing footnotes, as does its older and more intellectually conservative counterpart, *The American Scholar.* Prominent among *Raritan*'s editorial advisors and contributors are political scientists and anthropologists as well as humanists from several disciplines. Although neither *Critical Inquiry* nor *Raritan* limit their scope with any particular, topical specialty, many of the transdisciplinary academic journals focus on a narrow cluster of inquiries. Among the most widely appreciated journals with a topical specialty are *American Quarterly, Public Culture, Diaspora,* and *Modernism/Modernity.* Some of the transdisciplinary academic journals tilt toward the social scientific side of the academy. These include *Social Research, Contention,* and *Society.* But the bulk of them can be accurately described as humanities journals, with a largely literary base, that reach out to the most humanistic elements within political science, anthropology, sociology, history, and geography. This description applies to *October, Common Knowledge, Representations, Salmagundi,* and *Social Text.*

The increased role that transdisciplinary journals play in the professional work of members of many humanistic and social scientific disciplines is, in itself, an indicator of the much-noted weakening of disciplinary boundaries and loyalties. Nowhere did the theory wars and the identity debates proceed more fiercely than where academics confronted each other across disciplinary lines. These journals manifest a striking blend of *wissenschaftliche* and essayistic styles. Indeed, the transdisciplinary journals need to be distinguished from two other kinds of periodicals to which social scientists and humanists regularly contribute.

One is the disciplinary professional journal, of which *Journal of Philosophy, American Political Science Review, American Economic Review,* and *Proceedings of the Modern Language Association* are widely recognized examples of long-standing. The other is the more "journalistic" periodical that, while also read and written largely by professors, is ostensibly directed toward a wider public. These include *Commentary, Harpers, The Atlantic, The Nation, The New Republic,* and, somewhat more academic, *The American Prospect, Public Interest,* and *Dissent,* as well as, arguably, even academia's most popular "nonprofessional" periodical, *The New York Review of Books.* These "general circulation" periodicals are distinguished from the transdisciplinary "professional" journals in several crucial respects: they are less controlled by predominantly academic boards, they have fewer footnotes, they are more welcoming of frank political advocacy, and they are much less likely to be counted as "peer reviewed" when deans examine a faculty member's publication record.

Genuinely transdisciplinary academic journals were rare in the 1950s, although literary quarterlies with some pretense to transdisciplinarity were scattered widely around the country. By the 1980s, however, scholars with strong reputations within their own disciplinary communities proved eager to publish their work in the pages of *Critical Inquiry* and its analogues. And there were oodles of opportunities. Of the fifteen transdisciplinary journals I have mentioned so far, only five were in existence before 1970: *American Quarterly, American Scholar, Social Research, Society,* and *Salmagundi.* Of these five, moreover, two—*Society* and *Salmagundi*—dated only from the mid-1960s. *Partisan Review* was an exceptionally important forum from the 1930s through the 1960s, but it prided itself on its nonacademic past. Only gradually did it become what it is today: a not-quite-professional journal written mostly by and for professors, especially of English. Yet *Partisan Review*'s decline in relative significance is partly a consequence of its success and the prodigious increase in competition. This once-great quarterly was originally designed for "writers" and exemplified in the pre-1970 era one of two modes integrated in the plethora of journals founded after 1970. To write for Clement Greenberg's and Lionel Trilling's *Partisan Review* of old was to be "an intellectual," and this, for a great many humanistic and social scientific scholars of the 1970s, 1980s, and 1990s, was an idea not always supported by their disciplinary communities. The second mode was exemplified in the 1950s and 1960s by *American Quarterly;* contributing to it made one a "scholar," though this distinction was not to be limited by any of the traditional disciplines in which the cultural life of the United States was sometimes studied. This journal, founded in 1949, was always self-consciously academic, but its academic ambitions were long caught up in a struggle to make American studies into a full-fledged discipline. *American Quarterly* later outgrew this preoccupation and now functions as a "cultural studies" journal, very much like those whose transcending of any discipline-specific mission is a major point of their existence.

What actually went on the pages of the transdisciplinary journals between 1970 and 1995 is more various and extensive than I will attempt to describe here. But the desire to blend the essayist and *wissenschaftliche* modes was obviously bound up with a desire to retain something of what Carl Schorske calls the "rigorism" of the academic culture of the 1950s while addressing the normative dimensions of life that "rigorists" in the various disciplines were felt to have slighted. Humanists and social scientists of the post-1970 era proved reluctant to renounce a generically academic ethos but were determined, at the same time, to engage basic theoretical issues about society and culture that belonged exclusively to no discipline. Among these issues, none proved more deeply engaging to more scholars from more disciplines than the issues that came to be flagged with the term "identity."

Central to the identity debates was a drive to come to grips cognitively, and to some extent politically, with a set of enclosures the discovery of which was generally said to be a contribution of the 1960s. These enclosures, felt to have been ignored by the universalist, rationalist, and individualist biases of the previous generation, included the human body, language, class, gender, and, above all, the solidarities and confinements associated with ethnicity and race. Academic intellectuals of the 1940s, 1950s, and even the 1960s were felt by many of their immediate successors to have been incapable of appreciating the enabling function of groups and the diversity and particularity of the life sustained by groups. This incapacity was part of a larger failure to gauge the extent to which human lives were structured by race, class, and gender. The generation that flourished in the mid-century decades had dealt with identity as a matter of individual psychology rather than of collective experience and consciousness. That well-meaning but naive generation—this critique continued—had fallen victim to the conceit of a "God's-eye-view" of the world, and had thus failed to understand that even the most warranted of ideas owed much to the historical circumstances under which they had achieved their legitimacy. Knowledge, like the men and women who made it, needed to be "situated."

These blind spots of the previous generation were being corrected in the early and mid-1970s, often in a spirit of great confidence and conviction. An enhanced appreciation for groups, for particularity, for diversity, and for the power of historical circumstances was enthusiastically registered. Yet this appreciation, as it was developed and specifically applied, ran up against the Enlightenment conscience of many of its own partisans, who were unwilling to renounce altogether the old vision of the epistemic and moral unity of a humankind consisting of intrinsically valuable individual selves. Hence there followed, especially in the 1990s, a flurry of "neo-Enlightenment" attempts to prevent the hermeneutics and politics of identity from obscuring the agency of individuals, the epistemic authority actually earned by scientific communities, the emancipatory potential of intersubjective reason, and the legitimacy and value of civic and moral communities of broad scope transcending ethnoracial lines.

It is "disheartening," noted philosopher John Rajchman while introducing *October*'s special issue on the "identity question," that the rejection of Eurocentric models has sometimes, in its extremity, "reproduced some of the worst aspects of the organicist romantic conception of identity that flourished in Europe in the last century and that was to have catastrophic consequences in this one."[1] The popular notion of "cultural identity" as a replacement for "race" was actually a betrayal of antiracist commitments, argued literary critic Walter Benn Michaels in *Critical Inquiry*'s special issue. This notion served to perpetuate "racial thought," amounting to the self-contradictory "rescue of racism from racists."[2] In a special issue of *Social Research* in 1994, a group of political scientists embraced what one of their colleagues, Rogers M. Smith, described as "the proper task for liberals": to refuse the fashionable assertion of "the Enlightenment's demise," and to "see how the liberal project of enhancing human freedom and dignity can be strengthened and extended."[3] Two law professors brought out an anthology entitled *After Identity*; Michael Dyson, a prominent figure in African-American cultural studies, proclaimed the need for a "post-multiculturalism" designed to respect "the integrity of particularity" while seeking "race-transcending grounds of common embrace"; and my own book, entitled *Postethnic America: Beyond Multiculturalism*, criticized from a historian's perspective multiculturalism's implicit assigning of cultural identity to individuals on the basis of the physical marks of descent, calling attention to the historical specificity of the ethnoracial categories by which ideas and individuals had come to be "situated."[4] All this casting about for a more critical approach to identity bespeaks a frustration with a discourse in which the "context" for just about everything has turned out to be the salient ethnoracial and gender identities. Hence we may speak of a dynamic of "identity and its discontents," according to which the drive to come to grips with previously ignored or undervalued enclosures came up against residual universalist, rationalist, and individualistic values.

It is much too easy to say of this dynamic that it is "the playing out of the sixties." Although Ira Katznelson is correct to observe that many of the contributors to this volume have not given the movements of the sixties their due in the history of the disciplines, in most discussions of recent history the opposite is the problem. "The sixties," even more than "the fifties," has become a historiographic monster.[5] The sixties are said to explain almost everything that needs to be explained about the subsequent quarter-century. We will better understand the dynamic of identity and its discontents if we look a bit more specifically than we usually do at the early and mid-1970s.

In 1973, the Organization of Petroleum Exporting Countries doubled and then redoubled the price of oil, precipitating a series of far-reaching changes in the global economy that threatened the standard of living of Americans and Western Europeans. In that same year, the end of the Vietnam War finally removed from the agenda of contentions the one item that had done more than any other to structure the political discourse of the previous eight years. In 1973, too, the Endangered Species Act marked the maturity of the environmental movement, President Richard Nixon released the "Watergate tapes" that would lead to his resignation the following year, and *Roe v. Wade* introduced an era of intense political controversy over abortion and the degree to which women should have control of their sexuality and reproductive capacities. At the same time, American psychiatrists were brought under unprecedented pressure to drop homosexuality from their list of mental disorders, which they did the following year. Jobs in higher education took a dramatic nosedive after the flush 1960s; young men and women, who a few years before could have confidently expected several job offers, found that a Ph.D. completed in 1973 got them nowhere. Hayden White's *Metahistory* inaugurated the most extensive debate yet over the "fictional" nature of historical truth. Clifford Geertz's *Interpretation of Cultures* promoted a "cultural turn" in social science. Daniel Bell's *Coming of Post-Industrial Society* pulled together evidence that world-historical changes comparable in scale to industrialization itself were in progress. Thomas Pynchon's *Gravity's Rainbow* struck many critics as a literary breakthrough as portentous as that produced fifty-one years before by James Joyce's *Ulysses*. Gerald Graff's "The Myth of the Postmodernist Breakthrough" reinforced through negative critique the suddenly popular idea that the "modernist" epoch in the history of the Western mind was being replaced by one defined by a "postmodernist" sensibility.[6]

To be sure, a champion of any given year's claim to be among history's great turning points can come up with a list of exciting events. By the same token of deflation, it must be granted that the trajectories marked by the items on this or on most comparable lists do not necessarily propel themselves in the same direction.[7] But this particular list of well-remembered turns of 1973, executed in a variety of directions by a variety of actors in a variety of sectors beyond as well as within academia, represents only a first step toward understanding why the early and mid-1970s established a unique frame for the engagement of humanistic and social scientific scholars. A second step, which takes us closer to the engagement of this particular segment of the population of the United States, is to see the simultaneous, often synergistic action of four discrete intellectual forces during exactly these years.

We can call these four movements "Kuhn," antiracism, feminism, and "Foucault." The salient result of their far-from-harmonious commingling was an imperative to "situate" ideas and to recognize the "identity" of people, and to do so in light of certain assumptions about the constituent parts of situations and identities. Each of the four movements had taken on some of its shape during the vaunted decade of the 1960s. It makes some sense to treat these forces as "legacies of the sixties," but today's image of the sixties as a cultural and political monolith—fully as misleading as it is inescapable—risks homogenizing distinctive impulses that were then connected only episodically. Innumerable forces affected academic culture in the early and mid-1970s, including some that had defined themselves in the 1960s. Yet the coming together of these four, I want to suggest, created an intellectual setting decisive for the unfolding of the dynamic before us: the exploring of identity and the discovering of its limits. My point is not to pretend to do justice to these movements, but only to indicate how and when the most prominent features of these movements came into the position that enabled them to contribute to this particular effect. I speak in the tentative voice appropriate to any attempt to analyze the experiences of one's own generation.

By invoking "Kuhn" I intend to refer to the broadly based acceptance, of which Thomas S. Kuhn's *Structure of Scientific Revolutions* was by far the most influential example, of the dependence of knowledge on the workings of contingent, historically specific human communities. Geertz, too, became an agent of this historical self-awareness, as did Richard Rorty, whose *Philosophy and the Mirror of Nature* (1979) drew anti-foundational implications from the historicity of true belief much more radical than those that had been drawn by either Geertz or by Kuhn himself.[8] The story of this widening rejection of the "God's-eye-view" under the impact of Kuhn and his followers—sometimes recounted as the "hermeneutic" challenge to "positivist" or "objectivist" ideas—is familiar to readers of *Dædalus*. But its chronology and discursive location demand bold underscoring here.

The intellectual movement to historicize knowledge and the processes of its creation clearly predated the antiestablishment movements of the late 1960s. It was originally rooted in the supremely confident scientific culture of the 1950s of which Kuhn's book of 1962 was a relatively complacent product. Kuhn's protean work was put to service in numerous and scattered causes even during the 1960s, including some associated with the New Left. Eventually, the notion that learned communities had developed paradigms oblivious to the experiences of women and ethnoracial minorities became a common component of critiques of sexism and racism in the scholarly establishment. The additional idea that subaltern subjectivities possess their own ways of "knowing" could also be justified in Kuhnian terms. But we will misunderstand recent history if we forget that a project of situating truth in the historically particular experience of human communities had a formidable trajectory of its own, energized by a largely uncritical respect for the procedures and achievements of existing scientific communities. Only in the 1970s did the "strong program" of the Edinburgh school of sociologists take "science studies" in more "constructivist" directions,[9] and only in that decade did this trajectory become extensively entangled with the trajectories of antiracism, feminism, and Foucault.

Antiracism was a more direct and obvious extension of commitments declared and acted upon with unique intensity in the previous decade. Early in the new decade, antiracism fostered the expansion of affirmative action programs and inspired the proliferation of ethnic and minority studies. It also deepened sensitivity to the ways in which ethnoracial exclusions and inclusions had affected the destiny of individuals and of many ostensibly universalist endeavors, including some fields of scholarly inquiry. In so doing, the antiracism of academic intellectuals developed in close alliance with national priorities in social policy and with popular interest in the special circumstances of black Americans. The latter was displayed, for example, in the acclaim for Alex Haley's genealogical journey to Africa, *Roots* (1976). As early as 1971, Michael Novak's *The Rise of the Unmeltable Ethnics* gave voice to the feeling of some whites that the social and cultural particularity of Americans of many ethnoracial groups was being lost amid the clamor to do justice to the disadvantaged black population.[10] But such affirmations, even when embedded within a conservative "backlash" widely condemned as implicitly racist, fed the broadening impulse to attend carefully to the role of ethnoracial distinctions in every aspect of life.

Prevailing senses of what these distinctions meant underwent a change in the early and mid-1970s. The "color-blind" ideologies, according to which ethnoracial distinctions were largely barriers to a viable common life, gave way increasingly to competing ideologies of "color-consciousness." The latter gained credibility partly in response to the failure of empowered whites to act to integrate American society. Affirmations of ethnoracial identity also defended the particularity of cultural initiatives taken within minority ethnoracial communities. Color-blindness threatened to erase historic achievements attained under the ordinance of the color line, however invidiously drawn and manipulated. But color-consciousness increased also in relation to a quest for more aggressive antidiscrimination remedies. No incident in this quest looms larger, in retrospect, than the decision of the Office of Management and Budget in 1977 to instruct the federal census to count Americans by what amounted to the five classic color categories: black, white, red (American Indian), yellow (Asian or Pacific Islander), and brown (Hispanic white). The official consolidation of an ethnoracial pentagon was designed, of course, to facilitate the enforcement of voting rights and laws against employment discrimination. But this physically-based system of classification was easily conflated with culture at a time when educators were developing programs designed to teach and study cultural diversity. The panorama of cultural diversity could be conveniently reduced to the five parts of the pentagon, which came eventually to be denoted as African-American, Asian-American, European-American, Latino, and Indigenous. The "essentialism" that made culture a function of biology was widely criticized by many, including "minority" scholars. But the use of the ethnoracial pentagon as a basis for organizing the appreciation of cultural diversity proved hard to resist. It had a profound effect on colleges and universities and was reflected in the structure and title of a great expanse of new academic units. A person of Chinese, Japanese, Korean, or Cambodian descent, whatever his or her self-perception, discovered that he or she actually possessed an "Asian-American identity."

Identity by "gender" also proved to be a matter of intense discussion, going well beyond traditional talk of "roles" for men and women. Attention to gender expanded rapidly in the wake of the feminist movement, giving additional structure to efforts to clarify identity and to determine just what kinds of location were implied when one asked where somebody—especially a maker of ostensibly universal truth-claims—was "situated." Although feminist struggles against sexism derived some inspiration from antiracism and gained some popular support through the analogy between racism and sexism, feminism is a much more distinctly "seventies" phenomenon. Feminism owed much to events of the 1960s, including the publication of Betty Friedan's *The Feminine Mystique* (1963) and the founding of the

National Organization for Women (1966), but the bulk of feminism's crucial political and theoretical articulations date from the following decade. *Ms.* magazine was founded in 1972. There emerged in the early and mid-1970s a succession of popular feminist works of increasing theoretical ambition and sophistication, ranging from Kate Millett's *Sexual Politics* (1970) to Adrienne Rich's *Of Woman Born* (1976).[11] Most of these works were produced outside academia, but the founding of *Signs* in 1975—yet another transdisciplinary academic journal dating from this period—is a helpful marker of the emergence of feminism as an academic presence.

The meaning of the gender distinction was debated in terms that overlapped to some extent with the simultaneous discussion of ethnoracial distinctions. Differences between the world of men and the world of women could be construed as derived ultimately from biology, enormous in magnitude, and destined to remain in place even after women were liberated from the oppression that men had visited upon them. Or, the essential difference between male and female could be understood as not extending beyond sexual reproduction, in which case most of what passed for "masculine" and "feminine" were cultural constructions, at best, and, at worst, barriers serving to keep women from living lives as full as those routinely available to men. Disputes between what were crudely called "difference feminists" and "sameness feminists" were given a focal point in 1982 by Carol Gilligan's *In a Different Voice,* which argued that deeply structural differences between men and women could be discerned even in the moral reasoning characteristic of boys and girls. As feminism came to be informed by poststructuralism, these controversies took the form of more pointed debates over the nature and sustaining conditions of the female "subject" (and of the male). A point of these debates, as Judith Butler described it, is to ponder "what happens to the subject and to the stability of gender categories when the epistemic regime of presumptive heterosexuality is unmasked as that which produces and reifies these ostensible categories of ontology?"[12]

Butler spoke self-consciously in the idiom of Michel Foucault, which brings into play the fourth of our synergistic elements. In using "Foucault" to indicate the fourth of these trajectories, I intend simply to allude to the poststructuralist ideas developed by French theorists that were widely disseminated in the United

States. The impact of the abortive Paris revolution of 1968 on Foucault and his comrades enables one to construe this trajectory, too, as a "legacy of the sixties." But the peculiar Frenchness of the political dynamics of poststructuralism—entailing a reaction against varieties of Marxism and structuralism less deeply rooted in the American intelligentsia—renders this "sixties connection" less vital to any account of the generational pushes and pulls of American academic culture. The sudden and commanding influence of the French theorists in the United States is one of the most chronologically concentrated of the events that now enable us to see the early and mid-1970s as a distinctive historical moment. Some of the earliest works by American scholars advancing these ideas were, like literary critic Paul de Man's *Blindness and Insight* (1971),[13] absorbed primarily by a narrowly defined disciplinary constituency, but the French texts translated into English during these years were widely perceived to be prodigious in their implications for an enormous swath of social scientific and humanistic endeavors. This was especially so in the case of Foucault himself, whose *The Order of Things* (1970) was quickly followed by *The Archaeology of Knowledge* (1972), *The Birth of the Clinic* (1973), and *Discipline and Punish* (1977). Yet another Foucault title appearing in English in 1977, *Language, Counter-Memory, Practice,* clarified Foucault's concept of "genealogy." It was followed in 1978 by still another, the first volume of *The History of Sexuality.*[14]

Foucault and his coworkers accelerated the movement Kuhn had stimulated from "objectivist" to "constructivist" theories of knowledge. Any piece of knowledge was for Foucault not only a construction, but the embodiment of a certain dispersion of power. He spoke not of knowledge in relation to power, but of a single formation, "power/knowledge." Intersubjective reason, long regarded as a means of human liberation, was, for Foucault, a frequent instrument of domination. He declared, in a much-quoted aphorism, that "knowledge is not made for understanding; it is made for cutting."[15] A second relevant consequence of French theory was to undercut the faith in human autonomy and individual agency that many American intellectuals had sustained through the 1960s. Individuals achieve their "subjectivity" in their capacity as sites for the operation of categories of language that act prior to an individual's will. But the very categories that define the subject are themselves on the receiving end of power. The poststructuralist view that entities once thought to be features of nature are discursively constructed in a matrix of power is implied in Butler's comment, quoted above, to the effect that a "subject" such as "woman" and the very "categories of ontology" that endow us with the gender distinction to begin with might be the "products" of an "epistemic regime." Although this emphasis on the constructed character of vital categories provided a basis for mounting resistance to "essentialist" versions of identity, the game was indeed the game of collective identity: poststructuralists studied the naturalist subject, the lesbian subject, the Chicano subject, and a host of other subject identities.

Foucault, feminism, antiracism, and Kuhn thus together fostered the exploration of identity that "problematized" (as it was often put, to the horror of those valuing "good English") a number of ideas that the previous generation rarely felt obliged to defend. The ensuing debates drew heavily on the energies of historians, anthropologists, and sociologists, among others, but this collection is about the particular history of four other disciplines: economics, English, philosophy, and political science.

One could write an exceedingly detailed history of this entire episode without mentioning a single economist. This exclusion applies even to those economists who sometimes write about large and hard-to-solve problems for transdisciplinary audiences, such as Robert Heilbronner, Albert Hirschman, and Amartya Sen. This is neither to disparage economists nor to congratulate them. The clarity of disciplinary boundaries is sharper in the case of economics than in any other of the social sciences and humanities. This popular observation is resoundingly confirmed by the accounts offered in this volume by Robert M. Solow, David M. Kreps, and William J. Barber. Even in the setting of undergraduate programs where, as Barber observes, an occasional student would challenge the ability of a white professor to discuss economic development in Africa, this discipline's relative isolation remains beyond dispute. Its theorists, studying what Solow calls "greed, rationality, and equilibrium" through mathematical model-building, have so vigorously maintained the discipline's canonical version of the Enlightenment that it makes little sense to speak here of "neo-Enlightenment" initiatives. Epistemic universalism was never seriously challenged. Adam Smith's spirit had suffered few rebukes, even in the early and mid-1970s.

English is at the other extreme. In no other major discipline, including even sociology, anthropology, and history, did transdisciplinary journals play remotely as large a role in a "peer-reviewed" discourse as they did in English. Repeatedly, it was professors of English who founded, edited, and supervised these projects, and it was they who did most of the writing. It was professors of English, moreover, who dominated the proliferating humanities institutes of which the transdisciplinary journals were the textual counterpart. Literary scholars took the lead in affirming the importance of gender and ethnoracial minority cultures as matrices for the production of literature, and they took no less of a lead in the demonstration of the constructed character of any and all identities. As the essays of M. H. Abrams, Catherine Gallagher, and José David Saldívar detail, no discipline was more immersed than English in parsing the problem of identity, none was more engulfed by the tensions within American society that rendered the identity problem a public as well as an academic concern, and none was more politically divided by the endeavor.

What enabled literary critics to talk "professionally" about almost anything they pleased—to be "real intellectuals" while colleagues in other disciplines risked becoming "mere technicians"— was the textualization of the world. As more and more objects of inquiry were said to be "discursively constructed," the more sense it made for an expanding panorama of objects to be studied by specialists in discourse. "The special analytical skills" of literary scholars, as Gallagher puts it, were felt "applicable to all cultural phenomena, and only unadventurous critics would confine themselves to conventional literary texts." The culmination of this development was the inclusion of science in literature. This step produced an embarrassment for literary critics in 1996 when a physicist managed to place in *Social Text* a killing parody of the literary theorist's analysis of physical theory.[16] The field of "literature and science" has generated some rigorous work that genuinely enriched the study of science as a human enterprise, especially in the pages of yet another new transdisciplinary journal, *Configurations*. Nevertheless, the *Social Text* fiasco called widespread attention to a challenge Gallagher correctly represents as a consequence of the expansion of literary into "cultural" studies: the more broad the scope of study, the more one needs to ask what professional training or specialized knowledge would be required, and "how would that knowledge and training differ from that of intellectual or cultural historians or from cultural anthropologists, philosophers, or sociologists?"

From this dilemma political scientists were free, at least when it came to the identity debates. The discipline of political science had, among its classic fields, political theory. For political theorists, the identity debates were a standard professional activity. Hence the writings of Seyla Benhabib, William Connelly, Bonnie Honig, George Kateb, Judith Shklar, Michael Walzer, and Bernard Yack, among others, were able to speak to an audience beyond their own discipline even as they evaluated the competing claims of "communitarianism" and "liberalism." Unlike their counterparts in English, however, most of the political theorists operated within a relatively narrow, canonical frame. They conversed directly with Hegel and Marx, with Rousseau and Mill, and increasingly with Hannah Arendt, but were slow to recognize the relevance of Herder and List, thinkers from the past whose relevance to the identity debates was appreciated by historians and literary critics. The political theorists were a distinctive and often isolated subgroup within the discipline of political science. They did not, as Rogers Smith and Charles Lindblom make clear, constitute the core of the discipline. During exactly the years in which the dynamic of identity and its discontents was being played out, the attention of the discipline was more often captured, as Smith points out, by another of the discipline's most sharply defined subgroups, the rational-choice theorists.

The rational-choice segment of political science has been as far removed from the identity debates as have been the model-building economists. Arguments about the merits and drawbacks of both fall into similar patterns. Critics accuse the rational choicers of failing to illuminate anything of genuine significance to the study of politics, just as model-building economists are sometimes accused, as Kreps acknowledges, of avoiding the complexities of the real world with the determination of Methodists avoiding a local saloon. Rational-choice scholars responded, as Smith observes, "by insisting that they actually offered a general, impeccably scientific approach to all politics that promised to create a universal explanatory theory." Nowhere in the social sciences and the humanities is the Enlightenment flame of epistemic universalism kept with less respect for the concerns of thinkers who believe this flame to be a flash of artificial light.

Political science thus presents two antithetical faces to the identity debates. It has successfully professionalized these debates in a way that has proved difficult for English. On the other hand, political science has altogether avoided these debates, in the manner of economics. Neither of these persona can be credibly attributed to philosophy.

Philosophy presents a paradox more striking than any presented by the other three disciplines considered here. It polices its borders much more vigilantly that do most of the humanities and social sciences and maintains an image of great austerity. The vast majority of its practitioners remain aloof from transdisciplinary chitchat and are prone, in private moments, to make exceedingly uncharitable comments about their colleagues in other disciplines (e.g., that they are unable to distinguish an assertion from an argument). Yet much of the work done by mainstream analytical philosophers speaks directly, and some of it profoundly, to issues of the identity debates. A prime example is John Rawls. Rawls's *Theory of Justice* (1971) is the closest thing extant to a book that professional philosophers are "ashamed to admit they have not read," according to Alexander Nehamas. Yet the painstaking effort of Rawls and his followers during our era to predicate ethical claims on an "overlapping consensus" within "Western democracies with a certain political history," as Hilary Putnam rightly describes this effort, responds to the concerns that have driven the identity debates. Another example, also by a bona fide "analytic" philosopher, is Thomas Nagel's *Equality and Partiality* (1991), which nests an account of political legitimacy in an appreciation for the enduring cultural plurality and perhaps reducible economic inequality of the species.[17]

Rawls and Nagel are both "public" but not "popular," in Nehamas's useful distinction. Nehamas is right to complain both that intellectuals too often suppose that writing about matters of public concern must mean "popularization" and the "lowering of standards," and that many potential readers of philosophy "have no patience for any position that is not virtually self-explanatory." A philosopher who has risked being "popular" while trying to be "public" is Richard Rorty, whose relation to his discipline illustrates both philosophy's extraordinary capacity to instruct the rest of the humanities and social sciences and also that discipline's ambivalence about this role.

It was the fastidious disciplinary culture of philosophy that served up, in Rorty, one of the most loquacious and listened-to voices in the identity debates. Yet the more central Rorty became to the theoretical conversations of non-philosophers, the more he voluntarily separated himself from most philosophers and the more the latter were glad to return the favor. While the author of *Contingency, Irony, and Solidarity* (1989)[18] now strikes many philosophers as good stock gone to seed—having transformed himself from a respectable analytical philosopher into just another literary essayist who could quote Continental thinkers—Rorty's extensive constituency throughout the humanities and the social sciences has welcomed the discipline-honed clarity he has brought to conversations bedeviled by pretentious obscurity. In his eagerness to distance himself from an epistemological tradition he thinks bankrupt, Rorty may underestimate the intellectual capital he has inherited from a rigorous disciplinary tradition.

Rorty's case can be instructively contrasted to that of Thomas Kuhn, perhaps the most influential single thinker in the entire debate over the character and boundaries of epistemic enclosures. But was Kuhn, news of whose death arrives as I write these lines, "a philosopher?" Kuhn began as a historian (although trained, before that, as a physicist) and was gradually, if at first grudgingly, welcomed into philosophy while Rorty was finding, and being shown, the exit. Kuhn fled from the transdisciplinary discussion of his own work and in the process identified himself less as a historian and more as a philosopher. Analytic philosophers embarrassed by Rorty's frequent indiscretions could trust Kuhn to behave. Yet Kuhn's most creative work was accomplished when he was straddling the line between philosophy and history, building on the intellectual capital he had derived from his work as a historian, taking chances of the sort he later eschewed.

No clear lessons emerge from the contrasting trajectories of Rorty and Kuhn, nor from the larger story of the disciplines and the identity debates as told here. But one might conclude on behalf of disciplinary identity that there are some virtues to enclosures, especially if their boundaries are subject to critical revision. That was the soundest of the claims made in the name of "identity." Those of us who are living "after identity" would do well to remember its modest wisdom.

ENDNOTES

[1]John Rajchman, "Introduction," *October* (Summer 1992): 7.

[2]Walter Benn Michaels, "Race into Culture: A Critical Genealogy of Cultural Identity," *Critical Inquiry* XVIII (Summer 1992): 684.

[3]Rogers M. Smith, "Unfinished Liberalism," *Social Research* LXI (Fall 1994): 631–632.

[4]Dan Danielsen and Karen Engle, eds., *After Identity: A Reader in Law and Culture* (New York: Routledge, 1995); Michael Dyson, "Contesting Racial Amnesia: From Identity Politics to Post-Multiculturalism," in Michael Berube and Cary Nelson, eds., *Higher Education Under Fire: Politics, Economics, and the Crisis of the Humanities* (New York: Routledge, 1995), 343; David A. Hollinger, *Postethnic America: Beyond Multiculturalism* (New York: Basic Books, 1995). For an incisive summary of the state of "post-identity" discourse, see Ross Posnock, "Before and After Identity Politics," *Raritan* XV (Summer 1995): 95–115, esp. 101–106.

[5]I have expressed this complaint at greater length in the Introduction to David A. Hollinger, *Science, Jews, and Secular Culture: Studies in Mid-Twentieth Century American Intellectual History* (Princeton, N.J.: Princeton University Press, 1996), 4.

[6]Hayden White, *Metahistory* (Baltimore, Md.: Johns Hopkins University Press, 1973); Clifford Geertz, *The Interpretation of Cultures* (New York: Basic Books, 1973); Daniel Bell, *The Coming of Post-Industrial Society* (New York: Basic Books, 1973); Thomas Pynchon, *Gravity's Rainbow* (New York: Viking Press, 1973); Gerald Graff, "The Myth of the Postmodernist Breakthrough," *Triquarterly* XXVI (1973): 383–417.

[7]Yet a number of observers do find unusual coherence in a set of turning points we can now discern in the early and mid-1970s. David Harvey opens *The Condition of Postmodernity* (Cambridge, Mass.: Blackwell, 1989) with this sweeping claim: "There has been a sea change in cultural as well as in political-economic practices since around 1972," visible in "the rise of postmodernist cultural forms, the emergence of more flexible modes of capital accumulation, and a new found 'time-space compression' in the organization of capitalism." Ibid., vii.

[8]Thomas S. Kuhn, *The Structure of Scientific Revolutions* (Chicago, Ill.: University of Chicago Press, 1962); Richard Rorty, *Philosophy and the Mirror of Nature* (Princeton, N.J.: Princeton University Press, 1979).

[9]The Edinburgh journal *Science Studies* was founded in 1971. The chief programmatic books of the school's early leaders were Barry Barnes, *Scientific Knowledge and Sociological Theory* (London: Routledge and K. Paul, 1974), and David Bloor, *Knowledge and Social Imagery* (London: Routledge and K. Paul, 1976).

[10]Alex Haley, *Roots* (New York: Doubleday, 1976); Michael Novak, *The Rise of the Unmeltable Ethnics* (New York: Macmillan, 1971).

[11]Betty Friedan, *The Feminine Mystique* (New York: Norton, 1963); Kate Millett, *Sexual Politics* (New York: Doubleday, 1970); Adrienne Rich, *Of Woman Born* (New York: Norton, 1976).

[12]Carol Gilligan, *In a Different Voice: Psychological Theory and Women's Development* (Cambridge, Mass.: Harvard University Press, 1982); Judith Butler, *Gender Trouble: Feminism and the Subversion of Identity* (New York: Routledge, 1990), viii.

[13]Paul de Man, *Blindness and Insight* (New York: Oxford University Press, 1971).

[14]Michel Foucault, *The Order of Things: An Archaeology of the Human Sciences* (New York: Pantheon Books, 1970); Michel Foucault, *The Archaeology of Knowledge* (New York: Pantheon Books, 1972); Michel Foucault, *The Birth of the Clinic* (New York: Pantheon Books, 1973); Michel Foucault, *Discipline and Punish* (New York: Pantheon Books, 1977); Michel Foucault, *Language, Counter-Memory, Practice* (Ithaca, N.Y.: Cornell University Press, 1977); Michel Foucault, *The History of Sexuality*, vol. 1 (New York: Pantheon Books, 1978).

[15]Foucault, *Language, Counter-Memory, Practice*, 156.

[16]Alan D. Sokal, "Transgressing the Boundaries—Toward a Transformative Hermeneutics of Quantum Gravity," *Social Text* (Spring/Summer 1996): 217–252.

[17]John Rawls, *A Theory of Justice* (Cambridge, Mass.: Belknap Press of Harvard University Press, 1971); Thomas Nagel, *Equality and Partiality* (New York: Oxford University Press, 1991).

[18]Richard Rorty, *Contingency, Irony, and Solidarity* (New York: Cambridge University Press, 1989).